■ United States Holocaust
Jack, Joseph and Morton
Center for Advanced Holocaust Studies

Documenting Life and Destruction
Holocaust Sources
in Context

SERIES EDITOR

Jürgen Matthäus

DOCUMENTING LIFE AND DESTRUCTION

HOLOCAUST SOURCES IN CONTEXT

This groundbreaking series provides a new perspective on history using first-hand accounts of the lives of those who suffered through the Holocaust, those who perpetrated it, and those who witnessed it as bystanders. The United States Holocaust Memorial Museum's Mandel Center for Advanced Holocaust Studies presents a wide range of documents from different archival holdings, expanding knowledge about the lives and fates of Holocaust victims and making these resources broadly available to the general public and scholarly communities for the first time.

BOOKS IN THE SERIES

A project of the

United States Holocaust Memorial Museum

SARA J. BLOOMFIELD
Director

Jack, Joseph and Morton Mandel
Center for Advanced Holocaust Studies

WENDY LOWER
Acting Director

JÜRGEN MATTHÄUS
Director, Applied Research

under the auspices of the

Academic Committee
of the
United States Holocaust Memorial Council

PETER HAYES, *Chair*

This publication has been made possible by
support from

Claims Conference ועידת התביעות
The Conference on Jewish Material Claims Against Germany

The William S. and Ina Levine Foundation

The Blum Family Foundation

Dr. Alfred Munzer and Mr. Joel Wind

and

Dorot Foundation

Documenting Life and Destruction
Holocaust Sources in Context

JEWISH RESPONSES TO PERSECUTION, 1933–1946

A Source Reader

Jürgen Matthäus
with Emil Kerenji

Advisory Committee:

Christopher R. Browning
David Engel
Sara Horowitz
Steven T. Katz
Alvin H. Rosenfeld

Rowman & Littlefield
in association with the United States Holocaust Memorial Museum
2017

For USHMM:
Project Manager: Mel Hecker
Index: Jen Burton, Columbia Indexing
Maps: Aly DeGraff Ollivierre, Tombolo Maps & Design

Front cover: Photograph of the wedding of Salomon Schrijver (born 1917) and Flora
Mendels (born 1919) in the Jewish quarter of Amsterdam, no date (ca. 1942). Salomon
and Flora Schrijver were deported via Westerbork to Sobibor where they were murdered
on July 9, 1943. USHMMPA WS#08726 (courtesy of Samuel Schryver).

Published by Rowman & Littlefield
A wholly owned subsidiary of The Rowman & Littlefield Publishing Group, Inc.
4501 Forbes Boulevard, Suite 200, Lanham, Maryland 20706
www.rowman.com

Unit A, Whitacre Mews, 26-34 Stannery Street, London SE11 4AB

British Library Cataloguing in Publication Information Available

Library of Congress Cataloging-in-Publication Data Available

978-1-5381-0174-2 (cloth : alk. paper)
978-1-5381-0175-9 (paper : alk. paper)
978-1-5381-0176-6 (electronic)

∞™ The paper used in this publication meets the minimum requirements of American
National Standard for Information Sciences—Permanence of Paper for Printed Library
Materials, ANSI/NISO Z39.48-1992.

Printed in the United States of America

Contents

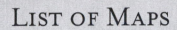

LIST OF MAPS

ABBREVIATIONS

AJJDC, AJDC	American Jewish Joint Distribution Committee, the Joint
Bund	Algemeyner yidisher arbeter bund (General Jewish Workers' Alliance), Poland
CENTOS	Centrala Związku Towarzystw Opieki nad Sierotami i Dziećmi Opuszczonymi (Central Office of the Union of Societies for Care of Orphans and Abandoned Children)
CV	Centralverein deutscher Staatsbürger jüdischen Glaubens (Central Association of German Citizens of Jewish Faith)
DP	Displaced person
Gestapo	Geheime Staatspolizei (Secret State Police)
GFHM	Ghetto Fighters' House Museum, Lohamei HaGeta'ot, Israel
HSSPFSS	General and Higher SS- and Police Leader
Joint	See AJJDC
LBINY	Leo Baeck Institute Archive, New York
LCSAV	Lithuanian Central State Archive, Vilnius
ORT	Organisation Reconstruction Travail (Organization for Rehabilitation through Training)
POW	Prisoner of war
Ring.	Ringelblum Collection, Jewish Historical Institute, Warsaw
RjF	Reichsbund jüdischer Frontsoldaten (German Jewish Veterans Organization)
RM	Reichsmark or mark
RSHA	Reichssicherheitshauptamt (Reich Security Main Office)

SA	Sturmabteilung (Nazi storm troopers)
SAM	Special Archive Moscow (Osobyi Archive; Rossiiskii gosudarstvennyi voennyi arkhiv, Russian State Military Archive)
SS	Schutzstaffel (Nazi Security Squad)
UNRRA	United Nations Relief and Rehabilitation Administration
USHMM	United States Holocaust Memorial Museum, Washington, DC
USHMMA	USHMM Archives
USHMMPA	USHMM Photo Archives
USSR	Union of Soviet Socialist Republics, the Soviet Union
WJC	World Jewish Congress
YVS	*Yad Vashem Studies*
ZAHA	Zentralausschuss der deutschen Juden für Hilfe und Aufbau (German Jewish Relief Organization)
ŻIH	Żydowski Instytut Historyczny (Jewish Historical Institute), Warsaw
zł.	Złoty
ŻOB	Żydowska Organizacja Bojowa (Jewish Combat Organization; also Jewish Fighting Organization), Warsaw
ZVfD	Zionistische Vereinigung für Deutschland (German Zionist Union)

INTRODUCTION

THIS VOLUME CONTAINS a concise selection of primary sources on the Holocaust featured and annotated in our larger series titled *Jewish Responses to Persecution, 1933–1946*.[1] With this reader we particularly aim to reach college students and instructors interested in exploring how Jews thought and acted during the Nazi era, what conditions they faced, and how oppression impacted their lives. One source included in this book, a photograph taken in June 1942 by exiled German Jewish painter Felix Nussbaum of his painting *Saint-Cyprien*[2] on the balcony of his Brussels apartment, encapsulates some of our goals: to show different shades on the diverse palette of human experiences in extremis, to raise awareness of the mediated nature of writing history, and to encourage readers to take a closer look beyond seemingly familiar settings. Denounced while living in hiding in Brussels, Felix Nussbaum and his partner, Felka Platek, were deported to and murdered in Auschwitz in early August 1942.[3]

Against all odds, victims left behind an astonishing yet highly dispersed abundance of diaries, letters, photographs, and other documents. In our five-volume series, with its roughly eight hundred documents, we have attempted to

---

1. *Jewish Responses to Persecution, 1933–1946*, 5 vols. Documenting Life and Destruction: Holocaust Sources in Context (Lanham, MD: Altamira Press/Rowman & Littlefield, 2010–2015).

2. Document 3-30.

3. See Eva Berger et al., eds., *Felix Nussbaum: Art Defamed, Art in Exile, Art in Resistance* (Woodstock, NY: Overlook Press, 1997). The photograph is printed courtesy of Felix-Nussbaum-Haus Osnabrück, Germany.

capture the power of this profound testament produced during the Nazi era. While most of the authors did not survive the war, some managed to escape the Third Reich's "final solution of the Jewish question," and others wrote as observers from outside the realm of German terror. Their words offer students of the Holocaust, if only for a moment, a faint glimpse of a time when the past was still the present and outcomes with which we are all familiar remained unknown.

Any history teacher knows the value of contemporary witness reports for imbuing historical periods and topics with a sense of immediacy. When it comes to understanding the Holocaust, however, contemporary documents, and particularly those stemming from victims rather than perpetrators, have significance and expressiveness beyond the general rule. They help recover the individuality of those too often seen merely as objects of Nazi policy. They bring to life the uncertainty, confusion, and disbelief of those confronting measures and processes that until then had been unimaginable and only in retrospect have become an irremovable feature of our mental landscape. Just as important, such individual sources rescue the diversity and individuality of millions of women, men, and children whom their tormentors tried to treat as a faceless mass. As Raul Hilberg, the doyen of Holocaust historiography, noted after a lifetime spent researching and writing on the destruction of European Jewry, we still have very little sense of how different groups within the Jewish community, "caught in the grip of destruction, reacted daily to restrictions and danger. What did coping look like? In their dilemma, what did lawyers do, or illiterates? How were family relations preserved or transformed? What was the significance of age? What role did money play? What might have been the personal budget of working Jews in the Berlin of 1941, or 1942 Saloniki, or the Theresienstadt ghetto of 1943?"[4] Only in the Nazi imagination was there one, undifferentiated "Jew."

Why focus on contemporary witness accounts—that is to say, on sources created close to the events by those discriminated against as Jews—and not on memoirs written in later life? In our introduction to the first volume in the *Jewish Responses to Persecution* series, we explore why hindsight is a challenge to Holocaust memoirists. After all, as many of the sources in this volume show, for much of the period of Nazi rule, contemporary observers had no idea where things would lead, even if some may have found themselves gripped by remarkably prescient forebodings. By contrast, those observers lucky enough to survive confronted throughout the rest of their lives the enormity of all that had befallen them. More than most memoirists of other periods, Holocaust survivors, after

4. Raul Hilberg, "Incompleteness in Holocaust Historiography," in *Grey Zones: Ambiguity and Compromise in the Holocaust and Its Aftermath*, ed. Jonathan Petropolous and John K. Roth (New York: Berghahn Book, 2005), 81–92 (quote, 88–89).

their reprieve from Nazi terror, lived and wrote under conditions vastly different from those of their former lives. Our series, including this book, thus emphasizes contemporary witness statements in the form of reports, memoranda, letters, diaries, poems, and photographs. We have given preference to documentation of Jewish provenance—that is, material from a variety of source types produced by Jewish organizations and individual Jews inside and outside the countries affected. And although we offer but a tiny selection, we hope these sources convey the richness, vitality, and depth of witness records preserved in archives and libraries across the globe.

Yet reliance on contemporary victim accounts does not spare us from grappling with particular features and difficulties of Holocaust documentation. In some cases, the conditions under which people wrote were so extreme, their survival so in doubt, that these texts, rather than simply offering specific details, speak to us about how a continued devotion to diaries and reports, how the very act of writing itself, functioned as a Jewish response to persecution. In other cases—in Germany in the 1930s but also later elsewhere—Jewish individuals and agencies operated in a strange space, sometimes enjoying unexpected freedom, precisely because the regime excluded Jews from all its efforts at mobilizing the people, yet at the same time increasingly surveilled, disempowered, and marginalized. Conditions were changing so quickly and so radically that past experience and frames of reference, be they religious, cultural, or political, often provided little guidance for the future. When exploring sources written under such circumstances, we should always bear in mind the circumstances of production and communication and do our best to read between the lines of texts penned under conditions of duress.

We intend for the selection presented in this reader not to favor one source over another but to showcase documents we found intriguing in and of themselves and in the context of others. As with our series in general, we have organized this volume chronologically, yet left room for topical, regional, or material clusters. Of course, chronological and geographic proximity differ from causal correlation. As but one example, mere weeks prior to the day Nussbaum photographed his painting in Brussels, a young Jewish man who had been deported from Germany to German-controlled Poland wrote a letter to his fiancée back in the Reich. He wrestled with what he was encountering and how to describe it: "What shall I write about? In terms of food and cleanliness the conditions here are more extreme than anything we imagined; it's simply impossible to put them into words. Words could never convey the reality of life here. The Wild West is nothing compared to this. The attitudes and approaches to life here are so incomprehensible. Anyone not firmly grounded will find himself spiritually derailed forever."[5] Meantime, in the Łódź ghetto, a woman deported from Vienna summed up in a notebook, staccato style, her family's misery since the beginning of 1942: "From late January to June, difficult days of hunger and cold. In that span of time, Leo [her husband] lost 20 kilos [44 pounds] and Irene [the author], 10. Ghetto diseases, rashes, attacks of dysentery, itchy scalps, etc. Flies a nuisance at 4 a.m. Weakness in feet, falling asleep from weakness, Bubi [her son] has temperature of 39°C [102.2°F], lots of vomiting, heartburn, dizziness."[6] Like Nussbaum, but each in their own way, the authors of these two accounts recorded what the Holocaust meant to them, face to face and day to day. None of them survived the war.

Despair, suffering, and death are synonymous with the Holocaust; yet not all sources project these experiences to the same degree. Unlike ex post facto observers, witnesses within the Nazi empire faced huge problems in trying to comprehend the shifting landscape around them and figure out how to act. In the early years of the Third Reich, observers in Germany found it difficult to untangle the strange mix of the normal and the abnormal, of the familiar and the unprecedented, of continued orderly rule from above and pressure from violent activists in the streets. What made it so difficult to perceive the big picture? Doubtless, the architects and practitioners of German anti-Jewish policies understood how to conceal their intentions. But the fluidity and contradictions of the persecution process reveal that even German protagonists had little idea of where events were leading: the Holocaust as we know it was neither a foregone conclusion nor, before the war, a clearly predictable one. In a situation as unprecedented as it was volatile, the struggle of discerning (or believing) the direction of anti-Jewish policy and, still more, of understanding why any human being would want to construct and serve such a murderous machine made taking action all the more challenging.

Studying this book and its sources may raise questions for readers about what constituted Jewish responses at the time, how they were documented and communicated, how we understand them now, and how they compare to the experiences of victims of other mass atrocities. Some of the statements and actions documented here undoubtedly reveal basic human behavior patterns that one might expect from any group or individual under threat. Others reflect the peculiarities of Jewish life in the first half of the twentieth century, with its specific political, religious, cultural, and social aspects. It goes almost without

---

5. See Document 3-24: Letter by Ernst Krombach, Izbica, Lublin district, Generalgouvernement, to Marianne Strauss, Essen, Germany, April 28, 1942.

6. Document 3-25: Diary entries by Irene Hauser, Łódź, Warthegau, for June–July 1942.

saying that the richness of Jewish tradition and the complexities of human interaction are reflected here only in fragments distorted by the pressure of persecution.

Yet we should also be aware that the images we carry in our minds about historic reality do not always match what actually happened. The understanding of Jewish resistance remains heavily influenced by preconceived notions and our expectations about how people should have reacted. Opposition, activism, and self-assertion encompass a far wider spectrum of behavior than armed engagement with the enemy. In addition to the many documentable instances of individuals and groups resisting, we should not lose sight of subtler, yet often no less life-threatening forms of Jewish reactions in the form of survival techniques, religious practices, diary or letter writing, and artistic or other cultural activities.

Different strata, segments, or subgroups within European Jewry behaved differently at different times, and even behavior within the subgroups was not uniform. Beyond established patterns of internal stratification, the documentation reflects the lives, problems, and perceptions of individuals, of "ordinary" Jews and members of elite groups, inside the urban centers of Europe as well as on the periphery. Anti-Jewish activists and bureaucrats stigmatized as Jews the authors of some documents featured here irrespective of their self-definitions; we include them partly because persecutors imposed on the individual their classifications and partly because we would lose sight of important aspects of persecution if we ignored the responses of those outside the scope of traditional Jewish affiliation, such as converts, persons of mixed ancestry, and individuals who chose not to identify as Jews for personal or ideological reasons. Also, the sources show that the overwhelming majority of both those who had previously seen themselves as Jews and those forced into a Nazi-defined Jewish category changed their self-definitions over time in response to surrounding circumstances.

In a variety of ways and with varying degrees of intensity, this volume's documents speak to a broad range of themes—such as age, gender, class, geography, nationality, leadership, religion, ideology, perception, and communication—that teachers of the Holocaust can and should explore. The possibilities and limitations inherent in our selection would make for fascinating class discussions. As useful as grouping sources according to topics or themes seemed, we decided against it so as not to preclude readers' own reflections about linkages between documents. To tap this collection's full potential, readers will have to consider what is gained and what is lost by highlighting one document, or one facet of a document, when, depending on how and from which angle we look at it, there are so many or so few.

We encourage readers to think not only about the material we present but—against the background of their own interests, expectations, and knowledge—also about the editors' role. No historian's account is objective; it involves making choices and abstracting—a process through which events tend to lose their specificity. The narrative presented through the documents featured here consists of many partly dissonant and conflicting voices that amplify our sense of the complexities of the past, particularly the diversity of Jewish experiences, perceptions, and reactions in their changes over time. Standard, often dichotomous parameters for defining Jewish responses—eastern versus western European, observant versus secular, rich versus poor, female versus male, young versus old, politically left versus right—are relevant in the context of the Holocaust; yet other, subtler and more transient forms of group differentiation also surface in the sources.

Because we focus on documenting Jewish responses, this book does not discuss how the Nazis and their allies designed and implemented the persecution process. Publications about this topic fill libraries; in our series we point to some of the literature produced by scholars from many disciplines on perpetrators, their actions, and their impact on victims. In this reader, we can neither duplicate these references nor elaborate on the documents' context, as this would require considerable space. In identifying sources, we have assessed their relevance, specificity, and context in terms of type, composition, style, content, and potential classroom value. We have also taken the relative importance of particular settings into account, especially in eastern and southeastern Europe, where most of the victims lived and where during the war the "final solution," defined as the systematic mass murder of Jewish men, women, and children, was implemented. We aim to present documentation from centers—urban and otherwise—and peripheries; where we had to choose between relatively well-known and underrepresented settings, semi-iconic sources and newly available documents, we opted for what scholarship has so far neglected.

For broader overall introductions, introductory sketches to each source, more annotation, further reading, and additional information (including glossaries and chronologies), we refer readers to our *Jewish Responses to Persecution* volumes. Some of the documents from this series reprinted here we have expanded or otherwise revised. The "List of Documents" serves also as a concordance to allow for cross-referencing this volume's selection with the larger set. Some of the documents featured here are also included in our new college-level teaching tool, *Experiencing History: Jewish Perspectives on the Holocaust* (experiencinghistory.com). An expansion of the *Jewish Responses to Persecution* print series, *Experiencing History* provides interconnected source collections in which each individual document is made available digitally (as image, video, or audio), together with teaching-oriented contextualization. The level of introduction and annotation allows for a well-informed classroom discussion, but we leave it to the college instructor to set the educational goal. This flexibility in disciplinary and methodological approaches, in addition to the hyperlinking allowed by the Internet, makes *Experiencing History* a cutting-edge teaching tool for the college classroom in North America, aiming to attract readers of this volume to the further study of the Holocaust, ideally by exploring different kinds of documentation held in many archives and now increasingly available in different formats.

We hope this volume meets our goals of conveying a better understanding of the open-endedness of the process of persecution in the minds of those who lived through it; of raising awareness concerning its unpredictability and consequences; and of highlighting the great diversity of perceptions as well as reactions by different strata and groups within the Jewish minority persecuted by Nazi Germany and its allies. Often missing from summary representations of the Holocaust, especially those that focus on how, when, and why the perpetrators did what they did, are the responses of the many who perished and the few who survived. Their reactions are uniquely suited to shed light on Jewish history and to deepen our understanding not only of Jewish agency under extreme circumstances but also of the forces that helped pass the threshold from persecution to genocide.

In compiling this concise volume that complements our book series, we have received invaluable assistance from a number of friends and colleagues. First and foremost, we would like to thank Alexandra Garbarini and Mark Roseman for their deep commitment to the project and their vital help with this book. Doris Bergen and Jeff Veidlinger provided most valuable advice and careful guidance. Our thanks also go to the reviewers, some anonymous, who commented on manuscript drafts and to the staff at Rowman & Littlefield, particularly Susan McEachern, Elaine McGarraugh, and Jennifer Kelland Fagan. Last but not least we are grateful for all the help we received in a multitude of ways from colleagues at the United States Holocaust Memorial Museum and the members of its Academic Committee.

This volume is dedicated to the memory of Raul Hilberg (1926–2007), one of the founders of the field of Holocaust Studies and a critical proponent of empirical research. He had helped nurture this book series, but died before it came to fruition. If this series is seen as valuable in stimulating further study of Holocaust history, we owe it to him.

PART I
1933–1938

DOCUMENT 1-1: Editorial in *Jüdische Rundschau* (Berlin), "Inner Security," on German Zionists' assessment of the Nazi takeover, February 3, 1933, 45–46 (translated from German).

Overnight the event that no one wanted to believe would happen has become fact: Hitler is Chancellor of the German Reich. This new development forces us to confront the reality of our underlying situation. [. . .] The truth is that pressure from the national socialists has affected life in Germany for some time. Quite apart from the fact that Jews are being systematically shut out of economic and cultural life, antisemitism has come to dominate the psychological atmosphere. This actually also has the effect that the Jew again knows that he is a Jew, for no one lets him forget it. But the feeling of being completely surrounded by people who take their spiritual cues from the [Nazi Party newspapers] *Angriff* and the *Völkischer Beobachter*, with their infernal agitation against Jews, is hardly a cheering thought. We were always convinced—and the *Jüdische Rundschau* repeatedly emphasized this—that the national socialist movement, for some time now no longer a mere political party, has become the authoritative source for public opinion and would in the end also seize positions of power. [. . .]

It would be ridiculous for us to say that Jews are perfect or that they have no faults. It is we ourselves who suffer most from certain phenomena in Jewish life. Zionism clearly recognized forty years ago that our community needed to renew from within. We know that we are dragging remnants of the old ghetto along with us. And likewise—perhaps even worse—we are burdened with the by-products of assimilation, an assimilation that gave us "freedom on the outside, but a feeling of servitude within." But we do now also have a <u>new Jewry</u> that seeks to free itself both from the remnants of the ghetto and also from the damage brought on by assimilation; a Jewry that has found its way back to itself, that knows its own worth, that fearlessly defends itself, that knows how to maintain distance and keep its composure, that confronts its enemies not with envy and arrogance but with a clear countenance. This new Jewry, internally secure, ignores all insults and assaults and keeps its head held high. To make this work, everything depends on freeing the Jews from their atomization and self-estrangement and drawing them together for the Jewish cause.

DOCUMENT 1-2: Press release by CV, Berlin, on reports of anti-Jewish acts in Germany, March 24, 1933, *CV-Zeitung*, March 30, 1933, 2 (translated from German).

[. . .] The CV, the largest organization of the 565,000 German Jews and faithful to the Fatherland,[1] hereby responds to the events of recent days:

According to German press reports, a variety of foreign newspapers claim, for example, that mutilated Jewish corpses are being regularly deposited at the entrance of the Jewish cemetery in Berlin-Weissensee, that Jewish girls have been forcibly rounded up in public spaces, and that hundreds of German Jews have arrived in Geneva, of whom nine-tenths—many of them children—were victims of severe abuse. All such claims are pure fiction. The CV emphatically declares that German Jewry cannot be held accountable for such irresponsible misrepresentations, which should be roundly condemned.

The German people have experienced enormous political changes in the past weeks. Acts of political revenge and violence have occurred, some of them against Jews. Both the Reich and the state governments have successfully taken steps to restore law and order as quickly as possible. The order issued by the

---

1. The Central Association of German Citizens of Jewish Faith (Centralverein deutscher Staatsbürger jüdischen Glaubens, or CV), founded in 1893, sought to defend the rights of German Jews while fostering the "cultivation of German sentiment" among its members. Its membership figures (72,500 in 1924), well-developed regional organization, and popular weekly journal, the *CV-Zeitung* edited by the head office in Berlin (with a circulation of 55,000 in 1933), attest to the CV's broad appeal among German Jews. After 1933, the CV reoriented its work toward assistance with emigration and material aid to those Jews remaining in Germany; the Nazi regime abolished it in the wake of the November 1938 pogrom ("*Kristallnacht*").

Reich chancellor [Hitler] to refrain from all isolated actions of this nature has proven effective.[2]

Recently in particular we have seen very clearly antisemitic goals being articulated in diverse arenas of economics and life, and this naturally fills us with grave concern. As before, the CV considers the struggle against these goals to be a domestic German matter. However, we are convinced that the equal rights of German Jews, which they have fully earned in war and peace by sacrificing life and property, will not be abrogated. Bound inseparably to the German Fatherland, German Jews will continue to work with all other Germans of goodwill for the advancement of the Fatherland.

DOCUMENT 1-3: Diary entry by Mally Dienemann,[3] Offenbach, Germany, for April 3, 1933, on the nationwide boycott of Jewish businesses, LBINY MM 18, 11a (translated from German).

Offenbach, April 3, 1933.

On Saturday [April 1] there was a boycott of all Jewish stores, doctors, lawyers. Black slips of paper with white dots were posted on Jewish stores and SA men stood in front of the buildings and stopped people from entering the stores or going to lawyers or doctors. [. . .] I thought, how unvarying is our fate; now we are [supposedly] harming Germany with fairy tales about atrocities, while in the Middle Ages it was we who were supposed to have poisoned wells, etc. I felt like my own ghost wandering the streets. Were we dreaming, or was it real? Could people really do this to each other? And why, why? Did any of those in power really believe that these Jews were to blame for spreading this so-called atrocity propaganda? [. . .]

---

2. See Jürgen Matthäus and Mark Roseman, eds., *Jewish Responses to Persecution*, vol. 1: *1933–1938*. Documenting Life and Destruction: Holocaust Sources in Context (Lanham, MD: Altamira Press/Rowman & Littlefield, 2010), 11–12.

3. Mally Dienemann (née Hirsch) (1883–1963) was active in Germany's feminist movement and the wife of Rabbi Max Dienemann. After the November 1938 pogrom her husband was incarcerated in the Sachsenhausen concentration camp. Following his release, the Dienemanns joined their daughters in Palestine, where Max died only months later from the aftereffects of his imprisonment. Mally Dienemann later emigrated to the United States.

DOCUMENT 1-4: Photograph of Beate Berger (center right)[4] and youth from the Beith Ahawah Children's Home on an excursion near Berlin, 1934, USHMMPA WS# 48874.

DOCUMENT 1-5: Account by Max Abraham,[5] Czechoslovakia, on his experiences in the Oranienburg concentration camp, first printed in *Juda verrecke: Ein Rabbiner im Konzentrationslager* (Templitz-Schönau: Druck- und Verlagsanstalt, 1934) (translated from German).

[. . .] The Jewish Company consisted of about 55 people, among them 39 boys from a Jewish education facility near Berlin. The Benjamin among the

---

4. Berta "Beate" Berger (1886–1940) trained as a nurse in Frankfurt am Main and in 1922 became the director of the Beith Ahawah Children's Home. Although she and a number of the children under her care managed to emigrate to Palestine in 1934, she continued to secure escape for those juveniles still in Berlin until her death in Kiriat Bialik in 1940.

5. Max Abraham (1904–ca. 1970) was a preacher in the small Jewish community in Rathenow, Brandenburg (Germany). Arrested in June 1933 on fabricated charges, Abraham was incarcerated for several months in Oranienburg and other concentration camps. After his release he escaped to Czechoslovakia, where in 1934 he published an account of his concentration camp ordeal, partly also printed in *Der Gelbe Fleck: Die Ausrottung von 500.000 deutschen Juden* (Paris: Éditions du Carrefour, 1936). Before the war began Abraham managed to emigrate to England.

boys was indeed called Benjamin, and he was <u>thirteen years old</u>.[6] [. . .] The children were beaten for hours on end in the cruelest manner and forced to perform extremely hard physical labor.

Thirteen-year-old Benjamin was naturally spared nothing. The school had accommodated physically weak and mostly psychopathic children with severe learning difficulties. The weakest was the thirteen-year-old, but he was mentally advanced enough to understand what was going on. The children often lamented their suffering and pleaded for help from me, their spiritual counselor. But how was I supposed to help, I, who was under the control of sadistic oppressors myself? My caring had to be restricted to comforting and occasionally supporting them in their physical hardship. [. . .]

The children from the school were incarcerated for six weeks. As a result of their experiences in the Oranienburg camp, many of them would be psychologically damaged for life. Even on the day prior to the release, a nineteen-year-old who was "parlor maid" for an SA man was severely abused. He was accused of having stolen a mark [one Reichsmark] from the SA man. He was first brought into Room 16, where he was supposed to make a confession. When he was beaten almost unconscious, he confessed to everything of which they accused him. He claimed to have buried the money in the yard, where he had to look for it for half an hour. He could not find the money there—since he had neither stolen nor hidden it. As he assured me later when I talked to him very seriously, he had only made this "confession" to gain time and to recover from the dreadful blows. I believed him; he was certainly not lying to me at that moment. He latched onto my encouragement like a drowning person onto a helping hand.

Since the mark was nowhere to be found, the boy was further brutally beaten and now said that he had hidden the money in a different place in the yard to be spared for half an hour longer. This was repeated three to four times. We older protective-custody prisoners could not watch this martyrdom any longer and slipped him a mark so that he could return the "stolen" mark and finally be freed from his torments. The last abuse of the boy happened in the evening. SA men entered the dorm around nine o'clock, asked for the location

---

6. "Benjamin" was a common German reference to the youngest among a group or family. Manfred Benjamin (1919–?) moved to Berlin after his release from the Oranienburg concentration camp and emigrated to the Netherlands in April 1939. He may have been the youngest prisoner held in any of the early concentration camps; his later fate is unknown. He and the other youth in the Oranienburg concentration camp had been arrested in June 1933 at a Jewish training home in the Brandenburg town of Wolzig; see Matthäus and Roseman, *Jewish Responses to Persecution*, vol. 1: *1933–1938*, 74–78.

of the bunk of the "thief," and hit the bare body of the weak young lad with rubber truncheons. We heard the cries of pain and the groans—and were power-less to intervene. [. . .]

DOCUMENT 1-6: Letter by League of Jewish Women, Berlin, to the Reich leader of the Nazi Women's League on the future of Jewish children in Germany, November 8, 1934, USHMMA RG 11.001M.31, reel 128 (SAM 721-1-2809, 57–58) (translated from German).

[. . .] In the name of the League of Jewish Women of Germany,[7] on whom the responsibility for Jewish youth is incumbent as the organized voice of Jewish mothers, we take the liberty of presenting to you, the leader of the German women's organizational network, our worries about the fate of this youth.

We Jewish mothers have always, and in full recognition of the burden assigned to us, expressed our unanimous commitment, to the extent that we can, to raise our children to be upstanding people, courageous adherents of our religion, and people who love Germany and are ready to make sacrifices for her. We are aware, however, that this can only be achieved if our children are allowed to grow up in an environment that does not present insurmountable barriers to the development of their moral selves. When honest effort and ambition are met with contempt and misunderstanding, when quality of achievement and goodness of character are not accepted as the criteria by which the individual should be judged, then those barriers are indeed in place.

We know that the NS Women's Association is inseparably bound to all the demands of national socialism. Therefore, we would never invoke motherly solidarity by asking the NS Women's Association to exert influence on our fate as citizens—whatever that may turn out to be—insofar as that is decided by the principles of national socialism and the authorities of the national socialist state. But when in front of a hundred thousand German boys and girls, hate and contempt for the Jewish people are praised as virtue and national duty, as hap-pened at the rally for youth in Aachen on July 22 and in Cologne on October 13, we cannot remain silent. Therefore, we, the mothers of the children whose right to live is threatened in this way, come to you, the mothers of the children

---

7. The League of Jewish Women (Jüdischer Frauenbund), founded in 1904 as part of the international women's movement, aimed at advancing Jewish women's rights both in the Jewish community as well as in German society at large. After 1933 the organization assisted in the training and retraining of Jewish girls as the employment landscape shifted dramati-cally. In the mid-1930s, the league had a membership of some fifty thousand women in numerous regional and local branches throughout Germany. It was abolished after the November 1938 pogrom.

who, from the seed planted in them today, shall someday build German life and the German state.

[. . .]

DOCUMENT 1-7: Note by Max Rosenthal on the bar mitzvah of his grandson, Hans Rosenthal, April 13, 1935, USHMMPA WS# 28738.

The dedication reads, "To my dear Hans on his bar mitzvah and to the everlasting memory of his loving grandfather Max. Memories are the only paradise from which we cannot be expelled. Max Rosenthal 13/4 1935." The card was inserted in a book, *Das Ostjüdische Antlitz* [The face of the eastern European Jew] by Arnold Zweig published 1920 in Berlin, that Rosenthal gave to his grandson for his bar mitzvah.

DOCUMENT 1-8: Letter by Julius Moses,[8] Berlin, to Erwin Moses, Tel Aviv, on his visions for the family's future, September 1935, translated from Dieter Fricke, *Jüdisches Leben in Berlin und Tel Aviv, 1933–1939: Der Briefwechsel des ehemaligen Reichstagsabgeordneten Dr. Julius Moses* (Hamburg: von Bockel, 1997), 370–71.

Berlin, Rosh Hashanah 1935

[. . .] There is so much I still want to do. For now I want to carry on writing down my many memories! As you see, I've started up again and hopefully won't stop. This time I'm doing it to give you something to read for the New Year!! Well, enjoy!! I imagine my grandsons Gad and Gill [Erwin Moses's sons] sitting together in brotherly fashion 50 years from now on the evening of Rosh Hashanah, already retired, respected, and established contributors to the building of Eretz Israel, surrounded by their own children and grandchildren. And I imagine the conversation turning to their grandfather and one of the brothers going into the next room and quietly returning with the "Memoirs." And Gad would begin to recount aloud to his grandsons the story told in these pages, almost as though it were the night of Passover. Yes, he would tell the stories in these pages aloud, for his grandsons are unlikely to be familiar with the German language and won't be able to read the "Memoirs" themselves: yes, it is thoughts such as these that give me a certain inner feeling of satisfaction, of well-being. I begin to indulge in them, embrace them, if I picture how Gad, somewhat quiet and calm, Gill more temperamental—like his father and grandfather—tell their grandkids how they were still born in Berlin, why and how their parents emigrated, and also give their grandchildren a picture of the bygone century through the "Memoirs." And I can picture how the grandkids will sit there with hot faces, hearing of the many battles and works performed by their forebears, their grandfathers Gad and Gill, their great-grandfather Erwin, and their great-great-grandfather, who wrote down these "Memoirs," and to which the writings of

---

8. Julius Moses (1868–1942), a physician by training and, during the Weimar period, a member of the German parliament (Reichstag) for the Social Democratic Party of Germany, retreated to private life in Berlin with Hitler's assumption of power. Moses had three children with his first wife, Gertrud Moritz. His son Erwin (1897–1976) left Germany for Palestine in May 1933 with his wife, Trude, and their two sons, Gad (Gert, b. 1924) and Gill (Günther, b. 1927), and corresponded regularly with his father in Berlin. Moses's daughter, Vera, was born in 1900; his second son, Rudi (1898–1979), a doctor dismissed by the Nazis in 1933, escaped to the Philippines in 1938. One day after his seventy-fourth birthday in July 1942, the Nazis deported Julius Moses to Theresienstadt, where he died a few months later. Gertrud Moritz and their daughter, Vera, were killed in 1942 after having been deported to Theresienstadt.

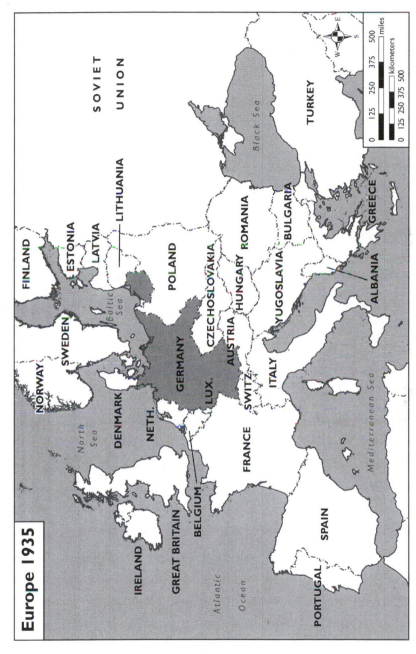

Map 1: Europe, 1935.

their great-grandfather Erwin, their own grandfathers Gad and Gill, then added and expanded upon, and to which the family archive assembled by their own father in turn added and supplemented. And then they will see for themselves from these stories that their forebears did not fight and suffer and battle in vain, and they will see why they have fought and suffered.

And if they compare the earlier stories with what has been achieved, they will see that the world has marched forward and how that happened, and how their own forebears did their part in bringing about that progress. And that will become an incentive for my great-great-great-grandchildren—I mean the grandkids of Gad and Gill—to seize the opportunity, in the spirit of their forebears, also to contribute to the great project of promoting progress in the world. And through this they will also contribute to the building of Eretz Israel, this Eretz Israel, which will at that point—around the year 2000 or so—look quite different from today: a free people on a free soil. [. . .]

DOCUMENT 1-9: Report by Bernhard Kahn, AJJDC,[9] European Executive Council, Geneva, titled "Jewish Conditions in Germany," November 29, 1935, AJJDC Archive AR 3344/629.

1. General Condition

At the setting up of the Jewish Laws issued in September [1935], the German Chancellor declared at Nuremberg, that these laws were purposed to establish a tolerable relationship between German and Jew.[10] Irrespective of whether this

---

9. The American Jewish Joint Distribution Committee (AJJDC, also AJDC, the Joint), founded in 1914 as an umbrella for aid organizations in the United States, provided assistance to Jews around the world, particularly in eastern Europe.

10. On September 15, 1935, during the annual Nazi Party rally and a specially convened session of the German parliament in Nuremberg, the regime promulgated the Reich Citizenship Law (*Reichsbürgergesetz*) and the Law for the Protection of German Blood and German Honor (*Gesetz zum Schutze des deutschen Blutes und der deutschen Ehre*). The first law restricted citizenship (and thus full protection under the law) to those of "German or related blood," while the second measure proscribed marriage and sexual contact between this group and Jews. Subsequent regulations defined a "Jew" as someone with at least three Jewish grandparents (according to their religious affiliation) or someone descended from two Jewish grandparents who him- or herself practiced the Jewish religion or was married to a Jew. Persons with two Jewish grandparents, but without Jewish religious affiliation and not married to a Jew, came to be defined as "mixed breeds" ("*Mischlinge*") of the first degree; persons with one Jewish grandfather or grandmother were labeled "*Mischlinge*" of the second degree. With clauses added during the war to facilitate the deportation and expropriation of German Jews, the Nuremberg Laws provided the legal basis for the Nazi regime's anti-Jewish policies.

statement was in earnest, it must be clearly stated that the condition of the Jews since the issuance of the Nuremberg Laws becomes daily more difficult, for the reason in fact that even at the very issuance of the Laws there were definite notifications that these would be executed to the full. About four weeks after Nuremberg, the Minister of the Interior Frick declared in an address that the not too distant fixing of the execution of the Laws would also limit the position of Jews from an economic standpoint. As of today, the execution of these Laws has not been set. What this will mean, when it does happen, one can hardly say. But the state of things which has in the meantime been created, becomes daily less bearable. Jewry is living in a state of the greatest insecurity and nervous unrest.

[. . .; Kahn refers to a multitude of other difficulties for German and foreign Jews; emigration is becoming more pressing and difficult for all groups.] If new and grand scale emigration possibilities are not quickly opened up, we fear that those countries bordering on Germany will be flooded with new refugees. The Jewish organizations are making every effort to quiet the excited, over-wrought, and alarmed people, and to warn them of imprudent flight into foreign countries; with the catastrophic deterioration of conditions these warnings will not have any permanent effect. [. . .]

DOCUMENT 1-10: Photograph of students from different Jewish schools in Berlin gathering around their banners for a sports competition, no date (1936–1938), USHMMPA WS# 12854.

The boy in front is holding up a sign from the Waldschule Kaliski, a well-known Jewish private school located in Berlin-Dahlem.

DOCUMENT 1-11: Philipp Flesch,[11] New York, "My Life in Germany before and after January 30, 1933," on the "Anschluss" of Austria in early 1938, LBINY MM 22/ME 132, 10–17 (translated from German).

[. . .] Vienna covered itself in swastikas. Since not enough badges were for sale, people wore badges they had made themselves from sheet metal, tin foil, and other material. There were also not enough flags, so the red-and-white flags of the Schuschnigg[12] era had to be waved again. Houses owned by Jews also had to be decorated with flags, contrary to the laws in Germany proper [*Altreich*].

Day and night, the SA took Jews and known Schuschnigg supporters out of their apartments. Mostly they had to clean the floors of party halls. On the streets, Jewish passers-by were stopped and forced to clean up Schuschnigg's campaign slogans.

[. . .; on the first day after the reopening of the school at which Flesch had been teaching for twelve years and had formerly been a student:] Colleagues stood around in the teachers' room adorned with the badges they had so long been prohibited from showing off publicly. About half of them wore the symbols of the "illegals" [i.e., the Nazi Party previously outlawed in Austria], which demonstrated that they had already worked secretly for the "party" under the old regime. [. . .] Nobody showed sneering satisfaction; everybody was uncomfortable when they saw me and the other "defeated" entering. Some of them even shook hands with us; everybody felt awkward. I felt quite dizzy, put my desk in order and emptied it, suppressed the swelling tears, and went with my companions in fate into the principal's office. There, instead of the "black" [i.e., Austro-conservative] principal who had succeeded the "red" [socialist] one, we now found the "brown" [Nazi] one: a young man who—as I heard later—came directly from Stein, a well-known prison, where he had been incarcerated for violent Nazi propaganda. Just like the other longtime "illegals," he was certainly friendly and announced to us simply that the municipal school administrator had ordered our dismissal. And so we went home. The female colleagues cried, and we, the men, did not feel any better since there is probably not a single teacher who is not connected with his job on a deep emotional level. [. . .]

In May [1938] or thereabouts, hundreds upon hundreds of Jews were

---

11. Philipp Flesch (1896–?) was a World War I veteran and scholar specializing in German philology. He taught at a public school in his home city, Vienna, and was detained after the November pogrom before emigrating to the United States via the Netherlands in 1939. Flesch submitted the text excerpted here to an essay contest solicited by Harvard University in 1940.

12. Kurt Schuschnigg (1897–1977) was Austrian chancellor from 1934 until the German annexation ("Anschluss") in March 1938.

arrested. Nobody knew why, and nobody could believe it, even when it was already clear that these people had been randomly sent to Dachau [concentration camp]. Only when the first urns with ashes arrived, mostly of physically fit young people who had only recently been seen walking around healthy and happy, did the terrible truth become obvious. "Your Jew is dead. Pick up the urn" was often the literal wording of the notification. I continued my life as usual, except that I always carried all my papers with me, three kerchiefs, ersatz glasses, and in my wallet a well-hidden razor blade—just in case. But I was not arrested. [. . .]

DOCUMENT 1-12: Report from files of the Jewish Telegraph Agency, Paris, by an unidentified author on the persecution of Jews in central European countries in the first half of June 1938, USHMMA RG 11.001M.25, reel 106 (SAM 674-1-109, 114–22) (translated from German).

Germany.

[. . .] Property must be registered by June 30. The forms and ordinances concerning implementation were issued during the first week of June.

The banking firm of M. Warburg & Co. in Hamburg has been made Jewfree.

Aryanization in Germany has proceeded at an increased pace.[13] [. . .]

The Gestapo informed the Jewish community in Saarbrücken that Saarbrücken must be free of Jews within three years. [. . .]

Hitler has ordered that the big synagogue in Munich be torn down to make room for a parking lot. Demolition began immediately, and only with considerable effort were the community's religious functionaries able to save the holy Torah scrolls and other religious articles.

Nazi officials have ordered immediate razing of the synagogue in Nuremberg in the middle of the city, a large structure built in the Moorish style. [. . .]

Austria

The suffering of Jews in Austria continues to increase. The persecution has no end. On the contrary: it becomes ever more vicious. [. . .]

---

13. The terms "Aryanization" and "Aryanize" (German: *Arisierung, arisieren*), derived from the vocabulary of *völkisch* antisemitism, denote the process of expropriating Jews and excluding them from the economy by legislative, administrative, and terrorist means. The "Anschluss" of Austria triggered a wave of exclusionary measures that culminated in the forced "Aryanization" of the remaining Jewish businesses later in 1938.

One day SA men mounted a *Stürmer* poster on the gates of the Rothschild Hospital. Despite entreaties from hospital administrators to show some consideration for the patients, the poster remained up. The administration was even obliged to hire officers from a private security company for two nights and pay them out of their own funds to protect the poster as it was assumed that Nazi provocateurs would tear down the poster and that the hospital administration would then face extremely harsh reprisals. [. . .]

Dr. David Schapira of 3 [Vienna's 3rd district] Hohlweggasse 12, a veteran frontline officer and blind from his war injuries, owned a law office and a tobacco and newspaper shop. The law firm had of course lost its clientele, and despite the assurances of some high Nazi officials, the shop was also taken away from him after the boycott. Guided by his wife, he then went to the ministry to hand in a petition, and he took all of his war decorations and medals for bravery along. He was nonetheless dismissed by a Nazi functionary with the following words: "Jewish scoundrel, you can shove that Habsburg stuff up your ass. Shove off, and don't come back, or I'll throw you down the stairs—maybe then you'll be able to see again." [. . .]

At the beginning of June, park benches for Jews appeared for the first time, namely, in the 9th district on the Elisabeth Promenade. Every fourth bench had white block letters written on it with the words "Jews Only." These benches were not painted yellow but brown [like the benches for non-Jews]. Needless to say, no one dares to sit on these benches for fear of being accosted. Soon these Jewish benches, whose introduction was announced in advance some time ago, will be found in all the parks.

During the first days of June, around 10,000 Jewish prisoners from Vienna were taken to Dachau concentration camp.

An estimated 6,000 Jews were arrested in Austria during the Pentecost week. [. . .]

A series of deaths have been reported from Dachau.

All Jewish lawyers have been forbidden from practicing their profession. They must wind up their business affairs within the next three weeks.

In the Burgenland the SA again violently dragged 40 Jews to the border. We have not been able to learn what happened to them since then. The Jews in the Burgenland are in a state of panic.[14]

---

14. Immediately following the "Anschluss," Nazi police agencies implemented a policy of expulsion across the border into Hungary that by the end of 1938 had driven roughly one-third of the thirty-six hundred Jews from the Burgenland province. On the expulsion of Jews, including citizens of Czechoslovakia, from annexed Austria later in 1938, see Saul Friedländer, Nazi Germany and the Jews, vol. 1: The Years of Persecution, 1933–1939 (New York: HarperCollins, 2007), 1:265–66.

Aryan lawyers in Vienna are not allowed to represent Jews.

Countless young Jewish academics have been sent to perform forced labor on the floodplain of Styria. [. . .]

An antisemitic newspaper is calling on the streetcar authority to institute special compartments for Jews, similar to the "Jim Crow" (Negro) compartments in America.

Well-informed circles are saying that the number of [Austrian] Jews who have been driven to suicide now exceeds 6,800. A furniture dealer in the 2nd district [in Vienna] killed himself along with his spouse, son, daughter-in-law, and five-year-old grandchild. The next day the SA affixed a poster to his shuttered business reading, "We strongly urge others to follow his example."

DOCUMENT 1-13: Diary entry by Ruth Maier,[15] Vienna, for October 2, 1938, on her Jewish identity, translated from Ruth Maier, *"Das Leben könnte gut sein": Tagebücher 1933 bis 1942*, ed. Jan Erik Vold (Stuttgart: DVA, 2008), 134–36.

[. . .] I was at the Chajes *Gymnasium* [Jewish high school in Vienna] today for the first time. The school is fervently nationalistic. This poses a considerable danger, and who knows, perhaps I'm not a Zionist just out of a feeling of opposition.

The principal gave a low-key, pleasant speech loaded with Jewish national consciousness. He is a small, worn-out man who tilts his head this way and then the other. He preached at us about our responsibility, about "bearing with dignity," and he expressed his conviction that we would all end up in Palestine. He hopes that the "baptized Jews and those without denomination" will find their way to the Jewish community.

It was a strange feeling to sit there, all of us young people, guys and girls, everything around us hostile and revolting; only us, relying on ourselves, on . . .

Well, that's where the danger lies: "the Jewish community." First my community was humankind. Now, suddenly, Jewishness [*Judentum*] is supposed to replace humankind for me? "A path leads from humanity through nationality to bestiality." I don't know who first said these words, but they have proven to be entirely true.

---

15. Ruth Maier (1920–1942) was born in Vienna and left Austria in January 1939 for Norway. Unable to join her sister and mother (who fled to England in April 1939), she was deported from German-occupied Norway, together with more than five hundred Jews, in late November 1942 and murdered on arrival in Auschwitz.

Today the principal said during a preparatory class, "It's possible to explain and excuse national socialism but still reject it."

I can certainly explain, excuse, and <u>understand</u> Zionism (which is clearly connected to nationalism), but I reject it. Precisely because, as Anny Schermann [a fellow student] today said quite correctly, I constantly and physically feel the consequences of nationalism.

Yes, right now I'm convinced that nothing could be further removed from me than nationalist feelings, etc. And yet, isn't it something completely negative and unhealthy to always long for "assimilation," for one's own disappearance, the disappearance of one's uniqueness? And so, I can't help but fluctuate between socialism and—though I <u>dread</u> having to write this—nationalism.

And maybe it's this, precisely this fluctuating position of Jews that has become the hallmark of being Jewish.

But to finally wrap things up on this issue: it's a fact that 75 percent of Jewish intellectuals and Jewish youth are being pushed toward Zionism. [. . .]

DOCUMENT 1-14: Letter by Gerhard Kann,[16] Berlin, to Heinz Kellermann,[17] New York, on the spiritual impact of persecution, October 24, 1938, USHMMA Acc. 2007.96, Kellermann collection, box 4 (translated from German).

My dear Heinz!

Your letter was simultaneously an expression of encouragement, hope, and resignation for us. Kind words that are a balm for this feeling of abandonment, of resigning oneself to an unavoidable fate.

It is truly very difficult to avoid being overwhelmed by a feeling of unending passivity.

Each day we see the walls around us grow higher, and each week brings new obstacles to leaving the country. Hopes and plans are buried, and the number of fellow sufferers in central Europe grows ever greater.

Germany, Italy, Czecho-Slovakia [*sic*] . . . the problems are becoming ever more daunting, and the need for an overall solution has continued to grow. The fate of individuals has become unimportant, trivial. And one can only hope that

---

16. Berlin-born Gerhard Kann (1910–?), a medical doctor by training, was interned in Dachau for over a month after the November pogrom. He managed to leave Europe before the war, landing in Palestine and eventually Bolivia.

17. Heinz Kellermann (1910–1998) was a leader in the CV's youth organization until his emigration to the Unites States in 1937, where he joined the diplomatic service.

the growth of the masses of people who are uprooted will make the world recognize the Jewish problem as one that it cannot ignore and not just a question that it can gloss over with a few conferences and speeches.

You on the outside don't of course see it with our eyes or hear what's going on with our ears; we don't share the same perspective. And that is a good thing. Human nature forces us to put ourselves and our own fate at the center of our concerns; only now and again does one realize that in the end a few hundred thousand Jews really don't play a very important role in the world.

And yet, as young, strong people we rise up against such feelings of resignation. And in this disintegration process affecting Jewry in Germany, we search for a meaningful position for as long as we are still here.

In the end, nothing is worse than being forced to sit around vegetating and waiting.

Regardless of all the energy I put into this serious, dogged search for a way to emigrate, I count myself lucky to be among the few people who still have a job and one that even involves work and responsibilities in our sector.

I know that there is still a need for my work [as a doctor treating Jewish patients] and that I can and must help others. And I derive some sense of satisfaction from the fact that I have been equal to the demands of this work.

Perhaps I am deluding myself; perhaps I am creating an ethical justification for my work so that I have any chance of carrying on. Yet I believe that were I working as a sales clerk—discounting any external factors—I would have a much harder time standing my ground.

Do you understand what I'm trying to say? It's also a form of spiritual self-protection that I have drawn upon.

What I have derived from this just in the past few weeks is trust in myself, a feeling of security in the face of others and events, a feeling that will hopefully continue to serve me.

As for day-to-day reality! I'm continuing to work, day and night, more demands on me than ever. Selma [his wife] is working in a private clinic, and we see each other for one or two hours at night and have a little private time. We are there for each other, help one another face the troubles, and hope that we can begin a life together somewhere else.

We do not know how long we will still be allowed to work. My livelihood is particularly uncertain. We are doing our work as best we can, as long as we can.

Our plans and hopes have more or less all come to naught. Despite registering at the consulate here, America seems like a very remote possibility, something you have said. There now appears to be some chance of going to Peru.

In any event, entering the country would cost four thousand French francs[18] per person, which would need to be raised for us abroad. Then we could get visas. I still have no idea how I could pull this off.

Is there some chance that you might look into this?

Perhaps there are some organizations or important people who could provide some assistance?

You are right when you say that I have dragged my feet a bit. But I believe that every person who is still here at some point failed to take advantage of an opportunity. *Kismet*! Islamic teaching says that everything is mapped out in the book of life. [. . .]

DOCUMENT 1-15: Letter by Emanuel Ringelblum,[19] Środborów, Poland, to Raphael Mahler, New York, December 6, 1938, on the fate of Jewish expellees in the Polish-German border region, Moreshet Archive D.1.4927 (translated from Yiddish).[20]

Dear Raphael:

I am in Środborów now to rest. I worked in Zbąszyń for five weeks. Apart from Ginzberg,[21] I am among the few who managed to hold out there for a long time. Almost all the others broke down, sooner or later. I have neither the strength nor the patience to describe for you everything that happened in Zbąszyń. Anyway, I think there has never been so ferocious, so pitiless a deportation of any Jewish community as this German deportation. I saw one woman who was taken from her home in Germany while she was still in her pajamas (this

---

18. In October 1938, four thousand French francs equaled roughly $100.

19. Emanuel Ringelblum (1900–1944), a Polish Jewish historian, in October 1938 helped organize humanitarian aid for the thousands of Polish Jews expelled from Germany and stranded near the town of Zbąszyń. With the outbreak of the war and the German occupation of Poland, Ringelblum used his experience at the Joint to coordinate a loose network of social organizations in Warsaw. To document Jewish life and society under the Nazi onslaught, he organized a ghetto-wide effort in Warsaw, code-named Oyneg Shabes. Ringelblum was killed in 1944, along with his family. See Samuel D. Kassow, *Who Will Write Our History? Emanuel Ringelblum, the Warsaw Ghetto, and the Oyneg Shabes Archive* (Bloomington: Indiana University Press, 2007).

20. The letter is published in Hebrew translation in Raphael Mahler, "Mikhtavei E. Ringelblum m' Zbonshin v'al Zbonshin," *Yalkut Moreshet* 2 (1964): 24–25. Raphael Mahler (1899–1977), historian from Nowy Sacz, was a close associate of Ringelblum's until his emigration to New York, where he taught Jewish history until his move to Tel Aviv in 1950.

21. Shlomo Ginzberg was, like Ringelblum, a teacher in a Jewish secondary school; he most likely perished in the Warsaw ghetto.

woman is now half-demented). I saw a paralyzed woman of over 50 who was taken from her house; afterward she was carried all the way to the border in an armchair by young Jewish men. (She is in the hospital to this day.) [. . .]

In the course of those five weeks, we (originally Giterman,[22] Ginzberg, and I, and after ten days Ginzberg and I, that is) set up a whole township with departments for supplies, hospitalization, carpentry workshops, tailors, shoemakers, books, a legal section, a migration department and our own post office (with 53 employees), a welfare office, a court of arbitration, an organizing committee, open and secret control services, a cleaning service, and widespread sanitation services, etc. In addition to 10–15 people from Poland, almost 500 refugees from Germany are employed in the sections I listed above. The most important thing is that this is not a situation where some give and some receive. The refugees look on us as brothers who have come to help them in a time of distress and tragedy. Almost all the responsible jobs are carried out by refugees. The warmest and most friendly relations exist between us and the refugees. It is not the decaying spirit of philanthropy, which might so easily have infiltrated into the work. For that reason all those in need of our aid enjoy receiving it. Nobody has been humiliated. [. . .]

We have begun to develop cultural activities. The first thing we introduced was speaking Yiddish. It has become quite the fashion in the camp. We have organized classes in Polish, attended by about 200 persons, and other classes. There are several reading rooms, a library; the religious groups have set up a Talmud Torah [religious school]. There are concerts, and a choir is active. [. . .]

Zbąszyń has become a symbol for the defenselessness of the Jews of Poland. Jews were humiliated to the level of lepers, to third-class citizens, and as a result we are all visited by terrible tragedy. [. . .]

Please accept my warmest good wishes and kisses from
Emanuel

---

22. Yitzhak Giterman (1889–1943) was director of the AJJDC in Poland on the eve of World War II and a mentor to Emanuel Ringelblum. In September 1939, Giterman fled to Vilna, in Lithuania, where he resumed his relief work. Later in Warsaw, he took active part in self-help efforts until his murder in January 1943.

DOCUMENT 1-16: Ovadia Camhy,[23] "Under the Sign of Satan," on pogrom violence in Germany,[24] *Le Judaïsme séphardi* (Paris), December 1938 (translated from French).

When the news broke that legation secretary vom Rath had been assassinated at the German embassy in Paris by a 17-year-old Polish Jew, Herschel Grynszpan, we felt a deep mixture of fear and pity. We feared that such a crime would provoke reprisals in Germany against the Jews, and we felt a profound pity for the young diplomat, an innocent victim.

Certainly, Grynszpan's crime was not a villainous one. His motive was not robbery or any other dishonorable objective. It was an act of despair. When one is 17 and overwhelmed by the horror of persecutions inflicted on one's own race and one's own parents, one quickly loses one's balance and, faced with the inadequacy of the civilized world and the impunity of tyrants, becomes obsessed by the desire for vengeance, or by the desire to cause a scandal capable of overcoming the silence of the world and centering world opinion on collective crimes that have been left in the shadows for too long.

Despite that, we condemned as strongly as possible the ill-considered act of Grynszpan, all the more so as it was likely to cause difficulties for France in its relations with Germany: for a France that, in offering a generous hospitality to refugees from other countries, has the right to expect better behavior from them.

After the success of the assassination, what could we do but express our deepest sympathy? The affair was henceforth a matter for French justice, and it was appropriate to await its verdict.

If the Reich had any shame, it would have waited for this verdict. In civilized countries, a crime is adjudicated and punished. In civilized countries, the

---

23. Ovadia Camhy (1888–1971?) worked as a journalist, was active in the foundation of the World Sephardi Federation in 1932, and edited its journal in France, *Le Judaïsme séphardi*.

24. On the night of November 9–10, 1938, the Nazi leadership staged Reich-wide violence to express "the German people's outrage" at the assassination of a German diplomat, Ernst vom Rath, in Paris by seventeen-year-old Herschel Grynszpan. Grynszpan's parents had been deported from Germany across the Polish border in late October, together with thousands of other Jews of Polish origin. During "*Kristallnacht*" synagogues, shops, and apartments owned or occupied by Jews were destroyed; at least twenty-six thousand Jewish men were arrested and incarcerated in the Dachau, Sachsenhausen, and Buchenwald concentration camps. The official death total of ninety-one people represents only a fraction of the overall casualties. After this event, a wave of anti-Jewish regulations swept Germany and forced more German Jews to emigrate. See Alan E. Steinweis, *Kristallnacht 1938* (Cambridge, MA: Belknap Press, 2009).

people, let alone the rabble, do not substitute themselves for justice. In civilized countries, only the person responsible is punished, and not the innocent.

But people in the Reich acted as they would have done in barbarian countries. [. . .]

The extreme cruelty of these measures and the desperate and inescapable situation of an entire community have roused the indignation of all the nations that have not yet been contaminated by the racist virus and that remain sensitive to human misery. [. . .]

Certainly, this general agreement on two continents to condemn the posture of a dictatorial Germany blinded by an implacable hatred is in itself a fine expression of human solidarity that gives us solace in such benighted times. But it is not only an expression. It is accompanied by steps aimed at ending the sufferings of Germany's Jews as they search for lands of asylum. [. . .]

The time has come to find an international solution to the alarming refugee problem. It must be understood that offering them aid alone is not enough. Aid that is distributed just for some period of time does not solve anything. They need to work, and work is forbidden them! They need to live, and life is forbidden them! The fate that often awaits refugees who leave the Nazi inferno is poverty in all its horror, accompanied by forcible repatriation or imprisonment.

The evil must be overcome at the root. We must combine all Jewish and Christian efforts to put *work* at the heart of all humanitarian aid to help the refugees.

DOCUMENT 1-17: Speech by Léon Blum,[25] Paris, delivered at the banquet dinner at the ninth annual meeting of the International League against Antisemitism, November 26, 1938, Centre de Documentation Juive Contemporaine fonds LICA, CMXCVI/série I/3.2.2, dossier no. 42, 2–12 (translated from French).

[. . .] We are witnessing phenomena that, I believe, we have not witnessed for fifteen centuries, since the collapse of the Roman Empire and the barbarian invasions.

I myself have lived since my youth, and all of you have lived, and many generations before us have lived, with the idea that mankind was above all governed by the law of progress; that indeed mankind is progressing pretty

---

25. Léon Blum (1872–1950) was, as head of the Popular Front government, the first Jewish prime minister of France (1936–1937 and 1938). From 1943 until April 1945 he was incarcerated in the Buchenwald concentration camp.

steadily and that its scientific progress—thanks to the increasingly great, power-ful, and definite influence of human reason on natural forces—[has marked its development], but that it is also marked by the development, by the blossoming, of a moral sense in man, of feelings of fraternity, solidarity, and equity. [. . .]

And now everything seems to have been placed in question again[;] not only is humanity no longer advancing, but it seems that suddenly an inconceiv-able, an inexplicable, decline is being imposed on it. Not only has everything been called into question, but everything seems to have been destroyed, and humanity seems to be in retrograde motion, moving backward, appears to be reverting suddenly to epochs of which we have lost all trace in our memory, that we can hardly understand or imagine accurately anymore, back to times of idolatrous fanaticism, from which all human civilization must have slowly escaped.

Yes, that is it, that is the terrible spectacle; it is seeing, I repeat, what we never thought possible: civilization is going backward. It is of that, that the Jewish people is the victim[;] it is of that, that hundreds of thousands of Jews are victims. They are not the only victims, however; do not forget, never forget it: they are the most public victims, but they are not the only victims.

How could this have happened? How will this real mental conundrum be solved? [. . .]

And so, what is the cause of all this today? It is a dogma, it is a dogmatic theory, an alien dogma, the racial dogma, the dogma that confounds the nation with the existence of pure, homogeneous, unalloyed race and that wants to propound the idea and implement the practice of a specific difference between races, of a difference between superior races, created for rule and conquest, and inferior races, condemned and made for one knows too well what.

I do not want to go at length here, tonight, into a critique of racial theories. You know that if a pure and homogeneous race were necessary to make a nation, then there would not be a single nation in the world [lively applause]. [. . .]

In France, with all the efforts in the world we could not arrive at that odd idea of a racial hypothesis. We could not submit to the same criterion a man from Provence and a man from Brittany.

Nevertheless, whatever its worth may be, it is that racial theory that is at the origin[;] it is in it that one must see the cause[;] it is its development, full of all kinds of fanaticism, that has led to this human regression that we are witness-ing today. [. . .]

But finally, my dear friends, whatever the causes—and I think I am provid-ing you with the essentials right now—the spectacle is here before our eyes. In a big European country, in several countries of Europe, hundreds of thousands of Jews today are destined for, condemned to the most miserable and atrocious fate. Will they be able to leave their prison, even stripped bare? I do not know. I am not sure of this. I am not at all sure that racism is not determined to keep its serfs and hostages, regardless.

But finally, for those who have already left and for those who are going to leave, one must find a refuge.

I will say here everything I'm thinking, even if I must offend the feelings of other Jews, even if I dispute the words recently uttered or published by men who, at least from a religious point of view, may pass for representatives of the Jews [bravo! bravo! very sustained applause].

I could not imagine anything in the world as painful and as dishonorable as French Jews taking great care to close the doors of France today to Jewish refugees from other countries [prolonged applause]. Let them not imagine that they can preserve their tranquility, their security in this way. There is no example in history of security being acquired by cowardice [applause], not for peoples, not for social groups, not for individuals.

As for me, things lead me to an idea that you perhaps will find quite simple, quite rudimentary, but I can't imagine these things any differently: You are at home, at night, in the country. Several kilometers away, a natural disaster strikes, a natural catastrophe, either a fire or a flood. There are men, there are women, there are children, fleeing across the fields, half naked, trembling from the cold, threatened by hunger. Your house may already be full, that's possible, but when they knock on your door, you open it to them [bravo! bravo!], and you don't ask them for their identity papers, their police record, or their vaccination certificate [enthusiastic applause]. [. . .]

Naturally, these unfortunates will not be able to stay forever, of course. Naturally, solutions of a stable and lasting kind will have to be found; but after all, for now, until they find themselves a safer and more durable refuge elsewhere, how are you going to refuse them shelter for a night? [. . .]

I know what the difficulties are today. I repeat with passion that I hope the conference which will soon convene in London will finally succeed in finding common ground between two branches of the Semitic family, the Arabs and the Jews, and that immigration can start again on a larger scale and that it can even spread to other regions of Asia, whether it be to Transjordan, to certain regions of Syria, or to Iraq.

Perhaps this will not suffice and new lands will have to be found instead. Let us look for them, find them, but by really doing what great democratic states must do in order for new cities really to be opened, with all the higher possibilities of human life. May they find there, at least, something that looks like a new fatherland and not international concentration camps [prolonged applause]. [. . .]

I do not believe that the catastrophe of mankind is irreparable. I am sure that civilization will return to its path. An eclipse may be prolonged, yet that does not mean that it completely gets rid of the sun. What are we facing? In the end, to me, it seems that what is happening all depends on details specific to a certain country, explicable by its domestic history, one of the forms of mental delirium that more or less hit all mankind after World War I. [. . .]

Don't be surprised; there is no disproportion between the facts and the cause. Since the war, mankind has experienced strange illnesses, and this is one of them in many respects and the worst of them all. But mankind will recover; mankind will recover because it must go on living. So one must withstand the ordeal with confidence, bear it with courage, without selfishness, without snobbery, without fear, without shame. One must rid oneself of all petty forms—so degrading—of complaint. One must be worthy of oneself. One must be worthy of one's past and of one's origins. One must be calm and courageous. One must have confidence in the future of mankind.

DOCUMENT 1-18: Account by Max Eschelbacher,[26] England, on his imprisonment following "*Kristallnacht*," written in spring/early summer 1939, translated from Max Eschelbacher, *Der zehnte November 1938* (Essen: Klartext, 1998), 41–54.

[. . .; Eschelbacher describes his assault and arrest during "*Kristallnacht*":] These fellows descended on me with clenched fists. One grabbed me and shouted at me that I should go downstairs. I was convinced that I would be beaten to death, went into the bedroom, took off my watch, put down my wallet and keys, and said good-bye to Berta [his wife]. All she said was, "Cha-sak!" [Hebrew: Be strong!].

[. . .; a description of his arrest and imprisonment follows.] Only one experience was positive in the twelve days that I was a prisoner. On Saturday, November 19, a warder appeared at the cell door. He pulled a long object wrapped in white paper out of his pocket and handed it to me with these words: "Your fellow sufferers are sending you this together with their greetings." At least 52 of us were being held in one large room down in the basement. Now they had

---

26. An expert in Jewish law, Max Eschelbacher (1880–1964) served as a rabbi in Bruchsal beginning in 1906 and later in Düsseldorf from 1913 until he left Germany. He spent nearly two weeks in prison after being attacked during the November 1938 pogrom and in 1939 managed to emigrate with his wife, Berta, to England, which became their permanent home.

sent me a huge meat sausage as a greeting. I thanked the jailer but told him I could not eat it and asked him to return it with my warmest thanks. He thought that the others might also want to eat it, whereupon I told him we had [our] dietary laws and each of us would have it on his conscience.

A legend grew out of this story, and it apparently left quite an impression at the jail. The story got around among the warders that my jailer had said, "But no one will see it," and that I had responded, "God will see it!" In this version the story appears to have really affected people. [. . .]

DOCUMENT 1-19: Letter by Georg Landauer,[27] Jerusalem, to Henry Montor, New York, on the mood among German Jews, December 2, 1938, Central Zionist Archive RG S25/9703.

[. . .] German Jewry is panic-stricken. They know they are lost. They fear they have no help, and what they think is that the Nazis are preparing a similar plot in America, presumably in the States. They, i.e., the Nazis, cannot continue feeding tens of thousands of Jews in the camps inside Germany. Although the persons in the concentration camps have to pay for their nutrition, according to the Nazi conception, they are paying with German money because all Jewish money belongs to the German State. They are not sure that other countries will take them out of Germany, and so far, they are not yet convinced that world Jewry will nourish them in Germany or pay the ransom hoped for by the German Government. Therefore, there are Jews in Germany who think that the intention is to arrange for a second plot and then to make short work of the Jews in Germany, or a considerable part of them.

Clearly, we cannot know whether the second part of the assumption is correct, but no one knows the criminal and insane phantasy of the Nazis, and it may be that perhaps only one percent of these apprehensions may prove to be correct. [. . .]

We think that the American press, the most important newspapers in any case, should bear this in mind that if something will happen to a Nazi official in America it should be understood in the light of what I have told you above. [. . .]

---

27. Georg Landauer (1895–1954), a German-born Zionist activist, moved in 1934 to Palestine, where he helped organize the settlement of German Jews.

DOCUMENT 1-20: Letter by Leon Gattegno,[28] Salonika, Greece, to the WJC Paris,[29] June 7, 1939, on the plight of Jews on refugee ships, USHMMA RG 11.001 M36, reel 107 (SAM 1190-1-299) (translated from French).

Dear Sirs:

We confirm our letter of May 12, 1939, and acknowledge receipt of your letter dated May 22, 1939.

The situation here is becoming more tragic every day, and we are literally overwhelmed and do not know how to relieve the immense misery spread out before us. The unfortunate 1,500 refugees on the ships *Agios Nikolaos, Astir,* and *Assimi* are well on the way to being struck by an attack of collective insanity as a result of the despair that grips them, and this thought makes us shudder. Until now, and despite the lateness of the season for our regions, the weather has been exceedingly mild, but we see with real anguish that the period of great heat is coming. It will torture our coreligionists, who are taxed already, as they are forced to sleep in overheated and stinking ship holds, and the slightest illness can provoke catastrophes.

The Jewish communities of Athens and Salonika have made every sacrifice and every effort to help them, but the task is far beyond our means and is becoming a superhuman effort for us. Help is indispensable and needed immediately, and we beg you to tell us ways to further our effort to feed these unfortunate people, to prevent them from sinking into madness, and, above all, to find a definitive shelter as soon as possible.

It is impossible to prolong their stay on these miserable little boats, which are cramped and unhealthy, and where they are penned up like a herd of animals headed straight to the slaughterhouse.

We are coming to you to let out a cry of anguish and to make you aware that this desperate situation cannot, must not, continue. A remedy must be found before it is too late!

With our hearts broken by compassion for the dreadful spectacle before us,

---

28. Leon Gattegno (1863?–1943) was a Jewish secondary school principal and the president of the Jewish community of Salonika from 1938 to 1941. In 1943 he was deported to Auschwitz, where he perished.

29. The World Jewish Congress (WJC), founded in 1936 and initially headquartered in Paris, worked to fight antisemitism and to organize relief for Jewish populations as well as rescue and advocacy efforts. The WJC moved its central office to Geneva with the outbreak of war and then to New York in 1940. After the war it supported efforts to rebuild European Jewish communities.

we nonetheless retain the hope that your organization will immediately do whatever is necessary to send financial assistance and to end this terrible martyrdom.

Please accept the assurances of our highest consideration.

The Secretary   The President
[illegible]   [signed] L. Gattegno

PART II

1939—1940

DOCUMENT 2-1: Testimony by an unidentified woman from Lipno, Poland, on the first days of war, recorded ca. 1940 in the Warsaw ghetto, USHMMA RG 15.079M (ŻIH Ring. I/854), reel 39 (translated from Polish).

[. . .] On the day the war started—it was a Friday, an ill-fated day—everything changed, as though someone had covered the town with ashes. Everyone's face turned gray, with smiles fixed on their pale lips that instinctively, instead of speaking, began to whisper; various pieces of news spread like wild fire around town, creating confusion, panic. [. . .]

Every day brought something new. On Friday the first of September [1939], enemy bombs fell on the town, on the railroad tracks in particular—an attempt to damage them so as to disrupt communication with Warsaw; there were no antiaircraft defenses whatsoever, people hid in basements and discussed what was going on. Polish forces moved in the direction of Pomerania. [. . .]

On Saturday the second of September, people from Pomerania began to flee with whatever and however they could, on wagons and crowded into trains, there were shortages of food and water too. Aid committees immediately sprang up, Polish and Jewish, antisemitism disappeared. Women ran through the streets with baskets as people threw bread, fruit, and tomatoes from windows and balconies and stores donated soda water, *kvas* [a beverage], etc. All of this was driven out to the station and distributed among the refugees regardless of religion. A great migration began; day and night, wagons were constantly in motion, cars sometimes flew by, everything was moving in the direction of Włocławek; Polish forces began to retreat in the night from Saturday to Sunday, the entire camp was returning, with thousands and thousands of people in tow. Fear of the enemy was becoming more and more widespread. The residents of Lipno, following the example of neighboring towns, also began to buy and to rent new wagons and horses and to pack things up to get ready to leave. One mother said to me, "I'm afraid, so I'm sending my daughters along with the camp, and when they leave I'll be calmer." [. . .]

[. . .] People continued to travel through Lipno, and the residents of Lipno were leaving too; my husband and I watched this with a heavy heart [. . .] our best and closest friends were leaving town. We, mainly my husband, decided to stay: "Let whatever is going to happen to me happen at home—I'm not moving until I'm forced to." It stayed like this until the following Friday; on September 8, X [the Germans]¹ entered the town. After they took control, a whole series of orders and prohibitions was issued. One could only be on the street until 5 o'clock, Jews had to wear yellow ribbons, and when these markings proved too small, Jews were ordered to pin yellow sashes onto their backs and chests. Walking on the sidewalk was forbidden; [there was] an order to walk on the road, to bow. A despicable little Jew from a neighboring town conveyed all these orders. [The Germans] began to round up Jews to clean the streets and squares, and you had to see how the Aryan overseers stood laughing as the Jews of the town swept the streets.

The Polish intelligentsia watched this with indignation and often spoke to the Jews, comforting them and advising them not to preoccupy themselves too much with what, according to them, was a temporary annoyance. All Aryan and Jewish organizations were disbanded.

---

1. Here, the author clearly crossed out what she had written and replaced it with an *X.* From the context, one can tell she meant to write "the Germans" but decided against it.

DOCUMENT 2-2: Shimon Huberband,[2] Warsaw, "The Destruction of Synagogues, Study Halls, and Cemeteries," no date (ca. 1941), USHMMA RG 15.079M (ŻIH Ring. I/108), reel 7 (translated from Yiddish).[3]

Będzin They [the Germans] marched into Będzin on Tuesday, September 5, 1939. The priest and both rabbis welcomed them [with the traditional] bread and salt. This was an effective gesture. No slaughter took place in Będzin, as had occurred in the neighboring Sosnowiec.[4]

On the evening of Saturday, September 9, 1939, at the same time as in Sosnowiec, a frightening dynamite explosion was heard across town. It was soon learned that the synagogue was on fire. A number of Jews, including Rabbi Yekhil Shlezinger, his two sons, and his son-in-law, Rabbi Yekhezkel Kon, raced into the burning synagogue to rescue the Torah scrolls. The arsonists shot at them and killed all of them. The martyrs were burned together with the synagogue and its Torah scrolls.

The Jews began to pour out of the surrounding houses to save themselves from the flames. The whole area, however, had been cordoned off by soldiers, and as soon as a Jew was spotted, he was shot. In a short time the streets near the *shul* [synagogue] were filled with the bodies of dead Jews.

At that point Jews no longer even tried to quell the fire. The blaze spread from one house to the next, and everyone inside knew that leaving the house meant certain death. People were driven mad by looking death straight in the eye and knowing that there was no way they could save themselves from death. The only choice left to them was how to die—burnt by the fire or shot by a bullet.

---

2. Shimon Huberband (1909–1942), born in Chęciny near Kielce, Poland, was a rabbi in Piotrków Trybunalski. His wife and child were killed in a German air raid in September 1939 during the Nazi invasion of Poland. Huberband returned to Piotrków Trybunalski but subsequently moved to Warsaw and eventually remarried. In Warsaw, Huberband began working with the self-help organization Aleynhilf, heading its religious section; he also collaborated with Emanuel Ringelblum on the Oyneg Shabes underground archive. In August 1942, he was sent with his second wife to Treblinka, where both were murdered.

3. This account is also printed in a differently worded translation in Shimon Huberband, *Kiddush Hashem: Jewish Religious and Cultural Life in Poland during the Holocaust*, ed. Jeffrey S. Gurock and Robert S. Hirt (Hoboken, NJ: KTAV Publishing House, 1987), 274ff.

4. According to Huberband (see his *Kiddush Hashem*, 287), as soon as German troops entered Sosnowiec (on the road from Katowice to Będzin) on September 4, 1939, they arrested three hundred Jews and shot all of them. The next day the Germans interned all male Jews in a camp, where they shaved beards and subjected the prisoners to brutal torture. An additional seven Jews were shot on the pretext that they had been trying to sabotage a German vehicle.

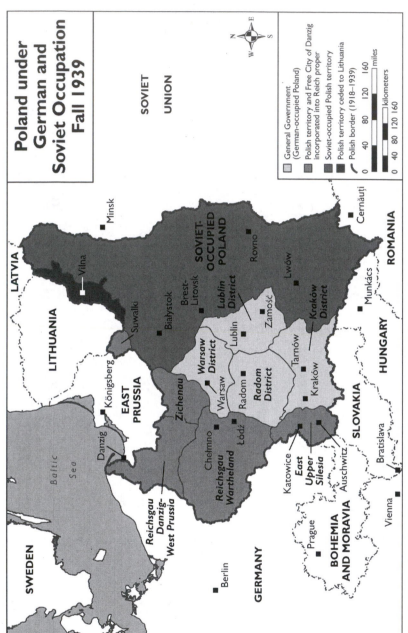

Map 2: Poland under German and Soviet occupation, fall 1939.

Women who ran out onto the street were not shot. But many women remained in their homes, although they could have saved themselves from the flames. They perished together with their families.

Fifty-six Jewish houses were burned down that day in addition to the synagogue. Nearly five hundred Jews died, either by being shot or being burned. The synagogue burned, the Torah scrolls burned, the bodies of Jewish martyrs, men and women, burned. But the heavens did not spurt out any fire to burn those who had caused the conflagration.

Only a few Jews managed to save themselves. One man clothed himself in a long dress and put a kerchief on his head. There were six men in all who rescued themselves in such a manner.

There was a church on a hill not far from the synagogue. A steeply curved street led from the Jewish quarter to the church. At a certain moment during the fire, the German guards left this street, and since it was curved and very steep, they couldn't detect from farther away whether anyone was moving there. Six Jews seized this moment, rushing out of a burning house and escaping into the church by way of this street. The priest and the worshippers welcomed the Jews very hospitably and kept them in hiding. As a result, the six were saved from certain death.

DOCUMENT 2-3: "Nazis Establish More Ghettos in Poland," *Canadian Jewish Chronicle* (Montreal), January 12, 1940, 5.

NEW YORK (WNS)

Establishment of ghettos in various towns in Nazi-occupied Poland not incorporated in the Reich, to segregate Jews in separate districts, besides the Jewish "reservation" in Lublin,[5] is reported to Jewish organizations in Paris, according to a Paris dispatch to the *New York Times*.

Warsaw Jews, who paid several million zlotys in November for postponement of the ghetto orders, now again are menaced with formal separation. Already certain streets in the centre of the city are closed to Jews. The dispatch

---

5. This refers to a German expulsion scheme in the Lublin district of the Generalgouvernement near the town of Nisko on the San river. In October 1939, Gestapo officer Adolf Eichmann organized transports of Jews from the newly annexed East Upper Silesia, the Protectorate of Bohemia and Moravia, and Vienna to Nisko, where the deportees were to build barracks for a large camp. Due to problems emanating from Nazi plans to "Germanize" Poland, SS chief Heinrich Himmler stopped these transports in early November, and the camp itself was closed in April 1940, when the Jews were returned to Austria and the Protectorate.

further disclosed that in Radom, Minsk and Mazowiech,[6] Jews already have been ordered to settle in separate districts. To these ghettos have been transferred many inhabitants from surrounding villages and townships.

Before ghettos are created, detailed registration of Jewish property is undertaken. Jews are compelled to deposit sums of more than 2,000 złotys and any valuables they possess.

Informed sources were of the opinion that this policy of separating Jews in various towns confirms recent information that the Nazis decided to slow down deportations to Lublin. According to the dispatch, Dr. Hans Frank, Governor General of Nazi-occupied Poland, visited the "reservation" recently and expressed dissatisfaction with the state of affairs there, asserting that the idea of the "reservation" is difficult to work out and too costly, as foreign Jews are unwilling to pour relief money into a reservation.

DOCUMENT 2-4: S. Moldawer,[7] "The Road to Lublin," on his deportation from Hamburg in October 1939, *Contemporary Jewish Record* (New York) 3 (March–April 1940): 120–21.

[. . .] Twelve hours in the foul and filthy car. Not even a drop of water to drink. The few scraps of food we were able to buy at Hamburg with our last couple of marks have long since been exhausted. What we had has been divided among the women and children or given to old people. We men have had nothing. For us it has been a real Yom Kippur [Day of Atonement].

Suddenly the door of the freight car is opened. The captain of the guard pokes his head in and orders us all to get out. We form fours on the platform. The chief of the Berlin Gestapo calls the roll. One hundred and twenty-two "pieces of baggage." "No one dead?" he remarks ironically. "Wait till they get to Lublin, and we'll put them to bed with a shovel."

It's the first time anyone has mentioned a destination. Now we hear it, we can scarcely believe our ears. What has Lublin to do with us? Naturally, we had heard of it. City in Poland. Once played a role in Jewish history. That's all. No one, of course, has the faintest idea that this is to be the capital of Hitler's "Ghetto-State," the republic that is somehow to rise from the ruins and smoke. For five weeks we have been cut off from the outside world and seen no papers.

---

6. This is most likely a reference to Minsk-Mazowiecki, near Warsaw.

7. The author's identity could not be clearly established. From his article it appears he had Polish citizenship but lived in Germany for more than twenty years and had been interned in 1938–1939 in the Buchenwald concentration camp. Released shortly before the war, he was again arrested in September 1939 and deported to Lublin; based on a U.S. visa, he was released in mid-November and subsequently made it to the United States via Italy.

The formalities are over. We are herded back into the car, into our living grave.

In heaven's name, we cry, what is to become of us? What does it all mean? Here we are, hungry and frozen, without a penny or a morsel of bread, without even a drop of water, and once again we are ordered out. This time they prod us in the back with the butts of their rifles. At four o'clock, they stuff us in again and padlock the door. The train moves off. So there is no reprieve.

In a corner of the truck, stifled sobbing. Every now and then a piercing shriek. Everywhere tears, everywhere terror. Presently pandemonium. People start knocking their heads against the walls. It goes on like this for a couple of hours. Then, a platform, crowds, human faces. People begin to hear us. They stop in their tracks. They look around.

The bolt slides back. The Gestapo officer comes in. He is livid with rage. He wants to know the reason for the din.

"We are hungry," cry some.

"We want to know where we're going."

"Where?" bellows the officer, foaming with rage. "To Lublin, of course, to the Jew state."

Is the world gone crazy? It's the second time we've heard that name. Lublin. We are going to Lublin. A Jewish state. What does it all mean? Are we dreaming? Are we mad? A Jewish state in Lublin? Hitler the Savior of the Jews? Hitler the Messiah?

An order is rapped out. Whoever has money can buy food. Whoever hasn't can rot.

We run through our pockets for our last few pennies and frenziedly hand them over. The Gestapo agent runs to the buffet. The place is cleaned out. Only sweets and chocolates. Better than nothing.

The train moves on. Over and over again the word Lublin is muttered. But now it is not merely Lublin. It is the Jewish state. The words ring like magic. Now, at least, our journey has [a] point. Instead of New York, Philadelphia, or Chicago, they are taking us to Lublin. One hundred and twenty-two Jewish souls packed in a filthy freight car. [. . .]

DOCUMENT 2-5: Photograph of Warsaw Jews, wearing armbands, selling their possessions out of suitcases in a makeshift market on a bombed-out street, December 1939, USHMMPA WS# 31515.

DOCUMENT 2-6: Letter by Jenny Marx,[8] Mannheim, Germany, to Max Marx and family, Jerusalem, on her daily struggles, January 14, 1940, private collection (translated from German).

My dear Three:

I thank you for your two letters and am happy that you all are well. Unfortunately, I cannot say the same of us. Papa is very gravely ill and is slowly declining. There is no chance for improvement, as cancer of the lung is incurable. He has had this illness for four years now, and he is bedridden, can no longer get up. He was in the hospital for 10 weeks without any improvement,

---

8. Jenny Marx (1906–1942?) was born in Mannheim, Germany. After internment in the Gurs camp, she was deported to Auschwitz, where she was murdered. Her mother, Ernestine (née Hess), was also sent to Gurs and died in early 1944 in Mâcon, France. Siegmund Mayer (1907–1942?), Jenny's fiancé, was deported to Gurs the same day as the Marx women and killed in Auschwitz. Max Marx, Jenny's younger brother, had emigrated to Palestine in 1933. The other persons mentioned in the letter could not be identified.

and the doctor tells us that the end could come fast.[9] We have to face the facts, because there is no sense in deceiving each other. Mother is also an old, sick woman; 70 years is no longer youth. The daily sorrows take their toll. I'm certain, dear Max, that you cannot imagine how poor we have become. I hope that you will always be spared such a sad condition. We are entirely dependent upon the Jewish community; otherwise, we have nothing left at all. Completely without means. You will also understand that this is hard on the nerves. Siegm. [Siegmund, her fiancé] and I carry the entire responsibility. It is very sad that we have to start building our new life in such poverty. To set up a comfortable home, from what? It is out of the question. Our bedroom is my white bed and your old bed, painted white, that is my home. I've gotten past it. Siegmund is unemployed at the moment, as work was stopped because of the cold weather.[10] But daily life goes on. One has to live, the rent has to be paid, and we have to have some heat. We sit here often without heat. Can you imagine that? I don't think so. [. . .] I think you couldn't stand this misery. This is my lot. Who wants impoverished people? Nobody. Nobody is left here, they all have emigrated. The only one with some human compassion is Uncle Schlösser. Uncle Josef also promised the parents that he will help, but nothing so far. Please remind him of his duty. Now you have a picture how poor we have become. Sometimes I would want to end my life, if I did not love Siegmund so much. Therefore I am making a sincere request of you, please send Uncle what is meant for us, because we are in dire need. Please write once more to Martin Dreyfuss, and ask that he get the matter of the house sale in Malsch in order. It is already a year since they left, and we're already dead as far as they are concerned. Uncle Salomon has owed us 1,000 marks for 10 years. He has yet to pay back a penny, and now we would need it desperately. Please see to it that they help us in whatever manner. Siegmund and I can no longer carry this burden alone. Otherwise there is little news. My in-laws visit us from time to time, they are also in bad shape financially. I have a question, has your affidavit for America expired? Are you still interested in it? If not, see whether it can be transferred to us, Siegmund has none, in the event that you cannot let us come to you. I thank you all for your congratulations on our wedding. It had to be postponed, since I have been very sick, we hope that we can do it this month. [. . .]

---

9. Jenny Marx's father, Herz, died of his illness later in January 1940.
10. Starting in 1938, Jews in Germany were drafted for forced labor.

DOCUMENT 2-7: Account by an unidentified woman on the German/
Soviet occupation of Zamość, no date (ca. 1941), USHMMA RG 15.079M
(ŻIH Ring. I/935), reel 42 (translated from Yiddish).

[. . .] Between Yom Kippur and Sukkot of the year 5700 [between September 23 and September 28, 1939], the Germans left the city, and we learned that
the Russians would soon come in.[11]

Jews were extremely afraid of pogroms and attacks by the Poles in the inter-
vening time, before the arrival of the Russians. Jews closed down their shops
and locked the gates. All the men took up positions by the gates, armed with
sticks, rods, axes, and iron tools, to defend themselves in case of an attack by
the Poles, but no attacks took place.

After three days, Russian tanks and a large military force entered the city. Jews
rejoiced and went out to the marketplace. The military forces continued beyond
the city. A city council was created and was composed of formerly arrested Communists, for the most part Jews. The local Jewish Communist, Hackman, was
appointed to be the head of the council. A militia was soon formed, which was
composed of some of the darker elements of the Polish and Jewish population.
[Food] products, which had been stored in a warehouse of the municipal authorities, were distributed by the city council among the poorer segments of the Polish
and Jewish population. Every night there was a meeting in the marketplace, Hackman and others gave Communist speeches in Polish, Russian, and Yiddish.

After a few days, we learned that the Soviets would leave the city and that
the Germans would return. Great panic and confusion gripped the Jewish population. Hackman called a special meeting in the marketplace and categorically
denied the rumors, but in the morning we found out that Hackman himself
had sent off his mother, wife, and child in a horse and carriage.

The next day the retreat of the Soviet forces began in the town. Many Jews,
out of fear of the Germans, also fled the city with the Russians. The soldiers
gladly picked them up and allowed the Jews to travel on their vehicles. Among
the Russian soldiers there were many Jews, among them a great number who
still remembered their Jewishness. With great longing, they asked about the
Jewish holidays, the Sabbath, and praying.

My husband and I also boarded a military vehicle. On Shemini Atzres of
that year [October 5, 1939], we arrived in Rawa Ruska.

---

11. Between the signing of the Molotov-Ribbentrop Pact on August 23, 1939, and the
German attack on the Soviet Union on June 22, 1941, the two countries divided the defeated
Poland and the previously independent Baltic states among themselves.

DOCUMENT 2-8: Letter by Moshe Kleinbaum,[12] Geneva, to Nahum Goldmann,[13] New York, on the situation in Soviet-occupied Poland, March 12, 1940, facsimile reprinted in *Archives of the Holocaust*, ed. Abraham J. Peck (New York: Garland Publishing, 1990), 8:112–13.

[. . .] I had an opportunity to observe at first hand the Soviet occupation for a period of six weeks in three important places, in Łuck, Lemberg, and Vilna, from September 18 to October 28 [1939]. I therefore have a right to claim that everything I say represents my own view and reflects the truth.

I saw the Red Army march into Łuck. Thick rows of people lined the main street through which the Soviet tanks, artillery, and mechanized infantry marched. Most of them watched the scene out of curiosity. Ukrainian peasants, who streamed in from the surrounding villages, and young Jewish Communists, particularly the girls, applauded and hailed the Army with friendly greetings. The number of Jewish enthusiasts was not very large, but they made more noise than all the others that day. This created the false impression that the Jews were the chief hosts at this festival. In Łuck, the Polish population consisted almost entirely of officials and the military. They and their families kept off the streets on that memorable day. I spoke with Jewish shopkeepers, with a tailor, a shoemaker, a teacher, a salaried man, an unemployed Jewish engineer, with Jews representing all sections, who expressed the reaction of the Jewish population, not to be confused with the tumult raised by a few dozen youthful Jewish Communists, in a clever comment such as issues from Jews in critical times. Already on September 18, the following remarks prevailed among the Jews of Łuck: "We were condemned to death, but our sentence has been commuted to life-long imprisonment." The Nazi danger meant the death penalty for the Jews. The Red Army came and rescued a million and a half Jews from a sure physical and civil death, but the Red Army rescued no more than the bare lives of Jews. The Jewish population views life under Soviet rule as a sentence of life imprisonment. Life continues, but with nothing more than black bread and water, and people are no longer free. You probably know that I am somewhat familiar with the spirit of the masses, and that the gauging of public opinion is, so to speak, my profession. I wish to declare, with the fullest conviction, that at least 80 percent of the Jews think that way, and that they accepted Soviet rule first with a sigh of relief, because of the weeks of anxiety regarding the threat of Nazi

---

12. Polish-born Moshe Kleinbaum (aka Sneh, 1909–1972) was a doctor and leading Zionist who emigrated in 1940 to Palestine, where he became the head of the Jewish militia organization (Haganah) and later served in the Israeli parliament.

13. Nahum Goldmann (1895–1982) helped create the WJC in 1936 and served as its longtime president.

invasion, and then with a sigh of deep concern: What will the morrow bring us? Whoever describes the reaction of the Jewish people in eastern Poland to the arrival of the Red Army otherwise, is falsifying the truth. [. . .]

DOCUMENT 2-9: Photograph of Willem Friedman,[14] a soldier in the Belgian army, posing next to a piece of artillery, winter 1939–1940, USHMMPA WS# 20481.

DOCUMENT 2-10: Eugen Tillinger,[15] "The Bridge of Hendaye: Eyewitness Account of the Mass Flight to Spain," *Aufbau* (New York), August 30, 1940, 2 (translated from German).

[. . .] Closed border

And now people are standing in line before the bridge. Before the bridge that has often been mentioned in the world press, before the famous bridge at

---

14. Willem Friedman, a Belgian Jew born 1919 in Antwerp, joined the Belgian army after finishing high school. He fought against the invading German army in May 1940 and was taken prisoner. After his release Friedman and his entire family managed to flee Belgium via France, Spain, and Portugal, eventually emigrating to the United States in 1940.

15. Journalist Eugen (Eugene) Tillinger (1908–1966) had worked for a German tabloid from 1928 to 1933 in Berlin before he arrived in late 1940 in New York, where he published extensively in *Aufbau* throughout the 1940s.

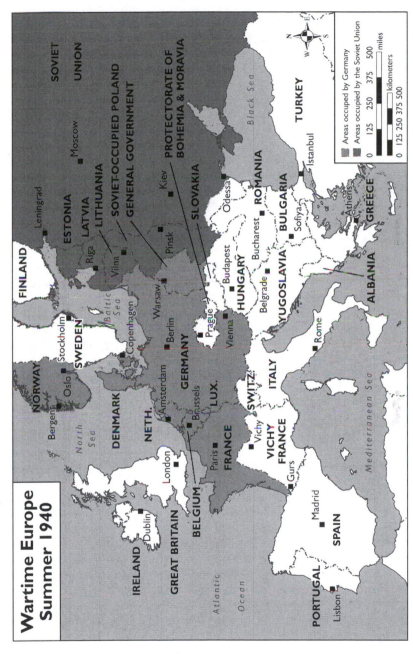

Map 3: Wartime Europe, summer 1940.

Hendaye [at the French-Spanish border]. Just a few meters ahead of us, the *tricolore* still flies. The French officials are unusually friendly. And barely a hundred meters [300 feet] away lies Spain. We hear the radio: the German troops are advancing, the cease-fire was signed yesterday.[16] Many people are growing impatient. Believe that the border could be closed any minute. One man, who is sent back because his papers are not in order, has a crying fit.

It is 1:00 in the afternoon now. Our turn has come. All the formalities are done with, we walk the few steps toward the French border barriers, show the official a white slip of paper; he takes it, says "Merci" one last time, and gives a signal with his hand. The toll bar rises slowly . . . One step and we're no longer in France. Just a few more steps . . . We look behind us. Stand still here in no-man's-land for a moment, quietly. We think back with melancholy: Adieu, France . . . Glorious, beautiful France! Why did it have to come to this? Why? Slowly we walk toward the opposite end of the bridge. And only a lively dispute abruptly rouses us from our dreamlike state. What has happened? . . . A few seconds later we catch sight of a man talking insistently to the Spanish officials and gesticulating energetically all the while. The discussion grows louder and louder. It is clear: the Spaniards are unwilling to let the man pass through. In vain, he shows his visas, his diplomatic passport . . . Nothing helps: Mr. Titulescu, Romania's former foreign minister, is not allowed to pass . . . He has to go back. Back to France. . .

And twenty-four hours later, as we arrive at the Portuguese border, the swastika flag is already flying at the Hendaye bridge . . .

DOCUMENT 2-11: Letter by an unidentified Jewish correspondent in Casablanca, French-administered Morocco, on local conditions, August 28, 1940, USHMMA RG 68.045M (WJC Geneva C 3/1), 203–4 (translated from German).

[. . .] Incidentally, Casablanca is the most curious city I have ever seen—an American-style cocktail with a shot of megalomania and a Moorish flavor that fits the area well. Directly after seeing skyscrapers, you again catch sight of the most splendid gardens, like something out of *1001 Nights*. One can find the grandest and most powerful American cars such as Packards here, and the small donkeys ridden by a Moroccan must tread cautiously so as not to be run over. Nowadays horse-drawn carriages straight out of grandma's day make their way

---

16. Germany had started its offensive against France, Belgium, Luxembourg, and the Netherlands on May 10, 1940. The German-French cease-fire was signed on June 22, 1940, to take effect three days later.

through traffic, since the fuel shortage has also arrived in these parts. And the elegant residential area here lies directly next to the old medina, the native quarter of the Arabs—but also of the Jews—who live in unimaginable misery. Apart from that, Casablanca during the last two decades must truly have been the city where people became millionaires overnight. [. . .]

The Jews of Casablanca have by and large attained a highly respected position. Not only in an economic respect; they also have had a knack for gaining the favor of the Moroccan dignitaries and of members of other faiths through their extraordinary charitable endeavors. The Alliance Israélite in particular has made a name for itself here by founding a series of charitable institutions that are viewed as exemplary. The Alliance also maintains a number of its own schools for the benefit of the poor Jewish population. Casablanca, like Algeria, remained completely untouched by the stream of Jewish refugees over the last seven years. This changed with the tragic days of June [1940], when the Germans swiftly advanced through France. A hundred ships lay anchored off Bayonne, Biarritz, and Saint-Jean-de-Luz on the southernmost Atlantic coast [of France] ready to take refugees onboard. It was precisely on those three critical days before the armistice that it rained horribly. The refugees stood in the downpour on the beach for hours, all night, because they were willing to board the ships only if they were truly going to depart. Some sailed to England, but these steamships mainly took only English passengers as well as whole units of Polish and Czech troops, while smaller and medium-sized French ships initially set course for Portugal. However, the Portuguese port authorities refused to let the ships offload their cargo of hundreds of refugees, including very many non-French Jewish refugees. The term "cargo" is fitting here because the people were penned up, there was in most cases nothing to eat, and some ships even ran out of drinking water. The Joint and HICEM[17] in Lisbon were not informed in time. Hundreds of passengers had to be transferred from the smallest ships to a larger cargo ship while out at sea but within the three-mile zone. Some of the steamers set course for Casablanca. Here, too, port authorities initially refused to let them disembark. Their position changed quickly after they learned that these were refugees from France, many of whom had served France loyally. The refugees were first placed in a quarantine camp. In a humanitarian gesture, the Moroccan Jewish community in Casablanca very quickly attended to the refugees, who stemmed from twelve different nations and included four Christian families. Alongside some French notables, the Alliance Israélite as well as members of the foreign colony provided financial guarantees, and a great humanitarian service was thus performed. Those [newcomers] who were not deemed

---

17. HICEM was an organization that aided emigration of European Jews. It was founded in 1927.

suspicious and who did not have a criminal record were by and by released [from the camp]. The Alliance set up sleeping quarters at its various institutions, families were housed with private individuals, and a communal kitchen was created to provide kosher meals three times a day for individuals without means. All this work showed the same initiative and generosity as the aid provided for the Austrians in Switzerland during the fall of 1938. Provisions were also made to ensure that the refugees obeyed all police regulations. No new steamers arrived after the armistice because the French government followed its provisions to the letter. A few stragglers still arrived, but only by land and having traveled in part through Spain. The Aid Committee is well organized and seeks to help above all emigrants who already hold visas (indeed, only genuine visas). And yet various difficulties have arisen, since France remains bound to certain conditions; for instance, men fit for military service may not leave, and, moreover, the English blockade has brought travel by sea to an almost complete standstill. Very occasionally merchant vessels set sail for Portugal. These belong to a Portuguese company and charge "only" 3,500 French francs for a passage to Lisbon but are of course already sold out.

That is how things stand here. Incidentally, a few good acquaintances from Switzerland are here as well. The head of the Aid Committee, incidentally, is a Zionist who represented Morocco at the last [Zionist world] congress, Herr Tuers or something like that. I intend to remain here for a period of time. Please send me the little green newspaper—one cannot get a Jewish paper here.

DOCUMENT 2-12: Report by AJJDC Warsaw about its relief work during the period September 1939–October 1940, USHMMA Acc. 1999.A.0154 (ŻIH 210/6), 10–12 (translated from Yiddish).

The First Steps in Providing Aid/The First Aid Efforts

During the first month of the war, September 1939, it was, of course, impossible to organize any formal relief assistance for the Jews in Poland. The military campaign had such a blitz character right from the beginning that any sort of normal activity was impossible. The bombs and shrapnel brought death and destruction to Jewish life and property. Just going out into the street put your life in danger. Each day brought new dead, new homeless, masses of people whose homes had burned down; some managed to survive, but they lost everything but the clothes on their body.

Under such circumstances it was difficult to organize an appropriate relief action for the tens of thousands of homeless. Those unfortunate from the first and second categories, who had no relatives in Warsaw, crowded in the dirty, stifling cellars, courtyards, and staircases, often holding their tiny, sick children in their arms. First it was necessary to put a roof over their heads and some cooked food for them, but there was no one to whom they could turn; there was not a single representative of a Jewish social organization willing to risk his life in order to organize the necessary help.

The Joint-Central in Poland was the first to do this. On September 14, the very day when terrible bombings took place in Warsaw, when dozens of homes on Nalewki, Genshe, Franziskaner, and other Jewish streets were destroyed and approximately two hundred Jews were killed, on this very day, the Coordinating Commission was formed. It was established on the initiative of the Joint Central Office, in the local office of the Joint on Jasna 11 (in Warsaw), with the money of the Joint and with the assistance of the Joint directors. The Coordinating Commission was created from a range of Jewish help organizations that the Joint had until then subsidized, e.g. CENTOS, TOZ, Tze-ka-be, the Help Committee for German Refugees,[18] and others. This commission immediately opened soup kitchens for the refugees, relief stations, and overnight shelters in synagogues, prayer houses, school buildings, and other public buildings in various locations. [. . .]

The Joint was able to launch a much more generous aid campaign only in October, when the military operations ceased and, as a result of forced expatriations, the second wave of Jewish homeless started to flow.

The Ten Commandments of the Relief Action
From then on, the relief action began to embrace the following areas:
Food for the hungry
Providing home for the homeless
Clothing
Fight against epidemics and other illnesses
Children's protection
Aid for the Jewish intelligentsia, clergy, artisans, and the working class
Constructive aid, individual aid, legal aid
Emigration
Contacts with relatives abroad
Organizing self-help action among Polish Jews.

Actions in all these fields were carried out in Warsaw and in the provinces simultaneously.

---

18. Polish Jewish humanitarian aid organizations.

DOCUMENT 2-13: Kalman Huberband,[19] Warsaw, "The 'March' into the *Mikveh*," October 1940, USHMMA RG 15.079M (ŻIH Ring. I/218), reel 11 (translated from Yiddish).

Among all the other cruel decrees which the evil regime issued was the one forbidding Jews to immerse themselves in the *mikveh* [ritual bath]. All the *mikvehs* were sealed, and a notice was hung on their doors, saying, "Opening or using the *mikveh* will be considered sabotage and will be punished by ten years in prison to death."

The rebbe[20] made a decision, an ironclad decision, that one must immerse himself in the *mikveh* before Yom Kippur. Members of his inner circle tried to argue that immersing in the *mikveh*, or even just approaching it, would endanger people's lives, and especially the rebbe's, but to no avail. The rebbe did not alter his decision, and we made plans to implement it. But how? As mentioned, all the *mikvehs* were sealed, and their use was subject to such dangerous consequences. Finally, after a number of secret consultations between the rebbe and a *mikveh* owner, the matter was arranged.

At dawn of the day on which the Thirteen Divine Attributes are recited [Yom Kippur], at exactly 5:00 a.m., the hour when Jews are first permitted to walk in the street, a small group of people, led by the rebbe, assembled and began the "dangerous march" to the *mikveh*.

Outside it is still pitch dark, to our luck. We wish that the darkness would thicken even more and last even longer. Maybe we can hide in the darkness, maybe they won't notice us and we can carry out this "dangerous expedition" successfully.

The distance between the rebbe's home and the *mikveh* is quite long. The wagon that we had ordered has not arrived. The clock is showing ten minutes past five already. The group is getting nervous, because everything had been planned to the exact minute. We decide to begin "the march" by foot, in the hope that the wagon might meet us en route. It would be rather difficult to find another wagon at this hour of day, and you can't trust just any wagon, since all the arrangements had been made in great secrecy, and the coachman we had hired already knew all the "strategic" information—how to travel, which streets

---

19. Kalman Huberband (1907–1942?), brother of Shimon Huberband, was murdered in one of the deportations from Warsaw. This account was also printed, using different wording, in Huberband, *Kiddush Hashem*, 199–210.

20. This refers to Kalonymus Kalmish Shapira (1889–1943), a Hasidic teacher and rabbi. At the beginning of World War II, Shapira's son was killed in the bombing of Warsaw; his daughter was later deported. His teachings written in the Warsaw ghetto were discovered after the war and published as *Esh kodesh* (Holy fire).

to take, and where to stop. Apparently he had encountered some sort of obstacle, as is so often the case.

Quietly, on our tiptoes, we walk down the stairs, but there is a new, unanticipated problem: the [non-Jewish] janitor doesn't feel like getting up so early to open the gate, and he wants to know why the Jews need to go out to the street so early. We grease his palm, and this softens his heart instantly; he agrees to let us through the gate.

We are walking with soft footsteps, in pairs, leaving some space between each pair. Our hearts beat like hammers. Our eyes straining, we are staring into the depths of the night, looking at each approaching silhouette, to see whether it isn't one of "them." When we hear heavy footsteps ahead of us or behind us, our limbs are numbed with fear. Suddenly an approaching night trolley is ringing. We run quickly to the station to get on the trolley, since it is going exactly where we need to go. But as we come nearer, we realize that it is an Aryan trolley—off-limits to Jews. It would be a long time until a "Jewish" trolley arrived, since Jewish trolleys do not run so early in the morning.

So we walk from street to street. Suddenly we hear the sound of an approaching automobile. Its blinding headlights shine into our eyes. We stop as if paralyzed, because meeting an automobile on the street can be very unfortunate these days. In most cases, one is "invited" to a place from which there is no return . . . There isn't a gate behind which to hide; they are all still locked, since it's very early. But we were graced with a stroke of luck. The automobile passes by without noticing us. Holding our breath, we manage to walk past the more dangerous points and reach the entrance to the *mikveh*.

The courtyard is pitch dark. Mysterious shadows are creeping along the walls and disappear into a cellar on the side. A secret emissary is already waiting for us. Without uttering a single word, just by waving his arm, he begins to lead us. We descend into a deep, dark cellar. The door locks above us. We are groping in the darkness. We have instructions to walk straight and then to turn left. We reach a chiseled hole in the wall. With great difficulty, we push ourselves through it and find ourselves standing on some wooden boards. After a successful jump we land in a corridor that leads to the steps of the *mikveh*.

Despite the great danger in which we found ourselves, we were mesmerized by the whole event. Our forefathers in Spain appeared vividly in our imagination—how they celebrated seders and prayed with a minyan in secret cellars, fearful of the Inquisition. They certainly never imagined that four hundred years later their descendants would find themselves in a much worse situation and that in order to immerse themselves in honor of a festival, they would be forced to follow the same kind of dangerous procedures.

In the *mikveh* we found a large group of people who had received secret word that the *mikveh* would be open for an hour. Silently and in great haste we undressed and immersed ourselves in honor of the festival. A few minutes later, we repeated the same procedure we had used to enter. By the time we reached the courtyard, day was beginning to break and we could see on the seal on the entrance to the *mikveh* the well-known notice: "Opening or using the *mikveh* will be considered sabotage and will be punished by ten years in prison to death."

DOCUMENT 2-14: Letter by Wilhelm Filderman[21] and Isac Brucăr,[22] Bucharest, to Ion Antonescu, Romanian prime minister, September 30, 1940, in *Documents Concerning the Fate of Romanian Jewry during the Holocaust*, ed. Jean Ancel (New York: Beate Klarsfeld Foundation, 1986), 1:528–30 (translated from Romanian).

[. . .] Through the regular application of the Jewish Statute Law, over 25% of the current Jewish population—at least 80,000 souls—will be starving by February 9, 1941, when the legal interval of six months allowed for the termination of professions forbidden to the Jews will expire. [. . .]

In reality, against the formal orders of Your Excellency and in violation of the current legal norms and of the Jewish Statute laws, some authorities extend, based on their [own] decisions, the list of professions forbidden to the Jews; others deny [the Jews] the right to carry out business throughout the legally established interval of 6 months; others cancel contracts, although the Statute explicitly stipulates their fulfillment; others have required the immediate closure of all Jewish stores in certain locations; others have demanded the closure of firms; others deny access to the customs offices at ports to Jewish merchants who wish to see or export merchandise; professional associations demand that the Jews be completely or indirectly excluded from professions, which the Statute allows them to practice; or require regulations that cancel lease contracts

---

21. Wilhelm Filderman (1882–1963) was a member of the Romanian parliament, the AJJDC representative in Romania, and leader of the Federation of Jewish Communities until its dissolution in December 1941. He continued to fight discriminatory measures and deportations of Romanian Jews and suffered expulsion to Transnistria for a time. Upon his return he intervened on behalf of other deportees to Transnistria, with some success. See Radu Ioanid, *The Holocaust in Romania: The Destruction of Jews and Gypsies under the Antonescu Regime, 1940–1944* (Chicago: Ivan R. Dee, 2000).

22. Born in Bukovina, Isac Brucăr (1888–1960) was a lawyer, journalist, and leading philosopher who served as a high official of the Federation of Jewish Communities until 1941.

[signed by Jewish individuals] etc.; others allow individuals to stand by the entrances to Jewish shops in order to prevent customers from entering; or by the entrances to residences and stores of Romanian manufacturers, in order to prevent them from selling their products to Jews, etc. [. . .]

Generally, every authority and every citizen seems to wish to appear more legionary than the Legionnaires, more puritanical than his neighbor, instead of following Your Excellency's decisions regulating the phased Romanization, beginning with those who entered the country—legally or illegally—after 1913. [. . .]

We cannot help but point out the legal and humane attitude of the Prefect of Dorohoi, who convened all leaders of the Jewish community and declared that he would guarantee the maintenance of order among all; and invited Jewish merchants to provision themselves with goods so that normal commercial activity may be reestablished. [. . .]

We hope, Mr. Prime Minister, that you will appreciate the sentiments that have compelled us to bring these facts to your attention and that you will be so kind as to ensure that Justice be dispensed to us. Please remain assured of our utmost consideration.

GENERAL SECRETARY, PRESIDENT,

Dr. I. Brucăr   Dr. W. Filderman

DOCUMENT 2-15: Diary entry by an unidentified man, Łódź, Warthegau, on the struggle for bread in the ghetto, December 15, 1940, USHMMA RG 02.208M (ŻIH 302/191) (translated from Polish).

It happened on Friday, November 1, 1940. For three days already there had been no bread in the house, the child was constantly wailing "give me bread, mommy!" but there is no bread in the house. For supper my wife put some potatoes in to bake, but because the flame was too weak, we couldn't wait for the potatoes [to be cooked]. After supper, the neighbors came by, and we agreed that early in the morning one of us would wake the other so that we could go together to wait in the bread line. We also decided to go to the Szmulewicz bakery, which is located at Lutomierska 8, since we could get there through the back entrance, i.e., from our courtyard at Zgierska 12 to Zgierska 14 and from there to Lutomierska 6. We worked all this out so that we could get up before 7 a.m. (*schper-schtunde*)[23] and avoid the barbed wire. All night long my little

---

23. This refers to the German *Sperrstunde* ("curfew"). The author apparently reasoned that if he and his companions were to reach the bakery before the nightly curfew had ended, they would have an advantage over those who could not or would not risk moving about during curfew hours.

daughter couldn't sleep because of hunger, and her crying prevented us from sleeping. At 5 a.m. our neighbor Ostrowicz knocked on the shutter, my wife and I got up, we quickly got dressed and went out into the courtyard. We placed the child in the bed of the elderly woman who lived in the first room. Suddenly our other neighbor, Zylbersztejn, also came down into the courtyard, and we together woke up the watchman to open the gate for us. Arriving a couple of minutes after 5, a considerable line of people was waiting for us near the bakery, one line in the direction of Zgierska Street and another in the direction of Stodolniana Street. We all joined the Zgierska line. We stood there without a problem until 7 o'clock. At 7 the crowd began to demand that the baker begin distributing bread. The baker did not want to give out any of the bread because, as he explained, there was no [police officer] there yet. A couple of minutes after 6 [*sic*; most likely meaning 7], six men arrived, all of whom were wearing navy blue hats, the same ones the Jewish police wore at the time, and began to violently push their way to the window of the bakery. I didn't know who the six were, but I heard that it was the "Berk" family[24]—well known in the area. They worked their way to the window, and the baker started giving them two loaves of bread each. And as soon as they had gotten their bread, the baker stopped handing it out. The crowd raised a cry, demanding that the baker keep handing out bread, and because the baker didn't want to, the crowd began throwing rocks at the bakery's windows, breaking a few panes and wounding the baker's apprentice. The baker then said that without the police there, he wouldn't hand out bread, and he didn't. The "Berks" had already managed to bring home the bread that they had received and then to come back. They began pushing again and beat up somebody who was standing in their way. Somebody from the line went to get the police, and two policemen came. The "Berks" together with the police began establishing order just as they pleased. And it was at this time that a cart arrived alongside the bakery, and the driver, wanting to get bread, got down from the cart. Since he was an acquaintance of the "Berks," he began to help them "establish order." One of the "Berks" then took the driver's whip and began whipping the people in the line to disperse them, and the police pulled people out of the line. I was among those pulled out of the line. They ordered us to form a chain and promised that we would get bread. We stood in the chain for about ten minutes, then four more policemen arrived. Feeling stronger now, they began to disperse the chain with truncheons, and I got hit by one several times. So, I went up to one of the two policemen who had first arrived

---

24. For unknown reasons, the author of this document put certain names in quotation marks. The editors were unable to find biographical information about persons mentioned in the document.

and asked him to allow me to return to the line I had been waiting in. The policeman's name was Fuchs (I learned the name later). He raised his truncheon and wanted to hit me, but I said to him, "Sir, I left a child at home who has not eaten bread for three days, but instead of bread you want to beat me." In the meantime, policeman no. 357 rushed up to me and hit me in the eye with his leather briefcase so hard that I went blind for a few minutes. And I don't know who it was, but a couple of the policemen beat me pretty badly. When my brother Mojżesz, who was standing in line, saw that they were beating me, he raised a cry. Then the police rushed over to him and began beating him. As I was regaining my sight, I saw that the police were encircling my brother from the other side of the sidewalk and that my brother was gushing blood. I ran over to ask why they were beating him, the answer: they were trying to take us by force to the police station. Being naive enough to believe that I would find justice at the station, I turned to the policemen who were leading us away and told them that I would go on my own to the station. And this is how we entered the reserve police station at 4 Kościelna Street. A policeman named "Görin" began to take down the report and, while doing so and in front of the noncommissioned officer, raised his hand and hit my brother in the face. I then asked whether it was permitted to beat people at the station as well. Then I got hit by a policeman too! As I was already at my wits' end by this point, I raised my hand and hit the policeman "Görin" in the nose—the one who had hit my brother while he was taking down the report. Forty policemen, who were in reserve, then began to rain blows down upon me and my brother. After I regained consciousness several minutes later, I had bumps on my head the size of an egg, my watch had been knocked off my wrist, and I didn't even notice until my brother told me that the watch was lying on the ground. I picked it up. They held us at the station for a few more minutes, then an escort led us off in wrist manacles to station no. 1. We were taken there by six policemen. The noncommissioned officer left the protocol at station no. 1. It was only while sitting there in the office that I found out that the police get the order to beat people as well as they can. For this was the order the policemen who went to the line at 20 Żydowska Street had gotten from noncommissioned officer Szpic. They weren't averse to beating us at station no. 1 either. The beating was led by Szpic himself. [. . .]

At the [ghetto] courthouse we waited while one case ended. The next case was mine. The court calls forward the defendants and the witnesses. Everyone takes their seats. The judge reads out the indictment and gives me the first word, and I respond by explaining what happened. My brother does the same, and my witnesses confirm what happened. Then comes the cross-examination of the police's witnesses. [. . .] Everything that the police's [witnesses] state is a lie, except that I hit the policeman "Görin" in the nose in my own defense and that of my brother. Everyone sees this, and the judge sees this as well, so I remain calm about the outcome of the case. [. . .] The court deliberates and returns. For a few minutes I sit as if turned to stone, not knowing what will become of me and whether I had misunderstood [the verdict]. Nine months and a tenth on top of that? [. . .]

PART III
1941—1942

DOCUMENT 3-1: Account by an unidentified person, Warsaw, on the eve of Passover in the ghetto, April 11, 1941, USHMM RG 15.079 (ŻIH Ring. I/1024) (translated from Yiddish).

The eve of Passover in the Warsaw ghetto, second year of the war, 1941

The daily struggle in Warsaw is a very difficult one. More prominent than everything else is the growing want, pain, desperation. The only solace for us Jews is the "yearning for the end of days" in accord with our own hopes and fantasies and particularly black-on-white, news, newspapers, random underground leaflets—this is the little spirit of life that alleviates the sufferings of the daily struggle. Close to the eve of Passover, Jews simply shook with joy nearly the entire week—wherever two Jews met, one noticed a smile, people wished and simultaneously believed that, with God's help, on the second day of the holiday they would celebrate at home in the shtetl. The spirit lifted, in Yugoslavia a revolution,[1] Jews make a toast, the season of our freedom [Passover] nears, groups of people stand on the street, one is even no longer afraid of the German. Peasants, people say, do not want to take Polish money, they want, people say,

---

1. Reference to the coup d'état of March 27, 1941, by pro-Western officers in the Yugoslav army who deposed the government responsible for Yugoslavia's joining the Tripartite Pact two days earlier. In retaliation, Germany and its allies invaded Yugoslavia on April 6. At the time of the document's writing on April 11, the war between Yugoslavia and its invaders was still raging; Yugoslavia capitulated on April 17.

rubles or dollars. A Pole meets a Jew, a friend, and calls him inside to have a drink; things are fine, he says, help is near. Things are no longer going so well for the Germans. In the evening, when people gather, each person has a chance to speak, each person provides a spark of hope. In each person one notices a certainty that just a month or two and we Jews will be saved. Jews are simply gladdened, and one does not have the sense that something in the air is strained, that something is going on, and simultaneously there is no time to think since there is only one more day until Passover, and a mist of sadness once again veils the face; one faces the daily question once again: where should one hold Passover? Only when the political news is good does the Jew feel satisfied and celebrate Passover without a cent of money, hoping to get potatoes, matzah on credit (on this Passover people were still hopeful), and at this point people learn lightning fast that at 9 o'clock in the evening information will be relayed by radio. Something must have happened, Jews do not rest. And thus despite the danger (because after 9 in the evening, it is not permitted to be on the street), many people gather around the radio. Before the radio program begins, we find out that food prices have increased. Bread is 8 złoty a kilo [2.2 pounds], potatoes are 2.50 a kilo, onions 4.50. The atmosphere becomes extremely oppressive, you cannot think for long, the speaker interrupts and announces that Salonika is surrounded by the Germans, they have met with success in fighting the Yugoslavs and Greeks. With this, he ends. The Jews quickly run home, everyone is overcome by fear that the situation has become more serious.

On the morning of [April] the 10th, a panic, a tumult, the food prices increase further, bread is 11 złoty for one kilo, potatoes are 4 złoty, onions 6. The shops are empty, people are scared to sell, and they keep and buy whatever they can. The atmosphere is like it was on the eve of the war, people are preparing and shopping, buying not only things necessary for Passover but whatever happens to be available; matzah costs 25 złoty a kilo, Jews do not give this a second thought—as long as beets are available, it will be enough. Only what is this supposed to mean? Questions fall from all sides. What is the reason for the increasing prices? People are silent. Earlier, when the political situation was favorable for the Jews, people found a justification for the increasing prices. Today, people are silent. On the one hand, the prices increase from hour to hour; on the other hand, [there are] frequent communiqués that Germany is advancing and capturing various territories in Africa, Greece, and Yugoslavia. In the street there is a racket, it might seem that this is because it is just before Passover, but no! People cannot sit in their homes, they run into the street to see, to hear, perhaps just in case. It is once again difficult to walk on the street, you're overcome by a shudder. German automobiles crowded with many officers and military men fill the streets. Several get out, they make use of their cameras with great pleasure and photograph the poor people by the walls with their stiffened, outstretched hands, and a half hour later cars of the burial society[2] quickly drive by and take away beggars from near the walls who have given up the ghost for hunger—and free up places for the others. The display windows are empty, there are no baked goods whatsoever. At first glance, one has the impression that the *chametz*[3] is being concealed, but no! It in fact turns out that the Jewish police requisitioned all the cakes and rolls for the dormitories and hospitals because there is no bread. And here a cart with potatoes again drives past, the wagon is besieged, tens of pale hands grab the potatoes, snatch them up, and eat them raw. On Solna Street, hungry people broke into several shops and looted them. Panic all of a sudden grows and grows. The pleas of the poor people become more and more desperate. Children wander about the streets, they beat with their little feet, they faint from hunger. The street singer's tune is sadder, the fiddlers by the walls play more weakly, and the prices get higher and higher. Bread with onions takes the top spot, and it has become a form of currency. Jews believe that when [the price of] a loaf of bread reaches fifty złoty, then redemption will come. The streets are full, satans move about—not men—and the words resound in one's ears: [the cost of] bread has increased, where can potatoes be had? Bread, bread, there is no bread. Amidst the throng, an acquaintance runs by with a black, torn-up eye—and smiles. He has drawn the ace of hearts. He says that he will not bow before them, there is no way he will remove his cap for the Germans. And behold a wonder: in the place where people speak of the vexed question of bread, he tells only how he encountered two Germans, walked in between them, and looked at them, and they at him, but did not remove his cap for them. Of course, they meted out a hell of a punishment to him. While bidding farewell he admits it, but he never did remove his hat for them.

On the morning of the eleventh, the prices fall precipitously—people say that a loaf of bread is back to 8 złoty, potatoes at 2.50—it is truly good fortune. The resigned nevertheless run to buy something to have something at home. The carts in the street are full, the people like flies, bargains are bought up—it is truly a stroke of good fortune. People snatch up, at the least, a kilogram of potatoes for Passover. After a difficult day, Passover arrived and brought new waves of want. The holiday of the season of our freedom reminded us of our continued exile. The only news that Passover of 1941 brought is the news of starvation!

2. Khesed shel emes: a Jewish communal society dedicated to ensuring proper burial for the poor.

3. Leavened foods, all traces of which must be removed for Passover in the homes of observant Jews.

DOCUMENT 3-2: Diary entry by Hermann Hakel,[4] camp Alberobello near Bari, Italy, for May 20, 1941, on a visit by Catholic dignitaries, Austrian National Library Vienna 221/04 (translated from German).

Yesterday was a big day in camp. We were chased from our beds bright and early by the head of the Carabinieri [Italian police] force in full dress uniform. Top-to-bottom cleaning! Everything that was lying and hanging around had to be stowed away, and the floor, tables, and benches had to be washed. Hurry! Hurry! That could mean only a prominent visitor. Exactly the same thing happened in Oliveto [a camp where Hakel had been previously], and at that time Cardinal B. [the apostolic nuncio to the Italian government, Francesco Borgongini-Duca] came and gave us splendid presents.

In fact, as I predicted, toward midday and just as we were involved in a game of nine-pin bowling, a big limousine drives up, and the huge prince of the church and his secretary get out. We step up and wait for the gifts I had publicized. The cardinal says a few words in greeting (this time, far less solemn) and gives each of us a postcard with the photo of His Holiness Pope Pius XII; in addition, everyone gets a sweet treat worth 3 lire. The disappointed faces turn in my direction, and I assert for the nth time that in Oliveto, only five months ago, each of us got 30 lire, 50 cigarettes, 20 decagrams [7 ounces] of cookies, and 10 decagrams [3.5 ounces] of tea.

Then His Eminence asks to be shown the building. He disregards my room, the first one in the hallway, and enters the second, where the Orthodox Jews are housed. The rivalry interests him. There is also a Torah there. The people wear *kippot*. His Eminence asks that he be shown the prayer books and then a passage from the Book of Daniel, which to everyone's amazement he reads aloud, translates, and interprets as proof of the birth of Jesus. It is a long-winded computation, but it adds up! Like a schoolmaster, the great man raises one finger of his heavily beringed hand and says that this, this little calculation, is the only difference between the two religions and that the Jews, as the guardians of the Bible, are owed the gratitude of all Catholics. (A feat of arithmetic as the only proof for the validity of the Catholic religion—!) The poor Orthodox Feintuch is utterly perplexed by this smooth calculation. And when David and his tribe are mentioned, Riebenfeld, a maliciously cunning Pole who also sleeps in the "temple room," pulls out his wallet and displays the photo of his son, who is also named David.

---

4. Hermann Hakel (1911–1987) was an Austrian writer and poet from Vienna. After a severe beating by the Nazis in 1939, he fled the Reich to Italy, where he was arrested in 1940 and interned in a number of camps. In 1947 he returned to Vienna, where he resumed his career as a writer.

Later, back in the yard, many people cluster around His Eminence's little secretary. They want the Vatican to help their Catholic wives living in Vienna get permission to come here. Obligingly, the stout little monsignor accepts all the scraps of paper with addresses, and by now the gentlemen are at their car (which is being examined in detail by our people). Polite words are spoken once again, the two servants of the Church of Christ wave at us as if we were children, and then, after one hour, it's all over.

DOCUMENT 3-3: "One Year Sosúa Settlement," on Jewish emigration to the Dominican Republic, *Jüdisches Nachrichtenblatt*[5] (Prague), May 2, 1941, 1 (translated from German).

San Domingo, February 1941

Though a year has now passed since the signing of the agreement for the settlement of 100,000 refugees in San Domingo [Dominican Republic], only 583 settlers have managed to make their way into the country thus far.

The Sosúa colony covers a 26,000-acre stretch of land that extends from the coast to the fertile plain of the Yassica River, about 14 miles from Puerto Plata. [General Rafael] Trujillo, the president of the Dominican Republic, made this land available to James Rosenberg, the head of the settlement association [Dominican Republic Settlement Association].[6]

The first group arrived in Sosúa on May 5, 1940. The great efforts and enormous sums expended to establish the settlement notwithstanding, only 583 emigrants came to San Domingo, and the number is unlikely to increase substantially over the course of this year.

Seventy percent of the Sosúa settlers are Jews from the various countries of Europe, while the rest are non-Jews. The settlers are young, energetic people who were carefully selected. There are more men than women in the settlement, as well as many families with children. All have pledged to remain permanently in Sosúa and to do agricultural work there.

The settlement association allocated each family 20 acres of land, on which

5. After the November 1938 pogrom, the Nazi regime restricted publication of Jewish journals in Germany to the newly created *Jüdisches Nachrichtenblatt* (Jewish news gazette) in Berlin, produced by Jewish authors under Gestapo control. Later, German officials established similar publications under the same name in Vienna and in Prague.

6. James N. Rosenberg (1874–1970) was a New York City–based lawyer and AJJDC official who struck an agreement with Dominican dictator Rafael Trujillo Molina for the Sosúa project.

facilities for cattle breeding and poultry farming are located. The settlers raise grain, tobacco, and Dominican potatoes and plant lemon trees.

Three of the settlers are physicians. A school is in place, and language courses are offered on an ongoing basis.

DOCUMENT 3-4: Leib Spiesman,[7] "In the Warsaw Ghetto," *Contemporary Jewish Record* (New York) 4 (August 1941): 357–66.

With the arrival in the United States of the sole Jewish newspaper published in the Generalgouvernement, more exact information has been made available about the life of Jews in Nazi-occupied Poland. The *Gazeta Żydowska* is a Polish-language newspaper published in Kraków every Tuesday and Friday since July 1940. It is issued by a private corporation and sells for 30 groszy (15 German pfennigs). In addition to the Polish title, the masthead also carries the Star of David and the words *Jüdische Zeitung* [Jewish newspaper] in small Hebrew characters.

While war news is limited to the official German and Italian communiqués, there seems to be little if any censorship of news about internal Jewish affairs, which fills most of the paper. These items are treated from a strongly religious and Zionist point of view. The rebuilding of Palestine and the problems connected with it are frequently discussed, while weekly language lessons in Hebrew, as well as a serialized novel by J. Burla[8] dealing with Palestinian life, serve to emphasize its Zionist character. Appeals for faith in Divine Providence and for a return to the traditions of Judaism testify to its religious character. The *Gazeta*'s question-and-answer department, with its replies to legal and emigration problems, reflects the life of Polish Jews and also helps to bolster their courage. In addition all decrees and ordinances affecting Jews are printed in full and carefully explained. Advertisements of all kinds fill one or two pages, although commercial notices predominate, the most striking of which are those advertising Jewish armbands made of celluloid. Yet, despite all these evidences of oppression and persecution, there is room from time to time for a children's section to which boys and girls contribute some surprisingly good poems. [. . .]

German, Yiddish, Hebrew, and Polish are the four official languages of the

---

7. The journalist Leib Spiesman (1903–1963) was active in the Zionist movement in the 1930s in his home city of Warsaw before seeking wartime refuge, first in Vilna and then late in 1940 in the United States, where he conducted Yiddish radio broadcasts and wrote extensively in Yiddish.

8. Judah (Yehuda) Burla (Bourla) (1886–1969) was a Jewish novelist famous for his portrayals of Middle Eastern Jews.

ghetto, and a knowledge of Yiddish is required of all community employees. An ordinance issued by the head of the Warsaw Council on January 20, 1941, fixes the Jewish Sabbath as the official day of rest. All business establishments must be closed on Saturday, Rosh Hashanah, Yom Kippur, and the first and last two days of Sukkoth and Shabuoth.[9] While Sundays and minor Christian holidays are ordinary workdays in the ghetto, important Christian festivals are also legal days of rest. Exempted from the compulsory Sabbath holiday are hotels, restaurants, pharmacies, the public utilities, and Jews of the "non-Mosaic" religion, i.e., converts to Christianity.[10] That this strict observance of the Sabbath is not considered an unmixed blessing by all can be seen from the petition presented to the [Jewish] Council by the photographers and barbers (*Gazeta Żydowska*, May 9, 1941), in which they asked to be exempted on the ground that it seriously harmed their business. [. . .]

Provisioning the ghetto is one of the Council's most serious problems. While food in all countries under German rule is rationed, Jews receive considerably less than either Poles or Germans. They are allotted only 60 grams of bread per day (approximately 0.13 pounds), half the amount that Poles may buy and less than one-third available to members of the German "master race." Similar gradations are the rule in the distribution of all other products, according to the regulations published in the *Gazeta Żydowska*. The issue of February 3, 1941, for instance, notified Jews that henceforth they would not receive any soap, eggs, or fruit juices. Meat has been entirely unobtainable by religiously observant Jews since the prohibition of *shehitah* [ritual slaughter] on October 26, 1939. One year in jail or concentration camp is the penalty for those found guilty of kosher slaughter. [. . .]

Compulsory labor, introduced by the Nazi authorities immediately upon the establishment of the Generalgouvernement, provides a number of Jews with a scant livelihood. In many cities and towns labor battalions are formed and sent out to work in various parts of the country. Failure to register is punishable by imprisonment at hard labor for up to ten years. These battalions drain

---

9. In 1941, Rosh Hashanah fell on September 22 and Yom Kippur on October 1; both are high holidays in the Jewish liturgical calendar, marking the beginning and the end of the Ten Days of Repentance. Sukkot, commemorating the biblical exile of the Israelites, fell on October 6–12, and Shavuot, celebrating the giving of the Torah on Mount Sinai, fell on June 1, 1941.

10. There were around two thousand Jews of Christian denomination in the Warsaw ghetto, roughly 0.5 percent of the ghetto population. See Havi Ben-Sasson, "Christians in the Ghetto: All Saints' Church, Birth of the Holy Virgin Mary Church, and the Jews of the Warsaw Ghetto," *YVS* 31 (2003): 153–73.

swamps, dredge lakes, and build roads. Much of the work was done in connection with military projects on the Russian frontiers. The number of Jews employed in forced labor can be judged by the fact that in Warsaw and its environs alone, over 25,000 were sent out, according to the *Gazeta Żydowska* of April 24, 1941. [. . .]

Relatively little is known about the health situation in the ghettos. It is certain, however, that the typhoid epidemics which followed the war affected Jews more than other elements of the population. [. . .] Since then, improved sanitary conditions have practically eliminated epidemics of this kind, as stray references in the *Gazeta Żydowska* testify. There is no doubt, however, that overcrowding, lack of parks, absence of recreational facilities, and particularly inadequate diets are exacting a serious toll on health and lives. Statistics gathered by the Lublin Council show that of 28,806 Jews over the age of fourteen registered in that community for compulsory labor, 10,330, or about 35%, were disqualified for physical labor because of the precarious state of their health. [. . .]

Examples of Jewish self-reliance and communal cohesiveness found in the pages of the *Gazeta Żydowska* do not at all dispel the horrors of the Nazi terror. A full picture of the situation of Jews in Nazi Poland would include the ghastly chapter of Lublin, the concentration camps, mass starvation and misery. It would also include a description of a different kind of torture, the petty annoyances by which Nazis seek to break the unyielding spirit of the Polish Jews. [. . .]

All the more amazing, therefore, is the stamina and courage of these men and women as seen in the *Gazeta Żydowska*. Despite terrible conditions, the inhabitants in this largest ghetto in Jewish history show an indomitable determination to outlast their enemies. Articles in the *Gazeta Żydowska* encourage them to endure their hardships even as their ancestors did in other critical periods of Jewish history. The tone of the paper is a proud one. There are no traces of groveling before the Nazis. Instead, national pride is emphasized, and faith in humanity and the brotherhood of mankind is kept alive.

The religious spirit, too, is much in evidence. A touching example of the sinking of the interest of the individual in the collective sufferings of the community is provided by a letter from a ten-year-old Jewish boy of Makow, published in the children's section of the *Gazeta Żydowska*. "O Lord, Thou who art omnipotent, show me how I may help my people," wrote the child. Also characteristic of the present attitude of the Jews of Poland is the old adage, published in the newspaper, about the rabbinical students whose ship was wrecked in a storm. They managed to cling to the debris until the waves cast them back on the shore. When they were asked how they had managed to save themselves, they explained that they had bowed their heads before each towering wave instead of resisting it.

To bow their heads before the engulfing waves of oppression is the present way of life of Polish Jewry.

DOCUMENT 3-5: Letters by Ruth Goldbarth,[11] Warsaw, to Edith Blau, Minden, Germany, on life in the ghetto during the first half of 1941, USHMMA RG 10.250*03, Edith Brandon collection (translated from German).

[February 26, 1941]

[. . .] A few days ago, Renia Nest was at my place. I feel terribly sorry for the poor girl. I've probably already written you that her sister, Mrs. Schmid, registered back then to return [to the Warsaw ghetto], in order to get the child, who is here. As a result, she was deported, and her husband had a heart attack and died within 24 hours. Now she is also somewhere in the interior, working in the forest like all the others, and is completely crushed. Her husband dead, the child so infinitely far away, and no hope of seeing the child again. One of Schmid's sisters lives here with Renia and her family (of course, all of them in one room) and to this day still knows nothing of her brother's death. It's an unbelievable tragedy . . . Oh, just don't think about it . . . [. . .]

Imagine, every day 5 to 8 złoty go for bread alone. Our monthly bread consumption (besides the bread we get with ration cards) totals 220 to 240 złoty. Where is this headed, anyway?! Really, Dita, the time is no longer so far off when we'll have to think about where we'll get food for the next day. Every day, hundreds of people arrive here, all of them destitute, with no possibility of earning anything here, with no prospect of getting even the bare necessities of life. Allegedly the Viennese also are already on the way here.[12] What will that be like?? There are rumors that starting on March 1, everything here will be even more tightly sealed, and every kind of communication with the outside is to be

---

11. Ruth Goldbarth (1921–1942) was born in Bydgoszcz, Poland, where she met Edith Blau (b. 1921) and their mutual friend Lutek Orenbach (1921–1942?). In January 1940, her father decided to move his family to Warsaw, where Ruth worked in her father's dental practice in the ghetto and corresponded frequently with Edith Blau (whom Goldbarth called "Dita" or "Ditlein"), then in Germany. Ruth and her family were most likely deported to their deaths in Treblinka in the summer of 1942; Edith Blau survived the war.

12. While the Warsaw ghetto received significant numbers of Jewish deportees from other parts of German-dominated Poland, there were no direct transports of Viennese Jews to Warsaw at any point during the war.

broken off; what then? The telephone, too, will supposedly be only for internal use. You can go mad if you think about it all. And yet we mustn't fall into despair now, we mustn't give up, we young ones. We have to live to see different times someday; after all, we have a right to that! [. . .]

[April 15, 1941]

[. . .] Dear, I can't possibly describe what joy your package has produced here. The people from the Point view it virtually as a miracle.[13] Many of them don't know you at all and simply can't grasp the idea that a totally unknown person is helping them in this way. I'm convinced that a collection of clothes for charity all over the city would not have yielded so many things, and above all such decent things. Not everything has been distributed yet, but the people are deliriously happy that they have a change of clothes, that they don't have to wear the same thing day after day, and that they have an opportunity to wash out some things occasionally. In some cases, we also swapped things; for example, Adas Dobrin got 2 pairs of stockings in exchange for 2 pairs that are too small for him and just fit a boy from the Point. In any event, the people are as happy as children. In the name of the people, the Committee, and the *Landsmannschaft*,[14] I've been asked to wholeheartedly thank you and all those who contributed something. And I myself would like to give you a very warm kiss, my dear. At last, through you, I've been able to help again. Edith, the misery is so dreadful! Sometimes I'd like to close my ears and shut my eyes and run far, far away so that I don't have to see and hear any more. Such pitiful creatures, of the kind found here on the street at every turn; wound only in a few rags, barefoot, half naked, and freezing, they slog along, and more and more people, often well dressed, simply collapse and lie there without moving—and the others walk past heedlessly, as if nothing had happened. Seeing it is enough to make you crazy—but you yourself are condemned to the same inaction. Because what can you do? Buy a kilo of bread (for 10 zł.) and give it to the poor man? Then he'll collapse again from hunger tomorrow. And who's able to feed the many who are in need!! You'd have to be a millionaire! Theft is routine nowadays. A few days ago, someone tore a loaf of bread from my hand in the street and

13. For the work of house committees and related charity initiatives ("Points") in the Warsaw ghetto, see Alexandra Garbarini et al., *Jewish Responses to Persecution*, vol. 2: *1938–1940*. Documenting Life and Destruction: Holocaust Sources in Context (Lanham, MD: Altamira Press/Rowman & Littlefield, 2011), 372–74.

14. *Landsmannschaft* in this context presumably refers to the Warsaw ghetto association of Jews from the city of Bromberg (German name for Bydgoszcz in Poland, annexed to Reichsgau Wartheland from 1935 to 1945), which Ruth Goldbarth was involved in.

wouldn't give it back, although several people were chasing him. A man from our building had his hand bitten so badly by a thief that you can still see the wound today. Recently I was at the hospital; it was about 12:30 p.m.; the patients still hadn't been given any breakfast. The conditions are so terrible that they can't even be described. So is it any wonder that the number of typhus cases is growing at an alarming rate? The day before yesterday I had an errand fairly far from here, in the downright poor area—entire streets are shut off because of the threat of typhus. Can the people take care of themselves when bread and potatoes are unaffordable treasures for them? (Using our cards, we've received 750 grams [26.5 ounces] of bread per person this month.) It's simply enough to make you crazy!! Despite all that, Uncle[15] continues to take his pick of the people he wants to hire (I wrote you about it last year); a great many have already started work and have determined that once again he's absolutely not keeping his promises regarding food, housing, and pay and that they have to put up with quite a lot of incivility and roughness besides. And Adi is also swaggering around like a savage. His old friends who were here until now have left, and the ones who have come are decidedly disagreeable.[16]—But enough of that for now! I've really moaned and groaned to you enough for the moment! Don't be cross, dear, but from time to time I simply can't stand it anymore, and you're my closest friend and the only one to whom I can tell everything. [. . .]

This evening is another holiday;[17] the dentist's office is closing earlier than usual, and I'll have free time tomorrow and the day after tomorrow in the afternoon. Terrific! At the moment it's fairly quiet in general. The lockdown of the building [due to typhus], the holidays, the rising prices, and the overall despondency have played a big role there. Anyway, there's not enough work: in March, there was really a lot to do [in the dental practice of Ruth's father], and something came of it: 60% of the expenses were covered. And that was an exceptionally good month.—But in the end: let's be glad that it's still like this! I have to tell myself repeatedly that I must not complain. Only 25% of the population—when things go well—are doing as well as we are. However: the lack of gas is slowly driving us crazy. For breakfast, at lunch, and in the evening, a fire has to be made in the hearth; we have no coal, the wood is always damp, the fire won't burn, and one after another we try our luck & the meals are never ready at the right time. [. . .]

---

15. "Uncle" and "Adi" are code for "Germans."

16. This is a reference to a change of the German police units guarding the ghetto.

17. April 15, 1941, fell in the middle of the Passover week.

[May 29, 1941]

[. . .] Ditlein, how I envy you the outings to enjoy the springtime! I don't even know anymore what a green tree looks like. In the narrow streets here, there's nothing but dust and dirt and "stinkis" (little fish that are sold on the street here in large quantities and have this beautiful name because of their strong odor. In the past few days, when it was so hot, you could pass out in some streets), flowers in only two shops, at insanely high prices. Do you know how much I would like to get out sometime, into the countryside, into the fresh air, hear birds singing, and see water! Viktor wants to take me along one day; just recently he has been allowed to go to Jurek again, but it's not worth the risk—he can allow himself to go without Mogen more easily than I can.[18]

But we're happy indeed about our balcony. From the street side we have sun until 11:30 a.m., and on the courtyard side until 3:30, and on all the floors a "beach life" is developing. Using an extension cord, we brought a light onto the rear balcony, and bridge is played there; in front, the young people get together (those who aren't playing bridge) and chat. And in addition, "our" café is now open. The passageway from our building hasn't been created yet, of course, but our residents are among the most grateful patrons. Admittedly, I haven't yet managed to go over there, although I had three invitations for Saturday and Sunday; I was just recently in the kindergarten next door, which has a swing, seesaw, sandbox, etc., with Marcyś and Henryś Kuschner. It's really nice there, even quite lovely for our circumstances, but I always think that in these times one shouldn't spend money on such things, money that can be used to help others. At any rate, I always have pangs of conscience whenever I think of going to such a café. And somehow I have a sense that I wouldn't feel comfortable there, either. [. . .]

[June 5, 1941]

[. . .] Dearest, I only wish there would come a time when I can thank you with something besides mere words for all your love & friendship, for all your letters, for every one of your warm and understanding words. As everyone knows, people can withstand a lot, but I think I would already have collapsed on various occasions if I hadn't had such firm support from you; merely the awareness that you, a brave little person, are there and demand of me the same strength and energy that you have to muster has given me new heart time and

---

18. "Going without Mogen" refers to taking off the yellow badge before leaving the ghetto part of Warsaw.

again. Lutek [Orenbach] is right when he writes: in this mass catastrophe, mass misery, and mass depravity, one feels so small and insignificant, so trampled on and beaten down to the ground, that one often has to summon up a lot of courage to keep from collapsing oneself. Anyone who hasn't been to the cemetery here, where 250–300 people are buried every day, anyone who hasn't seen the "Maska" movie theater, where the police bring all the starved, ragged beggars who sit and lie in hallways, on the sidewalk, and on the causeway, can't understand it at all. And you'd have to go insane if you could really still empathize and share the pain of all that. But, thank God, we are completely apathetic by now. [. . .]

DOCUMENT 3-6: Diary entry by Aron Pik,[19] Shavli, German-occupied Lithuania, for June 27, 1941, on the dangers facing Jews around the start of the German attack on the Soviet Union, USHMMA RG 26.014 (LCSAV R-1390), reel 58, file 170 (translated from Yiddish).

June 27, 1941

Yesterday (Thursday), in the evening, I suddenly saw from the window that Germans were walking about on the sidewalk opposite—my heart sank! Does this mean that four days after the start of the war the dogged Jew haters, the beastly murderers, were already able to penetrate into Lithuania?[20] If so, then the fate of the Lithuanian Jews has been sealed, too, like that of our unfortunate brothers in the other countries occupied by the Germans. The bitter experiences of Czechoslovakia, Austria, Germany itself, and so on reveal that very sad days await us and that boundless calamities and pain are in store for us. And all the evil afflictions gather over our heads after we have already suffered such a great deal. How much humiliation and persecution have we endured in recent years in our own blessed fatherland, Lithuania! In all areas, decrees and restrictions have rained down upon us like hail. [. . . ; a catalogue of discriminatory measures enacted in prewar Lithuania follows.] Government antisemitism went hand in hand with societal antisemitism, and they, together with the agitation of the

---

19. Aron Pik (1872–1944) was a physician living in Shavli with his wife, Dvora, and their son, Tedik David Pik. In September 1941 they were forced to move to the ghetto in Shavli, where Dr. Pik worked in the ghetto hospital and continued writing his diary. After Pik died in June 1944, David buried his father's writings, which consisted of three notebooks.

20. The German attack on the Soviet Union started on June 22, 1941. By early July Lithuania had been occupied; by September 1, the Wehrmacht controlled all the Baltic states as well as large parts of Belorussia and Ukraine.

antisemitic press, formed a nice "threefold chord,"[21] a triumvirate which, in time, created for us in Lithuania a complete pogrom mood.

[. . . ; looks back at start of the Soviet occupation in the summer of 1940:] From that day on the Bolshevik regime was established in our territory, and an immense change in our way of life and our psychology came about. And the hooligans and the pogromists disappeared. For the time being, many of them, so to speak, withdrew into themselves and "took on a second skin." And many became turncoats and, as it were, loyal communists, [and remain so] even today. In any event, we breathed more easily and felt equal to [other] people: from second-rate, inferior citizens up to that point, we became fully entitled, bold and active members of society, and many of us received very respectable positions and became materially well established. The workers and a large segment of society came to life! One cannot deny that the Jewish community on the whole paid dearly for all the freedoms since the majority consisted of merchants, industrialists, shopkeepers, and other so-called bourgeois exploiters, most of whose wealth was nationalized and expropriated; but the workers and the more conscious, who properly assessed the rights of the proletariat on the one hand and the unjust basis of the capitalist order on the other—they all felt that the sun of a new, free life shone with the Bolshevik regime. How great, therefore, was our desperation and heartache when, after one year of rule, the Bolsheviks suddenly abandoned us at the beginning of the war, and we were left defenseless in the teeth and claws of the wild, bloodthirsty German beasts!

Now, after the troubles with the Lithuanian regime and the unpleasantness of the Bolshevik upheaval for a large part of the Jewish community, the [illegible] begins; the German regime comes, with its unbounded hatred of Jews and its beastly wickedness, which hold a bleak future in store for us. *Gevalt!* Where will we find the strength and endurance to bear this all after all these experiences?

[. . .] The arrival in Shavli of large masses of soldiers immediately affected my situation as administrator of the polyclinic. A surgical unit of the Germans unceremoniously broke into the polyclinic, and their chief doctor immediately began to "boss [us] around," as though he was at home. His first accomplishment was to make the polyclinic free of Jews. At that time Dr. B . . . n, dentist W., and nurse L . . . n were in the polyclinic, all with typical Jewish appearances—brunettes with true "Jewish faces." He went to each of them and ordered them to leave as soon as possible: "You are a Jew, you must disappear immediately. I should never see you again." . . .

---

21. Pik used the Hebrew expression here (*hut hameshulash*), referencing Ecclesiastes 4:12: "Also, if one attacks, two can stand up to him. A threefold chord is not readily broken."

Now I sit at home idle, without work, and have ample time to write my recollections, more or less in detail. To go out into the street, to refresh oneself somewhat, one is in any event afraid to do (unless there is an important reason for doing so), so as not to run into the hatred of our brainwashed rulers, the Lithuanians. They were furious about the deportation of their families to Soviet Russia [by Stalin's police], which they considered to be the work of the Jews, disregarding the fact that more than a few Jewish families were also deported, suspected of being "counterrevolutionaries." They blamed all the deeds of the Bolsheviks on the Jews, whom they held responsible for everything that has taken place and that is presently taking place, including the war, according to the formula of the modern Haman and the clique of his followers. And in return, they have broken into the homes of those who ran from Shavli and robbed whatever their heart desired. A new beginning was initiated! Afraid of going out into the street, we sit already without milk, without meat, and without butter. What is going to happen next? Certainly, there will be no improvement, more likely it will get worse. [. . .]

DOCUMENT 3-7: Account by ghetto policemen in Kovno, German-occupied Lithuania, on the establishment of the Jewish police in the summer of 1941, no date (early 1943), USHMMA RG 26.014 (LCSAV R-973), reel 31 (translated from Yiddish).[22]

[. . .]

On August 10 [1941] it became known through the committee—already referred to as the Council of Elders [*Ältestenrat*, or Jewish Council]—that men were being accepted into the police force, priority being given to those who had served in the military. Twenty-six applications had been received, of which 10 were accepted.

The rank and file of the young people did not, in general, wish to join the police. It is also of interest that some in this group who participated in the almost daily meetings and consultations concerning the organization of the police were willing to help organize and structure the police force but were not willing to join it themselves.

The reasons for this attitude were as follows:

First, as noted, our future was clouded and veiled. We had no contacts with the [German] authorities, except for those instances when demands were

---

22. Also published in Samuel Schalkowsky and Samuel D. Kassow, eds., *The Clandestine History of the Kovno Ghetto Jewish Police* (Bloomington: Indiana University Press in association with USHMM, 2014), 78–80.

received for workers or if we happened to hear instructions concerning a new evil decree. We were completely in the dark as to the intentions of the authorities concerning us, not only with regard to general questions affecting the entire community but also as to their preferences concerning the establishment of the administrative life of the ghetto and the shape and duties of the offices. It was therefore feared that, outside the direct duties of the police to maintain peace and order in the ghetto, the force would be given other work and become a tool of the Gestapo and that all of our police officials would have to serve as their [i.e., the Gestapo's] functionaries.

Second, there was fear of the external administrative aspects, which could make each policeman individually responsible for any misunderstanding, any trivial matter.

Third, the very creation of a Jewish police was big news in the life of our community; we know from experience that Jews have difficulty getting along with Jews; that a Jew hates to obey a Jewish functionary. The members of the organizing group figured—with all due respect, but rightly so—that Jews would not obey, that there would be quarrels with everyone, such that the task would be difficult—indeed, thankless.

[. . .] Since there were very few applications [for leadership positions], it was decided to mobilize men with previous military service, sportsmen, members of the Maccabea [Jewish sports club], and war veterans. The mobilization was planned so as to recruit men from all classes and quarters of the population, without consideration of party affiliation, position, or social standing, so that neither this nor that tendency or group would have a monopoly in the police, so that it would be the protector and advocate of the entire ghetto.

And indeed, the attitude of those who either volunteered or were mobilized into the police during those first days was idealistic—to work for the good of the people, in contrast to the later times, beginning with the gold "action" [requisitioning of valuable items by Germans in early September 1941], when everything became so cheap and gray and very far from any kind of idealism. Initially, people worked day and night unselfishly for the well-being of the ghetto. These first weeks were the cleanest period for the police. Whether these good intentions had any practical significance is a separate question. [. . .]

DOCUMENT 3-8: Diary entries by Baruch Milch,[23] Tłuste, Galicia district, Generalgouvernement, written July–August 1943, on the persecution of Hungarian deportees in the second half of 1941, USHMMA RG 02.208M (ŻIH 302/98) (translated from Polish).[24]

[. . .] These condemned persons [Jewish deportees from Hungarian-occupied Transcarpathia] were torn from their homes with harsh ruthlessness and guile and driven to Ukraine on trucks along the path of Hungarian forces advancing along the eastern front. Some were taken from their jobs during the day; others were awoken from their sleep during the night and immediately loaded into cars. Some were allowed to take with [them] the most important [items], and others were not. Some were told that they were only being taken to be registered; a second group was told that they were being interned in *lagers* for a short time; a third group that they were being resettled to other areas of Hungary; and a fourth group that they were being taken to Ukraine, where housing and farmsteads had been prepared for them, as cities and villages had been deserted and emptied due to the Soviets' removal of the population.

Thus were they lied to and mystified, and in the end they were completely destroyed. It was a terrible sight how for two weeks in a row, groups of trucks, 5 to 10 cars together, loaded full of Jews, the elderly, cripples, women, and small children, were driven day and night under escort from the military or the Hungarian police in white gloves and comical outfits, in hats with long feathers tucked in. They were left to their fate in little towns and villages on the other side of the Dniester [River] starting all the way from Kamieniec Podolski [Polish spelling for Kamyanets-Podilsky]. Sometimes they were dumped from the trucks in some woods or in a field, from where they made their way in wave after wave to the nearest small towns. Often the Hungarian soldiers themselves robbed them of everything they had, but they were tormented the worst by Ukrainian peasants, who lurked everywhere, on roads and in fields, in entire bands, mercilessly attacking, robbing, and killing them.

Many of them, immediately after being let out of the trucks, realized what was happening and tried to cross back to the other side of the Dniester in order somehow to be able to return home, but a notorious Hungarian officer with the

---

23. Baruch Milch (1907–1989), a doctor in the Galician town of Tłuste, became a member of the local Jewish Council after the German invasion until the end of 1941. Germans killed his son in May 1943, and Ukrainians murdered his wife shortly thereafter. Milch wrote his memoir account in July and August 1943 while in hiding; in 1946 he submitted it to the Jewish Historical Commission in Poland before he left for Palestine.

24. The changes in tense here appear in the original.

last name of Simon stood on the bridge, a young snot, supposedly the son of some count or prince, who often arranged with these people that for a certain sum of money he would let them through, but when they arrived at the bridge, he robbed them of everything they had, threw them naked into the river, and shot at them. Far from the bridge, all along the banks of the river, bands of Ukrainians roamed doing the same thing, but in a still crueler way so that for a rather lengthy period of time the water of the Dniester was pink from blood, and Jewish corpses floated in it like dead fish.

One time, a wagon came for me from the neighboring village [Sicz], four kilometers [2.4 miles] away, with the request that I go see a sick peasant woman there. Although the times were very uncertain, I left immediately, as God forbid I might deny medical help to a Ukrainian. Prior to entering the village, I noticed from far away a mass of people gathered on one square, and I heard loud screaming and, from time to time, shots. It was already too late to go back, and when I entered, a boy from the village runs up to the wagon, to the man who had driven me there, a very dangerous man, and tells him that the Hungarian Jews have attacked the village and want to murder them. He answers that he'll show them right away, as he has a machine gun and hand grenades at home. I said to him that there must be some misunderstanding and, appealing also to his reason and conscience as well, that he should abstain from spilling blood, and I set out, after examining the sick woman, to clarify the situation.

[. . .]

On one side of the open square stood about 300 Hungarian Jews—women, the elderly, and children with bundles. A corpse, over which a young woman— the wife of the murdered man, as I later learned—was mourning, already lay in front of them, and the wounds of others—men and a woman—were being treated in primitive fashion next to them. On the other side, a little behind a fence, there stood a considerably smaller number of village peasants—since thirty-some people lived in the entire village—with scythes, rakes, axes, and other bandit's tools, and a few had rifles and hand grenades. Suddenly, a few Ukrainian residents of Sicz also arrived from the city with arms and wanted to do formal battle with these unarmed, unfortunate people.

I, feeling somewhat safe, since I had a sick woman next to me and, as the doctor of Sicz and an acquaintance of these villagers, I expected some respect, drove my wagon between the one group and the other. I stood on my wagon and, speaking to one group in German and the other in Ukrainian, I got them to agree, and I forbade any further shedding of blood. I worked for almost 3 hours, addressing and trying to convince the one group like the other[;] sweat was streaming down my face, and I didn't leave that spot until I had separated them.

The issue was that the Magyars had dumped a dozen Jews from the trucks in this village, telling them that "this village has been designated for them and these fields and homes will be theirs," and left, laughing into their fists. These Jews entered some homes, realized that people were already living there, and understood immediately that they had been deceived. Because it was harvest time, the houses were mostly full of women and children. They asked for water and a piece of bread, but since they didn't know the local language, they could not make themselves understood, so they perhaps allowed themselves to take some things. Thus arose the misunderstanding that the Jews had attacked them.

Later they wanted to go to our little town, i.e., the nearest one, yet Sicz did not want to let them in, and a misunderstanding arose once again, but what was worst was that the ignorant mob immediately wanted to exploit the situation for plunder and murder. I was at great risk then, but I was able to steer them to the nearest estate, and this under the escort of a few acquaintances from Sicz, who were paid. They [the Jews] spent the night there and later scattered in all directions. I took two wagons of things that they could not carry and gave them to the *Judenrat*; later some of them claimed ownership of them. [. . .]

In our little town [Tłuste], which numbered about 4,000 residents, there were more than 5,000 Hungarian Jews. That is why there was nowhere to place them, so they lived in basements, attics, synagogues, stables, chambers, and outdoors. More and more new waves of Jews arrived by foot because they had typically been released from the trucks outside the city, so the Ukrainian authorities ordered that they be driven farther. It was a terrible sight, the passing trucks carrying these crying, decrepit, unfortunate people, but even worse were the images of people driven on foot through Ukrainian Sicz who were not given the slightest moment in the city to stop and refresh their bodies. They were beaten and robbed of everything they had, and they were hounded from place to place in such a way that the Germans got involved and made of them a Caesarian section [meaning a mass execution].[25]

---

25. Between August 26 and 29, 1941, in Kamyanets-Podilsky—a month before the notorious massacre at Babi Yar near Kyiv—German SS and police units murdered 26,500 Jews, among them many expellees from Hungarian-controlled Transcarpathia.

DOCUMENT 3-9: Photograph of Jews led to their execution in Kamyanets-Podilsky, German-occupied Ukraine, secretly taken by Gyula Spitz,[26] August 27, 1941, USHMMPA WS# 28216.

DOCUMENT 3-10: Letters by Motl (Matvei Aronovich) Talalaevskii,[27] Kyiv, Soviet Union, to his wife, September 2 and 5, 1941, on his Red Army service, USHMMA RG 31.028.11 (Kyiv Judaica Institute) (translated from Russian).

Kiev [Ukrainian: Kyiv], September 2, 1941

Dear Klarusia!

Today I got your letter of July 31 that was sent through someone; as you see, the postal service is functioning better—yesterday I received your letter of

---

26. A Jewish cab driver from Budapest, Gyula Spitz was drafted into regular Hungarian army service, while many Hungarian Jews were forced into labor service. From 1940 to 1942 he transported valuables plundered from occupied territories by Hungarian officers. See Gábor Kádár, László Csősz, and Zoltán Vági, *The Holocaust in Hungary* (Lanham, MD: AltaMira Press in association with USHMM, 2013), chapter 2.

27. Matvei Aronovich Talalaevskii (1908–1978) was a Soviet Jewish author writing in Yiddish, Ukrainian, and Russian. During World War II, he served in the Red Army, both as

August 8. I've read and reread them. You're a brick! And that's just how a Soviet woman should think. I'm proud of you, and I love you even more. What is there to say about the people who prefer to lie low in the rear instead of taking an active part in the struggle against the fascist monster—the nation will make them answer for it! [. . .] The war takes away the tinge of everyday life, and the radiance of a soul, of a generous heart, becomes clearer. [. . .]

Ten weeks of war have gone by . . . Many things have already taken a turn for the better. All the monsters' expectations have fallen through. The temporary capture of individual towns does not signify victory; quite the reverse, it brings the enemy's downfall nearer. More than thirty thousand Germans have already been laid low close to Kiev. Kiev is standing firm, and no one will ever take it.[28] The people and the army are prepared and sturdily armed. Is there any danger? Of course there is; this is war. But we have to think about life. And among those of us who have stayed here, there is no thought of anything but living, winning, triumphing.

I have nothing from [illegible]. I've sent you the warm things. Unfortunately, the three bookshelves are in Kharkov [Kharkiv], and I couldn't gather up the more valuable things for you. Maybe they were stolen? Write me and tell me in detail what you took with you, and where are all the lengths of fabric? [. . .] In short, write and tell me about everything. As you see, on this little page I've written enough words to fill half a printer's sheet. Love and kisses to you and [illegible]. Kisses to Irochka.

Motia

[Postscript at the top of page 1: "Write and tell me how your pregnancy is going; I'm awfully worried about it."]

September 5, 1941, Kiev
Dear [Klarusia]

I've just sent you a telegram giving you my new address. I'm moving to Kharkov with the collective of the radio station. Upon arrival, I'll send you

---

a soldier and as a journalist. In the early 1950s, with the crackdown on Jewish cultural production, Talalaevskii was arrested and sent to a labor camp in Central Asia. After Stalin's death, he was released and returned to Kyiv. The authors have not been able to trace the later fate of his wife, Klarusia, their children, or the other people mentioned in the letters.

28. The Wehrmacht occupied Kyiv on September 19, 1941.

another telegram. It's been a long time since I received anything from you. As you already understand, I'm not exactly feeling like dancing—I can't bear to leave my dear Kiev. But I have great hopes! I'm convinced that the fascists will never take the city. It will be defended, and it is reinforced, so why are we leaving? The resources for printing are better there; it may turn out that we won't be able to transport paper into Kiev, and that's why it's better to move. My mood is bad because here I would at least have been at home, but this way I'm going to be a wanderer (again!). But for the Motherland, for victory over the monsters, over the cutthroats and rapists, I'm willing to make great sacrifices.

Today they recorded my voice on tape for the radio. This was done because there will be a big radio rally tomorrow, and I, the only Yiddish poet remaining at the front, am supposed to give a presentation at this rally. Since I'm leaving, my voice will be heard on tape. They taped the poem about Kiev. This is my latest work in Yiddish. It's almost three months now since I've written in this language. Hitler and Goebbels were not very glad to hear my Ukrainian voice; now let them hear my Yiddish one! If I'm killed, remember that on September 6, 1941, my poems were read, and you can hear my voice after the war. I'm joking here, of course. Nobody is going to kill me. There's a song that goes like this:

"a bullet fears a brave man,
a bayonet can't hit a brave man!"

And I'm a brave man, after all, especially now—if you could see me, you wouldn't recognize me! If we survive, you'll see for yourself and fall in love with me.

Today I did another big thing—this time for you. I went around to the savings banks and looked for both your savings book number and mine—I don't have anything, you see—and finally I established the number of my deposit, which I already had the right to make use of, and with my own hands I transferred the entire deposit to your name. [. . .] But I think there's no hurry anymore. My money will last you until the end of the war, and then we'll see. But use your own judgment and act accordingly.

I locked the apartment, and I have the keys, but where is the second bunch of keys? I took some things with me. I want to take the remainder—the LIBRARY! will be safe. But we won't be slaves to our belongings. We'll defeat the enemy, have our new cozy place, and acquire whatever was lost. The main thing is just for you and my dear [daughter] Irul'ka to survive. I dream about her all the time. Kiss her for me, and then give her another hug and kiss!

And you I'm asking for the hundredth time to write me more often. Two letters in 75 days of war—really, that's not many! [. . .]

DOCUMENT 3-11: Diary entry by an unidentified woman from her deportation to Kovno,[29] November 19–28, 1941, USHMM)14 (LCSAV R-1390), reel 65, folder 68 (translated from German).

. . . ; November 19, 1941]

The transport leaves tomorrow. Yesterday in the evening rumor had it that uld not travel until Sunday, but it is all in vain [Yiddish word used here:]. [. . .] Yesterday in the afternoon our visa number [for immigration to ited States] came, but it is no longer of use to us.

vember 20, 1941

ay we are supposed to travel. Thank god no order has come yet for . Perhaps the dear lord loves us and will not let us travel to Poland. have hope left. [. . . ; largely illegible page]

te, most likely November 28, 1941:]

train to the unknown.

no homeland, I have nothing in this world, my destination is unkn he grey [deleted: blue] sky is the roof over my head [literally, the grey sk y tent]. . . . "[30]

It i scribable how we are sitting here. Pressed together. Properly there should b y 6 people in the compartment, and we are 9. We have no inkling where we oing to and what awaits us there. We are not traveling to Poland. They say t ga. For the time being we are in Eydtkau[;][31] this is supposed to be the bord tation between Germany and Latvia. Sadly no one here has an atlas so that w are] without any orientation. Sunday at 6 a.m. we left Vienna. (Trucks took u o the train. Like cattle!) During the night we passed through Brünn [Brno][; hen we went on through Upper Silesia toward Poland. In Poland it is hope s. In general the entire region is monotonous like this.—Just now we traveled a oss the border. It is recognizable by wire barriers and bunkers. The houses re shot up. However they are already being built again. Just

---

29. The author, an unidentified young woman, was deported to Kovno (a destination unknown to her at the time she wrote her diary notes) together with 997 Jews from Vienna. German and Lithuanian police murdered all these deportees upon arrival. Fragments of the diary, with illegible sections, were found after the war near the Ninth Fort, the main Kovno killing site.

30. These are lines from a popular song penned in 1933 by Austrian composer and lyricist Friedrich Schwarz, titled "I Have No Homeland," with the subtitle "Jewish Tango."

31. Eydtkuhnen, renamed Eydtkau in 1938, was the border town between Germany and Lithuania (not Latvia).

we passed a military cemetery [soldiers' graveyard]. Here we are directly in war zone.—From Poland we are traveling to East Prussia, and we just now aveled across the Latvian [in reality: Lithuanian] border.

DOCUMENT 3-12: Lyrics by Khane Khaytin,[32] Shavli, German-occupied Lithuania, for "On a Begging Walk," no date (1942), USHMMA RG 26.014M (LCSAV R-1390) reel 63, file 54 (translated from Yiddish).

I stride with quick, with speedy steps,
A full beggar's bag along with me I drag,
And my legs are bending out of fatigue
And the water is seeping through my shoes.

I've already been on my begging trip today.
And a "shiny button"[33] I haven't yet seen.
And I received quite a good amount.
Oh, where does one get strength when one is weak?

Never thought I'd get a full potato sack
And a paper bag of barley also has worth.
Half a side of meat, large and thick.
A quarter loaf of bread—a treasure.

I walk with my beggar's bag and think:
Who stands at the gate today, God knows who?
I approach the gate . . . Oh, how awful!
It costs half a bottle [to bribe the guard] and soon becomes right.

I come into the house—it's cold and wet.
The children's appearance is yellow and pale.
As soon as the bag is brought, joy arises
All begin to grab pieces of bread.

We light a fire in the stove—let it be warm!
The barley and the meat into the pot.

---

32. Khane Khaytin (1918–2004) was a Lithuanian Jewish songwriter who wrote many popular songs in the Shavli ghetto until her deportation to the Stutthof concentration camp in the summer of 1944. Khaytin was liberated in 1945 and later emigrated to the United States.

33. Indicates the "shiny button" (badge) of a policeman.

The fire burns, crackles—oh, how good!
One forgets one's afflictions in this minute.

Beggars we have become today. . . .
Because we are Jews, we are hated,
Forever we shall sing the same song:
Oh how awful and bitter to be a Jew. . . .

DOCUMENT 3-13: Manifesto calling for resistance in the Vilna ghetto,[34] January 1, 1942, Moreshet Archives D.1.4630 (translated from Yiddish).

Let Us Not Be Led Like Sheep to the Slaughter!

Jewish youth, don't trust those who deceive you. Of 80,000 Jews in "Yerushalayim de Lita,"[35] only 20,000 are left. Our parents, brothers, and sisters were torn from us before our eyes.

Where are the hundreds of men who were seized for labor by Lithuanians?

Where are the naked women and the children seized from us on the night of fear? Where are the Jews of Yom Kippur?

And where are our brethren of the second ghetto?![36]

No one returned of those marched through the gates of the ghetto.

All the roads of the Gestapo lead to Ponar.[37]

And Ponar means death!

Those who waver, put aside all illusion! Your children, your wives, your husbands are no more. Ponar is no concentration camp. All were shot dead there.

Hitler conspires to kill all the Jews of Europe. And the Jews of Lithuania have been picked as the first line.

Let us not go like sheep to the slaughter!

---

34. The document, found in different versions held in several archives, remains contentious due to diverging postwar claims regarding its language, authorship, and dissemination. For a discussion of conflicting accounts and interpretations, see Dina Porat, "The Vilna Proclamation of January 1, 1942, in Historical Perspective," *YVS* 25 (1996): 99–136.

35. Eastern European Jews considered Vilna the "Jerusalem of Lithuania" due to its cultural and political significance.

36. On the murder actions in Vilna and the liquidation of the second ghetto in September–October 1941, see Yitzhak Arad, *Ghetto in Flames: The Struggle and Destruction of the Jews in Vilna in the Holocaust* (New York: Holocaust Library, 1982), 133–63.

37. Ponar, the Yiddish name for Ponary (Polish) or Paneriai (Lithuanian), was a mass-execution site near Vilna where an estimated seventy thousand persons, mostly Jews, were murdered.

True, we are weak and defenseless, but the only answer to the murderer is resistance!

Brothers! Better fall as free fighters than to live at the mercy of the murderers! Rise up! Rise up until your last breath.

January 1, 1942, Vilna ghetto

DOCUMENT 3-14: Diary entries by Eva Mändl,[38] Prague, for October–December 1941, on her impending deportation to Terezin, in Eva Mändl Roubíčková, *"Langsam gewöhnen wir uns an das Ghettoleben." Ein Tagebuch aus Theresienstadt*, ed. Veronika Springmann (Hamburg: Konkret Literatur Verlag, 2007), 52–54, 57, 62, 64–66 (translated from German).

[October 10, 1941]

Quiet in the workshop. Afterward at Mama's [her fiancé's mother, Marie Roubíčková]. A transport of Jews is leaving Prague, nobody knows where it is headed, some say to Poland. It's unimaginable. The first 1,000 people have to be ready as soon as Monday. One just must not lose one's head! It is terrible, we have to hope that we'll survive this too, one can endure a lot. A state of panic prevails everywhere. [. . .]

[October 13, 1941]

Political situation rather bad for the Russians. Several divisions have been trapped by the Germans. But what is important for us now is what they're going to do with us. The poor people in the first transport [summoned that day for deportation to Łódź] couldn't prepare at all, could not buy anything, and today they have to report to the Messepalais,[39] where they will be interned for several days before being taken away. They'll be examined, their hair will be cut off, and their bags will be searched. At work again, afterward everybody at Benny's [Benny Grünberger, a friend] listened to the phonograph. Zwi [Zwi Holzmann, a friend] quite depressed, he was assigned to assist with the transport and had to lug suitcases around all day. He saw terrible scenes. [. . .]

---

38. Eva Mändl (later Roubíčková, b. 1921) lived with her mother in Prague until December 1941, when they were deported to Theresienstadt (Czech: Terezin), where she kept her diary until her liberation. Theresienstadt, a former fortress town north of Prague, served since November 1941 as a destination for deportation transports from the Reich and other European regions. Of the roughly 140,000 Jews deported to Terezin, eighty-eight thousand were sent further on "to the East" to be murdered; more than thirty-three thousand died in Terezin itself.

39. This was a collecting place at Prague-Holešovice.

[November 30, 1941]

With Eva at Zwi's, he is already completely ready, then at Benny's, helped out some more. Zwi went to see the top people in the Community, all sorts of things were discussed. The situation doesn't look good, many people probably will not survive it, one should not despair, the young surely will survive it. One should say nothing to parents. These two good ones [most likely Zwi and Benny, who were about to be deported] are really very brave and courageous. Also packed up food, Frau Grünberger is incapable of getting anything ready. Eva very unhappy, she's never showed it but probably she does like Zwi best. It's all so sad. [. . .]

[December 13, 1941]

[. . .] Learned early today from the Jewish community [*Kultusgemeinde*] that our request [for exemption from deportation] was turned down, we have to go. Gi [her uncle Ernst Wolf] immediately volunteered. In the morning, all the bags were picked up. In the afternoon, the entire pantry was cleaned out, that was the biggest job. In the evening, a lot of other things were carried away, all the carpets, furniture swapped. All day long it was as if I was paralyzed. Thank God, there was no time for thinking about things, I feel as if I had been given an injection, I know that it must hurt, but I'm completely devoid of feeling. [. . .]

[December 14, 1941]

[. . .] Farewell to Prague. Just don't think about it. Have to join the others at 1 p.m. Saying good-bye to everyone [living in the apartment house] went very quickly. The gate was closed behind us, and from now on we're prisoners, not free human beings any longer. The Messepalais is a terribly large exhibition hall with various sections. The first impression is appalling. On account of Mutti [her mother], I couldn't show my feelings and appeared to be as cheerful as a lark.

The ground is covered everywhere with mattresses, only little pathways between them. One stays on the mattresses day and night. Some people are quite good-tempered, others are terribly agitated, withdrawn into themselves in misery. We're in the former group, and set out on a journey of discovery right away. I've run across lots of acquaintances. [. . .] At 4 p.m. a fatally ill man with a sobbing wife and a screaming child was suddenly brought in, we took a closer look, and it was Paul Mändl [a relative of her mother]. After a short time we managed to find out that he was only putting on an act, so that he'd possibly be sent home. Next to me on the other side, a girl of my age, apparently very nice, I immediately made friends with her. She's been married for six weeks and is going voluntarily in order to follow her husband. In front of the exhibition hall on one side are big pipes with water faucets for washing, on the other side, open to the air, is the kitchen, just covered with a roof. A little wooden shed with a wash basin for women to wash. The best is the toilet, a long wooden shed with pails that have to be carried out every day. Everybody is quite aghast and terribly unhappy about it, but I make little of it. My new friend is with me constantly, I'm glad that I have her. Very athletic, very jolly, everything is much easier when there are two. [. . .]

DOCUMENT 3-15: Drawing by Karel Fleischmann, Theresienstadt, Protectorate of Bohemia and Moravia, *Infirmary for Children*, 1942, USHMMPA WS# 28808, courtesy of the Jewish Museum Prague.

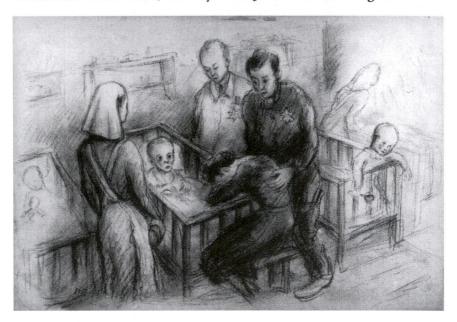

DOCUMENT 3-16: Diary entry by Nekhama Vaisman,[40] Romanian-occupied Transnistria, for January 27, 1942, on life in an unidentified ghetto, USHMMA Acc. 2010.264, Nekhama Vaisman diary (translated from Russian).

January 27, 1942

Tomorrow, the 28th, I'll turn 18. The 17 years I've lived are behind me, full of fire and life, seething and joyful. I was expecting to celebrate my 18th birthday after coming for summer vacation from the institute [i.e., university] . . . But life has turned around and cruelly lashed out at me. Fate is mocking me, like an old jester. Now I'm sitting at the table, in the faint light of an oil lamp, in a damp room in which water drips from the walls, and snow lies on the ground. This room seems like a palace in comparison with the hovels where the Jews who have been deported from Bukovina and Bessarabia by the flower of contemporary civilization now huddle. Filth, cold, hunger, epidemics. Every day in this small town, we have at least 30–40 and as many as 80 corpses, which, because of the impossibility of digging graves (it's -20–30°C. [-4°F to -22°F]), are thrown into the cemetery and freeze on the ground. [. . .] [W]hat will happen in the spring! [They] will be food for the dogs. I'm afraid to look at my relatives and acquaintances: they're unrecognizable. My mother and father are emaciated, have grown old. They always called me a child. The only daughter in the family, I lightheartedly had faith in life, and it always tossed the flowers of success to me. I passionately loved my homeland, the embodiment of the ideas of the great son of my people K. M. [Karl Marx], completely failing to notice the injustices and difficulties of the life of the proletariat and peasantry. I completed ten grades of school and earned respect and honor. With my outstanding abilities, I comprehended everything quickly and with excellent grades,

---

40. Nekhama Ioanovna Vaisman (1924–?) and her family were deported, after the beginning of the German-Romanian attack on the Soviet Union, from Bessarabia to an unidentified small town on the banks of the Dniester River in Transnistria, a region between the Bug and Dniester Rivers taken over by Romania in August 1941. Apart from Nekhama Vaisman's diary, the editors could trace no information on the fate of the family. Of the 210,000 Jews present in Transnistria on the eve of the German attack, an estimated 185,000 perished due to a combination of mass shootings, ghettoization, forced labor, and general privation. From September 1941 until October 1943, the Romanian regime deported approximately 150,000 Jews, most from Bessarabia and Bukovina, to camps and ghettos throughout Transnistria; 90,000 of them died. Beginning in December 1943, efforts by Romanian Jewish organizations resulted in the repatriation of several thousand deportees, but the majority remained in Transnistria until its liberation by Soviet troops in March 1944. See Radu Ioanid, *The Holocaust in Romania: The Destruction of Jews and Gypsies under the Antonescu Regime, 1940–1944* (Chicago: Ivan R. Dee in association with USHMM, 2000).

and got a gold medal with my high school diploma. I literally devoured the volumes of our Russian and western classics. Books were my best friends, but I also had many friends. But now I feel that after seven months of war I have become an adult, in the full meaning of the word. And I have come to know grief, hardship, and terror. I have seen a great deal of blood and many tears with my own eyes. My hopes have collapsed like a house of cards. And although my faith in the future, in a better future, is alive and intact, like a sacred thing, will I live to see it? Will some fraction of the persecuted Jewish people live? I do not know. It is not without reason that my dear mama says that I've aged five years. I still want so much to live and survive! But along the streets walk living corpses, covered with lice, miserable, unfortunate people. And alongside them are robbers, oppressors, people who have plundered, who have destroyed people and burned their corpses before my eyes. People who are animals that buried small children alive. Papa is groaning. In the damp, his rheumatism has flared up again and made all his bones ache. He is suffering, there are no earnings, and he has become nervous and irritable. Mama is calling me. I have to help, I'm stopping now.

DOCUMENT 3-17: Manuscript fragment by Đura Rajs,[41] Petrovgrad, German-occupied Yugoslav Banat, on his camp experiences, August 11, 1941, USHMMA Acc. 2012.35.1, Đorde (Đura) Rajs collection (translated from Serbian).

Introduction

I have dedicated this book to the "lager." Readers will be surprised and will wonder what a "lager" is, and what kind of word that is. It's a German word, which, translated into Serbo-Croatian, means camp. All Jews of Petrovgrad were resettled into that camp. Earlier the camp was an army barracks, which had been totally neglected and thus was full of lice and bedbugs. Before the Jews were moved into the barracks, it was a breeding place for infectious diseases. The courtyard was full of various military things that the retreating Yugoslav army left in great disorder. In the rooms, soldiers unloaded their things from

---

41. The Rajs family lived in Petrovgrad (today Zrenjanin in Serbia) in the German-occupied Banat region. In early October 1941, Đura's father was killed in the camp in a mass reprisal shooting. Eleven-year-old Đura and his mother were deported to the Sajmište camp near Belgrade, Serbia, where they and the remaining Serbian Jewish women and children were killed between March and May 1942. See Jozo Tomasevich, *War and Revolution in Yugoslavia, 1941–1945: Occupation and Collaboration* (Stanford, CA: Stanford University Press, 2001).

suitcases, trunks, etc. Bedbugs promenaded among those things just as people take an evening stroll in town. In a word, there was a big mess in this building, and the only inhabitants were lice and bedbugs. We, the children, still lived relatively well because we were together and we were able to play to our hearts' content all day long. But the adults could not boast anything like that. They worked and sweated very hard, and when they returned, the commissar would harass them. And so it went. This book cannot be written in the form of a novel, because it wouldn't have any content, and therefore I am writing in the form of short stories. The stories in this book are not fabrications but rather the plain truth which I lived through. Readers will see how a young boy of 11 feels and imagines the "lager." Because I am writing this book when I am only 11 years old.

So, let's begin . . .
Petrovgrad, August 11, 1941   Đura Rajs
Moving to the "Lager"

After the entry of German troops into Petrovgrad, all Jewish males between the ages of 18 and 60 were taken to a former elementary school and locked up there. They were escorted by guards every day to work at various places. My father was also among them. So it went for about a month. On May 2, 1941, a fateful day for the Jews, an order was issued that all Jews must resettle in the former Hungarian army barracks.[42] The resettlement began . . . Just to be safe we moved to the house of my grandmother, who was also alone because grandpa was also in the school, to await the day when we too would have to be resettled. That day soon arrived. On May 8 a police vehicle pulled over with two auxiliary policemen armed to the teeth. They showed us an announcement that said that we must immediately resettle in the barracks. Dad and grandpa then came to help with the move. My uncle Franja, a medical student in Zagreb, who, immediately upon arriving in Petrovgrad, went to the school and voluntarily signed up for labor, came along with them.

The policemen allowed us to bring along two beds, a sofa, and an armoire. Also, a table with four chairs, a wash basin, some food stuffs, and so on and so on. Then we loaded all of that on a cart, bid farewell to our acquaintances, friends, and relatives, and we took off in a carriage to our future apartment, actually to our future jail.

---

42. This region belonged to the Hungarian crown and was part of Austria-Hungary until 1918.

DOCUMENT 3-18: Letters by Hilda Dajč,[43] Zemun near Belgrade, to Mirjana Petrović, Belgrade, on conditions in the Judenlager Semlin, December 9, 1941, and early 1942, USHMMA RG 49.007, reel 5, file 2, and Historical Archives of Belgrade, IAB, 1883, 3126/II-XXIX-1122 (translated from Serbian).

[December 9, 1941:]

My dear Mirjana,

I'm writing to you from the idyllic surroundings of a cowshed, lying on straw, while above me, instead of the starry sky, stretches the wooden roof construction of Pavilion No. 3 [a barrack in the Semlin camp]. From my gallery (the third), which consists of a layer of planks and holds three of us, and on which we each have an 80 cm [31.5 inches] wide living space, I am gazing down on this labyrinth, or rather this ant heap of wretched people whose tragedies are as widespread as those who live, not because they think that one day things will be better but because they haven't got the strength to end it all. If indeed that is the case. [. . .]

Dear Mirjana, there are now 2,000 women and children here, including nearly a hundred babies for whom we can't boil any milk as there's no fuel, and you can imagine what the temperature is toward the top of the pavilion with the *košava* [a cold southeasterly wind in Serbia and the eastern Balkans] blowing as hard as it does. I'm reading Heine and that does me good, even though the latrine is half a kilometer [0.31 miles] away and fifteen of us go at the same time, and even though by four o'clock we've only been given a bit of cabbage that has obviously been boiled in water, and even though I have only a little straw to lie on, and there are children everywhere and the light is on all night, and even though they shout "idiotische Saubande" [German: stupid bunch of

---

43. Hilda Dajč (1922–1942) was the daughter of a well-to-do Jew, who, after the German occupation of Serbia, became vice president of the German-controlled representative body of the Jewish community in Belgrade. While exempt from deportation due to her father's position, in early December 1941 Hilda defied her parents' wish to stay with them and volunteered to go to the Judenlager Semlin to help nurse the sick. The camp, controlled by Germans, had been set up on the grounds of a former international exhibition to house the remaining Jews of Belgrade and Serbia after the shooting of thousands of male Jewish hostages in the fall of 1941. Hilda Dajč was murdered in the spring of 1942 in a sealed truck (gas van) brought to Zemun for the purpose of killing close to seven thousand Jewish women, children, and elderly in the camp. The editors could not find information on Mirjana Petrović and other persons mentioned in the letters.

pigs] and so on all the time, and even though they keep on having roll calls and anyone missing these is "severely punished." There are walls everywhere. Today I started to work in the surgery, which consists of a table with a few bottles and some gauze, behind which there is just one doctor, one pharmacist, and me. There's a lot to do, believe me—with women fainting and goodness knows what else. But in most cases they put up with it all more than heroically. There are very rarely any tears. Especially among the young people. The only thing I really miss is the possibility of washing myself adequately. Another 2,500 people are due to arrive, and we only have two washbasins, meaning two taps. Things will gradually sort themselves out—I have no doubt about that. The hospital will be in another pavilion. They frequently count us, and for the same reason the pavilions are surrounded by barbed wire. I don't regret coming here at all—in fact I'm very satisfied with my decision. If every couple of days I can do as much as I've done these first two, then the whole thing will begin to have some point. I know, in fact, I'm absolutely convinced that all this will pass (which doesn't exclude the possibility that it will last several months) and that it will all end well, and I feel good about this in advance. Every day I meet lots of new people and gain new experience—I get to know people as they really are (there are very few here who put on an act). Many of them are taken in as some sort of "commanding officers" [most likely to mean prisoners with supervisory authority]. Even though I would be up to this, it isn't for me—my ambitions don't point in that direction. My dear Mirjana, you'll still be able to recognize me—I won't change—it is only now that I realize from my presence of mind that I am strong enough not to let external things affect me. All I want is for my parents to be spared all this. [. . .]

[Signed] your Hilda
[not dated (probably early February 1942)]

My dear,

I could never have imagined that our meeting [over the camp fence], even though I was expecting it, would arouse in me such a flurry of emotion and create even more unrest in my already frenzied soul, which simply won't calm down. All philosophizing ends at the barbed-wire fence, and reality, which, far away on the other side you can't even imagine or else you would howl with pain, faces one in its totality. That reality is unsurpassable, our immense misery; every phrase describing the strength of the soul is dispersed by tears of hunger and cold; all hope of leaving here soon disappears before the monotonous perspective of passive existence, which, whatever you compare it with, bears no resemblance to life. It is not even life's irony. It is its profoundest tragedy. We are able to keep going, not because we're strong, but because we are simply not conscious all the time of the eternal misery that surrounds us—everything that makes up our life.

We have been here for almost nine weeks and I am still quite literate— I can still think a little. Every evening, without exception, I read your and Nada's letters, and this is the only moment when I am something else, not just a *Lagerinsasse* [German for camp inmate]. Hard labor is golden compared with this; we don't know why—on what charge—we've been convicted or how long we'll be here. Everything in the world is wonderful, even the most miserable existence outside the camp, while this is the incarnation of every evil that exists. We are all becoming evil because we're starving—we're all becoming cynical and count everyone else's mouthfuls—everyone is desperate—but in spite of this, no one kills anyone because we're all just a bunch of animals that I despise. I hate every single one of us because we've all fallen as low as we can go.

We are so near the outside world, yet so far from everyone. We have no contact with anyone; the life of every individual out there carries on as usual, as if half a kilometer away [from Belgrade] a slaughterhouse containing six thousand innocent people doesn't exist. Both you and we are equal in our cowardice. Enough of everything!

Even so, I'm not the antihero you might think I am from what I'm saying. I put up with everything that's happening to me calmly and painlessly. But the people around me. That's what upsets me. It's the people that get on my nerves. Not the hunger that makes you weep, not the cold that freezes the water in your glass and the blood in your veins, nor the stench of the latrines, nor the *košava* wind—nothing is so repulsive as the crowd of people who deserve to be pitied, but whom you are unable to help and can do nothing else but put yourself above them and despise them. Why do all these people talk about nothing else other than what is offending their bellies [meaning they only think of food] and all the other organs of their so highly esteemed cadavers. A propos, a couple of days ago we were laying out the dead bodies—there were 27 of them—in the Turkish pavilion, right at the front. I don't find anything repulsive anymore, not even my filthy work. Everything would be possible if only we could know what can never be known—when the gates of compassion will be opened. What do they intend to do with us? We are in a continual state of tension: Are they going to shoot us, blow us up, transport us to Poland . . . ? All that is of secondary importance! We just have to get through the present, which is not pleasant in the least—not in the least. [. . .]

You don't know, just as I didn't know, what it's like to be here. I hope you will never find out. Way back when I was a child I was afraid they would bury me alive. And now this is some sort of vision of death. Will there be some sort of resurrection? I've never thought so much about the two of you as I do now. I continually talk with you and yearn to see you, because to me you are that "paradise lost."

Love from your camp inmate

DOCUMENT 3-19: Uszer Taube,[44] "Protocol about the Events in the Koło Region," on the mass murder of Jews in Chełmno, Warthegau,[45] no date (after January 1942), USHMMA RG 15.079M (ŻIH Ring. I/1057) (translated from Yiddish).

[. . .] At the beginning of November 1941, a medical examination was conducted by district doctors throughout the Koło district of all Jewish men from fourteen to sixty years of age and of Jewish women from fourteen to fifty years of age. Insofar as a similar examination took place at the start of summer— for labor camp purposes—one must assume that the purpose of the second examination was completely different. Two weeks later, a head tax of four marks was imposed upon all Jews from the entire district who were incapable of working, and two days later a head tax was imposed upon the rest of the population as well. With the exception of Kłodawa, where the *kehillah* commissar [head of

---

44. Uszer Taube and his family lived in Klodawa, Poland, before the war. When, in January 1942, the Nazis deported the local Jews to their deaths at Chełmno, Uszer and his wife, Balcia, managed to escape from Klodawa to nearby Krośniewice with their daughter, Edzia. From there they eventually made their way to the Warsaw ghetto, where Uszer Taube recorded his protocol as part of the Oyneg Shabes underground archive. During the deportations of summer 1942 from Warsaw, Uszer and Balcia managed to save themselves by working in a brush-manufacturing shop, but Edzia died around this time. The parents of the Taube brothers were killed in Chełmno after the Nazi liquidation of Klodawa. The editors were unable to ascertain the fates of Uszer Taube, his brothers, or people mentioned in this document unless subsequently identified. See also Patrick Montague, *Chełmno and the Holocaust: The History of Hitler's First Death Camp* (Chapel Hill: University of North Carolina Press, 2012).

45. Chełmno (Kulmhof) was the location of a mass-murder site established in late 1941 by German officials in the Warthegau district of annexed Poland to kill the region's Jews, particularly the inhabitants of the Łódź ghetto, as well as other groups of "unwanted" people. Between early December 1941 and mid-July 1944, more than 150,000 men, women, and children, the vast majority of them Jews, including deportees from the Reich, were murdered in Chełmno by an SS unit, mostly by carbon monoxide poisoning and asphyxiation in a gas van. See Shmuel Krakowski, *Chełmno: A Small Village in Europe: The First Nazi Mass Extermination Camp* (Jerusalem: Yad Vashem, 2009).

the *Judenrat*], not wanting to provoke any consternation, covered the entire amount of the tax from the *kehillah* treasury and did not publicize this among the residents, the residents of the other towns in the Koło District were exactly informed about both the imposition of the head tax and the consequences it could have. A special messenger from Kłodawa—Golde Tabaczyńska—traveled to Koło to gain information on the expulsion, and, in fact, the Koło *Judenrat* was informed on that same day of its obligation to implement the head tax. In Koło, a certain *Hauptsturmführer* from the SS told the mayor of Bugitten [Bugaj] that by December 15, 1941, no Jews would be left in the entire Koło District. They all would be resettled in newly occupied areas.

On Friday, December 5, at 11 in the morning, 2 SS men from Poznań drove up in front of the *Landratur* [district administration] in Koło, and half an hour later they seized 30 healthy Jewish men off the street and immediately took them away in automobiles. At 2 o'clock, the systematic expulsion began. It was carried out thusly: using population records from city hall in alphabetical order, the SS men and the gendarmerie went from house to house and took out the Jews by families and put them in the *beys midrash* [study hall]. They remained there until Monday morning. Food was provided by the *kehillah*. Although the Jews were desperate, their blackest thoughts were tied to the prospect of expulsion. On the morning of Sunday, December 7, a truck arrived, and up to 50 people from Koło were loaded into it. I was told of the happenings in Koło by a resident of Bugaj by the name of Podkhlebnik who happened to be in Koło that day and subsequently was freed thanks to his certification. People and baggage were loaded separately. Severely ill individuals were placed on bed sheets and hoisted onto the automobiles with the help of several people. On Thursday, December 11, the last transport left, and along with it the chairman of the Jewish *kehillah*. People knew that they were being taken to "Chełmno" (called Kulmhof in German), a village between Koło and Dąbie. We in Kłodawa knew about this due to the following: the commissariat administrator from "United Aid Actions in Toningen," Gerardus Melchior, a Baltic German who had a reputation for being a friend of the Jews, instructed the *kehillah* commissar, who worked for him at his business, to go to Koło and find out where the Jews were being sent. From Koło he brought the news that Jews were being sent to Chełmno, where a Jewish village was being established in which all the Jews from the Koło District would live out their days. On that day there was rejoicing in the town. The Zagórów tragedy was still fresh for everyone,[46] and in this case,

---

46. In late September 1941, the remaining inhabitants of the Zagórów ghetto had been murdered in a nearby forest. See Evelyn Zegenhagen and Martin Dean, "Zagórów," in *The United States Holocaust Memorial Museum Encyclopedia of Camps and Ghettos, 1933–1945,*

having a safe haven (the Jewish village Chełmno), they wanted as quickly as possible to be done with the expulsion already and settle into the new residences.

On Monday, December 14, the deportation action of the Dąbie Jews (around nine hundred souls) was carried out.[47] They were all confined in the church. Insofar as, according to the population records, a considerable number of Jews were absent, everyone being held in the church was let go after one day so that on December 17, i.e., Thursday, the action could be carried out again. And this time, almost all the Jews were rounded up. From the church, they were sent in automobiles to Chełmno, just as in Koło.

In the meantime, the Jews from the remaining settlements did everything they could to find out what was happening with the Jews who had been taken away to Chełmno. We were unsettled by the fact that no food had been taken in that direction. Through Polish messengers we learned that the Jews were only at the Chełmno palace but were not present in the village itself.

The palace is guarded by SS men, and the neighboring forest is also guarded by SS men. The messengers did not see that the Jews could leave the palace, and in no way was it possible for so many Jews to live in one building (the palace). Our shtetl Kłodawa continually sent messengers to the palace to learn the fate of the Jews. No one was able to get close to the palace, but, based on conversations with Polish peasants from Chełmno, it seemed that the Jews there were being killed. Some Polish peasants from Chełmno came to us personally to convey this information. They did this in great fear, guarding against outsiders. According to them, the killing was taking place in the following manner: a specially constructed van would come to the palace several times a day, and Jews are hurled into it. Wails, cries, and screams can be heard from the van. From there, the van departs for the neighboring forest called Lodrutsk.

When the *kehillah* commissar conveyed this information to the German mayor Plev, he became very agitated and threatened with death the Polish peasants who spread horror propaganda. He calmed him, [insisting] that Chełmno is only a transit camp. The healthy are sent to labor camps, and the sick are transported to Łódź.

On Friday, January 2, the Kłodawa gendarmerie, using the population records of the Jews, took 30 solid, healthy men and detained them for an entire

---

vol. 2: *Ghettos in German-Occupied Eastern Europe*, ed. Martin Dean and Geoffrey P. Megargee (Bloomington: Indiana University Press in association with USHMM, 2009), 120–21.

47. The Germans carried out the deportation of Jews from Dąbie on December 14, 1941, but it was a Sunday, not, as Taube has it, a Monday. See Evelyn Zegenhagen, "Dąbie nad Nerem," in Dean and Megargee, *The USHMM Encyclopedia of Camps and Ghettos*, 2:50–51.

day in the gendarmerie. In the evening, a van arrived with field gendarmes (people called them white pelts because they dressed in pelts) and took away the 30 men. They drove off in the direction of Chełmno. This fact made a colossal impression in the town and caused great alarm. On the evening of Sunday, January 4, the same van came again and demanded another 20 men from the gendarmerie. They had to make do with 16 weak, sick, older men because the others were hiding. It must be mentioned that at the same time in Grabów and at the Kłodawa train station, groups of gypsies were seen passing through in automobiles from the direction of Łódź.[48] On Friday, January 9, 1942, at 2 o'clock in the morning, the Kłodawa gendarmerie, with the help of the SA, confined the entire Jewish population in the church. That same evening, some of the Kłodawa Jews had become aware of the following facts, which gave them much to think about: 1.) Two Jewish tailors, Hersh Nosek and Avraham Mishkovski, who worked in the village Zawadki for the commandant of the local SA, witnessed how a gendarme from Kłodawa came to the commandant with the request that he and his unit appear in Kłodawa at 2 o'clock in the morning. He did not know why they had been ordered to appear in Kłodawa. 2.) Busse, a former gendarme, while in the company of the Kłodawa Jew Yitzhak Leyzer, related that the expulsion of all the Kłodawa Jews was being prepared for that night. At the last moment (the curfew for Jews was 8 in the evening), some 40 men, women, and children fled. On Friday, January 10, automobiles arrived, and in the course of that Friday 750 people were taken in groups of 50 to Chełmno. The rest, about 250 people, were taken away on Monday morning. At the last moment, Gerardus Melchior, through his personal intervention with the Gauleiter Greiser in Poznań,[49] saved two families who were employed by him: Yakov Vanroykh and his family and his brother-in-law Perets Kohn and his family. That same Monday, January 12, the expulsion of Izbica and Bugitten took place and lasted until Wednesday. There, too, healthy men had previously been deported, as was the case with us.

On Sunday, January 18, and Monday, January 19, three young people, escapees from Chełmno, came separately to Grabów, namely: Viner and Rui from Izbica and Mekhl Podkhlebnik (a relative of the Podkhlebnik mentioned earlier) from Bugaj.[50] They were among the healthy who were typically seized earlier.

---

48. This refers to the murder in Chełmno in early January 1942 of forty-four hundred Roma ("Gypsies") deported to the Łódź ghetto in October 1941.

49. Warthegau Gauleiter Arthur Greiser; see Catherine Epstein, *Model Nazi: Arthur Greiser and the Occupation of Western Poland* (Oxford: Oxford University Press, 2010).

50. Szlamek Winer [Wiener] (of Zamość?), Abram Roj of Izbica, and Mordechaï (Mekhl, also Michał) Podchlebnik (1907–1985) apparently escaped from Chełmno on January 18,

They related the following events: the strongest ones in each town (30 men) are taken to the neighboring forest to dig large graves, wide from behind and narrow from above. They were taken to work before dawn, when it was still dark, and they were brought back to the palace when it was already dark [again]. Gold and documents were taken from the Jews who were brought into the palace. One of the SS officers holds a speech for each fresh group in which he announces to them that, since they are being sent to the ghetto, they have to undergo delousing. For the purported delousing the men are undressed down to their underwear and the women to their nightshirts, and soon after they are taken down into a cold cellar. Screams, shrieks, and moans were continually heard from the cold cellar owing to blows as well as the cold. A team of 150 SS men was active in the palace. A specially constructed van comes to the cellar that fits exactly into the door frame of the cellar. Fifty people are hounded into the van in a very violent way[;] then the van is hermetically sealed, and the driver presses a button. The automobile begins to make a loud noise, and at the same time terrible wails and cries of Sh'ma Yisroel[51] are heard from the van. The van stands like this for 15 minutes and then departs with its cargo for the forest. There, too, it stands for about 15 minutes, after which it unloads 50 dead bodies, which look wonderfully beautiful, and the faces are light and radiant.

The bodies are stiff. The people are laid 5 to a layer in the graves—lime is poured over each layer. In the course of a day, 750 people are killed. If one of the gravediggers pauses because he is exhausted from working, he is shot and [sometimes] even thrown into the grave while still alive. From January 2–10, gravediggers from Kłodawa buried 3,300 gypsies. After burying the gypsies, many of the Jewish gravediggers were shot on the grounds that the gypsies were poisonous, and they could spread the poison to the palace. Due to the shortness of the day, only 500 Jews from Koło were killed each day, but later the total was increased to 750 per day. If there were not 50 souls on the last transport of the day, then those remaining were killed in another savage way; for example: with the help of boards with nails hewn into them, rifle stocks, and so forth. A

1942. Mordechai Podchlebnik managed to survive the war and gave testimony in Poland in June 1945 and at the Eichmann trial in Jerusalem in 1961. In 1979, Podchlebnik was interviewed by Claude Lanzmann, who used parts of Podchlebnik's testimony for his film *Shoah*. The outtakes of the interview are available for research at the USHMM Steven Spielberg Film and Video Archive RG 60.5026, Tape 3294–97, and online at http://resources.ushmm .org/film/display/detail.php?file_num = 5088.

51. *Sh'ma Israel* (usually referred to as "Sh'ma") are the first two words of the Jewish prayer that takes an important place in daily morning and evening prayer services. The name of the prayer comes from Deuteronomy 6:4: "Hear, O Israel: the Lord is our God, the Lord is one."

fact: among seven Jews remaining in the cellar, a father, the merchant Kshevat-
ski, who had been beaten and who believed that the Germans would beat him
to death the next time they came, asked his 28-year-old son Yehuda to hang
him. He did not want to give the Germans the satisfaction [of killing him]. The
son hanged his father after the others gave him their word that they would do
the same with him.

While working, the gravediggers were not allowed to display the least agitation; for a wink of the eye, they would be immediately shot and flung into the
grave. Eyzen from Kłodawa, a forced gravedigger, buried his wife, his sisters-in-
law, and his parents-in-law. Another forced gravedigger, Getsl Tshonstkovski, a
solid Jew, buried his one and only son, a 15-year-old. The three forced gravediggers, Viner, Rui, and Mekhl Podkhmelnik,[52] escaped certain death under the
following circumstances: Mekhl Podkhmelnik was sent with five other Jews into
a second cellar to fetch straw. He squeezed through a small window in the cellar,
though he severely wounded himself in the process. He went into the open barn
of a German farmer and hid in the hay. A search was then conducted, but
unsuccessfully. Knowing the roads well, he successfully escaped to Grabów,
which he reached on Friday, January 17. The next morning, Viner and Rui
arrived, the former escaping in the morning and the latter in the evening by
breaking the small celluloid window of the automobile that was taking them to
work. They were aided by their fellow gravediggers, who were riding along with
them.

Every one of the young people who reached us separately told the same
story about the terrible act of extermination carried out by the German authorities against the Jewish population of Koło District.

---

52. In this paragraph, the surname is spelled consistently "Podkhmelnik," whereas above
it is spelled "Podkhlebnik." It is clearly the same person, namely Mordechai Podchlebnik.

DOCUMENT 3-20: Letter by Selig Brodetsky and Leonard Stein,[53] Joint Foreign Committee, to Władysław Sikorski, prime minister of the Polish government-in-exile, London, drawing attention to the plight of Jews, January 12, 1942, USHMMA RG 59.023M (Board of Deputies of British Jews), reel 24, frame 801.

To the President of the Meeting of Allied Governments,
St. James's Palace, S.W.
Your Excellency,

In view of the Meeting of the Allied Governments on the subject of Nazi atrocities against the populations of occupied territories,[54] the Joint Foreign Committee of the Board of Deputies of British Jews and the Anglo-Jewish Association desire to bring to the notice of the Allied Governments, some considerations relating to the atrocities committed by the Nazis and the German Army against the Jewish section of these populations.

The interval between the announcement of the Meeting and the Meeting itself has been too short for a full and detailed statement of all the evidence in our possession, but this will be prepared and sent to the Allied Governments in due course.

The Joint Foreign Committee had no desire to differentiate between the sufferings and brutalities inflicted by the Nazis on Jews and non-Jews, but as is well known, the Jews have as Mr. Winston Churchill recently stated borne "the brunt of the Nazis' first onslaught upon the citadels of freedom and human dignity . . . and continued to bear a burden that might have seemed to be [be]yond endurance."[55]

---

53. Selig Brodetsky (1888–1954) was a mathematics professor and since 1940 president of the Board of Deputies of British Jews. Leonard Stein (1887–1973) was a Zionist leader and president of the Anglo-Jewish Association (AJA) from 1939 to 1949. Until 1943, the AJA—considered the non-Zionist counterpart to the Board of Deputies of British Jews—cooperated with the Board of Deputies to form the Joint Foreign Committee, which documented the persecution of Europe's Jews and demanded action from the British government on their behalf.

54. This was a conference held on January 13, 1942, in London, presided over by Sikorski, with delegates representing the governments-in-exile of the Netherlands, Belgium, Luxembourg, Norway, Poland, Czechoslovakia, Yugoslavia, Greece, and Norway. The conference passed a resolution declaring punishment of German war crimes as one of their major goals. On the Polish attitude, see David Engel, *In the Shadow of Auschwitz: The Polish Government-in-Exile and the Jews, 1939–1942* (Chapel Hill: University of North Carolina Press, 1987).

55. This refers to a letter by British prime minister Winston Churchill to the *Jewish Chronicle* published on the front page of the November 14, 1941, issue commemorating the journal's one-hundredth anniversary.

In the course of the advance of the German Armies across Europe they have occupied territories, the Jewish population of which numbered over eight million souls, and particularly in Polish and Russian areas wanton and merciless destruction was wrought and calculated atrocities perpetrated in cities in which the Jewish population formed a considerable proportion.

Following mass executions and innumerable murders of individuals the Jewish population was either driven out or forcibly segregated in walled ghettos under conditions of physical starvation resulting in epidemics and an appalling rate of mortality. Any attempt at escape from the ghettos is punished by torture and death. There is evidence that in order to incite the non-Jewish population against the Jews, the latter have in many cases been compelled to destroy Churches and historic and national monuments.

The Joint Foreign Committee trusts that in the condemnation by the Allied Governments of the barbaric behaviour of the German Army in the occupied countries and in any measures which may be concerted in counteracting Nazi brutalities, due consideration will be given to the sufferings of Jews and to the part played by them in the common struggle.

We have the honour to be,
Your Excellency's obedient servants,
(signed) S. BRODETSKY.
L. J. STEIN,
Joint Chairmen.

DOCUMENT 3-21: Diary entries by Abraham Frieder,[56] Nové Mesto, Slovakia, for February 1942, on Jewish efforts to stop deportations to Poland, USHMMA Acc. 2008.286.1, Frieder collection (translated from German).

[. . .] Meanwhile, several anxious days elapsed. Then, on the night of February 25, 1942, that is, around 2 a.m. Wednesday morning, there was loud knocking at the front door of our apartment building. We heard nothing, but my housekeeper, Mrs. Elze Herzog, went to open the big door. Ludewit Tauber and Heinz Tauber had come to call on me; the latter was sent with instructions to

---

56. Abraham Armin Frieder (1911–1945), since 1938 a rabbi in Nové Mesto nad Váhom in Czechoslovakia, became a member of an informal gathering ("working group") of Jewish leaders in Nazi-allied Slovakia who, starting in early 1942, tried to stop the mass deportation of Jews to German-controlled Poland. After the German occupation of Slovakia in August 1944, Frieder was taken to a forced labor camp, from which he managed to flee. He died immediately after the end of the war.

see me and inform me that I should come to Bratislava immediately, for there was very serious talk of a plan to deport Jews to Poland. Thus: an expulsion of the Jews in the twentieth century, analogous to the forced displacements of Jews in the Middle Ages and modern era. Heinz Tauber had nothing to add, as he was only delivering the message and traveling on to Trenčin, on the same mission. I took the first train to Bratislava. In the meantime there was also a telephone call for me, but I was already on my way. I went to the UŽ [Ustredna Židov, the regime-appointed "Jewish Center"], where a room was made available for a meeting. When I arrived, I found the following already assembled there: from the Orthodox Jews, that is, representing the Orthodox Bureau, Rafael Levi from Bardejov,[57] Arnold Kämpfer from Bratislava, Salomon Gross and Geley from Topolčany, and Weiss from Nitra; representing the Neolog congregations [liberal Yeshurun group], Dr. V. Winterstein, Dr. Kondor, and Dr. O. Neumann; and nonaffiliated persons such as Dr. Fleischhacker, Dr. Tibor Kováč, and the architect Ondrej Steiner.

Dr. Winterstein was the actual chairman; that is, it was he who kept the discussion moving. He reported that there was a plan in existence requiring all Jews to leave the territory of Slovakia. The 14th Department had been established in the Ministry of the Interior for that purpose. It is supposed to collect statistics on all Jews and then proceed according to a certain schedule. First the young people, that is, our children, are to go, and then the adults, that is, the families, until all the Jews have been deported. No exceptions will be made; everyone must go. We were speechless, and dread and bewilderment were evident on every face. GERUSH GZERA [Hebrew: deportation decree], those were the words, the specters. We were aware of what it must mean to be sent to this enemy country. We could not determine, however, what dimensions it would assume. We expected various technical and organizational difficulties. After all, expelling 90,000 human beings and dealing with all the complexities of this undertaking is no small thing. We did not believe that it would be possible; nevertheless, we agreed that it was necessary to take action and to intercede [with various bodies] in order to do our job well and avert the great catastrophe. A very small committee was chosen—actually, not even chosen, as

---

57. Rafael Levi (1886–1944), president of the Orthodox Jewish community in Bardejov, Slovakia, had intervened with the Bardejov public health department to have a typhus epidemic (falsely) declared, which allowed many Jews marked for deportation to flee to Hungary or otherwise go into hiding. In conjunction with the Slovak uprising in 1944, Levi was captured by the Slovak fascist Hlinka Guard and deported to Auschwitz, where he was murdered. For further information on Levi and the other people mentioned in this document, see Gila Fatran, "The 'Working Group,'" *Holocaust and Genocide Studies* 8, no. 2 (1994): 164–201.

a group of six simply emerged, consisting of three men from the Orthodox Bureau and three from the Neolog Federation. The former were Raphael Levi, Salomon Gross, and Arnold Kämpfner; the latter were Dr. Winterstein, Dr. Kondor, and I. Of course, a great many people were arranged around this šestka, or group of six, as it was called, who had connections and contacts, and who were then supposed to lobby on our behalf according to uniform guidelines. The following guidelines were set:

1) To begin with, the community associations and the union of rabbis would submit a memorandum to the president of the Republic [Jozef Tiso].

2) An appeal would be made to all economic institutions, pointing out what this would mean for the Slovak economy and what damage the abrupt depletion [of manpower] would inflict.

3) An appeal would be made to the clerical leadership and regular clergy and to the Christian side, stressing what the disintegration of families and mass destruction in general would mean from a religious standpoint.

[. . .] The danger mounts with each passing day. On February 27, an Erev Shabbat [shabbat eve] before Parshat Zachor [the shabbat before Purim], I was granted an opportunity to express my views privately to Education Minister Jozef Sivák. In a meeting that lasted two hours, I talked over the entire situation and discussed all the details, and I saw that the situation was more serious than I ever believed. In particular, I was unwilling to believe that God wants to destroy us and that it is precisely the Slovak people, which after all has a Christian tradition, that is to be the Scourge of God, plunging us into the greatest distress. But now I learned that the matter has already been decided. Prime Minister Dr. Vojtech Tuka has decided the entire matter with the German embassy and with Advisor to the Slovak Government on Jewish Affairs SS-Hauptsturmführer Dieter Wisliceny, and the deportation must take place. There was no way for us to monitor the situation on the German side, because only one Jew has had access here: the engineer Karl [Karel] Hochberg, whom we have regarded as a grumbler and to whom we have had no access. He was with the advisor [Wisliceny] daily and formed a separate department at the UŽ, the so-called Department for Special Missions. He also carried out special missions conscientiously, by making statistically accurate material available like clockwork, in an unbelievably short time. Now the minister's well-meaning words more than answered my questions, and I was forced to realize that the Jews of Slovakia were utterly lost. I burst into tears during this meeting. The minister himself was very moved and wished he could help, but unfortunately the matter was under the jurisdiction of the minister of the interior, who completely shared the opinion of Prime Minister Tuka: Slovakia must be cleansed of Jews. We did not succeed in finding a direct contact to these two leading proponents of deportation, and all indirect contacts, too, broke down completely. So I saw both the imminent peril and the lack of any recourse.

[. . .]

After two hours, I left the minister and went to my group, where the six men plus Oscar Horvát from Nové Mesto were waiting for me.

I reported everything truthfully and in forthright terms, and we all burst into tears. For the first time I saw Dr. Winterstein, a strong man, crying as well. I could not help sobbing as I made my report; I finished it, and I will never forget Winterstein's words after I had finished my report: "I had been fearful before the Rav's [Frieder's] report, because I believed that he would give his report an undertone of his characteristic optimism, but now he has done the opposite. Therefore the situation is very grave, and we must try everything possible from now on!" [. . .]

DOCUMENT 3-22: Photographs and captions from Abraham Frieder's diary taken at the deportation camp in Žilina, Slovakia, no date (spring of 1942), USHMMA Acc. 2008.286.1, Frieder collection.

At Žilina, in the camp. People cluster around their fellow Jews who are destined for transport.

Under heavy guard, they leave the camp and, wearing numbers over their hearts and carrying parcels in their hands, walk to the train station, and they are beaten every time they fail to march quickly enough. The place is crawling with men on duty, providing supervision [including Hlinka guard members in uniform], although these [the deportees] are honest, upright folks, who, true to their people, are bearing their fate heroically. They all are on the move.

Regardless of whether someone has collapsed from illness and is unfit for transport, or whether someone has valid credentials in his pocket. No exceptions are possible; anyone who is not in favor with his commandants must go.

DOCUMENT 3-23: Abraham Lewin,[58] "In One Half Hour," on the spreading of news about murder actions in German-controlled Poland, Warsaw, March 26, 1942, USHMMA RG 15.079M (ŻIH Ring. I/1052) (translated from Yiddish).

The "news" that I heard in just a half hour of walking through the ghetto can serve as an example and illustration of how deep the sea of troubles in which we are drowning currently is. Today I left my home at one o'clock in the afternoon and went to visit a sick person on the former Kupiecka [Street], later Mayzel [Street], and today, in the times of German occupation, "Piner Street." In that home I met a girl of 19 to 20 who arrived today from the small town of Wawolnica in the Lublin region. The girl relayed to me the terrible news about the slaughter the Germans carried out there this past Sunday, March 22, 1942.

---

58. Abraham Lewin (1893–1943), teacher and historian, was a childhood friend of Emanuel Ringelblum with whom he worked in the Warsaw ghetto's Oyneg Shabes archive. The diary he kept from March 1942 until January 1943 was later published: Abraham Lewin, *A Cup of Tears: A Diary of the Warsaw Ghetto*, ed. Anthony Polonsky (Oxford: Blackwell, 1988), with a slightly different translation of the document printed here (see 61–62).

In that small town, a newly arrived ethnic German [*Volksdeutsche*] had been killed several days earlier; it was probably Poles who killed him as some sort of act of revenge. For the Germans, however, this was a sufficient pretext to attack and murder an entire community of Jews. This past Sunday three automobiles with Germans came down and brought all the Jews who had been seized, including the *Judenrat*, to the market square and shot them there. Because many Jews had hidden in the houses of Christians, the Germans went around to all the Polish homes, and wherever they found a Jew, they led him outside and shot him on the doorstep. As many as 90 Jews were murdered in Wawolnica. I did not receive a clear response to my question of how many Jews lived in the town [before the massacre]. The girl only stated that "all, all the Jews in Wawolnica were killed." I walked back by way of Nowolipki Street and encountered a Jew I knew from before the war who had just come from Słonim [in German-occupied Belorussia] two weeks prior. In the short conversation I had with him, he again revealed to me the terrible wound of "the story of Słonim."

"Right before me, right before my eyes," he says, "mothers with children were seized and slaughtered. I myself miraculously survived. In my house, where four families lived, I and an older Jew remained. Come to my home, he'll tell you, too. Nowogródek [in German-occupied Belorussia] was completely slaughtered, too." I arrange with the acquaintance to visit him several days later, and I continue on.

Coming to my street, on Nowolipie, I meet another Jewish acquaintance, who tells me several sad pieces of news which he had read from a letter. Here they are:

In Zduńska Wola this past Purim, 10 Jews were seized, and Jews were forced to hang them in the market square on 10 gallows.

The same thing happened in Łęczyca, too, which is also located in that region (the same is supposed to have happened in Brzeziny, too).[59]

All the local Jews, numbering 500, were deported from Izbica, in the Lublin region. 1,000 Czech Jews were brought in their place. The latter brought with them trunks with their belongings.

As Yehuda Ha-Levi says, "The cup of sorrows, long ago drained of its beauty, souls filled up with bitterness . . . "[60]

Truly a little too much for one half hour . . .

---

59. Zduńska Wola, Łęczyca, and Brzeziny were at the time located in the Warthegau region of German-occupied Poland.

60. This last section was written in Hebrew. Yehuda Ha-Levi was one of the best-known Jewish poets in Spain in the eleventh and twelfth centuries.

DOCUMENT 3-24: Letter by Ernst Krombach, Izbica, Lublin district, Generalgouvernement, to Marianne Strauss,[61] Essen, Germany, on the limits of communicating conditions in "the east," April 28, 1942, in Mark Roseman, *A Past in Hiding: Memory and Survival in Nazi Germany* (New York: Metropolitan Books, 2000): 175–76 (translated from German).

Dearest,

Sadly I have not yet had any mail from you. So I am waiting for something nice. What shall I write about? In terms of food and cleanliness the conditions here are more extreme than anything we imagined; it's simply impossible to put them into words. Words could never convey the reality of life here. The Wild West is nothing compared to this. The attitudes and approaches to life here are so incomprehensible. Anyone not firmly grounded will find himself spiritually derailed forever. There is neither culture nor morality, two things we once thought we could manage without. Once you experience the extremity of this place, you're cured of that particular view. It is terrible not to be able to help people. One is simply powerless in the face of it all!

I'm trying to give you some insight into what it's really like here. But it's impossible. I could fill 20 pages and you still wouldn't know. I'll save it until I can tell you face to face. Don't worry about me. I'm strong enough, and as long as I don't have the misfortune of going the way of all flesh, we'll see each other again. I know what to do, and the thought of you keeps me going too. [. . .]

Jeanne, I know that this is doubly hard for you. But if you trust me, you must be strong. I know that what's asked of us is almost inhuman, but we always wanted to achieve great things; so here it is, our first and probably hardest test. The word MUST stands above us and reunion is the goal that keeps us going.

I don't work—working is not the custom here. Where possible, I try to help, but the problems are so great and so many and my resources so limited that I can offer little in relation to what is needed. Every day I meet nice young people my own age so that I have something for myself. My love, I keep realizing that although comparisons are possible, there is no one who is right for me as you are. The difference is so great!

61. For information on Ernst Krombach, deported to Izbica in late April 1942, and his fiancée, Marianne ("Jeanne") Strauss, see Mark Roseman, *A Past in Hiding: Memory and Survival in Nazi Germany* (New York: Metropolitan Books, 2000). The transit ghetto Izbica was liquidated in April 1943, when all remaining Jews were deported to the Sobibór death camp; see Robert Kuwalek and Martin Dean, "Izbica (nad Wieprzem)," in Dean and Megargee, *The USHMM Encyclopedia of Camps and Ghettos*, 2:639–43.

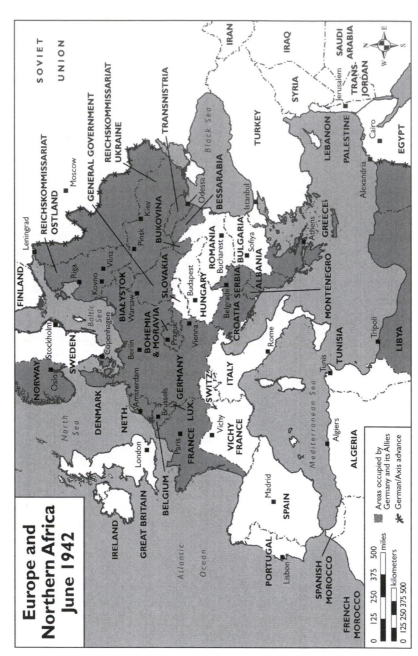

Map 4: Europe and Northern Africa, June 1942.

Postal orders are not always accepted. But we are allowed to receive money via letters, and letter-parcels do get here. It's probably better not to send proper parcels. It is possible to put old clothes in letter-parcels. It is possible to receive food.

You must be terribly curious about the appearance of this place. There are 7,000 Jews ruled by a Council of Elders, and the council is ruled by the Gestapo. That might sound fine, but the reality is different. You might be able to sketch a rough picture of the place, but I doubt it would bear much resemblance to the reality.

Now the page is used up, Jeanne!

DOCUMENT 3-25: Diary entries by Irene Hauser,[62] Łódź, Warthegau, for June–July 1942, on conditions in the ghetto, USHMMA RG 02.208M (ŻIH 302/299), reel 42 (translated from German).

[. . .] On January 21 [1942], Leo got his job putting the markings on watch and clock faces. From late January to June, difficult days of hunger and cold. In that span of time, Leo lost 20 kilos [44 pounds] and Irene, 10. Ghetto diseases, rashes, attacks of dysentery, itchy scalps, etc. Flies a nuisance at 4 a.m. Weakness in feet, falling asleep from weakness, Bubi has temperature of 39°C [102.2°F], lots of vomiting, heartburn, dizziness. Lungs affected. No sex since January 30, 1942. Today, June 15, Father's birthday, we're very hungry and have nothing to eat. Bubi and I have had diarrhea and fever for three days, had been at the baths beforehand. [. . .] Late June, menstrual periods have stopped [. . .] July 5, gold crown broken off. Leo annoyed because of Bubi's diarrhea. [. . .]

July 19, 1942.

Delivery of vegetables between 12 and 2 p.m. I come downstairs; it's changed to between 7 and 8 o'clock, so you run up and down the stairs for nothing, and every day this state of affairs. Standing in line for sausage for 5 hours. Bread, 5 a.m., in vain. Windows get ruined, that's how they carry on, it's a matter of life and death, the clerks are worthless, you can't get any information. Allegedly the people who were taken away from here between May 5 and 15 were gassed, that is, exterminated.

---

62. Irene Hauser (née Hacker; 1901–1942) was deported with her husband, Leopold (Leo, b. 1898), and son, Erich (Bubi, b. 1936), from Vienna to Łódź in October 1941. On September 11, 1942, Irene and her son were sent on to Chełmno, where they were murdered. Three days earlier she had written the last entry into her ghetto diary. Leo Hauser was deported from Łódź to Skarżysko-Kamienna in 1944 and survived a death march to Buchenwald.

July 23. [Leo] goes and sells the child's clothes. He wants to take everything, if only the end would come now, I lie here as if paralyzed, he's not willing to get a doctor because he doesn't want to pay, I feel sorry for the poor child. [. . .]

July 24. As of today we've been here 9 months, also a Friday. Two executions for stealing half a loaf of bread and 60 RM. 18-year-old young men are collapsing. My neighbors, woman of 40 and daughter of 17, 2-year-old child below me, starved to death, etc. We must be rescued soon or we'll all be dead, God help us. Mr. and Mrs. Fuchs [neighbors] help me in every way to lighten our dreadful lot, and Bubi gets many a bite to eat, he's so hungry. These people are my saviors. Leo is going today about the apartment, didn't go, decided we'll stay alone.

July 26. Sold summer dress for a little fat. All three of us completely exhausted, medicine and yeast have to keep us going one more week, have nothing left to sell.

DOCUMENT 3-26: Diary entry by Mirjam Korber,[63] Djurin, Romanian-occupied Transnistria, for July 4, 1942, USHMMA Acc. 2010.93.1, Mirjam Korber Bercovici collection (translated from Romanian).

It's already July, nine months have passed since we left home, and no end is in sight. A change in temperature like that experienced here on the Ukrainian steppe is an unusual thing. A July without heat, with a cool sun and wind. Everything is upside down. The latest restrictions give the finishing touch to the previous ones. But now there's talk of something even more humiliating. It's rumored that a ghetto will be built, that is, everyone will be resettled, moved out of the Zavod district [in Djurin] into the Jewish neighborhood. But in that case, what awaits us spells mortal danger. People crowded together, one on top of the other, frayed nerves, filth. The result: diseases. It's not enough for them that so many have died thus far, that hundreds of people go begging, that hundreds fast more often than they eat, to keep from begging, and that the ones who do eat, eat things they never even dreamed of in the past. It's not enough for them. They want to kill us all. And what is easier than killing a Jew or thousands of helpless Jews? Terrible stories are told about the brutal way thousands of Jews in the villages and towns of the [German-occupied] Ukraine were murdered. I never could have imagined that the civilization of the twentieth

---

63. In October 1941, Mirjam Korber (later Korber-Bercovici, b. 1923) and her family were deported from Romanian-controlled Bukovina to Transnistria. The family survived with the help of Ukrainians; after the war Mirjam Korber became a renowned pediatrician in Romania.

century would allow so much brutality in both thought and deed. "Quo vadis," the torments of the first Christians or even older examples, and even older events, the agonies and tortures suffered by the blacks at the hands of the ancient Egyptians,[64] nothing can compare with the present day: mothers and fathers killed in the presence of their children, children killed before their mothers' eyes, children thrown alive, along with their murdered parents, into graves where they were then beaten to death with rocks. And the world is mute, remains silent in front of the one man, the one evil spirit, who tyrannizes this world and is fighting to the death against a handful of helpless Jews. [. . .]

DOCUMENT 3-27: "To the Wide Jewish Masses," *Undzer vort* **(Paris), on mass roundups in Paris, September 1942, McMaster University Library Digital Collections (translated from Yiddish).[65]**

Brothers and sisters!

Since July 16, a hunt for Jews in Paris has continued. From Thursday, July 16, until Sunday the 19th, 20,000 men, women, and children were torn out of their homes with brutal force. The French police and gendarmerie, which [Vichy prime minister Pierre] Laval put in the service of the occupier, did not differentiate between old and young, between sick and healthy. The sick were dragged out of their beds, mothers had to take in their hands their children sick from scarlet fever, diphtheria, measles, etc. All were chased from their homes, not allowed to take with them more than a small suitcase and a covering.

The cruel, wild, inhuman, barbaric, and sadistic scenes from these "black days" will forever remain scored in the memory of Paris Jews and the whole population. Everything that took place in the houses and at the collection points cannot be compared with the organized mass murder of the Vélodrome d'Hiver,[66] where 12,000 persons were confined. It has been confirmed that the bloody Hitler bandits not only want to carry out an expulsion [*geyrish*] of Paris Jews but aim toward their complete physical extermination. Animals led to the

---

64. The meaning of this phrase is not clear. It is possible that the author is construing the slaves as "blacks" [*negrilor*] and that the scene of slavery in Egypt refers to the story of Israelites recounted in Exodus.

65. Available at "Unzer Vort [Notre Voix]," McMaster University Library, http://digital collections.mcmaster.ca/wwiijur/media/unzer-vort-notre-voix (accessed February 23, 2017).

66. The Vélodrome d'Hiver (also Vél' d'Hiv', v.H.) was a cycling arena in Paris, which in July 1942 served as the holding site for roughly thirteen thousand Jews as part of their deportation to the east. See Michael R. Marrus and Robert O. Paxton, *Vichy France and the Jews* (New York: Basic Books, 1981).

slaughter are treated more humanely than the Jewish mothers with their children in the Vélodrome d'Hiver. If not for the immediate, large protest storm of the French population, the Nazi murderers would continue the torment and torture of 12,000 Jews. In the v.H. on the 6th day, fathers were torn with force from their children and wives, in order to be taken away to the work camps of the Hitlerian tyranny. The women and children were taken away to the concentration camps of Pithiviers and Beaune-la-Rolande. Here the separation of mothers and children was prepared. All children, beginning at two years old, are pushed into a concentration camp, at the same time as their mothers are working someplace in Hitler-Germany.

The hunt, the "Jew catching," has not yet stopped, the wild Hitler beast takes as its goal the physical extermination of the Paris Jewish population. Until [now], only immigrant Jews have been affected, mostly from Poland. The same bestial plan, however, has also been prepared for all other Jews, French and immigrant. The beast is not yet satisfied, it needs to have more blood and more prey. Thousands of Jews who followed the warning and call of the Communist Party succeeded in saving themselves. There, where the police encountered barricaded doors, there, where the Jews enlisted their French neighbors, there where there was resistance, the "*khapers*" retreated,[67] and the Jews saved themselves. In those cruel days, the French people strengthened their friendship and solidarity with us. Strengthened by the active help of the French masses, the French Jews decided to put up active resistance against further attempts at deportation.

Cruel should be our revenge!

Avenging the barbaric crime is the holy obligation of every Jew today. How can our blood be quelled after such a cruel mass murder of our brothers, fathers, and children? Will we leave unpaid the breaking apart of thousands of families, the sentencing of thousands of men and women to death, the tearing of mothers away from their children? Will we let go unpunished the deaths of scores of innocent little Jewish children who died in their mothers' hands? [. . .]

This today is the very desire of every honest Jew, save for a bunch of dirty blackguards from the Nazi community who want to benefit from misfortune, in order to snatch souls and worker-hands by their brown waists. Their hands are spotted with the blood of our brothers. The Izraelovitches [i.e., Jewish traitors] took part in the preparations for carrying out the deportation. Today, they offer the tortured and tormented "liberation" for the price of becoming a volunteer slave, there at the murder of their closest and dearest. If, however, the brown Jews from the rue de la Bienfaisance[68] and the great patrons have no boundaries

---

67. The "snatchers," literally, "those who catch"; from the Yiddish verb *khapn* (to catch).

68. The rue de la Bienfaisance was the address of the Union Générale des Israélites de France (UGIF) headquarters. Brown was the color of the Nazi uniform; in this context,

in their shameful treason, the majority of the Jewish population remains firmly determined not to let themselves be dragged into the Nazi net. In the day of the final reckoning, they will get their dues, as is deserved by dirty traitors. [. . .]

To arms, Jews, brothers!

Jewish men, Jewish youth!

The Nazi executioners have not broken, rather strengthened our desire for battle and battle-cheer. We don't belong to those who capitulate right in the moment when victory is close. On par with the French people, let's take our weapons in hand, let us stand in the lines of the partisans, who are the avant-garde of the Jewish masses, the kernel of the Jewish battalions in the French people's army, which will be born in the decisive battle. Leave the ateliers and workshops, where you're working for the enemy! Destroy the machines, smash the equipment, help those who don't capitulate but rather fight on! Help the partisans! Help the families who saved themselves from deportation! Equip yourselves with weapons! Become closer to your French neighbors! Organize house-committees to put up collective resistance! Around the struggle, in order to avenge the torture that those closest to you have had to withstand, to avenge the murdered children, in order to put an end to the Nazi barbarism! To the fight for chasing out the occupier, for liberating all the oppressed and deported! For an independent France, without antisemitism and Jewish persecution, for the victory of the Soviet Union, America, and England over the bloody Nazi beast!

"brown Jews" refers to Jewish collaborators. In other words, Jewish Communists saw UGIF's work as collaborationist.

DOCUMENT 3-28: Drawings by "A. R.," an unidentified prisoner in the Westerbork camp, November 1942, USHMMA Acc. 2007.510.1, Moshe and Chaya Nordheim collection (translated from Dutch).

Women's hall, barrack 57, Westerbork, November 19, 1942.

"Do not throw paper on the floor. After use close cover."

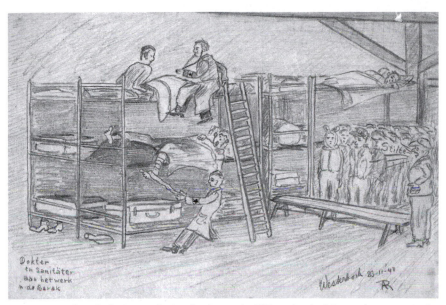

Doctors and orderly at work in the barrack, Westerbork, November 23, 1942 (the person on the right is yelling, "Quiet!").

DOCUMENT 3-29: Diary entries by Moshe Flinker,[69] Brussels, for November 24 and 26, 1942, on religion and events since mid-1940, in *Hana'ar Moshe: Yomano shel Moshe Flinker* (Jerusalem: Yad Vashem, 1958), 11–17 (translated from Hebrew).[70]

Kislev 15, 5703
November 24, 1942

[. . . ; looking back on events after summer 1940:] The Germans now controlled almost all of Europe. The only countries that were still neutral were

---

69. Moshe Flinker was born in 1926 the son of a wealthy, Polish-born, Jewish businessman living in The Hague. The family, with its seven children, escaped from the Netherlands to Belgium in July 1942. Arrested in April 1944 by the Gestapo, they were eventually deported to Auschwitz: Moshe and his parents were murdered, whereas his five sisters and his brother survived the war. See Dan Michman, ed., *Belgium and the Holocaust: Jews, Belgians, Germans* (Jerusalem: Yad Vashem, 1998).

70. This excerpt has been published in English in a different translation in Moshe Flinker, *Young Moshe's Diary: The Spiritual Torment of a Jewish Boy in Nazi Europe* (Jerusalem: Yad Vashem and Board of Jewish Education, 1971), 21–26.

Sweden, Spain, Portugal, and Switzerland. All other countries were occupied by Germany or her ally, Italy. There was one refuge still remaining, and this was the part of France that was not yet occupied by the Germans. Those who had enough money, and who did not want to be sent to Ukraine, fled from Holland to one of the countries that were still neutral. My father, who also has money, did not wish [to be sent] to a place specified by the Germans. He therefore investigated the matter of crossing the border [. . .] With God's help, our journey was successful,[71] and after traveling by bicycle, and afterward by trolley, and afterward by train, we arrived in Brussels, the capital of Belgium [. . .]

Although Belgium is also occupied by the Germans, we were not afraid here as we had been in Holland, because no one knew us (except for a few Jewish acquaintances). Therefore we did not fear at all to venture out without a [Jewish] "star" (mark of shame) and to do other things forbidden to Jews. During this war period in which we are living, it is almost impossible to buy anything without ration coupons: for example, for bread you need a bread coupon, for coffee, a coffee coupon, for soap, a soap coupon, and so on. In addition, everyone must have an identity card, stating who he is, where he works, where he lives, and so forth. If a person is found outside without this card, he is immediately taken to the police. Obviously, it is extremely dangerous to go about without this document. For this reason my father made a great effort to get us registered at the city hall. Naturally, we couldn't simply go to the city hall and say, "Here we are." Had he done so, the [man] sitting there to register people who had moved from another city or country would have asked, how did you get here, give me a moment to see if you have a stamp on your passport. Therefore my father turned to an intermediary, whose name he had gotten from someone. This intermediary took care of the matter for us, and we received a permit to stay in Belgium for three months. Naturally, this cost a lot of money, but my father doesn't care about the money. He always says, "The money is toward our atonement."[72] And so we are living in Brussels [. . .]

November 26, 1942

[. . .] As is known, people speak a lot of French here in Brussels. (I think more people here speak French than speak Flemish). So for that reason, and also because my sister[s] may not go out during school hours, and therefore I must keep them busy, my mother told me to try and teach them French. This took

---

71. The writer uses the phrase "[God] made our journey successful" (*hitsliakh darken*), a quote from Genesis 24:22.

72. Jews traditionally donate money as one form of ritual expiation before the Day of Atonement (Yom Kippur).

up half a day, and in the other half I quarreled with my sisters and read a little of the Hebrew periodical *Tekufah*.[73] I borrowed this volume [. . .] from the library. In Brussels there is a Hebrew-Yiddish library that belongs to the Jewish community. My father received the address of this library from a man who is also here. When my father gave me the address, I fell upon it as if I had found a great treasure because I would have had nothing to do or read if I had not found, or, better, if my father had not found, the address of this library. Every Sunday I borrow Hebrew books in order to improve my knowledge of Hebrew and general information [. . .]

Today, i.e., Nov. 26, 1942, I taught my sisters again in the morning. Before that I put on my phylacteries [and said my morning prayers]. I didn't do anything at all after teaching my sisters, except eat, read *Tekufah*, and play cards. So today, once again, I did not do much, but tomorrow I hope to borrow a volume of Talmud from someone. In fact, I should have received a volume of Talmud today from a certain butcher. My father went to him today, and I asked him to bring me back from the butcher the tractate "Hullin."[74] But as I should have thought, the butcher needs this volume, and so my father did not bring me anything. But tomorrow maybe I will receive "Hullin" from someone else, and if not, I'll borrow a different tractate from the butcher. The newspaper said today that things aren't going so well for the Germans in Russia. The Russians have opened a great offensive south of Stalingrad. Maybe they will succeed, and the Holy One Blessed Be He will save us in this way from our present plight. It seems to me that the time for redemption has already come. If the Lord wishes to save some of the Jews deported by the Germans, now is the time to do so. Because if they are forced to spend the winter in Russia, then, it seems to me, not many of them will be able to survive, God forbid [. . .]

We are in a very bad situation. Our sufferings have by far exceeded our wrongdoings. What other purpose could the Lord have in allowing such things to befall us? I feel certain that further troubles will not bring any Jews back to the path of righteousness. On the contrary! There is reason to believe that upon experiencing such great anguish they will think that there is no God at all in the universe, because had there been a God, He would not have let such things happen to His people, the ones He chose. I have heard this already from many people. And indeed, what does the Holy One Blessed Be He intend with all that is happening to us in this terrible period? It seems to me that the time for our redemption has already arrived, that is to say, that we are more or less worthy of being redeemed. (Tomorrow I shall continue further in a search for

73. *The Season* was a leading Hebrew periodical.
74. This is the tractate of the Talmud that deals with the laws of ritual slaughter.

an answer to this last question, because now I am very sleepy. It is already after midnight.)

DOCUMENT 3-30: Photograph by Felix Nussbaum[75] of his painting *Saint-Cyprien* on the balcony of his apartment in Brussels, no date (June 1942), printed with permission by Felix-Nussbaum-Haus Osnabrück.

---

75. Felix Nussbaum (1904–1944), German painter, was arrested in Belgium in May 1940 and sent to the Saint-Cyprien internment camp in southern France near the Spanish border. He later escaped and lived with his wife, Felka, in hiding in Brussels. In July 1944 they were discovered and deported to Auschwitz, where they were murdered on August 9, 1944. Felix Nussbaum's most famous paintings include *Self Portrait with Jewish Identity Card* (1943) and *Triumph of Death* (1944).

DOCUMENT 3-31: Account by an unidentified Oyneg Shabes activist on a conversation with David Briner[76] regarding his efforts to survive by looting in the Warsaw ghetto, December 1942, USHMMA RG 15.079M (ŻIH Ring. II/170) (translated from Yiddish).

Outwardly they are unkempt, raggedy, shabby, befeathered, always preoccupied, jealous of the time that could otherwise be spent looting, that is, stealing from empty houses. Here you have a few examples:

David Briner: a tall, solidly built lad, full face, black eyes, a soldier's yellow cap, a soldier's boots, torn overcoat, filthy clothing, hands as black as coal, 18 years old.

His life story: his father, the owner of a large carpenter's workshop on 11 Skaryszewska Street before the war, worked for the military. During the bombing of Warsaw the workshop burned down. The father then opens two workshops, one at 7 Miła Street that produces toothbrushes. The boy David worked with four other workers in the other at 19 Smocza Street. During the deportation, David goes to an outpost in Okecie.[77] He returns after two weeks. But he does not find his mother. He sat and cried for three days in a row. After the third day, he goes back to the outpost. After five weeks he comes back and does not find anyone from his family (five sisters, four brothers-in-law, three nephews, a brother, and his father—they were all taken during the selection on Miła Street). Without any money, without anyone from his family, he begins to go to the outpost in Praga every day. He has a little bit of money, 4,000–5,000 zł. He focuses his attention on food, a master of securing for himself the best food and, especially, drinks, a bottle, or at least half a bottle, every day. At the end of his term at the outpost, he begins to go looting with his buddy, Kaufman (by the name of Malina, the son of a wealthy, simple milkman).

This is what he has to say about his new trade: ["]We picked out the Pawia-Dzielna area as our area of action. Why this area exactly? Because Leszno-Solna-Orla [street triangle] is dangerous. There are too many Germans about there, but here it's relatively quiet. Every day, we go out together as a pair, casting about in every corner. We've come up with our own system: first cellars, then attics. Just last week, in the cellar of 24 Pawia, we landed a Persian carpet (I was the one who saw it). Then in an attic on the corner of 15 Dzielna—a rug. The

76. David Briner, an eighteen-year-old survivor of the mass deportations from Warsaw to the Treblinka death camp in the summer of 1942, lost his entire family to this German sweep. His later fate is unknown.

77. The writer uses the Polish word *placówka* here. We have translated it as "outpost," but its exact denotation remains unclear, be it a hiding place or labor site outside the ghetto.

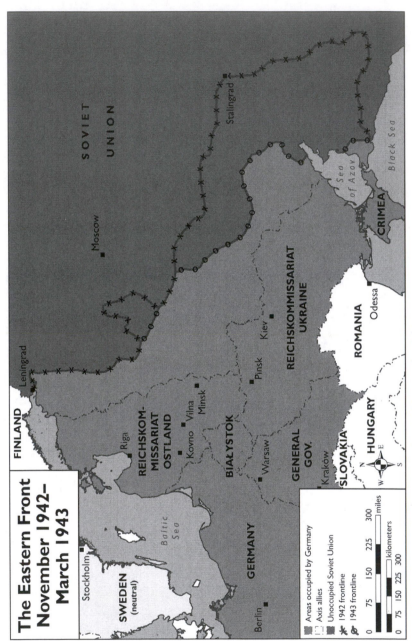

Map 5: The Eastern Front, November 1942–March 1943.

windowsills are the next stage. We know from experience that furs are usually hidden in them. In one windowsill, in fact, we found two furs made of paws. When we pull off something like this, we stash the loot at a friend's place and go out to eat something. Something in this case means spending up to 1,000–1,500 zł. and drinking three to four bottles of vodka. You know,["] he says, ["]how scared we are while we're working? Gendarmes are often out on the street. We crawl on all fours, listen for whether anyone has noticed us, and jump ahead. Then it's back on the ground, and so on.

["]Look at me and you might think that I've always been a looter, a wild boy. I was considered a quiet, reliable boy. What I want to experience is revenge. For what will become of me! Am I to forget my five beloved sisters, especially the youngest, Perl—so beautiful, tall, and well built—and my father. How I now miss his shouting, his angry look, even the beatings he would give me whenever I bungled my work. *Mensch*! (an expression from the Germans). Can all this be forgotten? What do I do now? So I eat and drink. Should I save money? Money is worthless. Should I bring some to Treblinka? Yesterday my dinner cost 220 zł (chicken, broth, apple, and a drink). I don't think about it. I don't want to know what tomorrow will bring. You ask me whether I'm interested in girls. *Mensch*, no! What do I need that trash for! What can a girl give me? Can she replace my dear family?["] [. . .]

DOCUMENT 3-32: Manifesto by Solomon Mikhoels and Shakhno Epshtein,[78] Kuybyshev, USSR, "To the Jews of the Entire World," December 21, 1942, USHMMA RG 22.028M (Gosudarstvennyi arkhiv Rossiiskoi Federatsii R-8114), reel 232, file 903 (translated from Russian).

To the Jews of the Entire World

A joint declaration of the governments of the USSR, Great Britain, the United States, and other allied countries,[79] as well as a communication from

---

78. Shakhno Epshtein (1881–1945), a Russian Jewish writer and editor, founded the Communist Yiddish newspaper *Freyheyt* (Freedom) in New York while in the United States in the 1920s. Solomon Mikhoels (1890–1948), director of Moscow's State Jewish Theater, trained actors for theaters across the Soviet Union. Both men were involved in the creation of the Jewish Antifascist Committee (JAFC), headed by Mikhoels, who traveled widely in the West, appealing to Jews in Allied countries to help the Soviet war effort. In addition to fundraising, the JAFC published a Yiddish newspaper, *Eynikayt* (Unity), and collected documentation of Jewish suffering during the war with the intention of publishing a "black book" of Nazi crimes. After the war, support by the Soviet regime for the JAFC ended and was replaced with political oppression. Mikhoels was assassinated in Minsk in 1948. See Shimon Redlich, *War, Holocaust, and Stalinism: A Documented Study of the Jewish Anti-Fascist Committee in the USSR* (Luxembourg: Harwood Academic, 1995).

79. This refers to a public proclamation issued on December 17, 1942, by representatives

the Information Office of the People's Commissariat of Foreign Affairs of the USSR, in defense of the Jewish people from Hitler's butchers, make it even more incumbent upon every Jew to perform his national duty to the heroic Red Army, to whom the main burden in the struggle against Hitler's murderous hordes has fallen.

These most distinguished historical documents have profoundly moved the broad Jewish masses of the Soviet Union. In all sectors of the struggle against the fascist monsters, the Soviet Jews, like all other peoples of our country, have doubled, tripled their heroism. At Stalingrad and on the central front, the Red Army delivers blow after blow to the accursed enemy. In these fierce fights, the sons and daughters of the Jewish people also give new examples of bravery and fearlessness. On the labor front, in factories and plants, in *kolkhoz* fields, and in social development, there are no sacrifices that the peoples of the Soviet country would not make.

The Jewish Antifascist Committee in the USSR appeals to the Jews of the United States, Great Britain, Palestine, Australia, Argentina, Uruguay, South Africa, Mexico, Cuba, and other countries to launch an even more intense campaign of all types of assistance to the heroic Red Army.

Brothers and sisters! In the name of saving the lives, honor, and liberty of our people, in the name of preserving its age-old culture, in the name of our great past and bright future, all of you, every last one, must not spare your efforts, your means, when your brothers and sisters in the Soviet Union are not sparing their own lives for the happiness of all mankind and for the happiness of the Jewish people.

Jews of the whole world! Let us not dishonor ourselves before all the freedom-loving nations, before our new Maccabees, before history.

THE JEWISH ANTIFASCIST COMMITTEE IN THE USSR
PRESIDENT OF THE COMMITTEE
People's Artist of the USSR S. Mikhoels
SECRETARY
Shakhno Epshtein
December 21, 1942

---

of Allied governments and the French National Committee and broadcasted on BBC radio, stating that Germany was systematically exterminating European Jews and that "those responsible for these crimes would not escape retribution." Quoted in Saul Friedländer, *Nazi Germany and the Jews*, vol. 2: *The Years of Extermination, 1939–1945* (New York: HarperCollins, 2007), 462.

PART IV

1943–1944

DOCUMENT 4-1: Correspondence between Jacob Katzenstein,[1] Hamburg, and Michael Chaim Gescheit,[2] Berlin, on ritual fasting, February 1943, translated from German and published in Yitzhak Arad, Israel Gutman, and Abraham Margaliot, eds., *Documents on the Holocaust: Selected Sources on the Destruction of the Jews of Germany and Austria, Poland, and the Soviet Union* (Jerusalem: Yad Vashem, 1981), 156–58.[3]

Question: Hamburg, Sunday of the [Torah] Portion "and let them make me a Sanctuary" [Terumah], 5703 [February 7, 1943].

To: The distinguished Rabbi in Berlin

I wish to tell you, Sir, what happened to us last week. During the winter we assemble to pray in one of the rooms in the Community House—and in

---

1. Jacob Katzenstein (1884–1963), born in Copenhagen, became a teacher and later director at the Talmud-Torah-Realschule in Hamburg. It is unclear whether he was a rabbi, though Gescheit addresses him as such. With protected status as a Danish citizen, he helped many Jews to emigrate. He returned to Denmark with his own large family in March 1943 and then fled to Sweden for the remainder of the war.

2. This was most likely the Hungarian-born rabbi Dr. Heinrich Mikhael Gescheit (1887–1945?), deported to the Buchenwald concentration camp in the autumn of 1943; his later fate cannot be traced.

3. Originally published as "She'elot u-teshuvoth ben Hamburg le Berlin" in *Bet Ja'akov, Yarhon le-inyene hinuh, sifrut u-machshava* 22 (1961): 23.

this room there stands a cupboard in which there are two large Scrolls of Law. We therefore brought a third, a smaller one, from the Synagogue, to exchange it. And when we looked at the small Scroll we saw that it had several imperfections, there were letters that had faded, erasures and corrections, and therefore we decided not to read from it in congregation. And when we took out another Scroll, it happened, may the Merciful Lord preserve us, that the small Scroll fell to the ground.

And now, according to the common custom we must declare a fast for all the people who were in the room and who saw what took place; and this matter touches upon another matter, which is this: the people who always or sometimes are concerned with the ritual cleansing and burying of the dead must try their souls [i.e., must fast] on the eve of the New Moon before the month of Nisan, and in my humble view this is a great trial, especially so because some of these people are not in sufficient health. I thought to myself that perhaps the two fasts should be observed together on the eve of the New Moon referred to above.

I beg forgiveness that this time, too, I trouble you with my question. But what shall I do? For my people look to me, and I knew myself that I was not fit to instruct them, and particularly as long as the voice of the Torah is heard in our land, praise be to the Almighty, from the mouth of his honor, who is distinguished in the Torah.

Set down by Jacob Hacohen Katzenstein.

Reply: With God's help, Berlin, Wednesday in the week of the Portion of Terumah 5703 [February 10, 1943].

We must not impose upon the people[;] on the contrary, because of and owing to the troubles and persecutions that are breaking our spirit this is not the time to torture ourselves. For this reason it is to be preferred to be sparing with scourging and torture . . .

With respect
Your faithful servant
Michael Chaim Gescheit

DOCUMENT 4-2: Account by Abram Jakub Krzepicki,[4] Warsaw, of the Treblinka death camp, recorded by Rachel Auerbach[5] under the title "A Fugitive from Treblinka," December 1942–January 1943, USHMMA RG 15.079M (ŻIH Ring. II/299) (translated from Yiddish).[6]

[. . .]

The doors of the train cars were opened by Ukrainians. There were also German SS men standing around with whips in their hands. Many people still lay on the floor, unconscious. Among them there might have been some who were already dead. We had been in transit for about 20 hours. If the trip had gone on for another half day, the number of dead would have been much greater. We would have been killed by the heat and the lack of air. As I learned later, entire transports arrived in Treblinka from which only corpses were unloaded.

When the doors were opened, some of the people who had been lying half naked tried to get dressed, but not all of them managed to get ahold of their clothes. At the command of the SS men, the Ukrainians leapt into the train cars and used their whips to drive the people out of the cars as quickly as possible.

"So Many Clothes! But Where Are the People?"

We exited the cars tired, exhausted. After traveling for so many hours in the half-dark train car, the sun blinded us. It was around 5 p.m., but the day's heat still burned at full strength. The first thing we saw was endless mountains of rags. The sight pierced our hearts: so many clothes—where are the people? The tales of [mass murder in] Lublin, Koło, Turek arose in our memories, and we said to each other, "This is no good, we're in trouble." They hurried us faster,

---

4. Abram Jakub Krzepicki, born ca. 1917, was deported to Treblinka on August 25, 1942. After eighteen days in the camp, where the Nazis had selected him for hard work, he managed to escape with three others by hiding under a pile of rags on an empty train and found a way back to the Warsaw ghetto. There, Krzepicki eventually joined the Jewish Fighting Organization (Żydowska Organizacja Bojowa, or ŻOB), which staged the famous ghetto uprising in April 1943 in which he was killed.

5. Rachel Auerbach (1903–1976) was a leading figure in Galician and later Warsaw Yiddish literary circles. During her three years in the Warsaw ghetto, she contributed reports to Emanuel Ringelblum's secret Oyneg Shabes archive and helped organize a soup kitchen. Auerbach escaped the ghetto in 1943, remained active in the Jewish underground, and survived the war. In recording Krzepicki's account, Auerbach also added editorial comments and subheadings (underlined) to Krzepicki's account.

6. Also translated in Alexander Donat, ed., *The Death Camp Treblinka: A Documentary* (New York: Holocaust Library, 1979), 77–145.

faster. Through a different entrance, guarded by a Ukrainian, we left the square by the side road and entered a fenced-off area where two barracks were located.

One of the Germans gave a command: "Women and children to the left, men to the right!" A little later, two Jews were stationed at that spot as interpreters and showed the crowds where to go. We men were told to sit down outside in the passage along the barracks on the right. The women all went into the barracks on the left, and, as we later learned, they were made immediately to strip naked and were driven out of the barracks through another door onto a narrow path lined with barbed wire that led through a small forest to the building that housed the gas chamber. Only a few minutes later we heard their terrible screams, but we could not see anything because the trees of the forest blocked our view.

[. . .]

Ten Thousand Corpses in One Place
The Field with Bloated Corpses
There we saw a horrible sight. Countless dead bodies lay there, heaped on top of one another. In my estimation there could have been 10,000 corpses.

A dreadful stench hung in the air, and most of the bodies had dreadfully bloated bellies, spotted brown and black, swollen, worms already crawling over the bodies.

The lips of most of the dead were strangely twisted, and the tips of their tongues could be seen between their swollen lips. It reminded you of the mouths of dead fish. As I came to learn, most of them had died in the boxcars due to lack of air, and their mouths remained open as if they were still struggling for breath. (K. demonstrates the facial expression of the dead and how he imagined their last struggle for air.—R. A.). Many of the dead also had open eyes.

We, the new group, fell into a panic. We looked at one another, to see if it was all real. But we were afraid to look around too much, in case we would be whipped. I didn't want to believe my eyes. I thought, maybe it was only a dream.

Work in the Corpse Yard

Five hundred meters farther, a machine was at work digging ditches. This machine, together with its motor, was as big as a railroad car. Its mechanical shovels scraped up heaps of dirt, loaded the dirt into a small wagon, turned the wagon around, and dumped it out to the side. Bustling work dominated the large field. Many Jews were already at work there. All of them were busy dragging corpses into the ditches that had been dug. We could also see Jews with carts, which carried bodies to the large graves at the edge of the field. There was that <u>smell</u> (I leave the incorrect yet characteristic expression—R. A.). They were all running, driven by Germans, Ukrainians, and even Jewish group leaders, so-called kapos (*Kameraden-Polizei*),[7] who all continually goaded them on: "Faster! Faster!" All the while, we could hear the crack of pistols and rifles and the whistle of bullets. But there were no cries or groans from those who were shot because the Germans shot them in the back of the neck in such a way that the person fell to the ground like lightning, without making a final sound.

There were different kinds of graves in that field. In the distance, running parallel with the outermost fence of the camp, one could see three giant open mass graves, in which the dead were arranged in layers. Closer to the barracks, a somewhat smaller ditch had been dug out where our sixty men were put to work. A group of workers walked around the field, dusting the corpses with chlorine powder, which they scooped from large barrels with buckets.

After I had watched the work for a while, an even greater panic fell upon me. I saw so many graves and so many corpses that I thought, in just a few days the war will have to be over.

("Why did you think that?"

"Because there were already so many dead Jews and so many graves."

When I ask [him] again to clarify, Krzepicki explains to me the connection between his view of the field and his hypothesis about the approaching end of the war. Since Hitler had said that at five minutes to twelve he would succeed in exterminating the Jews, and since there were such masses of exterminated Jews laying there, surely the twelfth hour had struck. Truthfully, I thought that this notion came from the fact that K was trying to say something unusual, so he was looking for a way to depict the powerful impression, but in his naïveté could find no other way. So he substituted this metaphor, which represented for him the big picture.—R. A.)

I should point out that they weren't burying those who had been gassed in

---

7. Kapos were privileged camp prisoners assigned by the camp administration to supervise camp inmates and perform limited administrative assignments. The origin of the word is unknown. It may be that, as Auerbach suggests, it is an abbreviation of *Kameraden-Polizei* (comrade police force). Other etymological suggestions include the French word for corporal (*caporal*) or the Italian word for head (*capo*). See Geoffrey P. Megargee, ed., *The United States Holocaust Memorial Museum Encyclopedia of Camps and Ghettos, 1933–1945*, vol. 1: *Early Camps, Youth Camps, and Concentration Camps and Subcamps under the SS-Business Administration Main Office (WVHA)* (Bloomington: Indiana University Press in association with USHMM, 2012), xxxvii–xl.

the field, only those who had died during transport or were shot on the spot before entering the showers.

Our sixty men were divided into three groups. Because I knew German I was made the leader of my group, and truthfully very soon I was yelling at my men and pushing them on. If I didn't, there was always a whip or a bullet threatening me.

[. . .]

DOCUMENT 4-3: Adolf Berman,[8] Warsaw, "The Problem of Resistance," January 17, 1943, USHMMA RG 68.112M (GFHM 20213) (translated from Polish).

The Problem of Resistance

(Facts and Reflections on the Jewish Population's Reaction to the Destruction of the Warsaw Ghetto in 1942)

The liquidation of the great Warsaw ghetto, carried out by the German authorities under cover of the so-called resettlement action, the murder in cold blood and with premeditation of more than 300,000 people in the course of two months—this was one of the most terrible social cataclysms history has ever known. The magnitude of the physical and psychological suffering of the Jewish people during this period exceeds anything the human mind might imagine. The action of physical extermination and mass destruction of the Jews was organized in a planned and systematic fashion and proceeded with the monstrous precision of a smoothly functioning machine. It did not come unexpectedly. It was preceded by the mass slaughter of Jews in the eastern lands, previously occupied by the Soviets, and in the western territories, annexed to the Reich [. . .] How could it then be that, when the "action" in Warsaw began, the Jewish masses did not defend themselves, that even their socially active elements did not offer the Germans resistance? This question occupied Polish society in its entirety[:] it was raised by nearly the entire Polish underground press irrespective of orientation[;] sharp accusations and words of sorrow beset Jewish society from

---

8. Adolf Berman (1906–1978) was active in the left-wing Zionist movement and headed the Central Office of the Union of Societies for the Care of Orphans and Abandoned Children (Centrala Związku Towarzystw Opieki nad Sierotami i Dziećmi Opuszczonymi, or CENTOS), the main organization devoted to the care of orphans in prewar Poland. One of the leaders of the Jewish underground, he left the Warsaw ghetto after the deportation wave of the summer of 1942 to hide on the "Aryan side," where he wrote his essay on resistance. After the founding of Israel, he served in the Knesset and testified at the Eichmann Trial.

many directions for its passivity in the face of extermination. This phenomenon, strange at first sight, cannot be fully understood by anyone who did not experience the entire "action" together with the Jewish masses [. . .] The considerations below have not been written with the intention of defending or condemning Jewish society[;] they are merely an attempt to explicate the phenomenon of Jewish society's passivity and to inform [the reader] of the dispositions and views that were present in Jewish society in respect to the question of resistance.

[. . .]

The "resettlement action" in Warsaw began on July 22, 1942. The German decree announced that all Jews, irrespective of age and sex, except for workers in German enterprises and in the Jewish Council, were subject to resettlement to the east [. . .] On that very same day, they began snatching up people off the street, evacuating refugee asylums and the homes of the poorest, and dispatching thousands of people into "the unknown." The previous day had been marked by mass arrests among members of the Jewish Council and random persons, principally from among the intelligentsia; these were hostages. The arrests had a powerful effect. The start of the "action," following upon the arrests, caused an enormous depression. The masses sensed the danger looming above them but still did not recognize how deadly the threat was. A mass panic erupted. People first reacted, understandably, by trying to save themselves by finding work in a German enterprise. A terrible run began on the "shops" (the two workshops) and the factories, which had grown "impromptu" like mushrooms after the rain in the course of the previous months. People fought over certification from such a firm or from any institution as if they were fighting for their lives. People still did not realize that these certifications, after a short time, would lose all value. People held on to them like their last chance at life.

After a few days of nearly ubiquitous panic, a conference on the situation that had come about was held that brought together representatives of all political groupings from across the board as well as independent social actors. Representatives of the groupings that belonged to the "antifascist agreement"[9] generally assessed the situation as the "beginning of the end," as the beginning of the complete destruction of the ghetto, as had happened in Lublin. They correspondingly called for resistance and vigorous action. The "Bund"[10] adopted

---

9. This refers to a group of political parties in the Warsaw ghetto that formed a joint antifascist bloc in March 1942 to organize resistance at an opportune hour.

10. This is short for General Jewish Workers' Alliance (Yiddish: Algemeyner yidisher arbeter bund), which advocated a Marxist-inflected socialism and stood for Jewish secular society in eastern Europe, with Yiddish as its common language. See Zvi Gitelman, ed., *The*

an analogous position, though rather more moderate. The leaders of the bour-geois groupings, above all Aguda[11] (the Orthodox) and the general (bourgeois) Zionists, opposed this position. Bourgeois social actors unattached to any party likewise judged acts of resistance to be premature. Neither was the opinion of the organized cadres and the periphery of the workers' parties, moreover, mono-lithic. The participants in the conference limited themselves to (a) forming a standing commission that was vigilantly to follow the course of the action and, at the appropriate moment, if it came about, to give the sign for active resistance, and (b) calling upon, through the organizations represented at the conference, the population to offer passive resistance to the Jewish police, which in its first phase was responsible for carrying out the "action." The individual organizations did in fact issue corresponding calls to the population and appeals to members of the so-called order service (the Jewish police) not to take part in the murder of their compatriots and not to carry out the Germans' orders. These calls and appeals, however, did not affect the course of events. Instances of passive resis-tance to the Jewish police occurred relatively often—they generally took place spontaneously when victims were seized at random off the street—but the police quickly liquidated them, and these incidents passed without much of an impact. It can be affirmed with complete certainty that during the first week of the action, the majority of the population was not inclined to offer active resistance, despite a certain ferment fostered by more militant elements and by refugees from those cities and areas that had already come to know "resettlement actions" firsthand (particularly refugees from Lublin and the Lublin region).

[. . .]

Both at the aforementioned conference of social groups and in numerous heated discussions and conversations among social activists of various orienta-tions during the initial phase of the action, a number of arguments and claims were made questioning the purpose and social value of active resistance in the conditions of the Warsaw ghetto. It was characteristic that these opponents generally stressed that they themselves individually burned for vengeance and a response and were prepared personally to rise to the battle, but they knew, when they assessed the situation "coolly," that a number of factors served as a brake. The fundamental, most frequently advanced doubts were the following:

Emergence of Modern Jewish Politics: Bundism and Zionism in Eastern Europe (Pittsburgh, PA: University of Pittsburgh Press, 2003).

11. Short for Agudat Israel (Union of Israel), an Orthodox Jewish political movement founded in 1912 that spread throughout Europe, Palestine, and the United States, growing particularly strong in Poland and Lithuania before World War II.

a) Struggle or an act of desperation?

In the concentration camp conditions that existed in the Warsaw ghetto, during the organized action of destruction of the <u>entire</u> Jewish population, even the smallest act of active resistance or an act of reprisal toward the Germans had to bring about an immediate, <u>comprehensive</u> massacre of the entire Jewish population, locked in the ghetto like in a cage. Given such a disproportionate disposition of forces as the one that prevailed between the Jews in the ghetto and the strength of the occupier's military might, any act of resistance would not have been an act of struggle; nor would it have led to a struggle. It would merely be a convenient pretext for the Germans to murder all the Jews, in their totality, without exception. It would have thus been an act of desperation, collective suicide rather than self-defense. Such an act can have great moral significance, could be a beautiful historical gesture, full of tragic pathos. But can the lives of not only hundreds but rather tens of thousands of people who may be able to live on be sacrificed for such a gesture? Can we take responsibility for their lives upon ourselves?

This argument was advanced at a time when even educated social circles had come to accept the near ubiquitous belief that about at least 100,000 to 150,000 people would remain in the ghetto. The adherents of this argument, however, stressed even after completion of the liquidation action at the end of September that they were correct. For if the tactic of armed resistance had been used, then even those 50,000 people who remained alive after the action would have been murdered. The lives of 50,000 people are worth more than a heroic gesture for history.

This approach was primarily linked with the argument that an act of resistance at that time would not have had even moral significance of any consequence for the struggle with the occupier. People did not believe that a collective suicide of this sort would find any resonance in the world or even in Poland; people did not think that it could play the role of a catalyst in the struggle. People judged that it would be a fruitless sacrifice. In this regard, people sometimes brought up the question of the social correctness of the educators led by Janusz Korczak,[12] who went to their deaths together with the children, even though some had the chance to save themselves. Psychologically, this step was completely comprehensible; ethically, it appeared very beautiful—the caregivers did not want to leave the children alone during their last moments, especially because they felt as close to their foster children as to their own families. But

---

12. Janusz Korczak (born Henryk Goldszmit in 1878), was a Polish Jewish doctor, progressive educator, and children's author deported to Treblinka in early August 1942, where he perished along with other staff members and the children of the Warsaw ghetto's orphanage.

from the perspective of society's interests, would it have not been more appropriate if Korczak and the dozens of other distinguished educators had remained alive and could have in the near future perhaps continued to serve society? Was the sacrifice of their lives not fruitless?

b) The sociopolitical aspect

Some workers' circles stressed the point that the German massacre, which would have been the result of acts of armed resistance, would have wiped out above all the workers' elements in the workshops that had a certain, even if minimal, chance at survival. The Germans would have assumed—correctly—that the acts of resistance came from among the workers. But insofar as there was any chance for workers in the shops to survive, would it be acceptable to condemn to an inevitable death an entire cadre of proletarians and an intellectual youth full of zeal and prepared to make sacrifices, that is, all the most valuable elements which could still play an important role in the true struggle with the occupier and with fascism in general, not simply through collective suicide? Ought one not to strive with all one's efforts to preserve the lives of cadres of workers, to save them from extermination for more important purposes than a beautiful exhibition in defense of our honor and dignity, for the true struggle for social and national liberation? (It is worth emphasizing that at the time these discussions were taking place, news reached the ghetto of preparations for a second front, of the German mobilization in France, etc.; there was a wave of rather optimistic predictions; workers' circles in the ghetto judged that the scales of military struggle would soon tip in favor of the Allies and the Soviets. Therefore, among a certain segment of the workers, there was an ardent desire to survive and await the moment when it would be possible to take active part in the struggle against the Hitlerites.)

c) The lack of arms and military equipment

One of the main impediments among social activists was the lack of arms and equipment, without which no larger-scale military action could be organized. Despite massive efforts on the part of the fighting organization, they did not succeed in acquiring a larger quantity of weapons.

[. . .]

DOCUMENT 4-4: Testimony by Leyb Rayzer,[13] Łódź, Poland, to the Jewish Historical Commission on resistance in the Grodno region, 1945, USHMMA RG 15.084M (ŻIH 301/555) (translated from Yiddish).

[. . .]

In the beginning of '42, an illegal partisan organization was created in [the] Grodno [ghetto]. It was divided in thirds, with three in a group. It had the task: get weapons and go off into the forest [. . .] The organization was strictly conspiratorial. Our organization was a communist one [. . .]

The delegates [of the partisans] arrived back in the ghetto and began to organize our circle into partisan fighters. We fashioned weapons. I stole out at night from the ghetto, I pried open the windows of the arms magazine of the military hospital on Zamkov Street, and I took out: 4 Parabellum [pistols] with [illegible] cartridges. We couldn't carry the rifles through the city. Avrom Kapulski[14] [. . .] got a Browning.

With the five revolvers, 26 persons slipped out into the forest: me, my wife Frume, with our five-year-old daughter Basye [. . .] We stole out through the wires at night, [illegible] on a Saturday night. The previous night, Mones and Pave had left, and they stood 2 km [1.2 miles] from the city at the Sekret forest and waited for us with 2 wagons. With the two wagons we went off on Shchuchin roads. We avoided the border between the Third Reich and Belorussia, and driving in snow up to the throat, we reached a spot where we stayed for a day.

The second night we drove once again. We spent the day in a *khutor* [Russian: a single homestead settlement], in the village Glebnitse near Vasileshok. The third night, we arrived in the Natcha forest. We drove to Kostia Buchko,[15] the organizer of the partisan unit in the name of Leninski Komsomol. [. . .] We were sitting in the bushes near the fire [. . .] Suddenly we heard a round of shots from machine guns [. . .] And an hour later, Germans rode through a couple of meters from us [. . .] We hid in the bushes.

---

13. Leyb Rayzer (b. 1910), his wife, Frumke (Frume), and daughter, Bashe (Basye), survived the war and later settled in New Zealand before they emigrated to Israel in 1973. Rayzer's memoir was published posthumously by Yad Vashem in 2009 and included his dedication from 1985, which he wrote shortly before his death. Beyond discrepancies in the chronology between the testimony recorded in 1945 and the memoir finalized in the 1980s, Reyzer's experiences with the partisans take a much more central position in the early testimony, in contrast to the memoir (despite its title). See Leib Reizer, *In the Struggle: Memoirs from Grodno and the Forests* (Jerusalem: Yad Vashem, 2009).

14. Kapulski later died in battle with the Germans.

15. Buchko later died in battle with Lithuanian collaborators.

Afterward it turned out that the Germans were going on a punitive expedition. They attacked Buchko's *khutor*. Buchko, his wife, and their two daughters, Zamia and Marusia, got away in time. Then the Germans burned down the *khutor*. In his *khutor* they caught his brother Sergei Buchko, and they forced him to lead them to the partisans. He led them to a group of partisans—at that time there were not yet uniform units [*otriad*] [. . .] Bringing them to the spot of the Jewish partisan group, Sergei told the Germans that the password of the partisans was a shot, and he advised them to give the password so that the partisans would think that their own were coming. The Germans fired a shot. The Jewish watchman immediately gave notice to the others, who slipped out of their huts, arranged themselves in battle formation, and under the leadership of the *politruk* [i.e., political commissar] Ilia, took up the fight with the attackers. They opened fire on the Germans with machine guns and rifles and put down 4 dead and 8 wounded. From their side there was one dead and one wounded. Sergei took advantage of the tumult and disappeared. The Germans, who hadn't planned on such a "welcome reception," grabbed their wounded and ran away, leaving the dead in the forest. The Jewish partisans had as trophies: 4 Parabellum, 4 rifles with cartridge pouches, 4 overcoats, 4 pairs of [illegible], and 4 bayonets [. . .]

With time, many Jews came to our group from Shchuchin, Vasileshok, Lide, Alke, Nayki, and other villages. Our group grew to 80 persons. The Leninski Komsomol unit, the head of which was the former secretary of the Skidel district committee and the current unit commander Stankiewicz. He treated us very well. He often visited us and took interest in our internal life. He often used to send us goods and literature. In general, the top [illegible] men of the partisan movement, especially party members, treated Jews well, as becomes Soviet citizens.

But misunderstandings happened often. So, for example, as commander of the group, I allowed my comrades to take from farmers only that which was essential for sustenance, potatoes, but meat only from those who had more than 3 cows.

Unfortunately, there could be found among Jews underworld types who used to take from the farmers meat, poultry, and clothes, and even things that were completely unnecessary for a person's life.

In these cases, the commander had to react and make me aware that I should not allow such acts. For such actions he once stood before a court Peysekh Mones, Zalmen Mednitski, and Berl Miller. He wanted to shoot them; but thanks to my intervention, he let them go, taking from them only their arms.

In the month of May 1943, the same commander Stankiewicz sent 10 Jews from his unit [. . .] to the Vilna ghetto to bring Jews from there. On the way, they stumbled on an ambush, and one was killed. Several comrades then came from Vilna. The majority of Vilna partisans went into the forests lying close by. In the month of May, the commander gave an order: select the youngest from our group, prepare them militarily, and integrate them into his unit. 35 men were chosen, out of which many [. . .] later distinguished themselves in battle with the Germans. On June 16 [1943], German airplanes attacked us and bombarded our camp for an hour. Fortunately, the bombs didn't harm us. German and Ukrainian infantry soon appeared. They encircled a part of our Natcha forest. There was panic in the camp. Everyone ran wherever they could. About half were killed in the raid—some were shot on the spot, and some were tortured.

[. . .]

After the raid, the Germans left behind their spies in the surrounding villages. The White Poles [members of the Polish Home Army (Armia Krajowa)] were especially active for the Germans, and their center was the village Kovalnik. At that point the unit decided to have a cleansing action in the village. The unit sent off about 120 comrades, half of whom were Jews. We encircled the village, shot several traitors on the spot, and brought back two [. . .] The commander interrogated them and let them live [. . .]

DOCUMENT 4-5: Diary entries by an unidentified person, Warsaw, on the ghetto uprising, April–May 1943, USHMMA RG 68.112M (GFHM 19773) (translated from Polish).

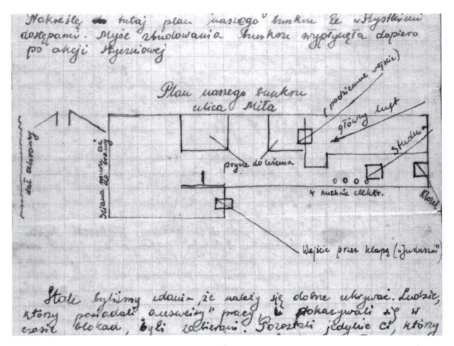

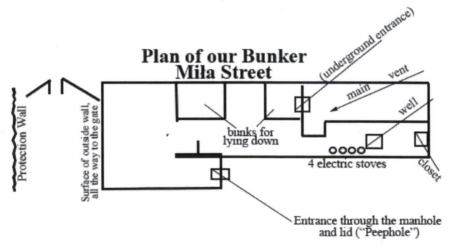

Plan of our Bunker Miła Street

(underground entrance)

Protection Wall

Surface of outside wall, all the way to the gate

bunks for lying down

main

vent

well

4 electric stoves

closet

Entrance through the manhole and lid ("Peephole")

The sixth day [of the uprising], April 24, 1943

Quiet until 12 o'clock. "Alarm," the Germans are in our building, luckily it passes and we sleep on. Our schedule is turned upside down, we sleep during the day, cook and eat at night. We are in an air-raid shelter, a great silence prevails. It's 8 p.m., steps can be heard outside the shelter. Someone knocks on the *Judasz* (a disguised observation hole), for several minutes there is great anxiety.

The people knocking at the door are Mr. Rosenheim and Miss Sonia. They raise the alarm that the building is on fire. All young people go out to the courtyard, the building is in flames, the front of it was set on fire. Apartments are burning, we set out to extinguish the flames. We immediately open tanks of water, which we pour on the apartments lying above us. We look through the window and see that the ghetto is burning, entirely in flames.

[. . .]

The eighth day, Monday, April 26th, 1943

Our building continues to burn. The building on the side of Zamenhof Street, where people were in hiding, is also on fire. People are running away from there and are coming to us, a difficult (catastrophic) situation is developing. The shelter has become crowded due to the large number of people, and more would like to enter. They storm the *Judasz* and beg to be let in. People shout and argue among themselves, they all want to get into the shelter. Meanwhile, giving any permission to enter is difficult. Around morning the situation clears up somewhat, many people are placed in other shelters. Others are placed in the shelter of Mr. Sowa and Mr. Rosenheim, the rest are placed with us.

[. . .]

The ninth day, Tuesday, April 27th, 1943

The owners of the bunker sit down for the first time for a conference. The topic of discussion is the people who arrived from other bunkers and have nothing to eat because they have no reserves of foodstuff. Aside from that, arguments reign in the bunker, and there's a great tumult. In the presence of Mr. Bychowski, who arrived with the other people, the following decision was made: Every day an additional bowl of soup and cup of coffee will be given out per person. The rations will be distributed by the eldest, those who prepare the food. A supervisor was chosen for the distribution of food who had engaged in this earlier. Everyone was satisfied with this arrangement of affairs.

Next, several people were chosen to impose order in the bunker, and in addition to this a guard duty was established, Mr. Mordecho was chosen to be in charge. In this fashion the day came to a close. At 6:30 [a.m.] everyone lay on the beds, if in our circumstances one can call them beds. In my bed they put a small boy. He was so agitated, he tossed and turned so much, throwing himself in his sleep, that my side began to hurt, but thank God, the day passed peacefully. Suddenly a crack, a hand grenade exploded nearby, people rise, but in the next moments the deepest silence prevails. The enemy is around our building, is looking for us. Our means of defense is to maintain the greatest silence [. . .]

The 11th day, Thursday, April 29th, 1943

It was a very dangerous night. At 4 p.m. the enemy threw a grenade at our basement. The effect was enormous. In the front wall, a hole opened up the size of a finger, they say that the enemy has laid an explosive device. Our neighbor, Sowa, had the same exact night. He had a hand grenade tear open his roof, thank God everything turned out fine. The day was normal. Hygiene is at the "highest level."

It seems that when a man awakens from a deep sleep, he begins to think realistically. He begins to think about escape to the Aryan side. Whoever has the opportunity begins to prepare for this; these are real thoughts but not accessible to everyone. Indeed, it is not possible to survive here in our basement for a long period of time. Above all, the air is unpleasant, and lice and crowding prevail. What is left to be done—to leave and risk your life or to die here? He who has the opportunity and has courage to escape should do that, but it is necessary to wait a couple of days. If the enemy retreats from his attacks, the opportunity for flight will increase. And for this we wait.

Friday, April 30th, 1943

The day passed normally, at night we all were terribly afraid, the enemy is searching for us everywhere. Listens in, knocks, circles about everywhere, our means of defense is to maintain the greatest silence and calm. On Saturday night we had such hours of unrest, the enemy was active from eleven o'clock in the morning. People could not sleep because of grenade explosions.

[. . .]

[Morning, Sunday, May 2, 1943] [. . .] Finally after 5 days I once again take up my pencil. 5 difficult and tragic days have passed, difficult from every respect. In this short time we have lived through much. Our living conditions from the moment we entered were very poor, and especially from the moment we took in 45 people. The majority had no food or provisions. The situation worsened, however, when on Monday at midnight the power station shut off the electricity. We now face a difficult problem: how will we be able to cook? The majority of our supplies cannot be used if not cooked. The reason is simple. We have no stoves that connect to the chimney. The leaders of the bunker discussed this problem for three days[;] in the meantime an argument broke out among them. The argument reached such proportions that brothers fought with their sisters, friends with friends. Hunger didn't spare anyone. The argument was so loud that it was certainly possible to hear it outside the bunker. The situation was both terrible and dangerous, and it didn't seem like there was any solution. All of our attempts were frustrated, we were helpless. All of our experts and people who had some sort of background in the matter gathered to confer: how to solve the problem of releasing the smoke.

The emotional state of people was critical. They can't withstand the situation, they lie on the ground in a partial state of unconsciousness. The children especially have been affected [. . .]

Another 3 days have passed, 3 days without hot food. This situation to a large degree affects disputes between people. The problem of the kitchen still has not been solved. Everyone was of a different opinion. Despite the long quarrels and arguments, the kitchen was finally set up, an exit was found for the smoke. It is forbidden for anyone to converse in order to maintain the silence. For every question one receives crude and offensive answers[;] people in the bunker, in contrast to their previous behavior, have adopted a very insensitive manner of behaving.

[. . .]

Our lives are currently in danger, and the quality of life is very low. People are half naked, badly dressed, they run by in a melancholy manner along the stone floor, they are not able to live, they are also not able to die.

[. . .]

I, myself, am surprised how it is possible that we have been able to live and survive 3 weeks in such conditions. We know very well what sort of action [akcja] this is because it was announced in advance. This is the liquidation of Warsaw Jewry and with it our end and our destruction. The Germans used to attack us this whole time at night, now they are broadening their attacks to the daytime, as well. Therefore we have to keep quiet on our plank beds, so that the enemy doesn't hear where we are. At night, however, it is possible to dare to go out to the street. The day passed well, to the sound of shots from machine guns and the explosion of grenades.

[. . .]

I go out to the street, it's burning. Everything around is going up in flames. The streets: Miła, Zamenhof, Kurza, Nalewki, Lubecki. In short, all the streets are on fire. The majority of workshops are burning, warehouses, stores, and whole buildings. The whole ghetto is a sea of flames. There is a strong wind that fans the flames and carries sparks from burning buildings to those that are not burning and immediately destroys everything. A shocking picture. The fire expands to such an extent that people do not have time to run from their homes and tragically die in them.

Because of the fire there is great traffic on the streets. People with bundles run from house to house and street to street, there is no hope for rescue, no one knows where to take shelter. They search desperately, but there is nothing—no salvation, no refuge, death prevails everywhere. The walls of the ghetto are completely surrounded, no one can exit or enter. Clothing is burning on people's bodies. They shout out from pain and cry. The buildings and bunkers are on fire, everything, everything stands in flames. Each person searches for rescue, each person wants to save his life.

People are choking because of the smoke. They all call for help. Many, almost all, call out to God, "O God, show your strength, have mercy on us." God, like a sphinx, remains silent and doesn't answer. And you nations, why are you silent, do you not see how they want to destroy us? Why are you silent?

[. . .]

The ghetto has been burning for four days, only chimneys and the skeletons of burned buildings remain. In the first moments of witnessing such a sight a person can't help but shudder: "Yes," this is the work of the Hitler vandals who want the whole world to look like this. They certainly will not succeed.

In our thoughts we retreat to the past. We have lost many things that we achieved through many years of work. The only thing left to us is our shelter. Of course it is not a safe place for the long term. We live by the day, the hour, the minute [. . .]

DOCUMENT 4-6: Diary entry by Aryeh Klonicki,[16] near Buczacz, Galicia district, Generalgouvernement, July 5, 1943, on life in hiding, translated from Hebrew in Aryeh Klonicki, *The Diary of Adam's Father: The Diary of Aryeh Klonicki (Klonymus) and His Wife Malwina with Letters Concerning the Fate of Their Child Adam* **(Jerusalem: Ghetto Fighters' House and Ha-kibbutz Hameuchad, 1973), 21–32.**

5.7.1943 [July 5, 1943]

In deciding to write this diary I was motivated by the desire to leave some remembrance at least to those of my brothers fortunate enough to be living in lands untouched by the hand of Hitler. Now that the knife of the slaughterer is resting on my throat, I find it difficult to concentrate on the chronological record of events.

It is not indoors that I am writing these lines but outside in a field of wheat where I am hiding with my wife.

We have come to this village near Buczacz, to a peasant whose wife was for several years a maidservant at the home of my wife's parents. We—myself, my wife, and my son—arrived here yesterday. In three days, on July 8, my son will be one year old.

My son's name is Adam. I chose it for its symbolic significance. I wanted to emphasize by this that the Germans, worse than all beasts of prey, yet who call themselves supermen and deny us the right to exist—will finally be conquered by humane beings.

Therefore I called him Adam [human being].

What a pity that I gave in to my zealously devout father-in-law and allowed my son to undergo circumcision! Now vengeance is being taken upon us in an awful way. Had he remained uncircumcised, there would have been no difficulty in finding a peasant to look after him till the war's end, but now they are afraid to do so. [. . . ; follows a description of anti-Jewish atrocities in the region under German occupation]

I have stopped writing for several hours. We are hungry. Our peasant has not brought us a meal. There are obstacles it would seem. But a few steps away

---

16. In the summer of 1943, as the Germans strove to murder the last remaining Jews in Galicia, Aryeh and Malwina Klonicki (nee Hertzmann) fled with their one-year-old son, Adam, from a village near Buczacz. While "hiding" in the open, over a period of roughly two weeks Aryeh wrote down the story of their wartime experience. The Germans murdered the couple in January 1944. It is unclear whether their son, Adam—who was baptized Taras, a common Ukrainian name—survived the war. For a summary of their story, see Saul Fried-länder, *Nazi Germany and the Jews*, vol. 2: *The Years of Extermination, 1939–1945* (New York: HarperCollins, 2007), 535–37.

from us peasants are at work without noticing our presence. Our nerves are taut. They just have to take a few steps in the direction of the grain crop and they will see us. We can hear their conversation quite distinctly. It is all about the Jews and their affairs. Mention is made of the hideouts ("bunkers") of the Jews and of the peasants who have enriched themselves on account of the Jews and are now able to buy themselves the most expensive suits.

[. . .]

It is difficult to write: the peasants' conversation upsets us. We hear of a peasant who had built a hideout for the Jews and that it was necessary to report this to the authorities.

We have already had several bitter experiences with the peasants. We had looked for a peasant, or any Christian for that matter, in town who would be prepared to accept our child against prearranged monthly payment. But it was difficult to find such a man. To put up a girl, that's not so difficult; when it comes to a boy, it's quite another matter. I had a feeling that in another day or two it would be impossible to continue living in town, since Buczacz was fast becoming "Judenfrei" [free of Jews] (little did I know that what actually took place was a process of liquidation spanning the entire territory under German occupation). Accordingly, I decided to call at the home of a Christian woman who was living next to the railway station. This is where I used to go daily when I was engaged in covering beets for winter storage. During mealtime it was too far to go home, and hers was the only place we could go to for our meal. She used to receive us Jews in a pleasant manner. This woman, whose name was Zosia Zasola and whose house was the last one on the road leading from Buczacz to Stanisławów,[17] used to comfort us and would ask me to take shelter in her house during the anti-Jewish "actions." Hence the trust I had come to feel toward her and her mother, who also lived in her house. It is to this woman that I went a fortnight ago asking for advice. She told me that it was possible to put us up with her mother, who now lived at the family estate in Tribokhowitz.

We came to an arrangement whereby I would hand over to her all our belongings. She would sell these and let us have the money, with which we would be able to make payments to her mother. Thereupon this woman and her mother came to us and received all our possessions. These they duly transferred to their own home. My wife dressed up as a peasant woman in order to call at their house. She was recognized and put into prison, but was fortunate enough to be freed after two days. When this happened, my wife and I, together with our child, once again went to the village. We made our way there hurriedly

17. Today Ivano-Frankivsk in Ukraine, some forty miles west of Buczacz (Buchach).

in the evening and got to the appointed place. On arrival, however, we were overtaken by an unpleasant experience. There, waiting for us, was a Ukrainian. We refrained from entering, waiting for him to go. Early the next morning this Ukrainian, whose name was Svistol, came again and, introducing himself as a member of the militia, bid us to follow him. We did not display sufficient eagerness to follow his order, and so he hit us. On the way he suggested that we give him one thousand złoty, and he would then consent to free us. We gave him this amount, whereupon he said that from now on he would look after our safety and would find a more suitable place for hiding. Afterward he told us that half the amount we had paid would go to the son-in-law of the woman we had been to, since it was he who had informed him of our arrival. Now it was quite plain that we had fallen into a trap. In the evening Svistol came to fetch us in order to take us to his house. While making our way there, we were suddenly surprised by two men who stopped us on the pretext of looking for arms but went on to rob us of all we had. They took our money and everything else we had on us, such as wristwatches, a pocketknife, string, shaving materials, etc. I understood immediately that this was the work of Svistol. Sure enough, we saw him join the two men and share the spoils, leaving us to our own devices.

We made a further attempt to come to an arrangement with another peasant in the same village, spending a whole night together with our child in his cowshed. His neighbors, however, became aware of the child's presence, since he could not keep his voice down. The peasant got frightened and sent us the next morning for a whole day into his field. This is where we remained, hungry and thirsty, because the peasant was afraid to bring us food, as I have already written.

Frustrated and full of despair, we returned to town. During the early morning hours, while on our way there, we called at the house of Franka Wanshik,[18] the maid in whose field we are quartered at the present moment, and requested her to find a place for our child. We spent the whole day with her while she came into contact with hostile peasants—to no avail. In the evening we returned to town. During the same night, an unusual "action" was launched here. It spelled the beginning of the liquidation of all the Jews. The raid lasted for two days, but even when it was over, it was no longer possible to go outdoors as before. Some nine days we spent in a hideout under the most appalling conditions. Here I had some heated encounters with fellow Jews who were in hiding. They demanded that I allow the strangling of my child. Among them were mothers whose children had already met this fate. Of course, I replied to them that as long as I was alive, such a thing would not come to pass.

---

18. This woman supposedly gave Adam to Catholic nuns; the Wanshik family preserved Klonicki's diary.

Meanwhile, I managed to send off a letter to Franka, who came here with the news that she had found a woman who was willing to accept the child. I received a loan of 1,500 złoty from my fellows in hiding (they were eager to be rid of my child), and so we arrived at Franka's house yesterday together with our son. Another day has already gone by, and our boy is still at the maid's home. The woman who was supposed to take him in seems to be in no hurry to carry out her promise.

Franka is really displaying considerable devotion toward us and very much wants to help us. But she is afraid. Posters have been placed throughout town announcing the death penalty for anyone caught hiding Jews. This is the reason for our being out in the field rather than at her home. We gave Franka all our money, amounting to 2,000 złoty and 15 *lokshen* [Yiddish: noodles (dollars)]. Should we succeed in finding a place for our child, we could stay here for some time—as long as our presence is not discovered in the village.

I sent Franka to Zosia Zasola in order to retrieve our belongings, but she refused to return them to us. Our position now is dreadful, as we have been left without any possessions. We have neither coats nor underwear for changing, having left everything with Zosia. The property handed over to her is worth some 7,000–8,000 złoty. As things have turned out, I am pretty certain that her suggestion that we go to her mother was made for no other purpose than that of laying her hands upon all our belongings. I shall once again try to write to her in the expectation that she might consent to return at least some of our things. There is no sense in attempting any open action against her as she could simply turn us over to the authorities.

We are listening to the conversation of the peasants working in our vicinity. Yesterday, we hear, twenty Jews were killed. After their burial, some Christians who were grazing their cows nearby heard the voice of a child calling, "Mother, mother, open the door, I'm suffocating!" This was followed by a woman's voice answering, "Calm yourself, my son, I'm mortally wounded and cannot do a thing." Just dry facts . . . They are burying children alive as well as adults who have not yet died. Is there a God in this world or is lawlessness at the very core of the universe?

DOCUMENT 4-7: Letter by Menahem Glitsenshteyn, Jizzakh, Uzbekistan, USSR, to Yerahmiel and Gitele Glitsenshteyn,[19] Ushtobe, Kazakhstan, USSR, on his experience as a refugee in Soviet Asia, June 12, 1943, USHMMA RG 02.208M (ŻIH 302/84) (translated from Yiddish).

My dears!

I know that one grows apprehensive from a distance. My blood boils when I know nothing of your situation and Efroim's, not to mention how the fate of Hanania and Mendel robs me of sleep, doesn't let me rest, although I have a clear conscience toward them, I help as I can, I helped them too after all, our little brothers! Certainly, help is more expensive [now]. It can't be expressed by tangible criteria. This is why you've become so dear to me, my dear, my radiant, my only ones; this is why I am not satisfied with the spoken word, this is why I often remain silent in light of the newly recognized truth. Pay heed that I am not responsible for my silence—responsible are the circumstances that have taken shape around me. I can't be accused of having any bad intentions, as you, my brother, are reproaching me. I'm driven by an evil fate, I don't have the necessary opportunity to stay in one place, although my God is my witness that I absolutely love to stay at home. I love the homey nest that warms, that nestles, like a mother, like a kind sister. The unfamiliar sears me, my dears, irritates me, and I often struggle to overcome this attribute of mine, that burning unease. No, not a single bad intention toward you [both]. But it hounds me, and I simply have no time to consider what's going on with me. Yerahmiel, you have to know that concern for the three of us weighs upon me, that it is not insignificant. That is why I was driven here, to Jizzakh in the steppe.

I was thrown out by the Tajiks only to wind up with the Uzbeks! I'm really seeing the world! I have to find a place to make a living, it's not easy anywhere—I don't mean that I've become spoiled, that I'm coddled, [it's just] my expectations of life have all of a sudden grown up. God forbid! I ought to be satisfied with trifles in order to be full, to fight my way through the day. All the golden mountains I foresaw in Leninabad have come to naught. It turns out that the Tajiks, whom we view as half savage, are actually smarter than we are. They promise you the pie in the sky just to get you on the hook—only later do you see: you've been had. I won't say that they're liars, eastern people. Only in

---

19. Menahem Glitsenshteyn and his siblings—Hanania, Efroim, Mendel, and Yerahmiel—fled their Polish homeland during the German invasion and ended up, after protracted journeys, in several places in the Soviet Union. Another brother, Chananie, was sent to the front; their parents ended up in a ghetto.

our expectations of their simplemindedness, it turns out, do we fool ourselves. In truth, they are no less wily than we are.

In your last letter, Yerahmiel, you lamented that you are tormented by the ghost of Poland. You abhor the Poland you know because, as far back as you can remember, they, your fellow citizens, persecuted you, humiliated you, your kind neighbors. They say to you, "Proszę pana" [Polish: Please, sir], yet don't let you enjoy the light of day. They want to mobilize you in the name of Polish patriotism, and you see this as a misfortune. I, you see, would be happy if they would take me, in the Polish army for example, in any army so I can go beat the *yeke* [German] fool black and blue. "Pole" is a rather broad term. It includes the attributes of the nobility, hollow conceit and pettiness; but don't forget that Poles are peasants, honest, warm peasants who live off the land and fear the evils to which they've been accustomed over centuries. And the Polish peasant silently hates the *pan* [Polish: lord or noble] for his haughtiness, for the peasants' want; Poles are also workers, sensible people, thoroughly plagued by the fires of fury and misfortune. Do not think, my dear, that "Poles" means only the rabble, the mob, which is always ready to kill, which knows nothing but liquor and "beat the Jew"! But why the splitting of hairs? Now is not the time to do so, and I won't convince you, but I know something substantial that concerns you. Do you know what I want to say to you? Efroim and I have come up with a plan for all of us to come together and jointly establish a household on the basis of weaving, which, you've written, reminds you of our dear house, the abandoned, old, eternally young home. Incidentally, my throat reflexively tightened, and tears welled up in my eyes. Yes, my dear, I have cried more than once while reading through a postcard from mom and dad in the ghetto which Efroim sent me. And again I am tormented: Hanania, Mendel . . . when will the end come? Will we finally succeed in harnessing together our lives, now in the land of the Uzbeks!? In the meantime, I'll search for an opportunity.

Be well and strong,
your Menahem

DOCUMENT 4-8: Testimonial letter by Elkhanan Elkes,[20] Kovno, German-occupied Lithuania, to Joel and Sara Elkes,[21] England, October 19, 1943, USHMMA Acc. 1999.86.1a–d (translated from Hebrew).

At the Viliampoli Ghetto (Kovno)
October 19, 1943
My beloved son and daughter!

I write these lines to you, my beloved children, after we find ourselves here, in the Valley of Tears,[22] the Kovno Viliampoli ghetto, for more than two years. We have learned that in the coming days our fate will be decided: the ghetto in which we are located will be cut and torn to pieces.[23] Only God knows if we will all be annihilated or if a small number of us will remain. We fear that only the slaves capable of working will remain alive, while the rest are probably destined for death.

Only a few remain here from many: from the thirty-five thousand Jewish residents of Kovno, there are now only about seventeen thousand, and from the quarter million Jews of Lithuania (including the region of Vilna), there remain now fewer than twenty-five thousand here in Lithuania and five thousand who were taken away in recent days, bare and bereft of everything, for slave labor in Latvia. The remainder were put to terrible deaths by those who carried out the will of the greatest Haman[24] in all generations and times. Many of the persons close to us are no longer living: Aunt Hanah and Uncle Aryeh were killed together with one thousand five hundred inhabitants of our ghetto on October

---

20. Elkhanan Elkes (1879–1944), before the war a well-known physician, after the German invasion in 1941 became the head of the Jewish Council in the Kovno ghetto. In the summer of 1944, he was deported to Landsberg, a subcamp of the Dachau concentration camp, where he died. See Avraham Tory, *Surviving the Holocaust: The Kovno Ghetto Diary*, ed. Martin Gilbert (Cambridge, MA: Harvard University Press, 1990).

21. Joel and Sara Elkes survived the war in England, where Joel trained as a doctor. Their mother, Elkhanan Elkes's wife, survived the Stutthof concentration camp and moved to Israel after the war. See Joel Elkes, *Values, Belief and Survival: Dr. Elkhanan Elkes and the Kovno Ghetto: A Memoir* (London: Vale, 1997).

22. Hebrew: *emek ha-bakha*; a biblical valley that later acquired symbolic significance as an expression of suffering and exile. The phrase is used in this sense in the Jewish liturgical song "Lekhah Dodi."

23. On October 26, 1943, the Germans deported some twenty-eight hundred Jews from Kovno. Able-bodied men and women were deported to labor camps in Estonia, while the rest were sent to their deaths in Auschwitz. The Kovno ghetto was subsequently turned into a concentration camp.

24. The villain and enemy of the Jews in the Book of Esther.

4, 1941. Uncle Tzvi, who was then in our hospital with a broken leg, was miraculously saved.[25] The rest of the patients, together with the doctors and nurses and the relatives of the patients who happened to be there, were killed or burned alive in the hospital, which was set on fire by soldiers from all sides, after the doors and windows were nailed shut so that no one could escape from the flames.

In the provinces, with the exception of Shavli, there is not one Jew still out in the open. Uncle Dov and his son Shmuel were killed together with the whole community of Kalvaria. Thanks to internal and external causes, our ghetto has lived its exilic life for two years in slavery and general forced labor, in hunger and without clothing (almost all of our clothes, property, and books were taken from us by the authorities two years ago)—but in relative peace.

The last great slaughter that befell us, with ten thousand victims in one blow, was on October 28, 1941. For all of that day, all of the community stood under the rod of the authorities: who for life and who for death.[26]

I am the man who saw the affliction of those chosen for death.[27] I myself stood early in the morning of October 29 among the crowd brought to the Ninth Fort for slaughter. With my own ears I heard the terrible symphony of crying, wailing, and screaming of ten thousand people, old, young, and infants, that tore open the heavens. No one has heard the like in all generations and all times! Together with many of the martyrs, I challenged, then, my Creator, and together with them, I cried out of a torn heart: Who is like unto you, O Lord[,] among the mutes![28]

And in my desire to save whomever I could, I was assaulted by the soldiers, and they beat me badly, and I was wounded, and having lost blood, I was driven out at the order of the Commander of the Guard. And fainting from weakness, I was carried out of the camp on the hands of my friends, and in the confusion,

25. Hirsch (Tzvi) Elkes (b. 1892), Elkhanan's brother, was liberated from the Dachau concentration camp at the end of the war. The editors could not identify the other relatives mentioned by Elkes.

26. This refers to the Jewish High Holiday liturgy and the *Unetaneh Tokef* prayer: "Like the review of a shepherd of his flock, passing his sheep under his staff, so do you pass and number and count and consider the soul of every living thing . . . who will live and who will die."

27. This refers to Lamentations 3:1: "I am the man who has seen affliction by the rod of his wrath."

28. This is an ironic paraphrase of the biblical exclamation "Who is like thee, O Lord, among the gods" (Exodus 15:11), with "the mute" (*ilmim*) substituted for "the gods" (*elim*). The phrase references a Talmudic discussion in which the rabbis describe God's seeming silence and indifference to the destruction of the Second Temple. See Tractate Gittin, 56b.

a small band of about thirty to forty people were saved with me. Firebrands plucked out of the fire.[29]

Our region was one of the Valleys of Slaughter[30] in the east. About two years ago, before our eyes and before the windows of our house, many, many thousands of Jews from southern Germany and Vienna, together with their property and large bundles, passed by the Ninth Fort, which is several kilometers from us.[31] There they were all killed with extreme cruelty. As we found out afterward, they had been completely led astray and were told in their [original] places of living that they were being taken to Kovno to settle with us in the ghetto.

[. . .]

In the most difficult moments of our life, you, my beloved ones, were always in our thoughts and hearts. During the long, black nights your beloved mother sits by my side, and we both dream of your lives and your future. We yearn to see you again, to embrace you, and to tell you once more how tied we feel to you and how our hearts throb when we remember you. And is there any hour, during the day and night, my dearest ones, when we don't remember? Standing at the edge of a pit, with a sharp sword at our throats,[32] we saw only your pictures, my beloved ones, and in the outline of your faces I saw everything. And you, my dearest ones, how have you lived during the last five years that were so difficult and filled with suffering and troubles for the Jews of Europe? I have no doubt that even located far from the area of destruction, you feel our pain, and gripped with agony and sorrow, you tremble at any news that comes from the Place of Tears, and in the depths of your souls you sense the terrible tragedy that has no equivalent in all of our bitter exile.

With regard to me, I don't have much to report. Over the past year I was sick with a bad case of rheumatoid arthritis, and I lay in bed for nine months. Even during the most difficult days of my ailment, I carried the burden of caring for my community, and lying sick in my bed, I actively took part in the work of my friends. I currently feel better, and it is now half a year that I am no

---

29. This refers to Amos 4:11.

30. This refers to Jeremiah 19:6.

31. In late November 1941, the Germans murdered 4,934 Jewish deportees from Berlin, Munich, Frankfurt, Vienna, and Breslau at the Ninth Fort. See Christopher R. Browning, with contributions by Jürgen Matthäus, *The Origins of the Final Solution: The Evolution of Nazi Jewish Policy, September 1939–March 1942* (Lincoln and Jerusalem: University of Nebraska Press and Yad Vashem), 395.

32. This refers to the Mishnaic Tractate Brakhot 10, the Hebrew phrase meaning "to be in great danger."

longer ill, although I have not quite returned to good health, but I can go on working without fatigue.

About six months ago we received the news via the Red Cross from Uncle Hans that all is well with you.[33] The small note that was written by a stranger took about nine months to arrive. We wrote and wrote again to you via the Red Cross and private individuals; have you received our letters? We regret and it pains us that during the time we have been here, in the Valley of Tears, we have not been able to get in touch with you and to tell you that we are still alive. Indeed, we know how much the doubt regarding our existence and survival oppresses you and how much strength and vigor the assurance that we were still alive would bring you. Certainty has given you courage for work and life with a fixed goal ahead. I greatly fear the despair and apathy that take an individual from this world, and every day I pray that you, my dearest ones, won't reach that point. I greatly doubt, my beloved ones, that I will merit to see you again, to embrace you and to draw you to my heart, and before I depart from this world and from you, my beloved, I want to say to you again and again how dear you are to us and how our souls yearn for you.

My beloved Joel! Be a loyal son to your people. Worry about your nation, and don't worry about the Gentiles. During our long exile they haven't given us the tiniest fraction of what we've given them. Delve, my beloved son, into this question, and return time and again to this matter.

Endeavor to settle in the Land of Israel. Tie your fate and future to our common future. If life there turns out to be a life of suffering because of the conditions, it will be filled with substance and meaning, a life that has everything. The strength of faith is great, it can move mountains. Don't stray to the right or the left, my son, walk straight ahead, and if you see sometimes your fellow Jews in their shame, in their contamination, and in their sins, then, my beloved son, don't lose heart. They are not at fault, my dear, but rather bitter exile itself. Truth, my beloved, should always be your guiding light, it will lead you and show you the path of life.

And with regard to you, Sara, my beloved daughter, read and consider what I said in my last words to Joel. I rely, my dear, on your lucid mind and your wisdom. Don't live a transient life, and don't seek flowers and blossoms on your way. They will wither and wilt as fast as they bloom. How beautiful is the pure life, the noble life, the life full of substance. Go, the two of you, all of your lives together, hand in hand. Let no distance separate you, and let no event of life keep you apart.

---

33. He probably meant Hans Malbin, Elkhanan Elkes's brother-in-law, who survived the war.

Remember, both of you, what Amalek[34] has done to us. Remember this, and don't forget it all the days of your life, and transmit a holy will and testament to the coming generations. The Germans killed, slaughtered, and murdered us with peace and with inner calm. I saw them, and I was standing near them when they sent many thousands of men and women, infants and unweaned children to be killed. How they ate then their morning bread and butter with appetite while laughing and ridiculing our holy martyrs. I saw them returning from the Valley of Slaughter, dirty from head to toe with the blood of our loved ones. In high spirits they sat down at the table, ate and drank and listened to light music on the radio. Professional executioners!

The soil of Lithuania has been wet with our blood by the Lithuanians themselves, with whom we have lived for many hundreds of years and whom we helped with all our strength to erect their independent state. Seven thousand of our brothers and sisters were killed here by the Lithuanians in the cruelest fashion in the last days of June 1941, and in the provincial towns, they, and not others, killed all the holy communities on the order of the Germans.[35]

With a special enjoyment they searched on their own in caves and walls, fields and forests, and they pulled out the survivors and gave them over to the authorities.

Do not wish them well all the days of your life. Let them and their children be cursed and ostracized for you and for coming generations!

I am writing at an hour when many broken souls, many widows and orphans, many naked and starving are camped at my doorstep asking for our help, and my strength is dwindling, and inside I am a barren desert, and my soul has flown away, and I am bare and empty, and I have no words to speak, but you, my beloved ones, you can read my heart and you will understand what I desired and wished to tell you at this time. For a moment I close my eyes, and I see the two of you standing before me. I hug and kiss you, and I say to you that I am your loving father until my last breath.

Elkhanan.

---

34. This refers to the ancient people who attacked the Israelites on their way out of Egypt (Exodus 17). The name has become synonymous with all foes of the Jews throughout the centuries. The reference here is to Deuteronomy 25:17: "You shall remember what Amalek did to you on the way, when you went out of Egypt."

35. During the first days of the German invasion of the Soviet Union, Lithuanians staged several dozen pogroms, most small-scale in terms of the number of Jews murdered, in the context of a rapidly emerging German anti-Jewish policy that until early July 1941 claimed the lives of an estimated four thousand Jews.

DOCUMENT 4-9: Account by Leib Langfuss,[36] "The Horrors of Murder," about the *Sonderkommando* at Auschwitz II–Birkenau, 1943–1944, transcript in Ester Mark, "Arba teudot mi-Aushvits-Birkenau: 'Bizvet hartsa,'" *Gal-Ed*, no. 1 (1973): 309–35 (translated from Yiddish).[37]

[. . .] Among the transports that arrived from Będzin and Sosnowiec was an older rabbi.[38] Being locals, they all knew they were being led to the death. The rabbi went into the dressing room, as well as into the bunker [gas chamber], with dance and song. He had the honor of dying for the sanctification of God's name [*kiddush hashem*].

A group of Jews were brought from a camp, thin, emaciated. They undressed in the courtyard and one by one went in to be shot. They were terribly hungry and begged for a piece of bread while they were still alive. Much bread was brought. Their eyes, which were dull and burned out from starving hunger, lit up with a wild fire of surprised joy, and with both hands they snatched a piece of bread and swallowed it with appetite, going up the steps right to be shot. They were so surprised with pleasure from the bread that death came much easier for them. This is how the Germans can torture people and conquer their psyche. It is worth emphasizing that they all had come from their homes just a few weeks before.

It was around the end of 1943. 164 Poles had been brought from the surrounding area, among them 12 young women. All were members of the underground. A group of SS men arrived. At the same time, several hundred Dutch Jews from the camp were brought to be gassed. One young Polish woman made a short, fiery speech in the gas bunker to all who were present, all already naked. She spoke against the murderous acts of the Germans and their oppression and ended[, "W]e will not die now, we will be immortalized by our people's

---

36. In early December 1942, Leib Langfuss (b. ca. 1910) and his family were deported to Auschwitz. Langfuss was selected for *Sonderkommando* work and took part in the uprising in Birkenau in October 1944, during which one of the crematoria was blown up. It is unclear how and when he died, but Ester Mark speculates that he was killed on October 26, 1944. See Ester Mark, "Notes on the Identity of the 'Anonymous' Author and on His Manuscript," in *The Scrolls of Auschwitz*, by Ber Mark (Tel Aviv: Am Oved, 1985), 166–70.

37. The translation here is based on the Yiddish transcript of the original published in *Gal-Ed*. Another translation appears in Mark, *The Scrolls of Auschwitz*, 206–15.

38. The final liquidation of the ghettos in Będzin and Sosnowiec, amid armed resistance actions organized by the ŻOB, took place in the first days of August 1943; some twenty thousand Jews were deported to Birkenau. See Aleksandra Namysło, "Będzin" and "Sosnowiec," in Dean and Megargee, *The USHMM Encyclopedia of Camps and Ghettos*, 2:140–43, 162–66.

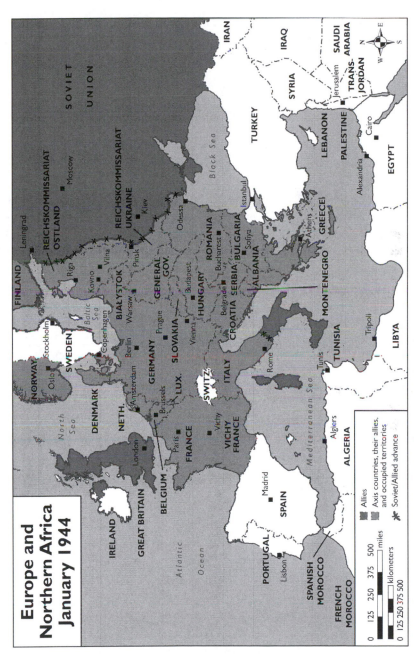

Map 6: Europe and Northern Africa, January 1944.

history. Our initiative and spirit live and bloom. The German nation will pay more dearly for our blood than one can even imagine. Down with barbarism in the form of Hitler's Germany! Long live Poland!["] Then she turned to the Jews of the *Sonderkommando*: ["R]emember that your holy duty is to take revenge for our innocent blood. Tell our brothers, our people, that we go to our deaths with much pride and deep conscientiousness.["] Then the Poles kneeled on the ground and solemnly said a certain prayer in an impressive pose[.] Afterward they stood up and together sang the Polish national anthem in chorus. The Jews sang Hatikvah.[39] The cruel common fate in that accursed corner melted together the lyrical tones of these very different anthems. With a deeply moving sincerity, they poured out their last feelings and their consolation and hope in the future of their people[.] Afterward they sang the "Internationale" together.[40] In the middle, the car [with a] red cross came and threw gas into the bunker. Their souls expired in the midst of their song and the ecstasy of a dream about brotherhood and improving the world.

[. . .]

It was toward the end of summer 1943. A transport was brought of Jews from Tarnów.[41] They asked where they were being led. They were informed they were being led to the death. All were already undressed. A tremendously powerful solemnity overtook everyone. All were deeply lost in thought, and quietly, with broken voices, recited confession [*vidui*] for the sins of their past. All feelings were smothered, and they became intoxicated by one thought, which swept them up, electrified them[:] spiritual stocktaking [*heshbon hanefesh*] before death. In the middle another group of Jews arrived from Tarnów. A young man stood up on a bench and requested that all give him their attention. It became suddenly deathly silent. ["]Jewish brothers!["] he called out, ["]don't believe that they are leading you to the death. It is impossible to think that something like that could happen, that thousands of innocent people would be led suddenly to a terrible death. It is out of the question, there cannot be such cruel, horrific murderous acts in the world. Those who told you this certainly had their reasons,["] etc. Until he had completely soothed them. Only when they were thrown into the gas did this moral preacher and deeply convinced man of conscience sober up from his naïveté. The arguments with which he had so

---

39. This Zionist anthem later became the national anthem of Israel.

40. This is the anthem of the international socialist movement.

41. The Tarnów ghetto was liquidated on September 2–3, 1943, when some eleven thousand Jews were deported. See Joanna Sliwa, "Tarnów," in Dean and Megargee, *The USHMM Encyclopedia of Camps and Ghettos*, 2:584–87.

persuasively calmed his brothers remained an illusion of self-deception. But he realized his mistake too late.

[. . .]

It was winter, the end of 1943. A transport of only children was brought [. . .] The leader of the [Sonder]kommando sent them to the dressing room, in order to undress the small children. A girl of eight years old undresses her little brother of a year old. A member of the [Sonder]kommando comes over to undress him. The girl calls out, ["]Go away, Jewish murderer! Don't lay your hand, drenched in Jewish blood, upon my beautiful little brother. I have become his good mother. He will die in my arms, together with me.["] A boy of 7–8 years stands nearby. He calls out[, "]You are a Jew after all! How can you lead such dear children in to be gassed, only for you to live longer. Is your life among a band of murderers really dearer to you than the lives of so many Jewish victims?["]

[. . .]

DOCUMENT 4-10: Letter by Zivia Lubetkin and Yitzhak Zuckerman,[42] hiding on the "Aryan side" of Warsaw, to members in the Hashomer Hatzair movement in Slovakia, January 6, 1944, USHMMA RG 68.112M (Selected Records from the Ghetto Fighters' House), reel 33, file 2001 (translated from Hebrew).

Dear friends.

We received your letter. Many thanks. We are touched by your concerns about our survival. To our regret, despite our desire, we will not all be able to come to you. We are engaged here in work of rescue and defense, the lives of thousands of Jews and our honor depend upon our work. We are thankful to you from the bottom of our hearts and to the rest of our friends who are there. Perhaps the day will come when we will see each other. Who knows. We will try to have Zivia come to you—may it only come to pass. [illegible] left over a couple of months ago for Hannover, to a concentration camp for foreign citizens, and there is no news of him. As we've heard, all the Jews have been

---

42. Zivia Lubetkin (1914–1978) and Yitzhak Zuckerman (1915–1981) helped build up the armed Warsaw ghetto underground, fought in the Warsaw Ghetto Uprising, and in 1944 fought with the ŻOB unit in the Polish uprising in the city. They emigrated to Palestine in 1946, got married, and cofounded the Ghetto Fighters' Kibbutz.

transported to Auschwitz and killed. Are you in contact with [illegible] in Switzerland and Yosef Kornianski in Hungary?[43] Do you have contact with the group of our members who arrived from Zagłębie [Dąbrowskie in southern Poland] and Hungary? We ask of you please to remain in contact with us as long as the conditions will allow. You are obliged to help us in the organization of the apparatus, in the search for border smugglers so that we will be able to send over to you children, young people, and a small number of activists who are still living. This man wanted to take only me and Zivia for free. For the others he wants 100 dollars in gold per person. This is an enormous sum. According to our finances we have about 65.00 [dollars] per person. Terrible and frightful. These sums will not allow us a mass exodus. And all of us want to live—if we've lived until now. Remember: the fate of the remnants of Israel in Poland hangs in your work. Do everything in order to help us. If there is a possibility, give news to the Land of Israel about us. We live and work on behalf of the Place [the land of Israel]. In the name of the survivors.

> Yitzhak Zuckerman
> Zivia Lubetkin
> January 6, 1944.
> P.S. Are there Hashomer Hatzair people among you?

DOCUMENT 4-11: "First Anniversary of the 'Tragedy,'" commemorating the deportation of Jews from Salonika, Greece, *La Vara* (New York),[44] March 10, 1944, 2 (translated from Judeo-Spanish).

The second week of March will always be a week of mourning for every Sephardic Jew, particularly for those from the city of Salonika, since it was on the day of March 10, 1943, that the national tragedy of the Jewish community of Salonika began—a tragedy that ended, regrettably, with the total annihilation of that community, once named the Zion of the Balkans.

It was in the middle of February of last year when the fatal and infamous Rosenberg commission[45] arrived in Salonika—this accursed committee, which had been charged by Hitler with the extermination of all of European Jewry.

---

43. Yosef Kornianski aided the Jewish resistance in Slovakia in 1941 and then in Hungary. He continued on to Palestine in early 1944.

44. *La Vara* was a Judeo-Spanish weekly published since the 1920s in New York by the Sephardic Publication Company.

45. This refers to the "Einsatzstab Reichsleiter Rosenberg," tasked with gathering artifacts for, among other things, Nazi research into the "Jewish question." After the German occupation of Salonika on April 9, 1941, this commission collected extensive information about the community that was later used in deportation efforts. See Rena Molho and Joseph Robert

In Salonika, the commission arrived along with a regiment of killers, who specialized in civilian populations.

The Rosenberg commission asked for and obtained the complete lists of all the Jews in Salonika with Greek citizenship. Those few Jews with Italian or Spanish citizenship were exempted from the lists.

In the first week of March, messengers shouted throughout the Jewish neighborhoods, ordering each individual—man, woman, and child of at least three years [of age]—to present themselves at the office of the Jewish community. Here from the morning until midnight, Gestapo agents registered every Jewish soul who thus received his registration number and the "yellow star of David," which from then on they had to wear on their chests.

On March 10 [1943], all Jewish families were ordered to abandon their homes and go to live within special ghettos, in quarters designated by Nazis. Four days were given for the completion of the general relocation.

If it weren't for the enormity of the calamities that would later befall the unfortunate Jewish community of Salonika, this relocation of an entire population, from their homes to ghettos, would have been itself a historic tragedy. The relocation occurred amid scenes of confusion, cruelty, and suffering. To make matters worse, during these four days, it rained without end, and the weather was particularly inclement.

The Nazis allowed Jewish families to carry only the most essential belongings. The rest—furniture, clothing, household goods, jewelry, etc.—was confiscated by the Nazis and sent to Germany.

From testimony of certain Greek officials, it is learned that for many consecutive days, lines of military trucks filled with Jewish belongings did not cease to exit the city at all hours of the day heading toward Germany.

Detachments of "Storm Troopers" were dispatched to all of the villages of Macedonia, of Greece at large, and of the islands, capturing each Jew from all corners of the country, to concentrate them in Salonika.

The city was divided into five ghettos, the barracks of the de HIRSCH[46] ghetto being the worst of the five. This center was converted into a true concentration camp, surrounded by barbed wire, guards at every end, and at night, powerful lights illuminating the area.

Later, the unfortunate Jewish community was to learn that the HIRSCH ghetto was the last stop between their native city, their repose, and exile, their very probable death.

White, "Thessalonikē", in Dean and Megargee, *The USHMM Encyclopedia of Camps and Ghettos*, 2:1844–48.

46. This was a Jewish neighborhood in the western part of Salonika established by funds contributed by Baron Maurice de Hirsch in the 1890s.

Toward the end of the month of March, the tragedy that began on the 10th began its final chapters. On a certain day—the exact date is not known—the first train of expelled[47] Jews left from the city. Three thousand souls, indiscriminately taken from among the residents of the de Hirsch ghetto, the first contingent, were thrown like animals into cargo trains. Seventy of them in each train car. Each individual was permitted to take with him only what he was wearing, one kilo of bread, and a little canteen of water.

Among those expelled were cripples, pregnant women, and the ill; the Nazis made no exceptions.

As soon as one contingent [was deported], hundreds of others from various ghettos received the order to relocate to the de Hirsch ghetto.

Since the de Hirsch barracks were near the train station, the deportations were accomplished without disturbing the city's [general] population.

The deportations thus continued through the month of April, the month of May, until June 10th. Of a population of sixty thousand in the community, more than fifty thousand disappeared; to where, God knows.

The strongest were subjected to cruel torture to make them confess where they had hidden their gold, their jewels, or other valuables.

The only Jews to remain in Salonika were those who, with the help of Greek workers' organizations (communists), succeeded in obtaining false identification papers with Greek names. Also, hundreds of children of a tender age were left behind by Jewish families with Greek families, who adopted the children as their own.

It is also known that four to five thousand youths, whose companies had seen [military] action against the Italians in Albania, fled to the mountains to constitute themselves into bands of guerrillas.

This is the history of the downfall of the Jewish community of Salonika, which we give here intentionally with utmost sobriety, so as to not break the hearts of our public too much. This week is the anniversary of this tragedy.

---

47. Here, this means "deported." Of the roughly forty-six thousand Jews deported from Salonika to Auschwitz II–Birkenau between March and August 1943, more than thirty-seven thousand were murdered on arrival.

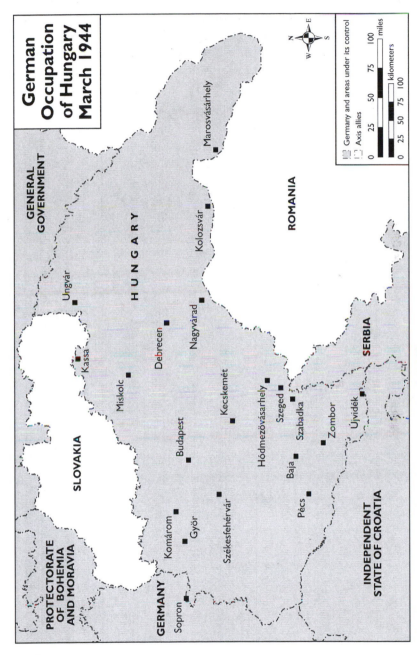

Map 7: German occupation of Hungary, March 1944.

DOCUMENT 4-12: Letter by Ede Buzás,[48] Óbecse, Hungarian-occupied Yugoslavia, to a Calvinist bishop in Budapest on his Christian identity, April 28, 1944, USHMMA RG 39.035 (Hungarian National Archives K 557, Papers of László Endre), reel 1 (translated from Hungarian).

To His Excellency
Dr. László Ravasz, Calvinist Bishop,
<u>Budapest</u>
Your Excellency,

I am Ede Buzás, the caretaker of the Calvinist church of Óbecse, and I am writing to you with a respectful appeal and request your intervention in the following painful affair:

My mother, Mrs. Sándor Buzás, widow, née Júlia Pollák, was born on February 6, 1869, as a member of the Jewish religion. However, on October 28, 1891, she was baptized according to the Calvinist Christian religion. She married, as a Christian, my late father, Sándor Buzás, who was of Calvinist Hungarian origin and his ancestors had been relocated to Ómorovica about 160 years ago, [and were baptized] by the late Sándor Tóth, Calvinist minister in the Calvinist church of Bácsfeketehegy according to the regulations of the Calvinist religion on December 1, 1891.[49]

My mother is considered Jewish according to the 1942 [Hungarian] Jewish Law, but she is not legally required to wear the distinctive yellow star because she is married to a Christian and has Christian children.

Today, a local German man, two gendarmes, and a German soldier showed up at her home, and she was taken away as a Jew[;] her apartment was sealed without an inventory being taken, as has been done in Jewish places by the local public administration representative. There was no such local public administration representative present at her home.

Together with her, my older sister Anna Buzás has also been taken away, even though she does not qualify as Jewish according to the 1942 Jewish Law because her parents are Christian, and she was born as a member of the Calvinist Church on December 6, 1894.

---

48. Ede Buzás, a Calvinist caretaker in Óbecse—in the area of Yugoslavia occupied in 1941 by Hungary (today Bečej in Serbia), 175 miles south of Budapest—was not considered Jewish according to Hungarian antisemitic legislation. The editors could not find more information about his fate or the fates of his mother and sister.

49. Ómorovica is today Stara Moravica in Serbia, some thirty-five miles northwest of Bečej; Bácsfeketehegy is now Feketić in Serbia, some twenty miles west of Bečej.

Those present were informed about this circumstance, but the German representative of Óbecse in civilian clothes did not respect it and took them away, quoting the law and saying that if my mother's husband were alive, she would not be taken away. But why did he take away my Christian sister!?

I have received several medals for fighting in the First World War. During the Serbian occupation, I proved at all times that I possessed a strong Hungarian national feeling.[50] I have been a devout Christian and the caretaker of the local Calvinist church since 1928, and every year I have organized, at my own expense, a Hungarian Christmas for Calvinist children.

I would like to respectfully request Your Excellency to intervene with the authorities in the interests of my mother and my older sister, given that they were taken to a place where they do not legally belong according to the existing laws.

As far as I know, they have been taken to Szeged to a place of collection together with the Jews, and they might be transported somewhere else from there.

I am again asking Your Excellency to intervene in the hope that I will meet my mother and my older sister again as soon as possible.

With respect,
Ede Buzás
Calvinist Caretaker

---

50. "Occupation" here refers to the interwar period, when this area became part of the Kingdom of Serbs, Croats, and Slovenes, later renamed Yugoslavia. Hungary occupied this region between 1941 and 1944.

DOCUMENT 4-13: Letter by Rezső Kemény,[51] Pestszenterzsébet,[52] Hungary, to an unidentified friend on his impending deportation, June 2, 1944, USHMMA Acc. 2000.78, Rezső Kemény collection (translated from Hungarian).

Pesterzsébet [Pestszenterzsébet], June 2, 1944.
My dear friend,

For two days now, I have been in the custody of a significant number of policemen in the ghetto at no. 11–13 in Lázár Street. Therefore, I have to prepare with my wife for the long road from which there will likely be no return. We have been separated from our children (Klára, nineteen years old, and Miklós, fifteen years old) for two days; they are employed as workers in the Lehr Domestic Textile Factory, against which, naturally, I have no objections.

I would like to say good-bye *rebus sic stantibus* [Latin: things thus standing] to those, here in Pesterzsébet, whom I have loved and respected.

Please allow me to greet, through you, all those whom I feel had goodwill toward me and were my friends. There is not enough time left to write to them separately.

Please express my deepest respect from among our colleagues to Dr. Dezső Suda, Benedek Sepsey, and Lajos Koncz, my greetings to Sámson and Reiszter.

I am sending my warm greetings to our friend Vazul Gunda.

I am shaken as I think of co-presidents Vitéz Lányi and Csathó and of judges Kachkovits and Halmi, to whom, especially to the first two, I am linked with gratitude and memories. They knew my legal stumbles and were understanding but also knew me as a human being. They, along with co-presidents Lányi and Csathó, were the last people that I shook hands with, from the world that I have appreciated and will always appreciate for its love for justice.

Since June 1, 1944, I have not met much justice, and I think I should not count on such a meeting in the near future. I have already [been subjected to]

---

51. Rezső Kemény, a Jewish lawyer, and his wife were forced into the Pestszenterzsébet ghetto near Budapest. Both were ultimately deported to Auschwitz and killed. Their son Miklós (Nick) survived, while their daughter Klára perished.

52. The Pestszenterzsébet ghetto was created on May 12, 1944, for roughly 4,600 Jews guarded by Hungarian police. On July 1, the Jews were transferred to the Monor concentration and entrainment center, from which they were deported to Auschwitz II–Birkenau on July 6 and 8, 1944. See Randolph L. Braham, "Pestszenterzsébet," in *The United States Holocaust Memorial Museum Encyclopedia of Camps and Ghettos, 1933–1945*, vol. 3: *Camps and Ghettos under European Regimes Aligned with Nazi Germany*, ed. Joseph R. White (Bloomington: Indiana University Press in association with USHMM, forthcoming 2018).

humiliation, ever since I [started] living in the ghetto, and I find it important that you, my friend, should not think that it is because of cowardice that I do not turn to the revolver. It is not cowardice, it is its opposite, because as long as my wife is alive, I feel like I cannot perform such an act. In any case, my revolver has been confiscated by the authorities.

I think the future of the homeland is dark. For temporary advantages, the leader[53] and groups around him have some years ago strayed a little from the fair road. This is manifested in their accusation (for domestic and foreign policy reasons) of Jews as the source of all trouble. After that there was no return, they got more and more entangled, and the feeling of responsibility was lost in certain circles. However, this damned world war will end, [and] even if the hoped-for German victory comes about, during the peace talks the Germans or any other power cannot be blamed for all inhumanity and morally questionable measures. The Finnish nation managed to retain its national sovereignty[;] it could enforce its national will. Unfortunately, this is not how it goes with us, and, sadly, this usually is expressed during peace talks.

But why am I boring you with my lengthy opinion on domestic politics[;] everybody sees these things differently. Furthermore, I wanted to entrust you with some of my private affairs today; please, if you have time, be so kind as to deal with this.

The issue is the following. My daughter Klára and my son Miklós are workers at the Lehr Domestic Textile Factory. For now, they have enough money (I gave all my money to them because, according to the order, we could not take a penny with us), but I think if they stay alive, the time will come when they will need a few pengő [Hungarian currency]. I am sending, enclosed in this letter, 6 bank deposit accounts, in the value of about 240P altogether. Please be so kind as to keep these and, if they need them, hand them over. Furthermore, I am sending, enclosed, a life-insurance bond in the value of $600, issued by the Hungarian General Insurance Company. If you hear news of my death, please collect this insurance sum for the children. The company also takes the war risk and pays double the amount in case of an accident. If I do not see you or write to you by December 31, 1944, please, my friend, inform the First Hungarian [Insurance Company] that I am unable to pay the 102P fee because I am prevented by my deportation to a foreign country, and in any case, the news is that I am already on another planet.

Maybe I will have an opportunity to thank you personally for your kindness toward me and my children.

---

53. Reference to Miklós Horthy (1868–1957), Hungarian head of state from 1920 to October 1944.

Now there is nothing left for me to do but say a friendly good-bye to you. Please give my deepest regards to her Excellency [the friend's wife?]. I wish you the best, good health, and strength for you and your family.

Warm regards,
Rezső

DOCUMENT 4-14: Postcard by Pál Justus,[54] Bor, German-occupied Yugoslavia, to his wife, Edit, Budapest, on his life in a Hungarian forced-labor battalion, July 9, 1944, USHMMA Acc. 2001.64.1, Eva Kovacs collection (translated from Hungarian).

July 9, 1944. My one and only, I know how impatiently you have been waiting to hear from me: it was not my fault that [the postcard] is only being sent now. With regard to correspondence, the situation is such right now that I am allowed to write to you twice a month on this card, and you can answer on the attached reply card. Sending packages is not yet possible. About myself: given the circumstances I am feeling excellent, I am working outside in mountain air and in the sun, I am enduring the work, which is healthy, quite well. I have become tanned and quite muscular. The food is excellent, my appetite is good. I am with Herbert, he is also feeling excellent, if it is possible please inform Magda about this. Of course I am very worried about you, I know how many difficult problems you have to solve, and it hurts me very much that I cannot stand by you. I do not know where, how, and when this card will reach you, please answer right away, I am incredibly impatient to receive news! Please kiss Évike [Éva] on her birthday for me and tell her not to forget her daddy, who, when he comes home, will tell her a lot of stories. Until then, you have to substitute for me in this respect as well. Please do not worry about me: I am fine, work is going, I am tanned, I have grown a mustache and got a haircut, no other changes. Take care of yourself and Évike: I want to see you again healthy. I greet our friends and embrace you, my dear. Pali

54. Pál Justus (1905–1965), a well-known Hungarian literary figure and socialist activist, was among the roughly sixty-two hundred Hungarian Jewish members of the forced labor battalions deployed in the Bor copper mines or on the railway line between Bor and Žagubica in 1944. He managed to escape from the Bor battalion and joined Tito's partisans; when he returned to Budapest, he was reunited with his wife, Edit, and their daughter, Éva, who both survived the war. Pál Justus became a prominent Communist politician but in 1949 was arrested and made a codefendant at the infamous Stalinist show trial against former minister of foreign affairs László Rajk and others. Sentenced to life imprisonment, he was released in 1955 and rehabilitated in 1956.

Is Márta with you still? I greet her.

[In different handwriting:] Warm greetings to you [from] Herbert. Pali and I are looking out for each other, we will go home together.

DOCUMENT 4-15: Diary entries by Selma Wijnberg,[55] Chełm, Poland, July and August 1944, on her life after hiding, USHMMA Acc. 2007.69, Saartje (Selma) Wijnberg Engel collection (translated from Dutch).

Wednesday 26 July [1944]

Did not write more yesterday. Chaim did not want me to write outside. Today I can, we are really free, unbelievable, and I am writing outside. Is it really true? Yes, we keep saying to each other. We are human beings again and can speak to people. Chaim spoke to two Russians this morning, and thanked them for liberating us. We walked to the village, to see a doctor. I am pregnant, we are almost sure, my tummy is getting bigger; what else could it be? The doctor did not say it for sure; he could not do anything for me since he was only a student. We went to Adam's brother-in-law. It hurts me to be treated like we are nothing. As soon as the front is through, we will go to the city to get paperwork for me. When we came back from our visit to the village, I could not walk anymore, it felt like my legs were filled with lead. God give me the strength and health to return to Holland and that Bram and his family are still alive and that we still have some good friends there who are willing to help us. I am so afraid that there is no more goodness in the world. Since we have been down from the loft, people have not been very friendly. It probably feels that way because I cannot understand the people. Chaim is helping Adam in the field, and I knit.

Shabbat 29 July

We are walking and working the last few days. I did laundry yesterday, and for the first time everything is clean. Also big news, I am pregnant, probably in my sixth month. My tummy is getting bigger every day. If the baby could only

---

55. Selma Wijnberg (Engel) was born in Groningen, Netherlands, in 1922. Discovered in hiding, she spent three months in an Amsterdam prison before she was deported in 1943 with other Dutch Jewish girls to the Sobibór death camp. Placed in Camp I, where she sorted the clothes of the dead, Selma met Chaim Engel (b. 1916 in Poland), her future husband. Selma and Chaim fled Sobibór during the uprising on October 14, 1943, and lived in hiding in Chełm, Poland. After the Red Army had liberated Chełm in July 1944, Selma and Chaim fled when the Soviets attempted to conscript Chaim. They eventually returned to Amsterdam just after the war and later emigrated to the United States.

be born in Holland and in good health, then we should receive this peace with
joy. It would have been better to have a baby a little later.

Chaim is helping in the field[;] he makes bundles from the wheat. We will
go to Chełm tomorrow, if everything is alright. Always something, they will not
give us anything for the ring. If only God does not leave us and luck stays with
us, we have 2 healthy hands to earn a living with. I cannot walk well yet, my
feet are swollen, that hurts. For as long as we have been down from the loft, we
have not received one friendly word from Stefka.

[. . .]
Sunday 6 August

We are already one week in Chełm. We have tried to find some money, and
I also went to the doctor. I am very weak and cannot walk. My feet hurt so bad
and are swollen and also my tummy is swollen and my pants are too small. I
cannot turn very well. We have the help from a captain from the hospital.
Maybe Chaim will work at the hospital and it will not be necessary to go away.
We are staying in a house with Jews. We sleep on top of the bedding covered by
our clothes. We are strong. I do not know where this is going. My feet hurt so
badly. If I had money and a good doctor. We do not sleep well, we wake each
other up. Is this living in peace? Is this what we longed for? God help us, we
cannot continue like this.

[. . .]
Sunday 13 August

We are already in Chełm for 14 days. Chaim is working for the Red Cross.
I am in the house with the Jews in a room full of straw and fleas. Life is very
difficult, and it is almost not possible to continue. At night late everybody still
speaks loud, and when it starts getting light in the morning again, I am so tired.
I burned my leg and have a large wound. It hurts. Is this the peace we longed
for, I cannot continue like this? I am so tired, do not feel like this is living
anymore, I am crying all the time. I guess I will not give birth to a happy child.
Chaim has to work tonight and I am always alone. Why do I have to suffer so
much?

Friday 24 August

[. . .] We have no roof above our heads, we walk from corner to corner to
find a place. We have no money, what to do. In two months, the baby will be

born. I cannot do this anymore, we are going back to Adam. I would like to have some rest, is that too much. God, let me die. I have had enough of this life.

DOCUMENT 4-16: Letter by the Pressel family,[56] Lyon, France, to Elie Schwerner,[57] New York, on their wartime fate, September 28, 1944, USHMMA Acc. 2007.413, Pressel family collection (translated from French).

Dear Uncle Elie,

"They are still alive! . . ."

Yes, we are still alive, and we can finally breathe in freedom. We are living in Lyon since the end of [19]42. The city was liberated on September 3 [1944]. We feel like the survivors of a cataclysm. The joy of feeling free is profound, but we have seen too much suffering, and we worry a great deal about all those dear to us whose fate is unknown, for this joy to be complete.

It is almost a miracle that we were able to survive safe and sound from this torture. For the past two years, human life counted for nothing. Perhaps later we will have the opportunity to tell you in more detail all that we went through. On November 11, 1942, we saw the arrival of the masses of German troops in Marseille,[58] and we had to wait until the month of August 1944 in Lyon, to see the withdrawal of this army, in endless file in front of our house, while being routed and pursued by the Allied armies coming up from the South of France. What a relief! We waited for so long and so fervently hoped for deliverance.

---

56. Upon the German invasion of Belgium in May 1940, the Pressel family—Joseph ("Jos"), Miriam ("Mir"), and their son, Philippe—fled to Marseille in southern France and in 1943 relocated to Lyon. In 1944 Philippe was sent to live with a former teacher in Vourles, just south of Lyon. On August 28, 1944, the family was reunited, and on September 2 the city was liberated. See Philip Pressel, *They Are Still Alive: A Family's Survival in France during World War II* (Pittsburgh, PA: Dorrance Publishing Co., 2004).

57. Elie (originally Elias) Schwerner (1887–1974), a manufacturer and Belgian national born in Konin (now Poland), had emigrated to the United States with his wife and three children in 1936.

58. The fall of 1942 brought the German occupation of certain areas of the previously "free" southern zone of Vichy France, including the city of Marseille, which had previously provided a refuge for thousands of Jews. In December 1942, deportations in the south increased, with the help of local French authorities. In January 1943, the Jews of Marseille, including both French and foreign-born, were rounded up. For more information, see Renée Poznanski, *Jews in France during World War II* (Hanover, NH: Brandeis University Press in association with USHMM, 2001), 356–72.

Our son was evacuated under mandatory order to the countryside last May in order to be sheltered from the bombings. We rejoined him on the 28th of August to be together no matter what would happen. The village where we found ourselves was already in the hands of the resistance, and all around the French army of the interior was attacking the German troops. Also, in the distance we could see the Allied planes diving and strafing the Germany convoys and releasing their bombs on the enemy trucks. The village was caught in a cross fire, and for several days we lived in an agonizing situation. Anyway the essential thing for the moment is that we can announce to you that we three are safe and sound and happy that we were able to save our little Philippe—who is now seven years old and who never lost hope and who had confidence in everything that we had to do to shelter him from harm.

Now concerning other members of the family. Since the [Allied] invasion of France, postal communications were halted and are still not normal, and we are waiting for news from various quarters. We were therefore very happy to receive news today in the form of a letter that Jacques and Jeanne Schwerner are in good health. They are still in Argenton-sur-Creuse. Ady is still in Toulouse and intends to rejoin her parents soon. Edmee is in Switzerland.[59] Harry [Schwerner], as you probably know, was arrested in 1942 at the Spanish border just as he was intending to resume his Belgian military service; he was interned for several months in a camp in Drancy (near Paris) and was subsequently deported.[60] We have not heard from him since. Licy, the eldest daughter, and her husband and two children are also safe and sound. We have not heard recently about the Kincler family. You probably don't know it, but unfortunately their daughter was deported in August 1942; little Irene stayed during this whole time with her grandparents; Jacques was also arrested but was able to escape in time and went underground; we last heard from him about two months ago. We hope that we will learn soon that he too was able to celebrate freedom with his parents.

We have not heard from Belgium for about six months. At that time my in-laws as well as Ella were still there, and we hope that they are safe and sound. My mother, unfortunately, was deported in 1942, and I have not learned her fate; my sister and her husband were also taken in 1942 to "a destination unknown."[61] Will I ever see them again? Norbert, his wife, and child underwent

59. Edmée Schwerner, born in Belgium in 1931, escaped across the Swiss border in May 1944.

60. Harry (Hendrick) Schwerner, born in Anvers, Belgium, in 1916, was the son of the aforementioned Jeanne and Jacques. He was deported from Drancy to Auschwitz in late June 1943.

61. Pressel's mother, Helen (Chaja), was deported from Mechelin, Belgium, on October

the same sad fate, as did Ella's husband, but he and Norbert have been able to communicate several times since.[62] My wife's uncles who were in France were deported . . . It is an unending list. My wife would have liked to go to Belgium immediately to see her parents except that travel by rail is not yet possible, and to go by road is an expense that we cannot afford.

Since I only have your address, Uncle Elie, I cannot write to any other members of the family; therefore I ask you to please convey this letter to my family in New York, to Miryam's two sisters, and to all the good friends who have asked about us during these hard war years.

We would like to know how you passed these last few years, if you are in good health, what you are doing, and what your plans are for the future? Where are Ruth and Sonia, how are the children, etc. . . .[63]

We do not intend to stay long in Lyon, but we do not know yet where we will go. Like before, we do know how long it takes for correspondence to go from France to the USA and back, so I ask you to please note that all correspondence sent to us should be temporarily sent to: Société Emile PRAT & FILS, for J. Pressel, 24 Quai Fulchiron, Lyon, France. If we leave here, the Société will forward our mail.

Hoping that we soon receive detailed news from you, we send you our best wishes and kisses.

Your,
Jos, Mir, and Philippe

[Handwritten addendum]
My dear all,

We have returned to life; let us hope that our dear parents are also safe and sound, as well as brother, sister, sister-in-law, brother-in-law, mentioning only the immediate family. You cannot realize the good fortune of all those who did not have to live in Europe for the last two years. As far as the future is concerned, we cannot make any plans, but I want to return to Belgium as fast as possible.

Write to us quickly if possible[;] it has been so long since we have heard any news from the family that every letter gives us a great deal of pleasure.

27, 1942, and killed at Auschwitz. His sister, Charlotte Hamel, and her husband, Naftali Hamel, died in Auschwitz.

62. Norbert Schwerner, possibly Elie's nephew and Joseph Pressler's brother-in-law, was born 1912 in Cologne; he was deported to Auschwitz, where he was probably killed.

63. Ruth (b. 1907) and Sonja (b. 1909) were Miriam's sisters and thus Eli's nieces, daughters of his brother Mozes (b. 1877?) and sister-in-law Lea.

A thousand kisses to divide among you all.

Your,
Mir

I would like to see you all again. I send you lots of kisses for both cheeks.
Philippe

PART V
1945–1946

DOCUMENT 5-1: Account by Meilach Lubocki,[1] Landsberg, Germany, on the liquidation of Estonian labor camps in the summer of 1944, September 20, 1945, USHMMA Acc. 1995.A.0793, Zalman Lubocki memoir (translated from Yiddish).

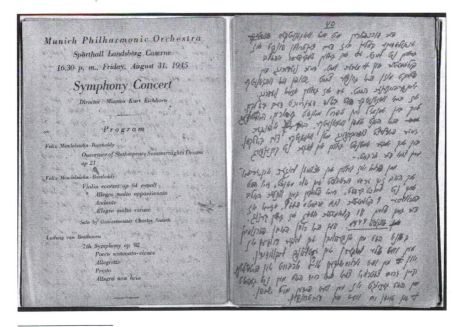

---

1. Meilach Lubocki (1901–1971), born in Vilna, survived the Kovno ghetto as well as forced labor camps in Estonia and later in Germany.

Map 8: Allied occupation zones in Germany and Austria, 1945–1946.

August 1944. When the Russians occupied Kovno, people in the camp began to say that all camps in Estonia would be liquidated, and we would be sent to work in Germany.[2] We had no great trust in these rumors. People said we would be taken by boat, and we would be drowned at sea. We were supposed to have departed the 5th or 6th of August, so several individuals in the camp hid, 5 men and 2 women. If we had indeed departed, they would have remained in their "hideouts." But it turned out that there were no means of transport available, so we remained to work further. And all those who had hid came out of their hideouts a few days later. On August 10th, the senior squad leader [*Oberscharführer*] and "famous" Dr. Betman came to the camp.[3] Ordered a roll call, lined us up, and said in a kindhearted fashion that our camp was being liquidated, and we would have to walk by foot for several days. They want to be good [to us], so the younger and older would go with them to the new camp by truck. And all the rest would go by foot to the new camp in several days. They had a list of those who were older than 50 years old. They didn't even look at these individuals and ordered them to stand off to the side. 8 men. Then they inspected our rows and stood 31 men and 3 women off to the side together. Among them were some younger persons but mostly middle-aged, strong, healthy men. So they thought they were being taken to a second camp. Because there was one case [person], there stood a father off to the side, about 45 years old. So his son of 18 years asked to go with him because he had a bad foot[;] it would be hard for him to walk. They granted him the favor, and he drove with them. A second case was where they stood a son of 17 years off to the side, so his father asked to go together with his son, gave the excuse that he felt weak; they took him with them as well. A third case was when a father went with them, and his son also wanted to go with them, so they took him for no reason at all. These 34 men were taken by truck (as we later found out) into a forest, and all were killed. They performed similar tricks like that in all the camps in Estonia prior to the evacuation. And they exterminated 10–15% of the Jews.

About 12,000 persons had been transported into Estonia from the Vilna ghetto and about 3,000 persons from the Kovno ghetto. Only 6–7,000 persons were transported out to Germany. All camps in Estonia were evacuated except

---

2. At that time Lubocki was in Port Kunda, Estonia. The Jews in this camp most likely worked in the town's cement plant and in a rock quarry. See Anton Weiss-Wendt, *Murder without Hatred: Estonians and the Holocaust* (Syracuse, NY: Syracuse University Press, 2009), 257, 297–98.

3. This is probably SS-Obersturmführer Dr. Franz von Bodmann (1908–1945), since the autumn of 1943 chief physician in the Vaivara camp in Estonia and its subcamps. Previously Bodmann had served as a doctor in various camps, including Majdanek and Auschwitz, where he developed use of phenol injections to kill prisoners.

for one camp, "Kloga"[4]; they had no time to transport people out, and exterminated everyone on the spot, about 1,800 persons (some survived). So that more than half of those who came from the ghettos died or were exterminated in the camps of Estonia.

August 17th, 1944. We were already at our workplaces when suddenly, around 11a.m., all have to go [back] to the camp. We came, and at 2 o'clock in the afternoon we left on a train in the direction of Reval [Tallinn]. On the evening of the 18th we arrived at the "Kloga" camp. They didn't let us in. Because there was no room. We stayed lying in the train cars. The next day, August 19th, they took us further in the same train cars, and we arrived at the port of Reval. A great freighter was already docked there. They let us out of the train cars, up onto the ship, and in the meantime, more Jews from other camps in Estonia arrived, so that it was tightly packed like herring, about 5,000 persons. And the ship departed.

Imagine my luck and joy when I met my wife on the ship, whom I had not seen for 10 months, since leaving the Kovno ghetto. She had been in Estonia in another camp, "Ereda."[5] The people from their camp had arrived at the Reval port two weeks earlier. They had already been on a ship but had to leave because the Wehrmacht requisitioned the ship for itself. These past two weeks they had been in tents several kilometers from Reval. And they were brought here again just now, on the 19th, and we had the opportunity to meet on the ship. Until we came to Danzig, on August 22nd.

In Danzig, we were transferred to other, smaller ships with 500 persons in each, and we went another 30 kilometers [18.6 miles]. I don't remember the place. It was already dark when we disembarked. All were once again lined up, in rows of four, and we marched wearily further. We saw that we were going in the direction of "Stutthof" [concentration camp] (it lies 35 km [21.7 miles] from Danzig). Coming closer to the camp, we saw from afar a modern camp, heavily lit. Surrounded with many rows of electric wires. It was not a pleasant welcome. SS guards already stood at the entrance and gate, and as we entered, they began to drive us in the dark into unfinished buildings without doors and without windows. They beat us and shouted familiar curse words. They pressed us together, and there wasn't even a place to sit[;] this is the way we suffered until early the next morning. After that, they sent us to the washroom for

---

4. Refers to Klooga, a subcamp of the Vaivara concentration camp in Estonia. See Ruth Bettina Birn, "Klooga," in Megargee, *The USHMM Encyclopedia of Camps and Ghettos*, 1:1501–2.

5. Ereda was part of the Vaivara camp system. See Ruth Bettina Birn, "Ereda," in Megargee, *The USHMM Encyclopedia of Camps and Ghettos*, 1:1497–98.

delousing. They let in about 30 men at a time. They let us in through one door, took everything that we possibly had. Examined even our mouths, ears, and elsewhere, to see if we had anything hidden. Sprayed us with cold water and let us out through a second door, gave us other things [i.e., clothes], and sent us in groups of 400–500 men to the barracks. In each barrack there were three levels of 50 beds each, so it came out that 3–4 men slept in a narrow little bed. You can imagine the sort of sleep we got. Then the next day we got up early at 4:30, were given a little coffee with a portion of bread; they called this a "paika" [Russian: ration or portion], about 150–175 gr. [6.2 ounces]. Drove us out to the roll call. The roll call used to be at 6:00 a.m.; they didn't drive us to work in the first couple of days. We stayed outside until the afternoon, until 12 p.m., then we were given about 3/4 liters [3 cups] of soup, without spoons. We remained outside until the evening roll call at 6 pm. Only after 6 would they let us into the barrack. Gave us again the paika of bread, as in the morning, with a little coffee for 3 men in one small bowl. Stutthof was a camp of about 30,000 persons, of various nationalities. Mainly Polish, criminals. From these "fine" men were chosen block and room elders, as well as "kapos" at the work stations.

The women were in separate barracks, and we were not allowed to meet with them. We used to make contact by going not far from the fence and throwing over a little note tied to a small stone. In this way, I was able to communicate with my wife until she left with a transport of 600 women for work, around September 10th.

When we came to Stutthof on August 22nd, we found some women and children, 14 to 17 years old, who had come from the Kovno ghetto, and they told us various things. After we had been deported [from Kovno to Estonia] on October 26th, 1943, no one knew where we had been sent and did not believe we were alive. They called it the Action of 3,500. News even came to the ghetto that we were working in Estonia, but no one believed this.

In November 1943, a part of the Kovno ghetto was sent to Shantz, Kazlove-Rude, and Ponevez.[6] In the ghetto remained mainly those who worked in the ghetto workshops and other such brigades, about 8,000–9,000 persons. On March 27, 1944, there was a children's action. They went from house to house and took all nonworking children and some men and women, about 700–800 persons, and drove them away in trucks, and alas, they were never heard from again. Among them were Dora Lamas, 8 years old, and Mia Blumberg, 12 years old. And other good friends and acquaintances of ours.

At the same time, they gathered together the Jewish police, mostly the

---

6. These are small Lithuanian towns near Kovno.

higher officers, and took them away to the Ninth Fort; there the Gestapo asked them to reveal where the children and elderly were hiding in the ghetto, in the bunkers or elsewhere. Those who surrendered this information would remain alive. A few of the Jewish policemen revealed where such persons were hiding and remained alive for the time being; they were later killed in the camps or elsewhere. 33 Jewish policemen and their chiefs nobly restrained themselves and were killed at the Ninth Fort at the end of March 1944.

In July 1944, when the Russian front was approaching Kovno, the Kovno ghetto was liquidated, and all were deported to Germany. Some were sent by train to Dachau [concentration camp], some by barges to Stutthof. Women with children under 14 years old were sent to Auschwitz a couple days after arriving in Stutthof. The same was done with transports that did not go to Stutthof, sent to Auschwitz. It is well known what happened to them; they were killed in the gas chambers (upon which hung a wretched sign, "Bath House"). Able-bodied men and women were for the most part immediately sent away to various work camps. So that when we came from Estonia to Stutthof, we found a small number of women in Stutthof.

In Stutthof we found boys from the Kovno and Shavel [Šiauliai] ghettos, 14–17 years of age. Afterward, around September 15th, they were transported together with the younger ones who had arrived from Estonia, about 400 children in total. Said they were sending them to work. Alas, nobody met any of them after the liberation. So, as it turns out, they were all killed somewhere in Germany.

When the Kovno ghetto was liquidated, many Jews hid in hideouts. Firstly, no one believed they were being sent to work in Germany. Secondly, they calculated that in several days the Russians would come into Kovno. Over 2,500 persons hid. Since it took over 3 weeks before the Russians occupied Kovno, the Germans had time to destroy everything. They blew up every house in the ghetto, so that all those who hid were killed. Around 40–50 persons were saved.

DOCUMENT 5-2: Account by Michal Kraus[7] on the death march from Auschwitz II-Birkenau in January 1945, written 1946/1947,[8] USHMMA Acc. 2006.51, Michael J. Kraus collection (translated from Czech).

[. . .] Chapter 10: Difficult Travel

In January—during the last year of the Second World War—I participated in the so-called death march. Yes, indeed, it was a death march because it claimed many victims, and only a few of us survived. We walked for three days. Ahead of us lay the victims of previous marches who had been shot, and behind us were guards who spent their time shooting prisoners who were not able to continue. They had a lot of work. It was a horrible sight because the SS shot the prisoners in the head at close range. At night they herded us into some kind of farm; some of us slept on hay, some in the stable, and the majority out in the cold. With the inadequate clothing many froze to death or were shot because their legs had given out. I remember a specific wretch whom the [*Unterscharführer*[9]] ordered to run ahead only so that he could shoot him from the back; but only the third shot in the head actually killed him. Our "supervisors" amused themselves with these and similar occupations! And again they herded us further, to Leslau [Włocławek, Poland], where they loaded us into a huge number of railroad cars. There wasn't even room to sit down. And so we rode four days without food in open railroad cars to a new concentration camp. At first we thought we were going to Gross-Rosen [concentration camp], because that is where the transports that had left before us were going. But when we arrived in Bohumín, they cut off the track, and we had to go back. The Poles treated us shamefully. They didn't give us anything. They didn't even react to the piles of corpses that were lying on the road and in the villages. And my opinion of the Poles has not changed to this day. In contrast our Czechs behaved well. In every station, in spite of great danger, they threw us rolls, bread, gingerbread, and other things. [. . .]

Many succumbed on the way. For a long time we did not know where they were taking us until we traversed the damaged Vienna[, when] we realized that

---

7. Michal Kraus, born in 1930 in Nachod, Czechoslovakia, was deported to Theresienstadt in December 1942 and in 1943 to Auschwitz II-Birkenau. Both of his parents were killed; Kraus survived Auschwitz, as well as a number of forced labor camps and death marches. See Daniel Blatman, *The Death Marches: The Final Phase of Nazi Genocide* (Cambridge, MA: Harvard University Press, 2011).

8. The account as a whole was rewritten ca. 1946/1947; this specific entry is dated May 7, 1945.

9. Identification of this SS rank is based on references in previous sections of Kraus's account.

they were taking us to the horrible concentration camp Mauthausen where so many of our people—from Nachod—perished.

DOCUMENT 5-3: Letter by Irving P. Eisner[10] to his father on his visit to Buchenwald, May 15, 1945, USHMMA Acc. 2012.16.1, Irving P. Eisner collection.

Wednesday, May 15th
Dear Dad,

I don't know how to begin this letter, but I'll try this. Today I visited "Buchenwald" (I hope that got by the censor). I learned a lot today about life and death at a concentration camp, for the past three, four, five, and six years for political prisoners. You know who those are—anti-Nazis by religion and nationality. Six years ago while I was in high school, millions of people were suffering and dying beyond approach of human thought. Today I saw where 51,000 people were tortured to death.[11] First I saw how they lived. They lived in barracks where we put 75 or a hundred men; by the thousands. Not in beds, but in shelves up to the ceiling. Three slept in a shelf room for one man cramped. They slept on top of each other. I saw their hospital. There was a room separate where S.S. doctors gave shots. A few minutes later the patient was dead. He was thrown out the back door into a pen full of bloody walls to be disposed of. I saw the kitchen where the turnip soup was made. A turnip was dragged through hot dish water. I also saw where they died. I saw the whipping posts where they were horse-flogged to death. I saw the hanging posts. They accommodated several poor devils at a time. And finally, I saw the crematory. I couldn't describe my impression of that building in 500 pages. As they entered they read in German, "You come in through the door and go out through the chimney."[12] I saw the remains of human beings after they were taken out of the furnaces. They were sent home in round boxes which would hold about a quart

---

10. Irving P. Eisner (1923–2001), born in Ohio, had enlisted in the U.S. Army in March 1943, was stationed in Germany at the time of writing this letter, and was released in April 1946.

11. Eisner's figure was a widely reported statistic, appearing in the *Philadelphia Inquirer* and *New York Times* in April 1945. For more information on this figure and its symbolic importance, see Barbie Zelizer, "The Liberation of Buchenwald: Images and the Shape of Memory," in *Cultural Memory and the Construction of Identity*, ed. Dan Ben-Amos and Liliane Weissberg (Detroit, MI: Wayne State University Press, 1999), 136–75.

12. The actual sign at the Buchenwald crematorium read (in German), "No loathsome worms should feast on my body. [Instead] the pure flames should consume it. I always loved the warmth and light, and for that reason you should not bury but cremate me." See USHMMPA WS #06494.

of water. The ashes I saw belonged to a 23-year-old Jew who was cremated five days before the Americans arrived. You may think I exaggerate, because I'm in the habit of doing that a little, but an American couldn't exaggerate anything like this because the mind can't construct things as bad, let alone worse. Everything we've read and I write is understatement, but it's the best we can describe this human brutality. Believe me Dad, I saw it with my own eyes, today.

I talked with two men today of my own race. They were from Hungary six years ago. One is only 20 years old now. The other was a married man with a four year old child and a two year old child (six years ago). He told me unbelievable stories. In me he found his first friend as a free man in all those years and he practically broke down. The hour I spent with those two men will remain with me for the rest of my life. He saw me take a member of Hitler Youth by the back of the neck and kick him in the back side out. He didn't believe that could be done by a man of his race. He was 30 but he looked like twice that age and acted like that too. This man told me how his mother, father, wife and two children had died. His wife and baby were gassed. His four year old boy was tortured to death. He told me how but we won't go into that. He told me what happened to young girls of that age too. I found myself grinding my teeth at how I'd have treated these goddamn Nazi whores. He told me he—himself was forced to cremate his father. Do you realize what I just wrote Dad. I don't think I do—it sounds impossible—and Dad you might think I've been given a good line of bullshit, but I don't, believe me, I don't!! It's the truth and worse has happened. The S.S. and Gestapo are described by words not yet invented within the dictionary or the vocabulary of any G.I.

Now Dad—I ask you to do me a favor for this man. He has an uncle in Cleveland. I can't give you his address, but you may find his phone number in the phone book. The name is Samuel Hellman. The man I talked to has the same name, and lives in Hust, Czechoslovakia.[13] Tell him your son in Germany met his nephew on the way home to Hust, from a concentration camp. If he asks about the rest of the family—tell him you don't know if you can't. Now, Dad I'll never see this man again, and he'll never know if we did him the favor or not. But if you'd seen his face when I told him I'd have you do that, and if you'd seen what I've seen today and heard his story, I think it would soften your heart like it did mine. It may be that his uncle won't even be interested or he may have died. Six years is a long time, but I'm sure this man has not forgotten. I sent him away with a few cans of C-rations I was saving for a rainy day, and a

---

13. Most likely Huszt, later Khust; the city changed hands several times. It was Hungarian before World War I, Czechoslovakian in the interwar period, and Ukrainian after World War II.

few extra packs of cigarettes. I felt I'd done my good turn for today and I can look anybody in the eye and say so. (Especially an S.S. superman).

Now Dad you may think I'm crazy for writing a letter like this, and maybe if I would have slept on it I wouldn't write like this, but it's all still fresh in my mind. I guess your [*sic*] the guy I tell all my troubles to release the load.

I'll close now—I'm your

Loving son

Irv

P.S. Still have no dope on whether I'm occupational or if we'll go to the Pacific. Will let you know as soon as I can.

DOCUMENT 5-4: Letter by Julius Lewy,[14] Linz, Austria, to his liberators on his persistent ill health, May 30, 1945, USHMMA Acc. 2005.120, J. George Mitnick collection.[15]

Linz, 30 May 1945

Dear Liberators!

I know well I have no right to trespass on your dutiful time—but before entering into the subject I think some introductory explanations would be of importance. In any case I shall try to be as concise as possible, although the very nature of my topic is likely to let my pen ramble far beyond any preconceived limits.

Who am I? A Polish Jew 28 years old, with University education; man deprived of everybody and everything, but instead rich of experiences; so that much more essential would be the question: who have I been?

From the very beginning of this most tremendous of all wars I have been living in Poland, under German occupation facing the hell on earth as martyr and witness in one person. There is not any suffering imaginable either moral, or physical or material I would not have gone through during these six fateful years.

Physically rather weak, I have had to my advantage another form of resistance: my spirit. To all this time I've never ceased to believe in the final victory of Humanity and Justice and never ceased to hope in my personal survival.

---

14. Julius Lewy, born in 1917 in Kraków, had been a forced laborer since at least September 1941. He was in the Plaszów camp near Kraków until early 1945, then spent two months in the Mauthausen concentration camp, and was subsequently forced to work in the "Göringwerke" factory in Linz.

15. This document, handwritten in English, contains many spelling and grammar mistakes retained here to preserve the originality of the letter.

The conscience of possessing some quantity of Anglo-Saxon culture—I studied English literature in Cracow under of greatest Polish Anglicist, Professor Roman Dyboski, has imparted to me the reassuring feeling that I am in a certain degree representative of Anglo-American potentialities. And it is, without a doubt, this psychological attitude of mine which is to be seriously taken into account when I try genuinely to explain the phenomenon of my personal survival.

It was not earlier than in the last period of my war biography, about two month before the end of the European cataclysm, that my physical organism collapsed: diarrhea, this mortal camp disease become my share too and in the course of following weeks I grew more and more exhausted and emaciated—till the miserable condition in which I was found by the Liberation. From then on a few days I was together with others transferred into the local hospital.

Since have passed several weeks . . . I was better already and I tried to descend steps. And then came a collapse with a heart disease.

For the time being I am far from being healthy, indeed I don't feel any bettering of my general state at all.

What are the reasons?

Here, in the hospital, all is lacking, all is failing. Medicaments as well as eating (quality and quantity!) treating as well as nursing.

Example: a daily ration: 1/3 of brown bread; never any butter or jam.

You are treated by a young German physician. An enemy of yesterday should be your benefactor of today?

It would take much time to enlarge on the subject; and I won't weigh you so long with my complaints.

My strongest wish now is to recover; to rejuvenate my breath not in the mere egotistical aim of enjoying my life, but to be able to serve and further my ideas and realize my life's aim: which consists in becoming a writer (I've got a nerve for it) in English language, nowadays a most universal means of literary expression (I already wrote several things in my Polish before the war).

That's why I've decided to address myself to you. I beg you, may I implore you, to help me out of my predicament by transferring to the hospital of yours.

For years I have dreamed about your victorious arrival and now when the longed for time is come—I am away from you, cut off from any contact with the civilization and culture that you represent and for which we have been so long and so desperately fighting.

The staying with you would prove, I presume—as most promoting my ultimate aims. I am ready to accompany you where you go and—as I know besides English and my mother-tongue Polish: German, French, Russian, Italian, Spanish, Jewish and Esperanto—I may be in Europe of some use to you (I've got a lot of practice as an interpret).

Who am I not? An orphan of the world. And you are in a position to restore the sens to my life: to create a new (first spiritual) home for me and the possibilities of fulfilling my life's aims.

I hope you won't refuse to make this salutary gesture . . .

Yours truly
Julius Lewy

P.S. I beg you very much for an immediate written answer; ill men are so impatient . . .

DOCUMENT 5-5: Diary entry by Dora Apsan,[16] Schildberg, Germany, for May 12, 1945, reflecting on the fate of her family, USHMMA Acc. 2005.166.1, Dora Apsan collection (translated from Hungarian).

Saturday, May 12

I am home. Marcel[17] is in the other room, but luckily he does not bother me. The whole afternoon I was lying exhausted, not from work but from my thoughts, my expectations, my fears. My little room is cool, I hear birds chirping outside, somewhere an accordion is being played, the sunshine is bright, the trees are blossoming . . . "It is May and the lilacs are blooming, it is May and my heart is freezing" . . . to what should I compare these surroundings? To Săpânţa [in Romania]? To the nursery in Cluj? Never mind, it is so pleasant, so sweet, so painful, I would rather stay here and not go home. Where would I go? To whom would I go? My God, is there anybody for me in Sighet? I would arrive on such a splendid May day, I would run home full of hopes and who

---

16. In the spring of 1944, Dora Apsan (born in 1921 in Sighet in what is now Romania) and her family were deported to Auschwitz, where she spent about eight months before being transferred to Weisswasser, a subcamp of the Gross-Rosen concentration camp complex in Lower Silesia (today Poland). After the liberation of the Weisswasser prisoners, Apsan moved to nearby Schildberg, where she wrote her diary. Both of Dora's parents—Herzl (Herman) Apsan (b. 1886) and Zali (Zissel) Apsan (née Basch, b. 1898)—were killed in Auschwitz. Dora's brothers Yancu and Esau survived the war and were reunited with their sister in Hungary; her older brother Moishi was killed at Auschwitz. Her brothers Abie and Yossie and half brother Mikki had managed to escape, respectively, to Palestine, Siberia, and Italy.

17. This was a member of a convoy of French prisoners also at Weisswasser.

will be there? Mother? Father? No, I can no longer feed myself with such illusions. My dearest parents! How much did I love you—only now do I know it. Why didn't I behave toward you as you deserved? Father, forgive me; mother, too: that I was not always good enough, that I caused you so many worries and aggravation. I am afraid that I am ready to forget this past year now that I am to embark on such a long journey. It seems as if I am returning home from an excursion and I am expecting you to be there waiting for me with open arms. God, why is our fate so cruel?

Dear little Yancu, maybe you will be home. Look, I even brought you a pair of shoes. You will like them, won't you, and you will be happy with the return of your sister who thought of you so often. Whom can I count on? Moishi, you are still my only hope, the only one whom I trust has survived. I implore you, don't cause me disappointment, I don't want to remain alive alone. Abie, my dear, where are you? Look at the tears that I was shedding writing these lines. I will look you up in Budapest even though I know that if you have survived these times you are probably home . . . but I don't dare to hope that I will find even a small family there. Part of the family . . . or just one person waiting for me. Lord, look how my demands shrink, how crushed I have become. Dear Edzu, did you have enough strength to endure? Yossie, are you alive, for five years we have not found out if you reached Russia? Alter, you will be there, maybe you are already working for a Jewish newspaper or at a theater? Do you think of me? And Miki . . . no, no. I am not allowed to deceive myself with such wonderful dreams of finding you home, because the disappointment will be so terrible. And it will be . . . oh . . . dear brothers, parents . . . my home, I am yearning so much, and it hurts so much that I cannot bear it.

Tzali,[18] I don't know what to say, but if I lose you then I had rather be taken to the gas chamber or run to the electric fence. Today memories are haunting me, our time in Cluj, the brick factory where we skied, all this was so very beautiful. You will be waiting for me, won't you? And you still love me.

Wouldn't it be better to stay here, to listen to the birds chirping and to deceive myself that I once had a Tzali, whom I loved so much, whom I see when I look at any man and who is waiting for me with outstretched arms, to hug me, to hold me. Maybe he even has a little room like this one, quiet, cozy, and he will love me as before . . . dreams of love . . . God, the disillusions are hurting me already.

"Come, my love, I am waiting for your coming only."

Why is this May so beautiful and so painful?

---

18. Dora's then fiancé and future husband, Zoltan Sorell (1921–2008), survived the war in Romania. After the war, they married; Zoltan became a mechanical engineer and Dora a physician. They emigrated to Brazil in 1961 and eventually to the United States.

DOCUMENT 5-6: Transcript of a voice-recorded interview with Polia Bisenhaus,[19] conducted by David P. Boder,[20] ORT School Paris,[21] on her experiences in the Bergen-Belsen concentration camp and postwar plans, Paris, July 29, 1946, Voices of the Holocaust Project, Paul V. Galvin Library, Illinois Institute of Technology, USHMMA RG 50.472*0002 (translated from Yiddish, German, and French).[22]

[. . .]

BODER: So in what sort of a camp were you in? Where were you in a camp?

BISENHAUS: I was in a camp in Poland, in a labor camp, and in Germany I was in an extermination camp.

BODER: An extermination camp?

BISENHAUS: [In French] Yes.

BODER: Alright. Tell me about the labor camp.

BISENHAUS: Well, we worked twelve hours a day, the whole day, and one week during the day, one week at night.

BODER: What work did you do?

BISENHAUS: Ammunitions. That is, well, ammunitions.

BODER: Ah, it was a factory.

BISENHAUS: . . . a factory. [In French] Yes.

BODER: Now then, and when you . . . what did they give you to eat?

BISENHAUS: Well, in Poland it wasn't bad, in Poland they gave us pretty good food . . . some days in the week it was meat, and in Germany it was very bad.

BODER: Aha. But that was in Poland. And [in English] how long . . . [in German] How long did you work in Poland?

---

19. The editors could not find biographic information on her; see also "Polia Bisenhaus," Voices of the Holocaust, http://voices.iit.edu/interviewee?doc = bisenhausP (accessed on February 24, 2017).

20. Russian-born psychologist David Boder (1886–1961) was a professor at Lewis University (later Illinois Institute of Technology). In 1946, Boder traveled to Europe for nine weeks to record about 130 interviews with Jewish and non-Jewish survivors of World War II living in displaced persons (DP) camps. The interviews were recorded in nine different languages, many of which were later translated to English. See Alan Rosen. *The Wonder of Their Voices: The 1946 Holocaust Interviews of David Boder* (New York: Oxford University Press, 2010).

21. These were vocational schools for Holocaust survivors, funded by the Organization for Rehabilitation through Training (Organisation Reconstruction Travail).

22. Transcript and alternative English translation accessible through "Polia Bisenhaus," Voices of the Holocaust, http://voices.iit.edu/interviewee?doc = bisenhausP.

BISENHAUS: In Poland, three years.

BODER: Three years? And why were you taken from there?

BISENHAUS: When the Russians got close, they . . . in Kielce, they sent us to Czestochowa, and then, when they got close to Czestochowa, they sent us to Germany.

BODER: To Germany?

BISENHAUS: [Answer not clear.]

BODER: Aha. Why did you say you were in an extermination camp? What camp was that?

BISENHAUS: Bergen-Belsen.

BODER: Bergen-Belsen?

BISENHAUS: [In French] Yes.

BODER: Ohhh. And what did you do there?

BISENHAUS: We did nothing there, we sat around and didn't get any food. Ten deca[grams] of bread per day, but some days no bread, either [phrase not clear] said that we stole from the stores of bread, so they didn't give us any food, and when the SS came and asked, "Why have you not received food today?"—they told the SS that we should say: we stole.

BODER: So, you should say . . .

BISENHAUS: Yes, we should say that we stole, and therefore today we get, we have a food punishment.

BODER: Aha.

BISENHAUS: And therefore they didn't give us any food. That happened many times during the week.

BODER: And how did you sleep, tell me [phrase not clear].

BISENHAUS: We slept on the ground, it was—we sat on the ground the whole day, on the same, it was straw, and afterward, at night, we slept in the same place. It was very dirty there, many died from the filth that was there.

BODER: What did the Germans say: why were you held there?

BISENHAUS: They told us nothing about why they were holding us there. They didn't tell us, but we knew, they were holding us because they wanted to exterminate us. But they didn't succeed.

BODER: All right. Did they exterminate other people there?

BISENHAUS: Yes, very many. When the people become weaker, because from day to day the people became weaker, because they didn't get any food, they took us, exterminated. It was a chamber there, where they gassed,[23] and after that burned, and this is well known after all, what the Germans did.

---

23. There was no gas chamber at the Bergen-Belsen concentration camp. The total number of victims who died in the camp is estimated at fifty thousand; see Thomas Rahe,

BODER: How do you mean, it is known? In America they know very little.

BISENHAUS: Ah, in America they know everything! Because the journals have already written much [phrase not clear]. Don't you know?

BODER: Yes. Some people know, some don't know. This is why I want . . .—do you have relatives in America?

[. . .; Bisenhaus and Boder discuss her brother in the United States and Boder's desire to interview him.]

BODER: How many weeks, how many months were you in Bergen-Belsen?

BISENHAUS: In Belsen I was . . . three months in Belsen.

BODER: Three months?

BISENHAUS: Three months.

BODER: Were many people exterminated there?

BISENHAUS: Yes, very many died because we, at roll call—do you know what roll call is?

BODER: Yes.

BISENHAUS: They called out people, they went completely naked, nothing on, this was . . .

BODER: Why did they have nothing on?

BISENHAUS: They took from us everything we had from home, all of our clothes, and they gave us these, with the stripes [phrase not clear], without clothes, without stockings, and this is how we went in the greatest—January, in the greatest cold, January, February [1945], this is the greatest cold, we went around completely naked, and that's why many died. Without food, not having slept, not having washed, and that's why many died.

BODER: Did the Nazis violate the women, did they . . .

BISENHAUS: Beat them?

BODER: No, I mean, were they indecent with the women?

BISENHAUS: Well of course, that's understood.

BODER: What do you mean, "it's understood."

BISENHAUS: Well, they treated the women very badly. And they beat them many times, when we weren't standing up straight at the roll call, because, when it was cold, we would lean on each other, so they beat us, over our heads, and like this [. . .]

BODER: Well, say for example: what did you do the whole day in Belsen? Let's say, you woke up in the morning—at what time?

"Bergen-Belsen Main Camp," in Megargee, *The USHMM Encyclopedia of Camps and Ghettos*, 1:278–81.

BISENHAUS: In the morning there was a roll call to get up, at four o'clock, three o'clock, five o'clock.

BODER: And?

BISENHAUS: So we went to wash, and "washing" was a room, very small, cold water. Completely cold, and we went in completely naked, and many caught cold, very many [pause]. And the organism is weak, you don't eat, you wash with cold water . . .

BODER: Were there men or women that

BISENHAUS: Women; these were . . .

BODER: No, no, I mean the Nazis.

BISENHAUS: The Nazis? These were women and men, but the women were much worse, they were much worse to us than the men were.

BODER: How come?

BISENHAUS: Well, the women beat us, very, just terribly. They beat us, they permitted, there were many Jews, Turkish and Rumanian, who were the camp leaders, camp elders [*Lagerälteste*]. And they were much worse than the Nazis.

BODER: You mean that there were Jewish camp leaders?

BISENHAUS: Yes.

BODER: And . . .

BISENHAUS: And the Jews were very bad to us. Very bad.

BODER: So the Jews were camp leaders, and they . . .

BISENHAUS: Yes, yes, they treated us very poorly.

BODER: To the other Jews.

BISENHAUS: Yes, very poorly.

BODER: Well, tell me: you got up at three, four in the morning, and you went to wash—then what.

BISENHAUS: Yes, afterward they brought coffee, black coffee, many times we didn't get this either, and without bread.

BODER: Without bread. Alright.

BISENHAUS: Afterward, twelve o'clock, eleven thirty, eleven o'clock, however it turned out, it was lunchtime. Lunchtime was: a little soup, three-quarters of a liter, sometimes a half liter, sometimes not even a half liter, and it was with turnips. If you found three pieces of turnip, that was very good, that was already a good soup. And afterward, five o'clock, four o'clock, sometimes six o'clock, there was bread. One piece of bread, this was a long bread, divided among ten people, twelve people. It came out to about eight deca[grams] of bread, ten deca[grams] a day. That was the food.

BODER: And then in the evening? And then, after eating, what did you do?

BIDENHAUS: Well, afterward, we sat some more. Like the rest of the day. [phrase not clear] lunch was after the roll call. The roll call was every day.

BODER: What do you call the roll call? What was the roll call?

BISENHAUS: The roll call is to count, whether anyone has escaped, or if anyone has died. This is so they would know exactly how many there are to give over further, how many are in the camp. How many women, men, it was, many times the roll call lasted four, five hours. And many people fell at the roll call, because they were—from the cold and fatigue, hunger—

BODER: And what was done with them?

BISENHAUS: Well, afterward, we went, many times after the roll call—after five hours of standing outside—they took us for work. The work was to carry sticks, various sorts of wood, from one place to another. That was—the work was nothing, but they beat us many times, when we couldn't run so fast, and so on.

[. . .; Bisenhaus and Boder discuss her deportation from Bergen-Belsen to Dachau, her transfer to Paris after liberation, and her desire to emigrate to Palestine.]

BODER: [. . .][24] [In German/Yiddish and English] This is a picture from a famous artist. From the last three years that you experienced, what do you think this picture means?

BISENHAUS: Well, this is a picture of a woman who, I believe, was deported and lost everything, and she is despairing, she is thinking of what to do, she has no way out.

BODER: And what do you think this picture is?

BISENHAUS: This is picture, this is also about the war, this is . . . the war, no?

BODER: Yes, go on.

BISENHAUS: This is, it must be [phrase not clear]

BODER: And what do you think happened to him?

BISENHAUS: Well, the same as before, he lost everything, his whole family, has been left alone, just like me, I am also the only one remaining from my whole family.

BODER: What is this?

BISENHAUS: Well, that is, I think—I don't know if this is right.

BODER: Yes, but naturally. What do you think?

---

24. Boder's note: "Here I showed her one of the TAT cards" (a psychological test used widely following World War II, especially with subjects who had undergone trauma; responses were evaluated as reflections of the subject's emotional state).

BISENHAUS: I think he is crying for his wife, she has died, or it is his daughter, I don't know for sure [phrase not clear]

BODER: And what do you think this is?

BISENHAUS: This? [phrase not clear]

BODER: Speak louder.

BISENHAUS: [phrase not clear] to run away, where to hide, and he has nothing.

BODER: And what do you think [in English] is this?

BISENHAUS: This, well, work, they're working in the field.

BODER: Where do you think this is?

BISENHAUS: Well, is it not Palestine? Perhaps, perhaps it is Palestine. Yes, this is very nice. He's working, yes? A *haluts* [pioneer] is working in the field. Yes, this is very nice.

BODER: Tell me, do you have a father and mother?

BISENHAUS: Well, my father and mother were deported, the whole family was deported.

BODER: When were they deported?

BISENHAUS: '42.

BODER: When you were still in Kielce?

BISENHAUS: Yes, when I was in Kielce. I was still at home. But I was sent from Kielce, they [phrase not clear] us from our town to a . . . it was called a "shop," that is, of all trades. Well, I went into such a shop, paid money, I was accepted, and afterward, after eight days, I was in the shop, afterward they sent me to Kielce. And my family was deported—I don't know where they are.

BODER: When was your family deported?

BISENHAUS: '42. That is, well, . . .

BODER: No, but I mean: how long after the Germans came did they deport your family?

BISENHAUS: Oh, the Germans came in '39. '39. And my parents were deported in '42.

BODER: Your parents were deported in '42.

BISENHAUS: Yes, '42.

BODER: Were you at home when they were deported?

BISENHAUS: No, I wasn't at home at all.

BODER: You were in Kielce. Did you have, do you have brothers and sisters?

BISENHAUS: I had [phrase not clear], today I have no [phrase not clear] six of the whole family.

BODER: How many brothers and sisters did you have?

BISENHAUS: I had two brothers and three sisters.

BODER: And where are they?

BISENHAUS: Deported! My two brothers were in Skarżysko[25] and are no more. They were probably murdered in Skarżysko. [phrase not clear]

BODER: What should I tell your uncle in Chicago?

BISENHAUS: Well, whatever you want to say. Well, you have . . .

BODER: Are you happy here?

BISENHAUS: Well yes, I have it good, at my aunt's, at my uncle's.

BODER: Aha. And you are studying here, you're learning at ORT.

BISENHAUS: Yes, I'm learning in ORT to make *soutien gorge* [French: brassieres].

BODER: What is that?

BISENHAUS: I'm learning to make *soutien gorge*.

BODER: What is that?

BISENHAUS: It is corsets, and well, *soutien gorge*, for . . . , for women.

BODER: And what do you do during the day? [Boder's note: The interview took place at an ORT night school.]

BISENHAUS: Well, during the day I don't do anything, today I'm not doing anything.

BODER: You don't work?

BISENHAUS: No, I don't work, I am with my aunt. [Boder's note: It was hard for DPs to get work permits in Paris.]

BODER: [In English] This is a record of Polia Bisenhaus taken at the ORT school, evening course, on July 29th, in Paris, 1946.

DOCUMENT 5-7: Account by Maria Gara,[26] May 21, 1945, on her rescue work in Hungary and subsequent deportation, recorded by AJJDC in Bucharest, USHMMA RG 68.087M, Nathan Schwalb papers/Hechalutz Office Geneva collection.

Statement No. 411

Made in the House of Refugees at 128, Calea Mosilor, Bucharest, on May 21st 1945, with

---

25. This refers to Skarżysko-Kamienna, a ghetto and labor camp not far from Kielce in German-occupied Poland. See Evelyn Zegenhagen, "Skarżysko-Kamienna," in Dean and Megargee, *The USHMM Encyclopedia of Camps and Ghettos*, 2:308–11.

26. The editors could not find additional biographical information on Maria Gara. Linguistic peculiarities in this document reflect the statement as translated into English from Hungarian by the AJJDC.

Miss Maria GARA

Born September 22nd 1924 in Budapest, who was deported to Thorn [Toruń, Poland] (No. 67,560), and who, appearing before us, declared the following:

During the spring and the beginning of summer 1944 I was working in an organization which provided Jews escaping from Hungary to Roumania with forged Christian documents. Many groups have been passed across the frontier this way, guided by smugglers. It was rather difficult and dangerous to organize this, as it was risky even to carry Christian papers in the interior of the country, and still more to travel with them. One of my collaborators was caught and the Gestapo started searching for me. I had to change my address. I took a new room where they suspected me. They investigated the address I gave in a false registration form as my previous one, and of course I was not known there. I had to move suddenly from my new room, too. By this time I was afraid to take a room and I was sleeping in the hills of Budapest for almost a week. These were difficult days, during the day I felt hot, but in the night I was freezing cold, and I could not wash. Thus I decided to pass over to Roumania with the next transport, but by accident I missed the group and went back to Budapest. With great difficulties I managed to organize a new transport but had no time to give them exact instructions before we started. This was my misfortune because I had to give them instructions for crossing the frontier when we were already on the train. All the men were dispersed in the train and I had to walk along it several times. Hereby I drew the attention of the conductor upon myself, who told a plain clothes policeman to watch me. I felt that somebody is observing me and just had time to tell some people of the transport that they should by no means get off the train together with me. It came as I thought, when I wanted to get off in Nagyvárad the detective arrested me and told me he would shoot me if I try to run away. He took me to the police station where my documents were examined. They almost accepted them for being correct but when they inspected my handbag they found too much money for a seamstress (I stated this as my profession) and besides there were some objects of gold there, which belonged to the group and remained in my bag. Until then I denied everything but when they said they would investigate in Budapest who I am, I saw that it is useless to go on lying, and admitted to being a Jewess. They locked me up in prison. During the questioning I told them my frank opinion about the then ruling system and I am astonished they did not shoot me. I told, among other things, that the Hungarian State should be ashamed to force honest people to forge documents, that it is ridiculous to imprison people just because they are defending their lives without having committed any crime. The police captain said I was right but he could not release me. Then I was conducted to the prison. For a day I did not get anything to eat, they did not even let me go to the W.C., and took away all I had. When they took me again to be questioned, I told them my opinion again which seems to have impressed the police captain for the treatment changed. I never got frightened and perhaps this was what saved me from many things. After 4 days I was transferred to Budapest, where I got back 700 pengős and my Christian documents. In Budapest I went to the prison, then to the internment camp of Jávar and from there I have been deported.

The whole lot of people who were still gay in Sárvár, became quite melancholy in Auschwitz. We suddenly felt what it was like to be pushed back to the state of beasts. It is depressing when one's hair is shaved, to dress in those rags and be dirty. It was so humiliating and shameful. The best example is that we were never called by name, just by our numbers. It was a characteristic feature of German methods to deprive the prisoners of everything that might recall human life. We could not keep a toothbrush, instead of human dwellings we had to live in dirty huts, our simple clean clothes were replaced by dirty rags, etc. Later, when we were taken to work, we got a piece of linen. We were quite happy about it. At home I never took so much pleasure in a piece of beautiful and costly clothing as in this plain cloth which at least was not ragged. I think there are some advantages in having lived in deportation, at least for those who did not perish. We have become modest and have learned to appreciate kindness and goodness better than before. We are looking at people from a new angle. We expect from them, and want to give them, warmth. Besides, there was a certain movement around us in the camp. Everything had to be done with speed. For instance, we were allowed to bathe for 2 minutes only. This of course is not enough to wash properly, but in any case, I am doing now everything much faster, for I have somehow brought along a sort of army spirit which was predominant in the camp.

The most depressing thing in Auschwitz was that the camp has been surrounded by a high-tension fence. We almost got mad when we looked out and saw the shining wires. We knew we are prisoners but this fence never allowed us to forget what was waiting for us.

Thorn camp was better insofar as there was no longer such a terrible electric fence. Nevertheless, it was impossible to escape. We did not speak the language, and with our hair shaved or very short everybody would have realized at once from where we are coming. Thus the Germans were sure we could stay. In spite of this, 2 girls once escaped. Of course they were soon caught. Had they not turned up, the camp would have been decimated.

I was block commander but finally I was deposed from this "post of honor" as I was not energetic enough. After this I worked for a short time, but the Russians approached rapidly, the Germans evacuated the camp and carried us on to Bromberg [Bydgoszcz, Poland]. Here the ground again became hot for them and in a night they just disappeared, leaving us behind. The next morning the Russians arrived and we were free.

Now I am waiting here in Bucharest for a chance to emigrate to Palestine. This was always the aim of my life which I hope will be realized soon. I must find a home country and a home to end all the vicissitudes I had to go through. (She states 13 names of survivors)

(signed) Maria Gara
We certify the above to be a true translation of the original.
Translated from Hungarian
Original by George Tolnai[27]

DOCUMENT 5-8: Report by Arthur Gold,[28] Montreux, Switzerland, to Gerhart Riegner,[29] WJC Geneva, on the care of Jewish orphans, July 1945, USHMMA RG 68.045M, reel 18, file 137 (translated from German).

STRICTLY CONFIDENTIAL
Dear Gentlemen,

After a thorough briefing with leading officials of Swiss and international Jewish organizations, I will permit myself to submit to you the following suggestions concerning the issue of Jewish children.

The Problem: In the case of caring for tens of thousands of children who were robbed of irreplaceable things—their parents—through war and deportation, the following considerations must take precedence:

  a. *Physical well-being* of the children from a medical standpoint (which will not be further addressed here).

---

27. The editors were unable to learn more about this person's role in the project.

28. Arthur Gold, born in 1924 into an Orthodox family in Leipzig, Germany, lived in France at the time of the German attack and was briefly held in Gurs. He crossed the Swiss border illegally in September 1942. While interned in Switzerland, he began working as a teacher and later pursued rabbinical studies.

29. Gerhart Riegner (1911–2002), a lawyer born in Berlin, served from 1939 onward as director of the WJC office in Geneva. In that critical location he obtained extensive information about the plight of Jews in occupied Europe. See Gerhart M. Riegner, *Never Despair: Sixty Years in the Service of the Jewish People and the Cause of Human Rights* (Chicago: Ivan R. Dee, 2006). Gold sent the statement to Riegner in early August 1945.

b. The emotional and psychological condition of the children who lost their parents.

c. The issue of religious-ideological-social training, that is, keeping them in and reintegrating them in the Jewish community.

Regarding b., the anguish that these "abandoned, parentless" children, besides their physical and material suffering, experienced and are experiencing has negative effects that are hardly noticeable but are ultimately very dangerous. The core of this problem, which in practice has been and continues to be given little attention, is often a total lack of selfless love, devoted caring, and a humane and loving atmosphere of trust in the care and upbringing of the children. This problem arose out of living apart from (the loss of) one's parents, whose nature it is to provide the vital factors for the growth and development of the child. These factors are not present, and thus the child lacks an emotional balance, and the children are being set in a psychological void that can cause resentfulness. Indeed, the child's distrust of these caregivers who are strangers to them is present from the outset. The educator does not understand how to gain the complete trust and devotion of the child, or s/he even offends the child's sense of justice, so that the child's initial distrust hardens into an emotional defense. Ultimately, hate can arise from the distrust, defensiveness, and bitterness. The child, retreating into their own small world, thus can develop a defensive disposition because of the behavior of just one or a few careless educators/caregivers— the child pulls back into himself and rejects even the most sensible measures (that the child often does not even grasp or refuses to comprehend anymore). The child's trust in adults is shattered, and the child is turned into a misanthrope. Incapable of any charitable work, the child thus belongs to the social classification "asocial." Through this emotional/psychological paralysis, which is strengthened by a spiritual emptiness and the absence of any alternative, the first preconditions for nihilistic, anarchistic, and finally criminal thoughts and behaviors develop. This enormous danger is firmly grounded in the laws of psychology and must not be overlooked.

Regarding c., in addition to this general, interdenominational problem that affects all orphaned children is the specific problem for us Jews of the revival and survival of our people—the existential problem of the children's <u>Jewish orientation</u>.

These children, who were spiritually hardened as a result of enormous suffering, can be the invaluable building material for our people's future. Our people's very existence was put in the throes of death in the bloodiest catastrophe of our history. The revival of our people requires a renewed and grand effort.

But the contributors to this effort are in great danger of being lost to us, indeed, even in danger of working against us. The issue today is not whether the children will become or remain more or less self-aware Jews, but whether they will count themselves among the Jewish community at all; yes, even whether we might be looking at a "small generation" of the worst—Jewish—anti-Semites.

Today we must be perfectly clear that Jewish children who are not being consciously raised Jewish, who are at best being raised with indifference to Judaism, are indifferent to all branches of Judaism. We know that many children—we cannot yet estimate their number—are being raised in a different faith and anti-Jewish. But all children who are not currently a part of the Jewish community will likely turn away from us in the future. They'll say, "We want no part of the Jewish community who did nothing to care for us." The consequences of the psychological condition described above and of the children's potential anti-Jewish upbringing will be a step from rejecting the community, from turning away from this community, toward actively working against it.

To what extent is the Jewish community today in the position to develop an answer to the large and important issues confronting them?

We unfortunately have to realize that we are ultimately responsible for our Jewish children—children whose last thoughts are of their murdered, innocent brothers and sisters in faith. If we are honest with ourselves, then it is mainly our fault. True, we lay the past behind us [ad acta]—we are thankful from the bottom of our hearts for the efforts of all the non-Jewish organizations that worked to save Jews and care for our children. But it is now of utmost importance that exclusively Jewish organizations assume the role of "protectorate" for our Jewish children. As was shown, we often had to ignore our more narrow Jewish interests and turn for help to interdenominational organizations. Today the Jewish community must see its most sacred duty as assuming the care of the children who are currently in the care of others. The various Jewish organizations of all ideologies are now prepared for the rescue work on behalf of our children. Financial resources are being obtained, technical preparations are being taken care of; in short, the fight for the Jewish child has begun. But exactly how this fight threatens to play out is evident in a terrible example of the differences among various Swiss organizations. The fight for the "minds of the children" has tremendously retarded the effort to find a temporary solution to the problem of child refugees in Switzerland. One thing is for sure: none of the existing Jewish organizations can <u>alone</u> deal with the daunting tasks. We must avoid at all costs a splintering of the minimal energies and abilities we can still muster to deal with the rescue of parentless, Jewish child-victims of war.

The most pressing requirement of the hour is the broad coordination of all possible forces that are willing to work on behalf of the Jewish child.

It is in the best interest of the various opposing sides to bury their differences at least temporarily and bridge their divides, because this is about not simply which ideology and in what type of care the children will be raised but the very existence of the Jewish community's future. Because it is a matter of rescuing the children's Jewish identity, it is a self-destructive argument that "in ideology there can be no compromise."

[. . .]

DOCUMENT 5-9: Diary entry by Rachela (Rachel) Bryk,[30] Bergen-Belsen, Germany, for September 22, 1945, on a day in the DP camp, USHMMA Acc. 2008.390.1, Ray Kaner collection (translated from Polish).

What happens in a given moment, no one realizes [illegible]. It is six in the morning. The sky is a beautiful blue, and the clouds are of various shades. In certain areas, the clouds are darker, lighter, and golden. On the bottom, across the fog, the outline of a mountain is visible. I am in the vicinity of a *lager*. Short and long barracks stretch out in front of me. The *lager* is beginning to wake up. In front of the *lager*, there is a sign, "House of Israel." There is indeed a mass of Jews here. It is our house, because there is no comfort like being among your own. Here, we do not feel that they do not like us. Above the *lager*, the Jewish flag is blowing in the wind—a blue-white sign. Our banner flutters like the others. Proudly. Looking at the flag, no one could tell that, although it is dependent on the wind like the others, it presents itself like banners of a different color. The banner flutters for a people oppressed for years. For the wandering Jews, chased from place to place, this moment was dreamt of during all of these years, and the most during the recent times in German captivity: the sight of the banner, which signifies freedom. Often, lying in the grass in [illegible] with a stupefied mind, I dreamt [illegible] to once see and feel freedom, and then to die. We survived. We saw freedom and we felt it. In the first moments, it was intense, but gradually everyone understood that our freedom is fictitious. That today, a man who has left the camp is a Jew. Our liberators treat us worse than the Germans, who were the cause of the loss of so many people, destruction, and ruin. It is true that no one likes us and will accept us. Our hopes are dying

---

30. Rachel Bryk, born in 1927 in Łódź, Poland, lived in the Łódź ghetto from 1940. While many in her family were deported to death camps or died in the ghetto, Rachel Bryk survived Auschwitz II–Birkenau and Bergen-Belsen, where she was liberated by British troops in April 1945. During this time, Rachel met Leon Kaner, whom she later married. Rachel and Leon Kaner emigrated to the United States in 1946.

that someone will open his arms for us. The borders are closed to us[;] will they ever open again? I thought about all of this waiting for Leon in front of the dining room. Leon is still sleeping. What a complicated character he is. He gets worked up about trivial things, but when it comes to serious matters, he is calm and balanced. His sister is in Bergen[;] she came there from Łódź. When I heard about this yesterday, I was so moved that my legs were shaking. I wanted to fly over like a bird to his job. And now, when I have been ready to leave for some time, he is sleeping peacefully. He is going to see his sister[;] I am going to find out the news and details of the death of my dearest brother. It saddens me that while he will be experiencing his happiest moments, I will be experiencing my most tragic ones. I will do my best to conceal what I am experiencing. How I dreamed about and waited to meet my brother. I thought a hundred times about our meeting. How will it go? What will I tell him? And how will he answer? Now I will never see my brother again[;] I will not even see a photograph of him, as I left behind all of my photographs in Auschwitz. Life is so cruel. Nature is so stern. I know that a time will come when I will not be able to evoke his image. What will be the worst, he will then be dead to me. Today, he died for the world. How often I see a boy who resembles him. I cry over the fate of my poor Levy.[31] Often, when I pronounce the name Levy, at once I see not the living one but one who is probably lying in the ground for some time now, or whose ashes were blown away a long time ago. How it hurts, how my heart stings me, when I write these cold, naked words. But I want to suffer, to torment myself in his absence so I can at least know what pain means. It is supposed to do me good in the moment that He died. My dearest Levy, I will never forget you, I will never get over the pain of losing You. I still wait for you in my dreams. How it hurts me, how I grieve for You, poor one, how sad I am that I will never see Your kind face, Your beautiful figure. Oh, my dearest. Why are you not here? So many survived, but why not You? I know that I am an egoist for thinking in this way, but oh well. You can have concern about the general state of affairs, but never as in the way of a private matter. If it pertains to you, it bites you[;] some bug sits inside of you and penetrates you. It is completely different from something that is happening near you, not inside of you. Yes, yes, Levy, I am going far away in order to tear out the mystery of your departure, without returning. [. . .]

---

31. This refers to the author's brother killed at Auschwitz in 1942.

DOCUMENT 5-10: Letter by Max Schweitzer,[32] Brăila, Romania, to his sister, Esther Williams, Cleveland, Ohio, on his family's wartime fate in Transnistria, April 10, 1945, USHMMA RG 10.374, Schweitzer family papers (translated from Romanian).

Brăila, 10.IV.1945
Dear sister Esther,

Some weeks ago I wrote you through the Red Cross the dates when our parents died. Now, after the post-mail communication between America and Romania has been reestablished, I want to write you more.

One morning in October 1941, the prefect of Câmpulung, Bucovina, arrived in our town, Gura-Humorului, assembled the elders of the Jewish community at the mayor's office, and told them, "You are all communists and traitors and must leave the country." He gave orders to all the Jews to be at the train station by two o'clock, with only hand luggage, and to leave the town in cattle cars. All the valuable things, like foreign currency and jewels, must be delivered to the mayor's office. If somebody did not obey the order, he would be shot. The mayor permitted no exceptions. All the Jews obeyed that order for fear of being shot, because the soldiers, armed with machine guns, waited to shoot the Jews.

Each one of us took only a rucksack with things, delivered the jewels and the key of the house to the mayor without receiving a receipt, and left.

After some days of suffering, we arrived at Atachi (at the frontier with the Ukraine). There the representative of the National Bank took our money and gave us rubles, exchanging 40 lei to 1 ruble. Before we crossed the Dniester, we were searched, and from the few things we had left, the most valuable were taken.

After we were robbed, we were thrown on the other border of the Dniester [into Transnistria]. What happened there, I think you read a little in the papers. I shall write you about our life there on another occasion. The family and I received permission to stay in Mogilev because Wumi and a few other skilled workers obliged themselves to work in a factory without a salary.

Our parents arrived after a month. Before they crossed the Dniester, they were forced to stay a day and a night in rain, water, and mud up to their knees.

---

32. Probably Max (also Mordechai) Schweitzer, born in 1899 in Gura Humorului (now Romania). In late 1941, he and his family were deported to Transnistria. Liberated in March 1944, Max Schweitzer subsequently went to Cyprus before emigrating to Israel in 1948. His sister, Esther Williams (b. 1894), was married to an American and had become a U.S. citizen.

When they crossed the Dniester, father could not walk. He was very weak and ill. I begged the officer to let them stay with us 3 days before they went further. If they had gone on without rest, they would have died on the road like thousands of other people who could not walk and were shot and left to be eaten by the dogs.

Anyway, the officer agreed to let them stay with us. I am going to conclude the letter:

Father died in the Mogilev ghetto on the 13th of Adar 5702 [March 1, 1942].

Mother died in the Vindiceni ghetto on the 12th of Adar Sheini 5703 [March 19, 1943].

Uncle Kiva died in Mogilev on the 21st of Nissan 5701 [April 18, 1941].

Father died from a cold and weakness. He was 84 years old. Mother, 73, and Uncle Kiva, 68. Both died of typhus fever.

I, Esther, and the children are staying with Emanuel and waiting to go to Palestine.

We are in a deplorable state, and we have nothing, are poor, and desperate.

We all kiss you,

Max Schweitzer

DOCUMENT 5-11: Report by Judah Nadich,[33] advisor to the U.S. Army theater commander on Jewish activities, October 22, 1945, on conditions in assembly centers for Jewish displaced persons, USHMMA RG 19.036, Rabbi Judah Nadich collection.

Headquarters, U.S. Forces, European Theater

Office of Military Government (U.S. Zone)

Displaced Persons Branch

OE-DP 383.7 (0.641)22 October 1945

SUBJECT: Report on Conditions in Assembly Centers for Jewish Displaced Persons.

To: Chief of Staff, Headquarters, United States Forces, European Theater, APO 757, U.S. Army.

Reference is made to report, same heading, to Chief of Staff, Headquarters, United States Forces, European Theater, dated 16 September 1945.

---

33. Judah Nadich (1912–2007), born to Russian immigrants in Baltimore, Maryland, was an influential conservative rabbi, chaplain in the U.S. Army, and postwar special advisor to General Dwight D. Eisenhower on Jewish affairs. In this position, he worked arduously, along with other chaplains, to alleviate the fraught conditions in place for displaced persons.

This present report is based on field trips made between 1–17 October 1945 to various assembly centers and towns in Bavaria and Czechoslovakia, U.S. Zone. Appendix "A" deals with conditions in German communities.[34]

Generally speaking, much improvement in conditions has occurred within the past several weeks. Steps have been taken to relieve the overcrowded conditions. Some improvement in food is noticeable. The supply problem is beginning to be solved, particularly as regards clothing, blankets, fuel. Frequent inspections are being made and a general tendency can be observed among officers of all ranks concerned with this problem to deal with it in the spirit desired by the Theater Commander. The alleviation of the situation is under way but it should be stressed that continuing and constant attention is called for and that several aspects of the situation still need further consideration.

As regards <u>housing</u> considerable improvement in the previously overcrowded situation has been secured by making Föhrenwald (Wolfratshausen) and Deggendorf all-Jewish camps, by adding a number of private houses to the camps in Feldafing and Landsberg and by opening a Jewish DP hospital in the village of Feldafing to which the Feldafing camp hospital has now been moved. However, while considerable improvement has thus been obtained, more remains to be done along such lines. At Feldafing, where the total census averages about 4,400, some 400 have been transferred to Föhrenwald, 27 houses in the village are occupied by between 500–600 people and 10 additional houses have been requisitioned, but not yet occupied. However, the number of people in the camp proper should be cut still further. Some rooms still contain as many as 25 and the wooden barracks, whose conditions have been referred to in the previous report, have been only partially evacuated. Additional houses in the village should be requisitioned, perhaps another 25. At Landsberg, with some 5,000 residents, some people have been transferred to Föhrenwald, a group of houses in the town are now occupied by 450 and 3 additional houses have been requisitioned. [. . .]

As regards <u>emigration</u> desires, the situation remains the same, with the overwhelming majority wishing to go to Palestine as soon as possible. A minority wish to go to the U.S., the U.K., and the British Dominions and South American countries, largely because of the presence of relatives in these lands. The only exception is the Deggendorf camp where two factors exist not true of any other camp: the average age is 50, with 350 being over 60, and 700 of the 1,000 residents are of German Jewish origin. However, even here a registration indicates that while the greatest single number 209, wish to go to the U.S., the second largest group, 170 are anxious to immigrate to Palestine. Generally

---

34. The appendices have not been included here.

speaking, the age level in all other camps is in the lower 30s with a very large number in the 20s. Some 811 children under 18 are at Föhrenwald and 56 children under 14 are at Deggendorf.

[. . .]

As regards <u>food</u>, the situation has improved. The caloric content varies in the different camps between 2000–3000. However, the same complaints are voiced as to the lack of balance in the diet, an overabundance of bread and potatoes and a lack of food rich in protein, minerals and fats. Desires are expressed for more fruits, vegetables, fresh meat, cheese, butter, fresh milk and eggs, sugar. At Deggendorf the caloric content is between 2000 and 2500, but the diet is starchy and because of the large percentage of the aged and ill more food, better balanced, is needed.

[. . .]

<u>Education and recreation</u> programs are developing but need further attention. An excellent Yiddish newspaper has been started by the Central Committee of Liberated Jews of Bavaria, located in Munich, and 15,000 copies of the first issue have been distributed gratis in the camps. A "People's University" was started on 4 October 1945 at Landsberg with courses offered by DP instructors (with no textbooks available) in biology, political economy, philosophy, Zionism, with over 100 students registered. A goodly number are enrolled in manual training courses, taking shop instruction by DP teachers in carpentry, metal work, radio, electricity, nurses aids, dental and laboratory assistants, shoe repair. A camp newspaper is soon to appear as in the case at Feldafing where a similar but less developed vocational training program is in effect. Here a dramatic group is organized and a band is planned but musical instruments are lacking. Each block of houses boasts of a day room and a number of radios are now on hand. At St. Ottilien there are school classes for children, including a kindergarten, which needs toys and educational materials. Literary evenings are held for adults. The St. Ottilien DP orchestra gives concerts for its own and neighboring camps and hospitals. Föhrenwald has organized a kindergarten and children's school and courses for adults in English, Hebrew, music, typing, nurses aids and health and beauty as well as a school of 80 students learning how to drive and service automobiles. The program also includes vocational training courses, a dramatic group, concerts, dances, and some athletics. Deggendorf has concerts, dances, a dramatic group which stages shows, a lounge, and radios have been promised. The former Commanding General, Third Army, has ordered projectors and screens to be made available for Föhrenwald and Feldafing as has the

Commanding General, 83rd Division for Deggendorf. What is required for almost all installations are the following: projectors, [illegible] and films, phonographs and records, radios, additional books (both textbooks and library books, especially in Hebrew and Yiddish), athletic equipment, such as ping-pong sets, soccer and volley balls, footballs, boxing gloves, musical instruments for the organizing of bands. It is also felt that many young people would welcome a program of calisthenics, drill and marching if arrangements could be made whereby U.S. Army personnel could act as instructors.

Religious activities continue to be well conducted under the guidance of a council of 12 DP rabbis, who form a department in the Central Committee of Liberated Jews of Bavaria. Academies of religious learning are conducted at Landsberg, Föhrenwald, Feldafing, and St. Ottilien. Kosher Kitchens are supervised at those 4 camps. The mass cemeteries are being put in order. A central registration for marriages is being organized. In this latter connection questions are asked as to proper procedure for marriages among DPs and clarifying instructions are needed. At present the couple to be married appears before a rabbi for the religious ceremony. Information is asked for also concerning registration of births.

Morale and discipline are always factors to be considered among people living in camps which at its best constitutes abnormal living, particularly when such people are former inmates of German concentration camps where law and order meant Nazi law and order. Added is the factor of much idle time. In view of all this the number of undesirable incidents among Jewish DPs is amazingly low and is a source of gratification. Morale has been considerably lifted by the personal appearances made in DP camps by the Theater Commander and by the publicized expressions of his generous spirit, as well as by the personal interest evinced recently by the Third Army Commander, Commanding Generals of the Corps and Division concerned and by the local Commanding Officers. Even more improvement in morale and disciplines can be obtained by placing more responsibility upon local DP camp committees, by drawing them more into the problems of camp management and granting them more autonomy—a practice suggested by our American philosophy of democracy—by further encouragement to the Central Committee of Liberated Jews of Bavaria in its various useful functions, and by expansion of the work and leisure time programs as suggested in paragraphs 12 and 13 above. The removal of armed guards, except for night security, the lifting of the pass system, and removal of "off-limits" restrictions on German towns and villages have all contributed toward raising morale as have, of course, the improvements in the clothing supply. Morale could be given a further boost by the early instituting of an easy workable method whereby these people could communicate by mail with relatives in other camps and in foreign lands. New situations have been recently created by the discovery by some residents of camps that children or/and wives are still alive in Poland or the Baltic countries. A great humanitarian work could be wrought by the establishment of a procedure whereby these remnants of families could be reunited within our DP camps. The Jewish DPs, the remnants of millions of Jews exterminated by the Nazis, would like to be permitted to send an official representative to the forthcoming War Crimes Trial at Nurnberg.[35] It would be a dramatic symbol that justice is being done to those who suffered longest and worst from the criminals and would raise the morale of every Jewish DP. Such a representative should be an ex-inmate of a concentration camp and might possibly be selected by the Central Committee of Liberated Jews of Bavaria.

[. . .]

A general summing up of the situation indicates a steadily growing improvement in almost all respects. So much was happening during the last several days of this officer's visit to Bavaria that many of the remarks made in this report may already be out-dated. Much has already been accomplished in what is and will undoubtedly continue to be a complex and difficult problem. But the U.S. Army and UNRRA[36] are evincing the will to do the job and it no doubt can be entertained that the job will be done.

JUDAH NADICH
Chaplain (Major), USA
Advisor to the Theater Commander on Jewish Activities

---

35. This refers to the International Military Tribunal held by the four major Allies in Nuremberg from November 20, 1945, to October 1, 1946, against Hermann Göring and other key German officials deemed responsible for the perpetration of war, war crimes, and crimes against humanity. Until 1949, American military tribunals conducted thirteen more trials against roughly two hundred German defendants in the city.

36. Founded in 1943, the United Nations Relief and Rehabilitation Administration (UNRRA) provided social and economic aid to the liberated countries of Europe. In October 1945, UNRRA assumed responsibility for the displaced persons population. In 1946, at the height of its activity, UNRRA operated with a staff of 25,000 people to care for 850,000 DPs, often in affiliation with Jewish organizations. When in the summer of 1947 UNRRA became inactive, the International Refugee Organization assumed care of DPs.

DOCUMENT 5-12: Dr. Zalman Grinberg,[37] "Nürnberg," on Allied trials and postwar justice, *Undzer veg* (Munich, Germany), November 20, 1945, USHMM Library microfilms 0377.

It is not coincidental that the city from which stemmed the laws which disfranchised, belittled, and finally destroyed European Jewry should be chosen as the Seat of Justice for the criminals who conceived and executed the Nürnberg Racial Laws. The murderer should be brought to justice in the city in which he fashioned his murderous decrees.

Yet, it is not these alone who are responsible for the merciless destruction wreaked upon an innocent humanity for a period of twelve years. The entire German population bears that guilt. The numbered criminals summoned before the bar of justice spoke in the name of the people and perpetrated their crimes with the consent of that people. The German way of death, designed by the masters in Nürnberg[,] was accepted by the entire German people.

It is difficult to prosecute an entire people. Cities cannot be summoned to the witness chair, especially when the penalty of death is the only verdict for those summoned.

We, the remnant of European Jewry, though we have not been called to the prosecutor's table, are convinced that we are the ones who should point an accusing finger. It is our voice, we know, that should be the first to be lifted against those who stand accused. Not being called, we exploit this opportunity to express our feelings and make our demands. Feelings and demands that should be supported by a humane and moral world.

During the past twelve years we have witnessed a people slavishly following their Fuhrer. There was hardly a protest against the ways into which he led them and hardly an attempt was made to destroy his evil plans. Instead, songs of praise were sung to the honor of the Fuhrer and in their pseudo-German heroism, they promised to follow him into the grave. At the ledge of the grave they remained standing, they would go no farther. It is this people which now maintains that it was not they who gave the Fuhrer his power[;] nor was it they who supported his grandiose schemes for destruction.

Who was it then?

Where are the 80,000,000 who voted for the Nazi party?

---

37. Dr. Zalman Grinberg (1912–1983) had been director of the Kovno ghetto hospital and survived the Dachau concentration camp before he became chair of the Central Committee of Liberated Jews in the U.S. sector of Germany and set up a hospital in St. Ottilien staffed by other camp survivors. After living in Israel, he emigrated to the United States in 1955.

Are they no longer alive? Or were they never in life?

The answer is that they live and will continue to live as National Socialists in their minds and in their actions. At present, under the dominations of military authority they fake the appearance of innocent sheep. They cringe and humble themselves before the victorious armies. And it is right that they should belittle themselves[,] for the soul of a slave quickens the German body.

We have been dealt with by a slave people, which became a master people. "Woe unto the nations of the earth," when the slave becomes master. His warped brain and hardened heart break open[,] and all the hate and venom that had been stored up through the years, strangles and poisons all those about him. The German people must remain the slaves! Never again shall they be permitted to rise and threaten humanity!

We, the small remnant of Jewry[,] condemn the German people to death as they condemned our people to death and carried out their condemnation. The Democracies, sitting in judgment, may choose to be more than generous to the German people. Whatever their verdict, our moral sentence of the German people must be made known to the world.

We demand full reparation for all Jewish property confiscated and destroyed. We do not make this demand in the sense that the German destruction inflicted upon our people should be made good. There is no force in the world that could conceivably make good that which was undone by the German people. The monies realized from the reparations would be set aside as a "Rehabilitation Fund" which would guarantee, in a sense, the future of the surviving Jew.

The best of our people lie in unmarked graves in the desecrated European soil upon which Spring flowers will soon blossom. Let not the flowers deceive you! You Mighty of the Earth! Together with the ascending scent goes forth a heartrending cry for justice. The fate of humanity is dependent upon whether or no[t] we are granted justice. For the Jew is the barometer which gauges the peace of the universe. Should the world bypass the Jew and his problems and go on to concern itself with supposedly greater issues, like a moral atom bomb, the barometer will explode and again will Humanity come to grips with death.

The Nürnberg laws were our death sentence. From the Nürnberg Trials we await the proclamation of our rights and the vindication of our claim to free and equal rights as individuals and as a people in the world of peace and humanity.

DOCUMENT 5-13: Editorial in *Unzer Sztyme: Organ of the Sharith Hapletah in the British Zone* (Bergen-Belsen, Germany), on disappointments since liberation, January 1, 1946, USHMM Library Microfilms, LMO251.

And so 1945 is fast a-dying, with its withered leaves and sharp winds. The year that had been born on so wonderful a promise, and we know full well that before the year is completely dead decisions will have been made, orders given, that will profoundly affect us. It is right therefore for us to attempt a summing up of this 1945, and perhaps we might even lift the curtain of darkness that still envelopes us and attempt to reach into the dim light of tomorrow.

Eight months have passed since the Day of Liberation. We have long ago lost the feeling of ecstasy of that wonderful day. We are no longer drunk on sheer Joy, and the thrill of existence has lost its momentum. We are attempting this analysis when every day troubles, and normal life tears at us with its usual cruel fangs. We want to dispel "to-day" in order to be ready for "to-morrow." We know that that accuracy of our vision is normal, and we are not leaning on the goodness of people of the outside world, and the simple faith of our brethren abroad. We realize that our situation will not improve, nay, everything points to the fact that we are being dragged into a deeper and darker abyss.

And so the last act of the war is brought to its conclusion. Millions who were enslaved by Hitlerism have returned to their homes. Soldiers who were torn away from kith and kin are beginning to rebuild their lives amidst their loved ones. Presidents and Prime Ministers, Foreign Secretaries are in solemn conclave, the great Captains depart. Life is approaching normality. Our problem still exists. We the ashes, the clinkers, the residuum of the furnace of War. Who is interested in ashes? And who will take unto him a heap of refuse? So we remain beggars, withered and grey, clothed in rags and we dutifully gnaw at the bone called liberation, and the World, the snug comfortable World warming itself at the grateful blessing of peace is expecting us to be ever so thankful for that bone.

Liberation! A word which we had lingered on for long, long years, a word, that had shrieked at us to pray for an Allied victory, this word has become the most inhuman of disappointments to us, the living flesh of the word has shrunk away but the bone remains.

We fought so well when we could fight. We had no tanks, no rifles, no flame throwers, no machine guns, but we fought with everything we had. With fists and boots, with sticks and clubs, with scalding water, and with our souls. We fought like Bar-Cochba, and we suffered like Job. We ask not for flowers to be strewn in our paths, we want no pacans of praise, but we do want to live, just to live a normal private life, to come and go, to eat and sleep and to be able to look men in the eye.

The Nazi fences are destroyed, but another is being built around us, a bigger and better [Bergen-]Belsen. The "free" Jews of Germany are being invited to return to this new Ghetto, in the heart of black Germany. We did not believe that it would ever be possible that in this first winter of liberation we should have to face such searing and bitter prospects after the liberation. The World is reading with mild interest the long tale of Nazi atrocities, they are but putting the past on trial, we ask that the future, our future be put on the throne of Justice.

Where are the voices of the World, perhaps they are dead. Has Hitler laid his evil touch on them? Can not their mouths speak? Has [*sic*] the brains of the thinking World been fossili[z]ed? We are dumb, and must we be but a silent stricken folk, lost in the corridors of an echoing world? Where are the democrats, the liberals of the World? Has their faith been changed into a dumb contemplation of their navels, and we know not, this may be Nirvana?

We are small in numbers, a remnant of a great people, and we live here in silent, futile contemplation, and we see no Nirvana this side of Belsen!

DOCUMENT 5-14: Certificate of widowhood issued by the Central Bureau of Orthodox Communities in Budapest to Golda Leitman Weiss,[38] May 14, 1946, USHMMA RG 10.522 (translated from Hebrew).

בית דין מיוחד לתקנות עגונות
בלשכה המרכזית לקהלות האיסטאראדאקסיית
במדינת הונגריה

כתב היתר

מספר 1424/250

לאנינו ביד המויחד לתקנות עגונות דחתום מטה באה גבית עדות בדבר מיתת האיש ר' מֹשֶׁה טֻוֹבִּי׳ בֶּן ר'
יְהוֹשֻׁעַ וַייִם ע"ה, בעלה של האשה מ' גָאלְדַא בַּת ר' אַבְרָהַם יַעֲקֹב בּוּרְדֹאפַּעסט
ועים הגב"ע הזאת נשאנו ונתנו בדבר ע"פ השולחן עריך והפוסקים. ועים התקנות היסודיות שנתקבלו מרבני מדיענו
להלכה נחלט מאתנו להתיר את האשה מ' גָאלְדַא בַּת ר' אַבְרָהַם יַעֲקֹב לייטמאַן הנ"ל מכבלי העיגון
וכן נתברר לנו שהיא אֵינַה זקוקה ליבם, וגם שהיא אֵינַה נרושה רְלֹא חלוצה מכבר
ע"כ הרי היא מותרת להנשא לכל גבר דתתיצבין בלי חליצה רֹאפִּילִּר לכדין.
ובכן ניתן מאתנו הרשות לכל רב ומורה לסדר לה קדושין כדמי', אם אינו מתנגד להקי המדינה.
רֹלֹא תכֹנֹא להעד ר' יַעֲקֹב דוד קלַיין

פֹעֹסֹטֹם יום יְגֹלְחרש אַייֹר שנת תשז"ו

Special Court to Adjudicate Abandoned Wives
Permit # [typed] 1424/250

Conducted in the main office of the Orthodox congregations in Hungary (God willing).

Appearing before the special court to adjudicate abandoned wives was the undersigned, who gave evidence regarding the death of [typed] *Moshe Toby, son of Yehoshuah Weiss*, who was the husband of [typed] *Golda daughter of Abraham Jacob* residing in [typed] *Budapest*, and according to this testimony and in line

---

38. Olga (Golda) Leitman Weiss was originally married to László (Moshe Tovia) Weiss, who, in 1944, was taken from Budapest to a slave labor camp. In 1946, following the decision of the rabbinic court printed here, Olga married her first cousin, Eliezer Avraham (Albert) Freedman, who had lost his entire family in the Holocaust. In 1949, to avoid religious persecution by the Communists, the Freedmans fled Hungary via Vienna to a DP camp in Hallein in Austria. Eliezer Freedman became head of the camp and remained in that position until they emigrated to Canada in January 1951.

with the laws in "Shulchan Aruch" and fundamental religious judgments provided by Hungarian rabbis we decided to release the woman [typed] *Golda daughter of Abraham Jacob Leitman* from the shackles of abandonment.

Thus it became clear to us that she [typed] *was neither* divorced [typed] *nor* dependent, and is allowed to marry any man, and even to a Cohen.

Thus, we give permission to any rabbi to preside over her marriage, if the latter does not conflict with the state laws.

In witness is [signed] *Rabbi Jacob David Klein.*

The [typed] *13th of Iyar* [May 14], 1946, central offices of the Orthodox congregations, Hungary.

DOCUMENT 5-15: Report by Becky Althoff,[39] Föhrenwald, Germany, June 7, 1946, on her assessment of child survivors in the DP camp, USHMMA RG 10.146, Henry Holland collection.

June 7, 1946
To: Miss Ethel Ostry, Principal Welfare Officer[40]
From: Becky Althoff, Psychiatric Consultant, AJDC
Re Children's Home

As indicated in my last report of 5/24, this two week period was the completing of my work at the Kinderheim,[41] initiate a random sampling of Kibbutzim at Hochland Lager, and continue to accept individual referrals. As discussed with you, in our weekly conferences every child and wherever possible [the responsible] relative has been interviewed at the Kinderheim.

Because of lack of time and secretarial assistance, I am unable to give full case histories of each child, but will give in writing in summary, a short review of each child and the disposition. You will also remember that in addition each

---

39. The family of Russian-born Becky Althoff (née Machanofsky, later Adelson; 1909/1911?–1997) had emigrated to the United States when she was still very young. After having worked at the New York Department of Welfare and obtained a master's degree from the New York School of Social Work at Columbia University, she joined the AJJDC in late 1945 and later served as a psychiatric consultant in the Föhrenwald DP camp.

40. Ethel Ostry (b. 1901) was a Russian-born Canadian citizen working as a welfare officer for UNRRA.

41. The *Kinderheim*, or children's home, consisted of the orphanage at the Föhrenwald DP camp. It was run by both AJJDC and UNRRA workers, who evaluated the children's physical and mental "rehabilitation" for immigration purposes. For more information, see Margarete Myers Feinstein, *Holocaust Survivors in Postwar Germany, 1945–1957* (New York: Cambridge University Press, 2010), 159–97.

child has been examined by the visiting psychologist, and where possible, I have discussed the findings with the relative. We started with 13 children in the Kinderheim, the following have been removed to their own parents or relatives, after discussion with me,

D., Sonia[42]—Mother at Missouri 12 [DP camp section]
D., Pepa—   "   "   "   "
S., Chaskel—two brothers and sister-in-law at Florida 8

Of the remaining ten the situation is as follows:

W., Mila, Chana, and Moniek—The father of these three children [was] interviewed. He is vitally interested in the children and is anxious to establish a home with the three of them. As the Mother is deceased, and since the ages of the children are 12, 11, and 10, he felt that his married sister could assume responsibility for them, with his help. The brother-in-law is also willing to be of assistance.

The psychologists' report indicates that they are for the most part mentally retarded, with shallow affect. All the children expressed a keen desire to return home with their father and relatives.

The doctor's findings indicate that Mila and Chana are suffering with closed TB lesions, and suggest a rest home for both under the supervision of the aunt. We are awaiting approval from the UNRRA Doctor to send the two children and aunt to Hochland Lager, where they can get the necessary diet, rest and fresh air. The billeting officer has been informed of the need for a room to accommodate 6 people, and as soon as the physical condition is taken care of, will endeavor to find suitable living arrangements for the[m].

M., Riwka, has a 20 year old brother in Dorfen, who is employed as a cook. He brought her here, about a month ago, with a friend placed her in the Kinderheim, awaiting emigration to Palestine and the arrival of the rest of the family. A mother and three sisters are still in Poland.

The boy has an affidavit to go to America, and is undecided as to plans concerning his sister. He refused to be parted from her, and would not consider Ansbach. Today we heard through the Welfare Officer at Dorfen that the rest of the family have arrived, staying at Camp Föhrenwald, unregistered. It is possible, that the family will be registered here or go to another camp where registration is not closed and take Riwka with them.

H., Lutke, has a father here in camp who is working as a bookkeeper. He

---

42. The editors have anonymized all last names in the interest of privacy.

was conflicted about taking the child to live with him. When, however, we told him that afternoon play groups were established, and that a 12 year old girl should definitely be accommodated, he seemed somewhat relieved. Here too, the question of new living arrangements was discussed. He is scheduled for another interview, and was reassured that change of residence would [in] no way interfere with his child's emigration to Palestine, he was relieved. Since the children now get their noon meal at school, and the evening meal he could share with the child. A later deposition will be forthcoming.

F., Basia and G., Lea, aged 8 and 12 respectively, both have aunts living in Munich. It is my feeling, that at one time, the relatives lived here at the camp, but found it more convenient to live in Munich and utilize the Kinderheim as a sort of boarding home. Neither children profess to know the address of the aunts, although both visit them frequently. I have asked to see the aunts on their visit to Föhrenwald and although both visited on a weekday, and the supervisor of the Kinderheim knew of my desire to see them, they did not appear. It is my feeling that more strenuous action is indicated. Either we plan to send the children to Ansbach, where they rightly belong, or we ask the aunts to take the children with them to Munich.

G., Pepa, has a mother at camp who works in the kitchen. She is anxious to continue working, but would consider doing so on a part time basis. In view of your own interest in Mrs. G. with regard to the recent suicide, another interview is scheduled in which we will plan to find living quarters for the deceased's daughter, Mrs. G and Pepa. The mother is not adverse to sharing a home with the daughter, and interview with the child reaffirmed the fact, that the child feels neglected and rejected at the Kinderheim being more anxious to live with the mother than at the Home.

G., Julia, has a mother who works in the Kitchen at Dorfen. The mother is anxious to live with the daughter, as is the daughter to live with her, but Mrs. G. informs me that she is able to provide better for her daughter with the zulage [German: added ration] as a worker than without. Discussions revealed that the mother felt she would [be] depriving her daughter of going to Palestine, or the "advantages" of group living, if she asked the child to live with her. Another appointment is scheduled, the Messing Officer at Camp, would be willing to have Mrs. G. work here, even part time, to enable her to be closer with the daughter. This too will involve different living arrangements, but further disposition will be contingent upon our second interview with Mrs. G.

F., Zosia, has an aunt and putative step-father to live with. Because of family disagreement, as to who shall assume responsibility, the child is residing at the Kinderheim. The child is conflicted herself, and does not know where she should go. Both relatives profess great interest in the child, who visits both frequently. To my mind, the aunt seems to be the better guardian, but since there is a religious matter involved, it will await my discussion with the Rabbi.

My own thinking about the Kinderheim is that it should be dissolved since it has outlived its usefulness. I question its original purpose, as we do not have the space, trained personnel, or equipment to carry on a Children's Home at the Camp. The purpose has been somewhat missed, in that the family situation, instead of being strengthened, has been weakened by the needless separation and dissolution of family ties. It has served to alienate children from the responsible relatives, needlessly, without giving the child substitute relationships which would be constructive for growth and development. It has relieved the parent of the care and companionship of the child without purpose, and has been used as a boarding home for those who wish to continue hold of the child, for visiting purposes only. It would appear therefore that upon subsequent interviews with the responsible relatives, that the children go back to live with the families, and that the Kinderheim, which consists of many more rooms than are now being used, be turned into living space which is so badly needed now.

DOCUMENT 5-16: Moyshe Feygnboym,[43] "Why Do We Need a Historical Commission?," *Fun letstn khurbn* (Munich, Germany), August 1946 (translated from Yiddish).

M. J. Feygnboym
Head of the Historical Commission
Why a Historical Commission?

Many among us ask: Why do we need the Historical Commission? Is the Nuremberg trial not inundated with a deluge of documents on the Jews? What can we Jews, to put it delicately, contribute? Have the great powers not compiled a huge amount of material on the Nazi era? Given this, what sort of an impact could a modest book of documents of the sort we seek to collect have?

Indeed, during the Hitlerite occupation we certainly never dreamed of occupying ourselves with such work, so difficult was it to imagine that we would

---

43. Moyshe Feygnboym (1908–1986), born in Biała Podlaska (now Poland), escaped from a deportation transport to Treblinka in 1943 and went into hiding in his home city. Initially attached to the historical commission in Lublin, he moved to the American zone in Germany in 1945 and eventually emigrated to Israel. For a history of these commissions, see Laura Jockusch, *Collect and Record! Jewish Holocaust Documentation in Early Postwar Europe, 1945–1957* (New York: Oxford University Press, 2012). This document is available digitally at https://perspectives.ushmm.org/item/moyshe-feygnboym-why-historical-commissions (accessed February 24, 2017).

even survive. Those who would like to write the history of our tragic days, we believed, would not be constrained in their work. Among the nations in countries where we were persecuted, there would be a sufficient number of witnesses to the atrocities the brown murderers inflicted upon the Jews in such a public fashion. With complete objectivity, they would convey for the historical record our tragic experiences from those days and the destruction we faced. This was our understanding of the matter.

But soon after taking the first steps we were disappointed. It became clear that not only are our neighbors unwilling to provide objective accounts, facts, and impressions, but also—on the contrary—they strive to diminish the Jewish tragedy, to whitewash it, and even—where possible—to denigrate it.

And we do not have to go very far to find this. We do not need to refer to facts from a Pole, for instance. It is sufficient simply to cite the declaration from former prime minister Churchill before the English parliament in February 1945, when Churchill declared that the Nazis, "as people were saying," had supposedly murdered upward of three million Polish Jews.

This was said by the prime minister of an empire that holds the entire world tight in the grasp of its spy services and that knows of even the smallest occurrence in the world. This was said by a statesman at a time when Poland up to the Vistula had been free for seven months . . . The Jewish Central Committee in Poland must first have the honor of calling it to Churchill's esteemed attention that it was not just "as people were saying," but unfortunately it is a sad truth that the Nazis killed 3,250,000 Polish Jews.[44]

This fact alone communicates enough, rendering reference to further examples superfluous.

The great powers have indeed compiled a huge amount of material. Yet they did not have the Jewish problem in mind, far from it. They have, first and foremost, their own interests in mind. We do not at all know whether the secret documents will remain secret. Doubt is certainly not out of place as to whether a Jewish historian will enjoy access to them. Many documents that directly pertain to us Jews are not at all being compiled by the great powers, and whose responsibility is it to do so?

Let us simply presume that they are collecting all the documents and the Jewish researcher will also have access to them. But what do the documents actually consist of?

All these documents make up only a fragment of our tragedy. They only

---

44. For a discussion of the number of Polish Jewish victims, see Raul Hilberg, *The Destruction of the European Jews*, 3rd ed. (New Haven, CT: Yale University Press, 2003), 3:1308–13.

show how the murderers dealt with us, how they treated us, and what they did with us. Did our life in those nightmarish days consist only in such fragments?

Upon which foundation will the historian be able to create a picture of what took place in the ghettos? How will he be able to fix in place our life, full of suffering and pain? From whom will he be able to learn about our heroic deeds, and how will he be able to discern our relationship with our tormentors?

Before the war, in order to fix in place Jewish life, the historian had at his disposal the Jewish press, popular creative output, record books, literature, archival material, pictures, etc. Yet today all this has disappeared.

We, the survivors, the surviving witnesses, must create for the historian documentation that will take the place of the aforementioned sources so that he may create for himself a clear picture of what happened to us and among us.

Therefore, the testimony of every surviving Jew is of immense value for us. Every song from the Nazi area, every proverb, every anecdote and joke, every photograph, every creative work, whether in the realm of literature or art. In short, anything that can in the slightest illuminate the martyrdom of our tragic generation.

It is clear that we Jews must document this bloody era ourselves. This is why the Historical Commission is needed.

The Historical Commission, however, is not only a site for compiling materials for the scholar and the researcher but also an instrument that must be used by our Jewish organizations that fight for our tomorrow in the international arena.

The Historical Commission holds materials that can be used by Jewish organizations as a weapon on behalf of our interests.

It is the duty of every Jew who tore himself away from the murderous grasp of the Hitlerites to make himself available to the Historical Commission whenever he may be asked to do so.

DOCUMENT 5-17: Testimony by Asher Zisman,[45] Munich, Germany, on German war crimes in Brest, Belarus, April 3, 1946, USHMMA RG 68.095M, reel 1, images 532–34, file 158, Yad Vashem Testimonies (M.1.E) (translated from Yiddish).

Testimony.

Taken in the Historical Commission at the Central Committee [of Liberated Jews] in Munich, April 3, 1946, from Asher Zisman. Born in 1905 in Brest-on-the-Bug.

---

45. The editors could not find further information about Zisman and Volf Glicksman, the person recording the testimony.

Taking the protocol: Volf Gliksman.

Regarding the SS General Rohde, who was the commander of the ghetto in Brest-on-the-Bug[46] from the year 1941 to the liquidation in October 1942.

When the Germans came into Brest-on-the-Bug on June 22, 1941, they caught Jews in the street, led them away to Kostełne, a suburb of Brest-on-the-Bug, ordered them to undress completely, and then shot them. Several hundred Jewish men perished at that time.

On July 12, 1941, the Wehrmacht, under the direction of the SS and Gestapo, encircled the whole city, and with the pretext that they would take Jewish men for labor, they searched through almost all Jewish apartments and took 4,870 (four thousand eight hundred and seventy) Jewish men, according to the registration of the local Jewish community. These persons were led out to the outskirts of Kostełne to the brick factories, and there they were ordered to undress completely and were shot. At the execution, they had [illegible] wolf dogs for help, which bit into the throat of every Jew who wanted to save himself by running away and pushed him right into the grave. From the peasants who lived in that area, they found out that only the Jews in the first rows were shot, while those in the back rows of the grave, whom the bullets did not succeed in hitting and killing, were buried alive. As the peasants relate further, the ground over the graves heaved for three days.

In order to efface the traces of the crime, the Germans let three Jews live of the 4,870, drove them in cars through the Jewish quarter, and forced them to shout out loud "that all those who were taken away are healthy, are living and working." But the evidence that the Jews were murdered was that later, the clothing of those who had perished was brought to the city warehouses on [illegible] street, and later the worse things were sold to peasants through auction and the better ones sent to Germany.

At the end of the year 1941, a ghetto was created, and Rohde decreed that closed Jewish workshops should be created there for Jewish tradesmen. And in order to divert attention of the Jews (who found out about the slaughters of Jews that took place in our parts of eastern White Russia) from running away to the Jewish partisans or procuring arms in the ghetto, Rohde decreed that all Jewish tradesmen who were employed in the workshops would receive special identification cards with his [Rohde's] stamp. And all the Jewish craftsmen who possessed such a card with his stamp would survive the war and would not be subject to any anti-Jewish actions.

---

46. This ghetto is also known as Brześć, located 215 miles southwest of Minsk in what is today Belarus. See Alexander Kruglov and Martin Dean, "Brześć," in Dean and Megargee, *The USHMM Encyclopedia of Camps and Ghettos*, 2: 337–39.

Rohde also created an empty square in the ghetto in Brest-on-the-Bug, between the streets Długa and Dabrowskiego, and ordered a Jewish furnace maker to make a large pit on that square and also to erect a brick fence that would embrace the locked artisan workshops and the pit that had been dug. At the same time, Rohde affirmed that the Jews who would work on the so-called Rohde-Platz would be spared from every anti-Jewish action.

Rohde also distinguished himself with his cruel acts against Jews, at the smallest instance, as he viewed it, of not properly fulfilling his orders. So, for example, whipping of bare skin until death. Heavy contributions of valuable items, gold, furs, jewelry, which for the most part went into his own pocket. Rohde himself shot many Jews, driving around with his car in the villages surrounding Brest-on-the-Bug.

On the night of the 15th to 16th October 1942, the Gestapo and the local SS police under his order encircled the ghetto, led all the Jews out to Broni-Góra [Belarusian: Bronnaia Gora; Polish: Bronna Góra], and murdered them there, explaining through the local Brest radio [loudspeaker] that Brest-on-the-Bug had been finally liberated from the Jewish pestilence and was now free of Jews. Even the Jews who worked in the workshops, whom Rohde had assured would be spared from every action, were also shot. The witness [Zisman] was hidden in a basement not far from the so-called Rohde-Platz for about three months, and over the course of that time, he could observe that the Jews who had hid before the slaughter and were later discovered by the Germans were led to the pit and shot there. Near the so-called Rohde pit was a small stall, in which every Jew had to undress completely before he was shot. Beautiful Jewish women, who had to undress completely there at the order of the German hangmen, were raped by the wild German beasts before they were shot.

[Note added by Gliksman:] *The witness lived in Brest-on-the-Bug before and during the war. He was there until its liquidation and hid in the ghetto. From the Brest community, which numbered 27,000 persons before the war, fourteen persons were miraculously saved. The witness is a son-in-law of Rabbi Lipe Klepfish, of blessed memory.*

DOCUMENT 5-18: Extracts from the file of Chaim Chajet,[47] Warsaw, on accusations of wartime collaboration, September–December 1946, USHMMA Acc. 1996.A.0223, RG 15.189M, Central Committee of Jews in Poland, People's Courts collection, SYG 313, file 14 (translated from Polish).

[Letter from engineers Wiktor Chelem, M. Vogelbaum, and Michał Prużan, Katowice, September 9, 1946, to the Central Committee of Polish Jews in Warsaw:]

We, the undersigned, as former inhabitants of the city of Wilno [Polish spelling; Lithuanian: Vilnius] resident in the prewar period and during the German occupation of Wilno, hereby affirm in relation to the report on the conference of Leaders of Jewish Committees placed in issue 31 of the journal *Dos naye lebn* on 6 September 1946 that the accusations raised by citizen Haber, secretary of the Jewish Voivodeship Committee in Katowice, are in respect to citizen Chaim Chajet, head of the Economic Central department in Katowice, fully fabricated and baseless and bear the marks of libel.

We are thoroughly familiar with citizen Chaim Chajet, his conduct, and his activities both before the war and during the occupation, and on this basis we affirm that he was not a member of the Jewish Council, he always conducted himself beyond reproach, and he was considered and is considered an upstanding person whose activities did not conflict with the law.

We hold that the interests of the Jewish community demand that the person who in such a shameless manner libeled his confrere, who underwent all the torments of the German executioners' concentration camps, be called to account and that the aggrieved party be granted redress.

[Letter from Chaim Chajet in Bytom, Poland, to the editors of *Dos naye lebn* in Łódź, September 10, 1946:]

On the basis of article 32 of the press codex in connection with the placement in issue 31 of the journal from 6 September 1946 of a report from the conference of Leaders of Jewish Committees regarding a speech given by citizen Haber, a member of the Voivodeship Committee in Katowice, I request that the following rectification be placed in the next issue of your journal.

---

47. Most likely Chaim Chajet, born in Vilna in 1891, was a survivor of the Vilna ghetto and the Kailis, Kaiserwald, Stutthof, and Burggraben camps. He was liberated in March 1945 and eventually emigrated to Israel after the war. For context, see Laura Jockusch and Gabriel N. Finder, eds., *Jewish Honor Courts: Revenge, Retribution, and Reconciliation in Europe and Israel after the Holocaust* (Detroit, MI: Wayne State University Press, 2015).

The accusation directed at me by citizen Haber, seeking to blacken my unblemished past and intended to degrade public opinion of me by accusing me of behavior contrary to legal principles and principles of honesty, bears the marks of libel, an investigation of which I am directing against citizen Haber along the appropriate legal channels.

I am firmly convinced that the judicial authorities will mete out to the perpetrator a fitting punishment for the wrong done to me.

[Letter from Chaim Chajet in Katowice to the administration of the Economic Management Board "Solidarność" in Warsaw, September 11, 1946:]

In issue 31 of the Jewish journal *Dos naye lebn* from 6 September 1946 in a report on the conference of Leaders of Jewish Committees, there appeared a notice with the following content:

"Citizen Haber, a member of the Jewish Voivodeship Committee in Katowice, demands the unmasking of a number of harmful and criminal elements that have infiltrated Jewish civic institutions. He tells of a certain Chajet, who worked in an authoritative position in the Economic Central and who turned out to be a collaborator of the *Judenrat* and a common speculator and con man."

Insofar as citizen Haber's utterances are libelous and mendacious, I request that you defend me against these accusations, that you facilitate [Haber's] being called to account via the Central Committee of Polish Jews in Warsaw, and that you demand citizen Haber immediately prove the substance of the accusations raised against my person.

Considering citizen Haber's position as secretary of the Voivodeship Committee, a civic position that requires corresponding ethical qualifications, I demand that the consequences of citizen Haber's unworthy behavior, compromising the committee, Jewish institutions, and their leadership, be drawn.

[Transcript of Emanuel Haber's testimony, given before the court secretary of the Central Committee of Polish Jews in Warsaw, November 13, 1946:]

I got to know Chajet when he worked in the Voivodeship Committee in Katowice in the Economic Central. I did not know him prior to this. That Chajet was a member of the *Judenrat* in Wilno, I heard from citizen Groll, whom I have summoned as a witness. During the occupation, I was in the Soviet Union. One time in a conversation with me [and] in the presence of engineer Rostal, chairman of our committee, and Aychenbaum, an official of the economic department, Chajet boasted that he had sold several carloads of yeast brought in from Berlin a few months prior (our conversation took place in

September of this year).[48] It is my belief that a transaction of this sort constitutes speculation and disqualifies the person in question from conducting authoritative work at a civic post. Immediately after the events in Kielce,[49] while among several people (approximately ten) at the committee's meeting place, Chajet said that the Jewish Yishuv in Poland is being liquidated and several million złoty are going into the pockets of individual members of the presidium of the Central Committee [of Polish Jews]. At the moment I don't remember who the people were in whose presence Chajet expressed himself in this way. At the conference of responsible secretaries, I made a statement along the lines that it is my belief that persons such as Chajet cannot hold authoritative positions in our civic organization, and I cited the two aforementioned cases. I did not claim at the conference that Chajet was a member of the *Judenrat*.

[Verdict of the Court of First Instance in Warsaw on libel charges brought by Chajet against Haber, presiding judge J. Szlaskiewicz, December 11, 1946:][50]

[. . .] This statement [Haber's accusations at the conference of Leaders of Jewish Committees that Chajet was a member of the *Judenrat* in Wilno] was summarized and appeared in print in the journal *Dos naye lebn*, a statement that may subject Chaim Chajet to a loss of the confidence required for his position and lower public opinion of him, an action addressed in article 255 of the Criminal Codex. Verdict: Emanuel Haber is found guilty of the act of which he is accused and will be punished in accord with articles 255 and 61 of the Criminal Codex with one month of arrest and a fine of 1,000 złoty with suspended implementation of the jail sentence for a period of three years. One hundred

---

48. Here the writer blends accusations of both wartime black-market activities and postwar profiteering.

49. This refers to mob-like violence on July 4, 1946, against Jews residing in a community building in the city of Kielce, Poland, resulting in the killing of forty-two Jews and the wounding of dozens of others. It was preceded by similar acts of collective violence in other cities and led to a wave of Jewish emigration from Poland. For more information, see Jan T. Gross, *Fear: Anti-Semitism in Poland after Auschwitz: An Essay in Historical Interpretation* (New York: Random House, 2007).

50. Following Chajet's appeal in the face of the libel charges, the "Solidarność" board requested that a Citizen's Court affiliated with the Jewish Central Committee take up the issue on September 18, 1946. On November 7, Haber wrote to the same court, stating that he was not the author of the original statement. Nonetheless, Haber was called to court as a witness on November 14. On November 30, the Jewish Committee of Katowice called on the Citizen's Court to bring Haber to the non-Jewish Magistrate Court of Warsaw, this time as the accused (by Chajet). Thus, the case was adjudicated before two courts simultaneously, which probably explains the delay. After the Warsaw Magistrate Court had found Haber guilty on December 11, 1946, the Jewish Central Committee's Citizen's Court dropped all charges against Chajet on August 27, 1947, for lack of evidence.

forty złoty are to be collected from the convicted as a court fee, and the convicted is adjudged [responsible] for reimbursement of the costs of conducting the proceedings.

DOCUMENT 5-19: "Spoils, Restitution, Reintegration," *Bulletin du Centre Israélite d'Information* **(Paris), December 1, 1946, USHMMA RG 68.066M, reel 50 (Selected Records from the AJJDC Archives, Jerusalem) (translated from French).**

[. . .]
Bad Faith Occupants

Annette Joubert, in the November 28, 1946, *Fraternité* [periodical], having shown that there are still too many despoiled persons without a roof over their heads, turns her attention to the situation, particularly worthy of attention, of Jews who have had the opportunity to assess the shortcomings of justice in their regard. It suffices for the adversary of the despoiled person to be a tactician of the law to succeed in turning to his advantage the circumstances that are legally the least favorable to him. Annette Joubert cites the two following cases:

["]I was going to see Mme L., boulevard Magenta, who, as a repatriated deportee and wife of a deportee who has disappeared, appeared to have a right of priority over the tenant of her lodging.

That's what I thought, myself, she said, and she told me her story:

When I came back from deportation, I brought an action to be able to regain my lodging. At the end of six months, it was announced that I had won, but I was forbidden to evict the tenant.

The tenant was probably a victim?

He had actually succeeded in making that believed, but it was very simple to show that he had made use of the damaged villa of his parents. Now since 1938, he possessed another apartment in the same house, in addition to mine. If he had really been a victim since 1940, as he says, where did he live until 1943, since it's just at that time that he entered my place?

I knew, quite simply, that he had lived in his second lodging. For that matter, he always owned it, but the concierge didn't want to attest to that.

And you yourself, how did you live?

For a year and a half now, I have lived with my son and the two children of my brother, whom I have kept with me since the deportation of their father, at my parents' expense. We live, ten of us, in their three-room apartment. I tried to work as a salesperson in a store, but after I went to the medical examination at the police headquarters, the doctor ordered me to stop, because, since my return from deportation, I am at risk of developing tuberculosis.

I ask only one thing, you know, that is to regain at least my four walls. I will never find my furniture and my machines, but I may be able, with the help of some friends, to restart the fur workshop that we had before, and my son could work there.

But have you spoken before the Commission of Rehousing to get a requisition?

Yes, actually. But it's a rather vague hope. Here is what happened to me recently: I heard one day that a tenant in my house was dead and that his lodging was empty. So I wanted to have it requisitioned for my benefit. But the heirs intervened, saying that the daughter of this woman wanted to move in there. Thus I had to withdraw, and today the lodging has been rented to a tenant who has nothing to do with that family.

Mme L seemed weary from all this, weary of always finding herself back in the middle of this vicious circle. She will appeal, but her action will not go to court until sometime in 1947.

[illegible] she will have to be patient. She will have to wait, always wait.["]

Therese G. has had no luck either. For two years, she has dragged herself from hotel rooms to garrets, the apartment of her parents, who died during deportation, now occupied by a single woman who does not want to give it back. The lawsuit, after a year of maneuvers from agency to agency, just ended like many others: no eviction. Here are the facts, according to Therese G.:

["]This woman, installed in my parents' lodging,["] she says, ["]has naturally used all the means in her possession to remain there. She lived there before as the common-law wife of a man who was deported. When that person came back, she declared herself the wife of another deported person, and the lawsuit has proceeded on that basis.

As for me, I have had endless difficulty proving that this apartment was that of my parents and that I, a minor at that time, lived there too. The owner of the house, a former collaborator, has never wanted to provide me with an affidavit. Only after numerous investigations have I been able to prove it.["]

These examples are taken at random, but how many others could be cited of human beings whom the war has placed "on the margin of the life of others."
[. . .]

DOCUMENT 5-20: Selection from the memorial book for Jewish victims in Tunisia edited by Gaston Guez, *Nos martyrs sous la botte Allemande. Ou' les ex-travailleurs juifs de Tunisie racontent leurs souffrances* (Tunis: G. Guez, 1946) (translated from French and Judeo-Arabic).[51]

[Opening]

This work has been undertaken following the loss of my poor brother at the Jewish forced labor camp of El-Aouina[52] and particularly traces the life of the Jewish forced laborers under the German occupation of Tunisia.

As a result of the appeals of many of my coreligionists and, most particularly, the parents of certain Jewish forced laborers who died at the camp, I have gathered the photos of these poor martyrs and have continued in Judeo-Arabic rather than in French since it is the daily language of the laborers.

I believe that I have thus contributed to relieving the parents of the murder [victims] belonging to the Tunisian ghetto and who read predominantly in Judeo-Arabic.

Preface

This work, titled "Our Martyrs under the German Boot," is not a defense presented by an abettor or a revelation of certain glorious facts but a living story of a life, during the German occupation of Tunisia, of my brothers, the "Jewish ex–forced laborers" in different German camps.

---

51. Gaston Guez, a mohel (the person required to perform the ritual circumcision ceremony for Jewish boys) of the Tunisian Jewish community, created a memorial book for his brother, Simon-Chalom Guez, who died during the bombing of the El-Aouina, and for other Tunisian men who died or were killed as a result of forced labor. The book is separated into several parts, in both French and Judeo-Arabic. The French section includes a brief description about the phenomenon of Jewish forced laborers in Tunisia during the war, an explanation about the editor's motives in creating the book, and extensive lists of the dead and how they died. Guez also includes lists of the forced labor camps that existed in Tunisia during the Nazi occupation, plus diary and letter transcriptions that speak to the Tunisian experience, along with an *ashkavah* service, a Sephardic memorial service. Featured here are the opening and conclusion of the book, which establish its primary purpose. Guez's narrative traverses a fine line between rage and restraint to avoid running afoul of postwar government censorship, in 1946 still run by wartime antisemitic Vichy officials. For more information on Jewish forced labor in wartime Tunisia, see *The USHMM Encyclopedia of Camps and Ghettos*, 1933–1945, 3 (forthcoming).

52. El-Aouina was an airfield near the city of Tunis. A photo and short description of Gaston Guez's brother Simon-Chalom appeared in the book. He died on February 24, 1943, from injuries sustained in an Allied bombing of El-Aouina. See *The USHMM Encyclopedia of Camps and Ghettos, 1933–1945*, 4 (forthcoming).

The loss of the flower of the age to the abominable suffering of my brother Simon-Chalom, forced laborer in El-Aouina, prompted me to write the present work.

Many were like him, underwent the same thing, and had to suffer not only injustice, cynicism, and German tyranny but also a horrific death as a result of their forced labor.

While feeling the pain of the loss so dear of my brother and understanding that families are tried by the same grief, I have faithfully retraced in this work the journeys experienced by many among us.

Then compare, our readers here, the serious misconduct by some, the unqualified egoism of many others, and the combined prejudicial nature of many rogues to the heroism and devotion of many of our coreligionists.

In the memory of the poor fallen martyrs of the front, in their youth, health, and vigor,

Pray for the peace of their souls,

Amen.

F. H. G. Guez, mohel

[. . .]

Conclusive moral of "the work":

We can observe that the worst with which we were overwhelmed lasted only a little while and cannot be compared with the countries of Europe.

Each of us has a duty to God, and every believer must love God and emulate His example of justice.

One must adore him, for he gives grace and protection to us.

Please pray now for his assistance, in these hours of distress, with our numerous needs.

We must have a sense of recognition of a boundless God, under whose protection the people [of] Israel escaped slavery in Egypt, Babylon,[53] and the extermination of the race under the "German boot" and have survived all the overwhelming pain and oppression through the centuries.

But we will not forget that this point is essential:

"Love your neighbor as yourself."[54]

What does this mean?

Next, listen to us, everyone, of every origin, race, or religion.

---

53. This refers to the exodus from Egypt and to the Babylonian exile, during which the Babylonians subjugated the Jews of ancient Judea.

54. This refers to Leviticus 19:18.

As it is prescribed in the "oral law,"[55] take part in the future life of justice for all the nations.

We must impose upon ourselves the necessity of justice and charity.

Our religion recommends particular love and respect for all who are superior in "wisdom, experience, and virtue."

A particular pity to the wounded, the infirm, the orphans, the widows.

This remains the great duty, the duty to our mother, the homeland.

The homeland is the country where one is born, where one lives under its protection, and where one rests upon death.

All Israelites must love their homeland, France, contribute to its material and moral prosperity, subordinate themselves to the interests of their country.

Also, one must defend his homeland, at risk to his life, against all aggressors.

As it is said in Jeremiah XXIX[56]

Contribute to the salvation of the state from which I have been transported . . .

Pray God for its [France's] happiness, because your prosperity depends on her.

Amen.

The Last Hour

To those who were kind enough to respond to my call:

In response to my call released on the 11 and the 15 of June, given a delay to the 20 of June 1946, many relatives of the dead wanted to write me.

I thank them and take note.

To my great regret I cannot include in my work their communications:

The work is finished, their letters were received after the delay indicated.

Concerning only the Jewish ex–forced laborers, I cannot, in fact, speak about deportees assassinated or those who disappeared. All of them are also our martyrs, but given the multitude of these cases, the work would have been delayed and could not, moreover, represent the sense set out in the preface.

---

55. This refers to the Mishnah, or the "oral law" of Judaism, which captures rabbinic interpretation and codification of Jewish law dating to the third century CE.

56. This refers to Jeremiah 29:7, Jeremiah's letter to the exiles, in which God implores the people of Israel living in Babylon, "Seek the welfare of the city to which I have exiled you and pray to the Lord in its behalf; for in its prosperity you shall prosper" (Jewish Publication Society translation).

DOCUMENT 5-21: Lyrics by Samson Först,[57] *Der Grager. Gesriben in Lager* **(Bucharest, 1947), for the Purim holiday, USHMMA Acc. 2010.343 (translated from Yiddish).**

"Samson Först, *The Gragger*[58], written in the Camp, for Purim, a brochure full of satire on Hitler's carcass and his great strength, Bucharest, 1947."

---

57. Samson Först (1888–1968), a folk poet and performer, was born in Novoselitsa, Bukovina. He also published *Geklibene lider* (Czernowitz, 1922) and *Truvadurishe lider* (Bucharest, 1962). One of his song-parodies appears with music in the anthology *15 cântece idis popularizatee* (Bucharest, 1946). The text translated here was written in Yiddish using Romanian orthography.

58. A gragger is a traditional Purim noisemaker.

For the Purim holiday, a brochure
With nothing but satire
For Jews, a compromise:
On Hitler's carcass
And his great strength,
It's the GRAGGER
From inside a former camp[59]

[. . .]

A Great Purim Sensation

How Haman had an audience with God.

According to the latest radio reports on Rosh Chodesh Adar,[60] the following Purim sensation is reported specially for our Purim *Gragger*:

We draw the attention of our *Gragger* readers to the fact that everyone ought to read this article attentively and ought not to think that this is simply a fabricated Purim tale to entertain the people a bit during Purim season.

Two weeks before Purim, a grandson of the famous Indian poet Rabindranath Tagore,[61] the famous fakir and spiritualist Ordmulz Tagos, came from India to Schischam-Haborn. As soon as he checked into the Karmalecho Hotel, he found a waiter who was a great medium. When the great spiritualists there became aware of this medium, the spiritualist association invited him to a séance. And here we present every word the spirit of Haman the Evil said to the medium:

"Spiritualists, my friends, you ought to know the spirit that speaks to you from the other world is I, the renowned Haman the Evil, the former prime minister of the historic King Ahasuerus,[62] who lives together with his beloved wife, Ester-Hamalku,[63] and his dear father, the Zadik Moredechai,[64] in Gan

---

59. Although the writer does not specify which camp he means, it was most likely one in the Transnistria region.

60. This is the first day of the month of Adar, which in 1947 corresponded to February 21.

61. Rabindranath Tagore (1861–1941), a famous Indian poet, was the first non-European to win the Nobel Prize for Literature in 1913.

62. This was the king of Persia, as noted in the Book of Esther. King Ahasuerus marries Esther (Hadassah) and begins the narrative of the Purim story.

63. Literally, "Esther the Queen"; this phrase is an honorific that refers to Esther's role as the savior of the Jewish people in the Purim narrative.

64. Literally, "Mordechai the Wise"; this phrase is an honorific that refers to Mordechai's role as Esther's uncle, guardian, and counsel. His refusal to bow down to Haman inflames the latter's anger toward the Jewish people.

Eden.[65] I can only tell you that all three are, *baruch hashem*,[66] healthy and living a princely life and prospering. They convey greetings to all the Jews and all say amen. Perhaps you'd like to ask me when I, the renowned Haman, suddenly turned into a *zadik* in a fur coat[67] who bestows greetings upon the Jews. Have a bit of patience as I'll tell you how my hellish life was transformed, after so many years of broiling and baking in hell, thanks to the Hitleriade with its fascist Hamans who are now in hell and are occupying all the sections until more chambers can be built. We, the old Haman prisoner-villains, like Titus,[68] Pare, Bilem,[69] Bulok, Nero,[70] and from modern times Lueger,[71] Purishkewich,[72] Kru-jewan, Petlura,[73] Codreanu,[74] Totu, Cuza, Goga, Antonescu, etc., etc., whose names the devil may know. But as soon as I rested a little from such a long period of torment in hell and recovered a bit, I got up several weeks ago and went to my friend Moredechai and asked him to urge Paul[75] to grant me an audience at the Beit Din Shel Maalah[76] because I had a brand-new Purim project. Moredechai received me in a very friendly manner and explained to me he was very pleased that after such a long time I hadn't forgotten that a nation of Israel exists. And after so much hell, I even wanted to present a project to God to expand and beautify their Purim. It didn't take long to convince Moredechai, and he left with me for Gan Eden Street and introduced me to the king that

---

65. This Hebrew reference to the Garden of Eden is a common reference to the "world to come," the reward of the righteous.

66. Literally, "blessed be the Name"; this is a common Hebrew reference to God.

67. This refers to the image of a wise scholar.

68. The Roman emperor Titus (39–81 CE) raided and conquered the city of Jerusalem and was responsible for the sacking of the Holy Temple in 70 CE.

69. This is a biblical enemy of the Jewish people.

70. The Roman emperor Nero (37–68 CE) is commonly held responsible for the burning of Rome in 64 CE.

71. This refers to Karl Lueger (1844–1910), Austrian politician and founder of the anti-semitic Austrian Christian Social Party.

72. Vladimir Purishkevich (1870–1920) was an antisemitic Russian politician in the years prior to the Bolshevik Revolution.

73. Symon Petliura (1879–1926) was a Ukrainian nationalist and politician known for his antisemitic views.

74. Corneliu Zelea Codreanu (1899–1938) was leader and founder of the Romanian Iron Guard, a nationalist, antisemitic, and local fascist party that briefly staged a coup in 1941. On the other authoritarian Romanian politicians mentioned in this sentence, see Radu Ioanid, *The Holocaust in Romania: The Destruction of Jews and Gypsies under the Antonescu Regime, 1940–1944* (Chicago: Ivan R. Dee in association with USHMM, 2000).

75. This refers ironically to Paul the Apostle, who was known to have loosened rabbinic law and prohibitions.

76. Literally, "the heavenly house of justice."

stands before the gate of the Beit Din Shel Maalah with his fiery sword. Moredechai displayed his business card, [and] we were immediately led into a corridor full of diamonds. The king there, Gavril,[77] instructed us to sit on two diamond chairs, demanded for us a roll of parchment, and asked us to write down what sort of a request we had. After a few minutes, we were led into a large chamber where a council of kings and *zadiks* [wise men] sat. One of the kings said to me in a very friendly tone:

'Do not fear, my child, and say what you request.' And I introduced myself: I am Haman, and I suffered for so many years in the hellish camp for nothing, only because one Purim I got drunk and had an incident with our friend Moredechai—here he stands before you, heavenly lords! Let him say it. Did I even touch him with my hand? It's only because I felt insulted as minister when my friend Moredechai saw me on my way to the royal court and didn't greet me. And this is why I gave the order that all the Jews from throughout the country should leave for Eretz Israel. And what the consequences were, oh my lords, you certainly read in the Book of Esther, and how I suffered a bitter defeat. And thanks to my defeat, the Jews got a holiday, our dear, beloved Purim. And every year when the Jews read the Book of Esther and when my name Haman is mentioned, I really hear it from the Jews, partly with graggers, partly by tapping feet, and my head becomes so confused that I don't know what sort of world it is I'm in. And this is indeed why I want to ask God to forgive me my sins against his people Israel. I now want to convert to Judaism and to change my name from Haman the Evil to Haman HaZadik, and the entire Book of Esther starting with the current Purim should be changed to the Book of Hitler, and instead of Hamantaschen[78] with three points, Hitlertaschen with 12 points should be made,[79] and Purim should not be in the middle of [the month of] Adar but rather on the day the Red Army strolled into Berlin and destroyed Hitler, the Haman of the world, together with his SS bandits. And now we all have a happy Purim.

Your grateful friend,
Haman HaZadik[80]"

---

77. This refers to Gabriel, the archangel, who serves as the messenger of God.

78. This is a triangular cookie eaten on Purim that mimics the three-cornered hat of Haman.

79. This refers to a double six-pointed star to represent the Magen David.

80. The signatory, "Haman HaZadik," translates to "Haman the Wise." The writer uses this tongue-in-cheek title to reverse Haman's status from pariah to wise rabbinic scholar.

DOCUMENT 5-22: Letter by Rachel Nordheim,[81] near Leiden, the Netherlands, to her children in the Kfar Hassidim settlement, Palestine, December 19, 1946, USHMMA Acc. 2007.510.1, Moshe and Chaya Nordheim collection (translated from Dutch).

Dear Children!

Although I haven't received any mail from you, I do write this letter. There is a sharp frost. During the day 7 degrees and 0 at night. There is skating on all the canals. The whole week there was a terrible wind. Therefore the ice was unreliable [unsafe] for a long time. The Ijselmeer was not navigable; the Wadden Islands are once again isolated. Almost everywhere on the big rivers shipping is at a standstill. The room cannot get warmer than 55 degrees. I walk around with 2 sweaters on top of each other and long slacks. The cold is the reason why I still haven't been to Leiden. There is a thaw in the forecast, so next week I will be able to travel. We have little gas for cooking because of a shortage of coal. My meals are not elaborate, so that doesn't bother me much. As you can gather from this letter, there is no El Dorado here in Holland. There hasn't been any snow yet. Lucky, because overshoes are not available, and our shoes are not waterproof.

In the meantime it's Chanukah, so I wish you many more years. You will understand that I pass these days without any cheer. At school there was a big celebration where children were well entertained. On the radio there were 2 broadcasts in honor of Chanukah. There are efforts from all sides to propagate [our] traditions. There are due to be a variety of meetings that are arranged through the Central Committee of the Jewish community and JNF [Joods Nationaal Fond, Jewish National Fund]. If the program is very good, then people will definitely come. You have to have lots of energy in this cold weather to go there.

How are things now with Moshe? Is his fever gone completely and the diarrhea as well? Have you as a result of his illness been able to achieve anything concerning a visitor's visa? From Holland there is no way to achieve anything, and applications that are filed here are forwarded to Palestine for review. That

---

81. Rachel (Chelly) Nordheim, born in 1914 as daughter of a prosperous Amsterdam businessman, had been deported with her husband, David, and two of her four children to Bergen-Belsen via Westerbork. David Nordheim died shortly after the family's liberation; their children, Moshe, Batsheva, Rivka, and Shimon, left in June 1946 to live in Kfar Hassidim, a religious settlement near Haifa. Rachel Nordheim wrote her letter while waiting for her visa to join her children. She later remarried in Israel and had three additional children.

means that however often I try, my name always appears before the same person with the same set of eyes. But the gentlemen at the consulate will not even accept an application made in Holland. It's still not very easy here.

Can you imagine what it is like to live all alone under such a nerve-racking strain? From time to time I have the desire to smash everything to bits and pieces.

Last Shabbat I was the guest of the Hartog Jacobs family. They can't understand why I don't visit them more often. But even if I weren't busy, I am too apathetic to walk all the way to the stadium. After my visit with them, I also stopped by the old Jacobs couple in the Harmony Hof. The *zij* [wife] is laid up with a nerve inflammation in her back. Otherwise they are doing well. I think often that these people are waiting for their deaths because they will never get to go to Palestine.

[. . .]

As you can see, I don't have much to talk about. The non-Jews here talk only about *Ling gadjatie* (Indonesia),[82] something that doesn't interest me enough. The parliamentary debates dominate the radio all day. That too doesn't interest me. I don't hear much about certificates, and that is all I want to know about. But perhaps there will be some light shed on that issue soon. So much for now. All the best and kisses and a speedy *Lehitra'ot*.[83]

Chelly
[. . .]

DOCUMENT 5-23: Jacob Pat,[84] *Ashes and Fire* (New York: International Universities Press, 1947), 248–54, on the Jewish past and future in Poland.

[. . .]

I think back to the things I have seen, and the talks I have had. I run through my catechism: What would the Jews of Poland do if they had freedom

---

82. This refers to the Linggadjati, or Cheribon, Agreement, which declared Indonesian independence from the Netherlands on November 15, 1946.

83. This is Hebrew for "see you later."

84. Jacob Pat (1890–1966), a renowned Yiddish writer and educator, had directed Poland's secular Central Jewish School System before he left for the United States in 1938. He served as executive secretary of the Jewish Labor Committee from 1939 until 1962; based on his visit to Poland after the war, Pat published his travelogue first in Yiddish in 1946 and one year later in English under the title *Ashes and Fire*. He authored over twenty books and helped found the World Congress of Jewish Culture, which sought to revitalize Jewish cultural life in the postwar years.

of action?—They would leave Poland. What do they do while they are prevented from leaving?—They try to rebuild Jewish communities. What would Poland's 80,000 Jews do if they were presented with 80,000 certificates for Palestine?—They would have themselves shipped to Palestine with the least possible delay. What would they do if they were given 80,000 visas to America?—They would sail for America with the least possible delay. Almost all of the 4,000 Jews who gave me letters to their relatives in America begged for visas and affidavits. At the same time the manager of a Palestine bureau told me that Jews come in thousands and ask for Palestine certificates. Is it Palestine they want then, or America? Do these facts contradict each other? No, for the Jews' urge to leave Poland is stronger than their preference for this or that place.

And yet, stronger even than their longing to emigrate is their urge for immediate reconstruction. Simultaneous with their frontier sneaking, towards Germany and the Displaced Persons camps, towards Palestine and the beckoning Eden of America, goes the upbuilding of producer-cooperatives—30 of them to date—of trade courses, schools, kindergartens, newspapers, magazines, and theaters. Łodz is the best example; every Jewish problem goes into the Lodz melting pot where Zionism, escapism, and reconstruction coexist in a single compound.

[. . .]

Yes, it is true that the Government disapproves of anti-Semitism. It is true also that in 1945 it contributed 92,000,000 zloties (then worth about 180,000 dollars) to various Jewish institutions. But it is false to say that only "sinister elements" engage in Jew-baiting. The Polish people as such is rotten with anti-Semitism.

[. . .]

But there is hope and comfort in the Jews themselves and in their brave new beginnings. Perhaps there is comfort also in the 150,000 Jews now pouring back from Russia. Some 200,000,000 zloties are required to set them up again; 100 large new homes are needed for them, thousands of ruined buildings have to be put back in condition; 40 more hostels must be set up, to say nothing of more cooperatives, schools, kindergartens, hospitals. The dreams come easily, airy castles that represent Jewish revival and reconstruction with 150,000 Jews from Russia lending a hand, with all of America's Jews lending a hand.

Where is the truth? Shall I find it in the Zamocz forest where twenty-two Jewish partisans were left unburied by their Polish murderers? Shall I find it on Savinsko Street in Tarnov, where a Jew was shot behind a sentried door? Or shall I find it in the thirty new cooperatives of Jewish tailors, carpenters and bakers; and in the reconstituted Jewish communities of thirty Polish cities?

[. . .]

I have with me a photograph taken just after the Germans had blown up the world-famous Central Synagogue of Warsaw. Flanking the entrance to the Synagogue were two massive pedestals, each supporting a gigantic carved menorah, the ancient Jewish seven-armed candelabra. On Sabbath and festival nights these great menorahs blazed with fourteen lights. They were ancient traditional symbols, replicas of the great menorah which two-thousand years ago illuminated the Temple on Mount Zion, which was carried in triumph through the streets of Rome and which still graces the Triumphal Arch of Titus, sacker of Jerusalem. Through two millennia the menorah burned in every pious Jewish home.

. . . A few moments after the Germans lit the fuse, the stately edifice was razed to the ground. By some quirk of chance the two menorahs remained standing, their arms still upraised as though waiting to be lit again.

LIST OF DOCUMENTS

PART I: 1933–1938

DOCUMENT 1-1:[1] Editorial in *Jüdische Rundschau* (Berlin), "Inner Security," on German Zionists' assessment of the Nazi takeover, February 3, 1933, 45–46 (translated from German).

DOCUMENT 1-2:[2] Press release by CV, Berlin, on reports of anti-Jewish acts in Germany, March 24, 1933, *CV-Zeitung*, March 30, 1933, 2 (translated from German).

DOCUMENT 1-3:[3] Diary entry by Mally Dienemann, Offenbach, Germany, for April 3, 1933, on the nationwide boycott of Jewish businesses, LBINY MM 18, 11a (translated from German).

DOCUMENT 1-4:[4] Photograph of Beate Berger and youth from the Beith Ahawah Children's Home on an excursion near Berlin, 1934, USHMMPA WS# 48874.

The following footnotes offer a document number concordance with our five-volume series *Jewish Responses to Persecution, 1933–1946* (2010–2015):

1. *Jewish Responses to Persecution*, 1:*1933–1938*, Document 1–2.
2. *Jewish Responses to Persecution*, 1:*1933–1938*, Document 1–5.
3. *Jewish Responses to Persecution*, 1:*1933–1938*, Document 1–11.
4. *Jewish Responses to Persecution*, 1:*1933–1938*, Document 3–3.

DOCUMENT 1-5:[5] Account by Max Abraham, Czechoslovakia, on his experiences in the Oranienburg concentration camp, first printed in *Juda verrecke: Ein Rabbiner im Konzentrationslager* (Templitz-Schönau: Druck- und Verlagsanstalt, 1934) (translated from German).

DOCUMENT 1-6:[6] Letter by League of Jewish Women, Berlin, to the Reich leader of the Nazi Women's League on the future of Jewish children in Germany, November 8, 1934, USHMMA RG 11.001M.31, reel 128 (SAM 721-1-2809, 57–58) (translated from German).

DOCUMENT 1-7:[7] Note by Max Rosenthal on the bar mitzvah of his grandson, Hans Rosenthal, April 13, 1935, USHMMPA WS# 28738.

DOCUMENT 1-8:[8] Letter by Julius Moses, Berlin, to Erwin Moses, Tel Aviv, on his visions for the family's future, September 1935, translated from Dieter Fricke, *Jüdisches Leben in Berlin und Tel Aviv, 1933–1939: Der Briefwechsel des ehemaligen Reichstagsabgeordneten Dr. Julius Moses* (Hamburg: von Bockel, 1997), 370–71.

DOCUMENT 1-9:[9] Report by Bernhard Kahn, AJJDC, European Executive Council, Geneva, titled "Jewish Conditions in Germany," November 29, 1935, AJJDC Archive AR 3344/629.

DOCUMENT 1-10:[10] Photograph of students from different Jewish schools in Berlin gathering around their banners for a sports competition, no date (1936–1938), USHMMPA WS# 12854.

DOCUMENT 1-11:[11] Philipp Flesch, New York, "My Life in Germany before and after January 30, 1933," on the "Anschluss" of Austria in early 1938, LBINY MM 22/ME 132, 10–17 (translated from German).

DOCUMENT 1-12:[12] Report from files of the Jewish Telegraph Agency, Paris, by an unidentified author on the persecution of Jews in central European

---

5. *Jewish Responses to Persecution*, 1:*1933–1938*, Document 3–8.
6. *Jewish Responses to Persecution*, 1:*1933–1938*, Document 4–3.
7. *Jewish Responses to Persecution*, 1:*1933–1938*, Document 6–10.
8. *Jewish Responses to Persecution*, 1:*1933–1938*, Document 7–3.
9. *Jewish Responses to Persecution*, 1:*1933–1938*, Document 8–2.
10. *Jewish Responses to Persecution*, 1:*1933–1938*, Document 8–19.
11. *Jewish Responses to Persecution*, 1:*1933–1938*, Document 10–4.
12. *Jewish Responses to Persecution*, 1:*1933–1938*, Document 10–7.

countries in the first half of June 1938, USHMMA RG 11.001M.25, reel 106 (SAM 674-1-109, 114–22) (translated from German).

DOCUMENT 1-13:[13] Diary entry by Ruth Maier, Vienna, for October 2, 1938, on her Jewish identity, translated from Ruth Maier, *"Das Leben könnte gut sein": Tagebücher 1933 bis 1942*, ed. Jan Erik Vold (Stuttgart: DVA, 2008), 134–36.

DOCUMENT 1-14:[14] Letter by Gerhard Kann, Berlin, to Heinz Kellermann, New York, on the spiritual impact of persecution, October 24, 1938, USHMMA Acc. 2007.96, Kellermann collection, box 4 (translated from German).

DOCUMENT 1-15:[15] Letter by Emanuel Ringelblum, Środborów, Poland, to Raphael Mahler, New York, December 6, 1938, on the fate of Jewish expellees in the Polish-German border region, Moreshet Archive D.1.4927 (translated from Yiddish).

DOCUMENT 1-16:[16] Ovadia Camhy, "Under the Sign of Satan," on pogrom violence in Germany, *Le Judaïsme séphardi* (Paris), December 1938 (translated from French).

DOCUMENT 1-17:[17] Speech by Léon Blum, Paris, delivered at the banquet dinner at the ninth annual meeting of the International League against Antisemitism, November 26, 1938, CDJC fonds LICA, CMXCVI/série I/3.2.2, dossier no. 42, 2–12 (translated from French).

DOCUMENT 1-18:[18] Account by Max Eschelbacher, England, on his imprisonment following *"Kristallnacht,"* written in spring/early summer 1939, translated from Max Eschelbacher, *Der zehnte November 1938* (Essen: Klartext, 1998), 41–54.

---

13. *Jewish Responses to Persecution, 1:1933–1938*, Document 9–6.
14. *Jewish Responses to Persecution, 1:1933–1938*, Document 11–5.
15. *Jewish Responses to Persecution, 2:1938–1940*, Document 1–1.
16. *Jewish Responses to Persecution, 2:1938–1940*, Document 1–7.
17. *Jewish Responses to Persecution, 2:1938–1940*, Document 1–8.
18. *Jewish Responses to Persecution, 1:1933–1938*, Document 12–10.

DOCUMENT 1-19:[19] Letter by Georg Landauer, Jerusalem, to Henry Montor, New York, on the mood among German Jews, December 2, 1938, CZA RG S25/9703.

DOCUMENT 1-20:[20] Letter by Leon Gattegno, Salonika, Greece, to the WJC Paris, June 7, 1939, on the plight of Jews on refugee ships, USHMMA RG 11.001 M36, reel 107 (SAM 1190-1-299) (translated from French).

PART II: 1939–1940

DOCUMENT 2-1:[21] Testimony by an unidentified woman from Lipno, Poland, on the first days of war, recorded ca. 1940 in the Warsaw ghetto, USHMMA RG 15.079M (ŻIH Ring. I/854), reel 39 (translated from Polish).

DOCUMENT 2-2:[22] Shimon Huberband, Warsaw, "The Destruction of Synagogues, Study Halls, and Cemeteries," no date (ca. 1941), USHMMA RG 15.079M (ŻIH Ring. I/108), reel 7 (translated from Yiddish).

DOCUMENT 2-3:[23] "Nazis Establish More Ghettos in Poland," *Canadian Jewish Chronicle* (Montreal), January 12, 1940, 5.

DOCUMENT 2-4:[24] S. Moldawer, "The Road to Lublin," on his deportation from Hamburg in October 1939, *Contemporary Jewish Record* (New York) 3 (March–April 1940): 120–21.

DOCUMENT 2-5:[25] Photograph of Warsaw Jews, wearing armbands, selling their possessions out of suitcases in a makeshift market on a bombed-out street, December 1939, USHMMPA WS# 31515.

DOCUMENT 2-6:[26] Letter by Jenny Marx, Mannheim, Germany, to Max Marx and family, Jerusalem, on her daily struggles, January 14, 1940, private collection (translated from German).

---

19. *Jewish Responses to Persecution*, 1:*1933–1938*, Document 12–18.
20. *Jewish Responses to Persecution*, 2:*1938–1940*, Document 2–19.
21. *Jewish Responses to Persecution*, 2:*1938–1940*, Document 4–6.
22. *Jewish Responses to Persecution*, 2:*1938–1940*, Document 4–10.
23. *Jewish Responses to Persecution*, 2:*1938–1940*, Document 9–3.
24. *Jewish Responses to Persecution*, 2:*1938–1940*, Document 9–2.
25. *Jewish Responses to Persecution*, 2:*1938–1940*, Document 10–4.
26. *Jewish Responses to Persecution*, 2:*1938–1940*, Document 8–15.

DOCUMENT 2-7:[27] Account by an unidentified woman on the German/ Soviet occupation of Zamość, no date (ca. 1941), USHMMA RG 15.079M (ŻIH Ring. I/935), reel 42 (translated from Yiddish).

DOCUMENT 2-8:[28] Letter by Moshe Kleinbaum, Geneva, to Nahum Goldmann, New York, on the situation in Soviet-occupied Poland, March 12, 1940, facsimile reprinted in *Archives of the Holocaust*, ed. Abraham J. Peck (New York: Garland Publishing, 1990), 8:112–13.

DOCUMENT 2-9:[29] Photograph of Willem Friedman, a soldier in the Belgian army, posing next to a piece of artillery, winter 1939–1940, USHMMPA WS# 20481.

DOCUMENT 2-10:[30] Eugen Tillinger, "The Bridge of Hendaye: Eyewitness Account of the Mass Flight to Spain," *Aufbau* (New York), August 30, 1940, 2 (translated from German).

DOCUMENT 2-11:[31] Letter by an unidentified Jewish correspondent in Casablanca, French-administered Morocco, on local conditions, August 28, 1940, USHMMA RG 68.045M (WJC Geneva C 3/1), 203–4 (translated from German).

DOCUMENT 2-12:[32] Report by AJJDC Warsaw about its relief work during the period September 1939–October 1940, USHMMA Acc. 1999.A.0154 (ŻIH 210/6), 10–12 (translated from Yiddish).

DOCUMENT 2-13:[33] Kalman Huberband, Warsaw, "The 'March' into the *Mikveh*," October 1940, USHMMA RG 15.079M (ŻIH Ring. I/218), reel 11 (translated from Yiddish).

DOCUMENT 2-14:[34] Letter by Wilhelm Filderman and Isac Brucăr, Bucharest, to Ion Antonescu, Romanian prime minister, September 30, 1940,

27. *Jewish Responses to Persecution*, 2:*1938–1940*, Document 5–9.
28. *Jewish Responses to Persecution*, 2:*1938–1940*, Document 5–10.
29. *Jewish Responses to Persecution*, 2:*1938–1940*, Document 7–8.
30. *Jewish Responses to Persecution*, 2:*1938–1940*, Document 7–14.
31. *Jewish Responses to Persecution*, 2:*1938–1940*, Document 7–16.
32. *Jewish Responses to Persecution*, 2:*1938–1940*, Document 6–1.
33. *Jewish Responses to Persecution*, 2:*1938–1940*, Document 12–1.
34. *Jewish Responses to Persecution*, 2:*1938–1940*, Document 8–3.

in *DOCUMENTs Concerning the Fate of Romanian Jewry during the Holocaust*, ed. Jean Ancel (New York: Beate Klarsfeld Foundation, 1986), 1:528–30 (translated from Romanian).

DOCUMENT 2-15:[35] Diary entry by an unidentified man, Łódź, Warthegau, on the struggle for bread in the ghetto, December 15, 1940, USHMMA RG 02.208M (ŻIH 302/191) (translated from Polish).

PART III: 1941–1942

DOCUMENT 3-1:[36] Account by an unidentified person, Warsaw, on the eve of Passover in the ghetto, April 11, 1941, USHMM RG 15.079 (ŻIH Ring. I/1024) (translated from Yiddish).

DOCUMENT 3-2:[37] Diary entry by Hermann Hakel, camp Alberobello near Bari, Italy, for May 20, 1941, on a visit by Catholic dignitaries, Austrian National Library Vienna 221/04 (translated from German).

DOCUMENT 3-3:[38] "One Year Sosúa Settlement," on Jewish emigration to the Dominican Republic, *Jüdisches Nachrichtenblatt* (Prague), May 2, 1941, 1 (translated from German).

DOCUMENT 3-4:[39] Leib Spiesman, "In the Warsaw Ghetto," *Contemporary Jewish Record* (New York) 4 (August 1941): 357–66.

DOCUMENT 3-5:[40] Letters by Ruth Goldbarth, Warsaw, to Edith Blau, Minden, Germany, on life in the ghetto during the first half of 1941, USHMMA RG 10.250*03, Edith Brandon collection (translated from German).

DOCUMENT 3-6:[41] Diary entry by Aron Pik, Shavli, German-occupied Lithuania, for June 27, 1941, on the dangers facing Jews around the start of the

---

35. *Jewish Responses to Persecution*, 2:*1938–1940*, Document 11–9.
36. *Jewish Responses to Persecution*, 3:*1941–1942*, Document 10–2.
37. *Jewish Responses to Persecution*, 3:*1941–1942*, Document 1–11.
38. *Jewish Responses to Persecution*, 3:*1941–1942*, Document 1–14.
39. *Jewish Responses to Persecution*, 3:*1941–1942*, Document 2–5.
40. *Jewish Responses to Persecution*, 3:*1941–1942*; collated from Documents 2–6 to 2–11 and 2–13.
41. *Jewish Responses to Persecution*, 3:*1941–1942*, Document 4–2.

German attack on the Soviet Union, USHMMA RG 26.014 (LCSAV R-1390), reel 58, file 170 (translated from Yiddish).

DOCUMENT 3-7:[42] Account by ghetto policemen in Kovno, German-occupied Lithuania, on the establishment of the Jewish police in the summer of 1941, no date (early 1943), USHMMA RG 26.014 (LCSAV R-973), reel 31 (translated from Yiddish).

DOCUMENT 3-8:[43] Diary entries by Baruch Milch, Tłuste, Galicia district, Generalgouvernement, written July–August 1943, on the persecution of Hungarian deportees in the second half of 1941, USHMMA RG 02.208M (ŻIH 302/98) (translated from Polish).

DOCUMENT 3-9:[44] Photograph of Jews led to their execution in Kamyanets-Podilsky, German-occupied Ukraine, secretly taken by Gyula Spitz, August 27, 1941, USHMMPA WS# 28216.

DOCUMENT 3-10:[45] Letters by Motl (Matvei Aronovich) Talalaevskii, Kyiv, Soviet Union, to his wife, September 2 and 5, 1941, on his Red Army service, USHMMA RG 31.028.11 (Kyiv Judaica Institute) (translated from Russian).

DOCUMENT 3-11:[46] Diary entry by an unidentified woman from Vienna on her deportation to Kovno, November 19–28, 1941, USHMMA RG 26.014 (LCSAV R-1390), reel 65, folder 68 (translated from German).

DOCUMENT 3-12:[47] Lyrics by Khane Khaytin, Shavli, German-occupied Lithuania, for "On a Begging Walk," no date (1942), USHMMA RG 26.014M (LCSAV R-1390) reel 63, file 54 (translated from Yiddish).

DOCUMENT 3-13:[48] Manifesto calling for resistance in the Vilna ghetto, January 1, 1942, Moreshet Archives D.1.4630 (translated from Yiddish).

---

42. *Jewish Responses to Persecution*, 3:*1941–1942*, Document 7–3.
43. *Jewish Responses to Persecution*, 3:*1941–1942*, Document 6–6.
44. *Jewish Responses to Persecution*, 3:*1941–1942*, Document 4–5.
45. *Jewish Responses to Persecution*, 3:*1941–1942*, Document 9–5.
46. *Jewish Responses to Persecution*, 3:*1941–1942*, Document 4–9.
47. *Jewish Responses to Persecution*, 3:*1941–1942*, Document 11–7.
48. *Jewish Responses to Persecution*, 3:*1941–1942*, Document 9–6.

DOCUMENT 3-14:[49] Diary entries by Eva Mändl, Prague, for October–December 1941, on her impending deportation to Terezin, in Eva Mändl Roubíčková, *"Langsam gewöhnen wir uns an das Ghettoleben." Ein Tagebuch aus Theresienstadt*, ed. Veronika Springmann (Hamburg: Konkret Literatur Verlag, 2007), 52–54, 57, 62, 64–66 (translated from German).

DOCUMENT 3-15:[50] Drawing by Karel Fleischmann, Theresienstadt, Protectorate of Bohemia and Moravia, *Infirmary for Children*, 1942, USHMMPA WS# 28808, courtesy of the Jewish Museum Prague.

DOCUMENT 3-16:[51] Diary entry by Nekhama Vaisman, Romanian-occupied Transnistria, for January 27, 1942, on life in an unidentified ghetto, USHMMA Acc. 2010.264, Nekhama Vaisman diary (translated from Russian).

DOCUMENT 3-17:[52] Manuscript fragment by Đura Rajs, Petrovgrad, German-occupied Yugoslav Banat, on his camp experiences, August 11, 1941, USHMMA Acc. 2012.35.1, Đorde (Đura) Rajs collection (translated from Serbian).

DOCUMENT 3-18:[53] Letters by Hilda Dajč, Zemun near Belgrade, to Mirjana Petrović, Belgrade, on conditions in the Judenlager Semlin, December 9, 1941, and early 1942, USHMMA RG 49.007, reel 5, file 2, and Historical Archives of Belgrade, IAB, 1883, 3126/II-XXIX-1122 (translated from Serbian).

DOCUMENT 3-19:[54] Uszer Taube, "Protocol about the Events in the Koło Region," on the mass murder of Jews in Chełmno, Warthegau, no date (after January 1942), USHMMA RG 15.079M (ŻIH Ring. I/1057) (translated from Yiddish).

DOCUMENT 3-20:[55] Letter by Selig Brodetsky and Leonard Stein, Joint Foreign Committee, to Władysław Sikorski, prime minister of the Polish government-in-exile, London, drawing attention to the plight of Jews, January

49. *Jewish Responses to Persecution*, 3:*1941–1942*, Document 4–12.
50. *Jewish Responses to Persecution*, 3:*1941–1942*, Document 11–2.
51. *Jewish Responses to Persecution*, 3:*1941–1942*, Document 6–3.
52. *Jewish Responses to Persecution*, 3:*1941–1942*, Document 3–3.
53. *Jewish Responses to Persecution*, 3:*1941–1942*, Document 6–7.
54. *Jewish Responses to Persecution*, 3:*1941–1942*, Document 12–8.
55. *Jewish Responses to Persecution*, 3:*1941–1942*, Document 7–13.

12, 1942, USHMMA RG 59.023M (Board of Deputies of British Jews), reel 24, frame 801.

DOCUMENT 3-21:[56] Diary entries by Abraham Frieder, Nové Mesto, Slovakia, for February 1942, on Jewish efforts to stop deportations to Poland, USHMMA Acc. 2008.286.1, Frieder collection (translated from German).

DOCUMENT 3-22:[57] Photographs and captions from Abraham Frieder's diary taken at the deportation camp in Žilina, Slovakia, no date (spring of 1942), USHMMA Acc. 2008.286.1, Frieder collection.

DOCUMENT 3-23:[58] Abraham Lewin, "In One Half Hour," on the spreading of news about murder actions in German-controlled Poland, Warsaw, March 26, 1942, USHMMA RG 15.079M (ŻIH Ring. I/1052) (translated from Yiddish).

DOCUMENT 3-24:[59] Letter by Ernst Krombach, Izbica, Lublin district, Generalgouvernement, to Marianne Strauss, Essen, Germany, on the limits of communicating conditions in "the east," April 28, 1942, in Mark Roseman, *A Past in Hiding: Memory and Survival in Nazi Germany* (New York: Metropolitan Books, 2000): 175–76 (translated from German).

DOCUMENT 3-25:[60] Diary entries by Irene Hauser, Łódź, Warthegau, for June–July 1942, on conditions in the ghetto, USHMMA RG 02.208M (ŻIH 302/299), reel 42 (translated from German).

DOCUMENT 3-26:[61] Diary entry by Mirjam Korber, Djurin, Romanian-occupied Transnistria, for July 4, 1942, USHMMA Acc. 2010.93.1, Mirjam Korber Bercovici collection (translated from Romanian).

DOCUMENT 3-27:[62] "To the Wide Jewish Masses," Undzer vort (Paris), on mass roundups in Paris, September 1942, McMaster University Library Digital Collections (translated from Yiddish).

---

56. *Jewish Responses to Persecution, 3:1941–1942*, Document 6–8.
57. *Jewish Responses to Persecution, 3:1941–1942*, Document 6–9.
58. *Jewish Responses to Persecution, 3:1941–1942*, Document 5–5.
59. *Jewish Responses to Persecution, 3:1941–1942*, Document 8–4.
60. *Jewish Responses to Persecution, 3:1941–1942*, Document 5–3.
61. *Jewish Responses to Persecution, 3:1941–1942*, Document 12–5.
62. *Jewish Responses to Persecution, 4:1942–1943*, Document 1–10.

DOCUMENT 3-28:[63] Drawings by "A. R.," an unidentified prisoner in the Westerbork camp, November 1942, USHMMA Acc. 2007.510.1, Moshe and Chaya Nordheim collection (translated from Dutch).

DOCUMENT 3-29:[64] Diary entries by Moshe Flinker, Brussels, for November 24 and 26, 1942, on religion and events since mid-1940, in Hana'ar Moshe: Yomano shel Moshe Flinker (Jerusalem: Yad Vashem, 1958), 11–17 (translated from Hebrew).

DOCUMENT 3-30:[65] Photograph by Felix Nussbaum of his painting *Saint-Cyprien* on the balcony of his apartment in Brussels, no date (June 1942), printed with permission by Felix-Nussbaum-Haus Osnabrück.

DOCUMENT 3-31:[66] Account by an unidentified Oyneg Shabes activist on a conversation with David Briner regarding his efforts to survive by looting in the Warsaw ghetto, December 1942, USHMMA RG 15.079M (ŻIH Ring. II/170) (translated from Yiddish).

DOCUMENT 3-32:[67] Manifesto by Solomon Mikhoels and Shakhno Epshtein, Kuybyshev, USSR, "To the Jews of the Entire World," December 21, 1942, USHMMA RG 22.028M (GARF R-8114), reel 232, file 903 (translated from Russian).

PART IV: 1943–1944

DOCUMENT 4-1:[68] Correspondence between Jacob Katzenstein, Hamburg, and Michael Chaim Gescheit, Berlin, on ritual fasting, February 1943, translated from German and published in Yitzhak Arad, Israel Gutman, and Abraham Margaliot, eds., Documents on the Holocaust: Selected Sources on the Destruction of the Jews of Germany and Austria, Poland, and the Soviet Union (Jerusalem: Yad Vashem, 1981), 156–58.

DOCUMENT 4-2:[69] Account by Abram Jakub Krzepicki, Warsaw, of the Treblinka death camp, recorded by Rachel Auerbach under the title "A Fugitive

---

63. *Jewish Responses to Persecution*, 4:*1942–1943*, Document 2–13.
64. *Jewish Responses to Persecution*, 4:*1942–1943*, Document 1–13.
65. *Jewish Responses to Persecution*, 3:*1941–1942*, Document 1–16.
66. *Jewish Responses to Persecution*, 4:*1942–1943*, Document 1–1.
67. *Jewish Responses to Persecution*, 4:*1942–1943*, Document 9–2.
68. *Jewish Responses to Persecution*, 4:*1942–1943*, Document 12–3.
69. *Jewish Responses to Persecution*, 4:*1942–1943*, Document 2–1.

from Treblinka," December 1942–January 1943, USHMMA RG 15.079M (ŻIH Ring. II/299) (translated from Yiddish).

DOCUMENT 4-3:[70] Adolf Berman, Warsaw, "The Problem of Resistance," January 17, 1943, USHMMA RG 68.112M (GFHM 20213) (translated from Polish).

DOCUMENT 4-4:[71] Testimony by Leyb Rayzer, Łódź, Poland, to the Jewish Historical Commission on resistance in the Grodno region, 1945, USHMMA RG 15.084M (ŻIH 301/555) (translated from Yiddish).

DOCUMENT 4-5:[72] Diary entries by an unidentified person, Warsaw, on the ghetto uprising, April–May 1943, USHMMA RG 68.112M (GFHM 19773) (translated from Polish).

DOCUMENT 4-6:[73] Diary entry by Aryeh Klonicki, near Buczacz, Galicia district, Generalgouvernement, July 5, 1943, on life in hiding, translated from Hebrew in Aryeh Klonicki, The Diary of Adam's Father: The Diary of Aryeh Klonicki (Klonymus) and His Wife Malwina with Letters Concerning the Fate of Their Child Adam (Jerusalem: Ghetto Fighters' House and Hakibbutz Hameuchad, 1973), 21–32.

DOCUMENT 4-7:[74] Letter by Menahem Glitsenshteyn, Jizzakh, Uzbekistan, USSR, to Yerahmiel and Gitele Glitsenshteyn, Ushtobe, Kazakhstan, USSR, on his experience as a refugee in Soviet Asia, June 12, 1943, USHMMA RG 02.208M (ŻIH 302/84) (translated from Yiddish).

DOCUMENT 4-8:[75] Testimonial letter by Elkhanan Elkes, Kovno, German-occupied Lithuania, to Joel and Sara Elkes, England, October 19, 1943, USHMMA Acc. 1999.86.1a–d (translated from Hebrew).

DOCUMENT 4-9:[76] Account by Leib Langfuss, "The Horrors of Murder," about the *Sonderkommando* at Auschwitz II–Birkenau, 1943–1944, transcript

---

70. *Jewish Responses to Persecution*, 4:*1942–1943*, Document 5–1.
71. *Jewish Responses to Persecution*, 4:*1942–1943*, Document 6–10.
72. *Jewish Responses to Persecution*, 4:*1942–1943*, Document 5–5.
73. *Jewish Responses to Persecution*, 4:*1942–1943*, Document 4–4.
74. *Jewish Responses to Persecution*, 4:*1942–1943*, Document 9–7.
75. *Jewish Responses to Persecution*, 4:*1942–1943*, Document 11–12.
76. *Jewish Responses to Persecution*, 4:*1942–1943*, Document 2–6.

in Ester Mark, "Arba teudot mi-Aushvits-Birkenau: 'Bizvet hartsa,'" Gal-Ed, no. 1 (1973): 309–35 (translated from Yiddish).

DOCUMENT 4-10:[77] Letter by Zivia Lubetkin and Yitzhak Zuckerman, hiding on the "Aryan side" of Warsaw, to members in the Hashomer Hatzair movement in Slovakia, January 6, 1944, USHMMA RG 68.112M (Selected Records from the Ghetto Fighters' House), reel 33, file 2001 (translated from Hebrew).

DOCUMENT 4-11:[78] "First Anniversary of the 'Tragedy,'" commemorating the deportation of Jews from Salonika, Greece, *La Vara* (New York), March 10, 1944, 2 (translated from Judeo-Spanish).

DOCUMENT 4-12:[79] Letter by Ede Buzás, Óbecse, Hungarian-occupied Yugoslavia, to a Calvinist bishop in Budapest on his Christian identity, April 28, 1944, USHMMA RG 39.035 (HNA K 557, Papers of László Endre), reel 1 (translated from Hungarian).

DOCUMENT 4-13:[80] Letter by Rezso Kemény, Pestszenterzsébet, Hungary, to an unidentified friend on his impending deportation, June 2, 1944, USHMMA Acc. 2000.78, Rezso Kemény collection (translated from Hungarian).

DOCUMENT 4-14:[81] Postcard by Pál Justus, Bor, German-occupied Yugoslavia, to his wife, Edit, Budapest, on his life in a Hungarian forced-labor battalion, July 9, 1944, USHMMA Acc. 2001.64.1, Eva Kovacs collection (translated from Hungarian).

DOCUMENT 4-15:[82] Diary entries by Selma Wijnberg, Chełm, Poland, July and August 1944, on her life after hiding, USHMMA Acc. 2007.69, Saartje (Selma) Wijnberg Engel collection (translated from Dutch).

---

77. *Jewish Responses to Persecution*, 5:*1944–1946*, Document 1–1.
78. *Jewish Responses to Persecution*, 5:*1944–1946*, Document 11–4.
79. *Jewish Responses to Persecution*, 4:*1942–1943*, Document 10–9.
80. *Jewish Responses to Persecution*, 4:*1942–1943*, Document 10–12.
81. *Jewish Responses to Persecution*, 4:*1942–1943*, Document 10–4.
82. *Jewish Responses to Persecution*, 5:*1944–1946*, Document 3–3.

DOCUMENT 4-16:[83] Letter by the Pressel family, Lyon, France, to Elie Schwerner, New York, on their wartime fate, September 28, 1944, USHMMA Acc. 2007.413, Pressel family collection (translated from French).

PART V: 1945–1946

DOCUMENT 5-1:[84] Account by Meilach Lubocki, Landsberg, Germany, on the liquidation of Estonian labor camps in the summer of 1944, September 20, 1945, USHMMA Acc. 1995.A.0793, Zalman Lubocki memoir (translated from Yiddish).

DOCUMENT 5-2:[85] Account by Michal Kraus on the death march from Auschwitz II-Birkenau in January 1945, written 1946/1947, USHMMA Acc. 2006.51, Michael J. Kraus collection (translated from Czech).

DOCUMENT 5-3:[86] Letter by Irving P. Eisner to his father on his visit to Buchenwald, May 15, 1945, USHMMA Acc. 2012.16.1, Irving P. Eisner collection.

DOCUMENT 5-4:[87] Letter by Julius Lewy, Linz, Austria, to his liberators on his persistent ill health, May 30, 1945, USHMMA Acc. 2005.120, J. George Mitnick collection.

DOCUMENT 5-5:[88] Diary entry by Dora Apsan, Schildberg, Germany, for May 12, 1945, reflecting on the fate of her family, USHMMA Acc. 2005.166.1, Dora Apsan collection (translated from Hungarian).

DOCUMENT 5-6:[89] Transcript of a voice-recorded interview with Polia Bisenhaus, conducted by David P. Boder, ORT School Paris, on her experiences in the Bergen-Belsen concentration camp and postwar plans, Paris, July 29, 1946, Voices of the Holocaust Project, Paul V. Galvin Library, Illinois Institute of Technology, USHMMA RG 50.472*0002 (translated from Yiddish, German, and French).

---

83. *Jewish Responses to Persecution,* 5:*1944–1946,* Document 7–3.
84. *Jewish Responses to Persecution,* 5:*1944–1946,* Document 1–5.
85. *Jewish Responses to Persecution,* 5:*1944–1946,* Document 1–10.
86. *Jewish Responses to Persecution,* 5:*1944–1946,* Document 2–1.
87. *Jewish Responses to Persecution,* 5:*1944–1946,* Document 2–4.
88. *Jewish Responses to Persecution,* 5:*1944–1946,* Document 3–1.
89. *Jewish Responses to Persecution,* 5:*1944–1946,* Document 12–7.

DOCUMENT 5-7:[90] Account by Maria Gara, May 21, 1945, on her rescue work in Hungary and subsequent deportation, recorded by AJJDC in Bucharest, USHMMA RG 68.087M, Nathan Schwalb papers/Hechalutz Office Geneva collection.

DOCUMENT 5-8:[91] Report by Arthur Gold, Montreux, Switzerland, to Gerhart Riegner, WJC Geneva, on the care of Jewish orphans, July 1945, USHMMA RG 68.045M, reel 18, file 137 (translated from German).

DOCUMENT 5-9:[92] Diary entry by Rachela (Rachel) Bryk, Bergen-Belsen, Germany, for September 22, 1945, on a day in the DP camp, USHMMA Acc. 2008.390.1, Ray Kaner collection (translated from Polish).

DOCUMENT 5-10:[93] Letter by Max Schweitzer, Brăila, Romania, to his sister, Esther Williams, Cleveland, Ohio, on his family's wartime fate in Transnistria, April 10, 1945, USHMMA RG 10.374, Schweitzer family papers (translated from Romanian).

DOCUMENT 5-11:[94] Report by Judah Nadich, advisor to the U.S. Army theater commander on Jewish activities, October 22, 1945, on conditions in assembly centers for Jewish displaced persons, USHMMA RG 19.036, Rabbi Judah Nadich collection.

DOCUMENT 5-12:[95] Dr. Zalman Grinberg, "Nürnberg," on Allied trials and postwar justice, *Undzer veg* (Munich, Germany), November 20, 1945, USHMM Library microfilms 0377.

DOCUMENT 5-13:[96] Editorial in *Unzer Sztyme: Organ of the Sharith Hapletah in the British Zone* (Bergen-Belsen, Germany), on disappointments since liberation, January 1, 1946, USHMM Library Microfilms, LMO251.

DOCUMENT 5-14:[97] Certificate of widowhood issued by the Central Bureau of Orthodox Communities in Budapest to Golda Leitman Weiss, May 14, 1946, USHMMA RG 10.522 (translated from Hebrew).

---

90. *Jewish Responses to Persecution*, 5:*1944–1946*, Document 12–5.
91. *Jewish Responses to Persecution*, 5:*1944–1946*, Document 3–5.
92. *Jewish Responses to Persecution*, 5:*1944–1946*, Document 7–10.
93. *Jewish Responses to Persecution*, 5:*1944–1946*, Document 7–6.
94. *Jewish Responses to Persecution*, 5:*1944–1946*, Document 5–1.
95. *Jewish Responses to Persecution*, 5:*1944–1946*, Document 8–3.
96. *Jewish Responses to Persecution*, 5:*1944–1946*, Document 2–9.
97. *Jewish Responses to Persecution*, 5:*1944–1946*, Document 7–11.

DOCUMENT 5-15:[98] Report by Becky Althoff, Föhrenwald, Germany, June 7, 1946, on her assessment of child survivors in the DP camp, USHMMA RG 10.146, Henry Holland collection.

DOCUMENT 5-16:[99] Moyshe Feygnboym, "Why Do We Need a Historical Commission?," *Fun letstn khurbn* (Munich, Germany), August 1946 (translated from Yiddish).

DOCUMENT 5-17:[100] Testimony by Asher Zisman, Munich, Germany, on German war crimes in Brest, Belarus, April 3, 1946, USHMMA RG 68.095M, reel 1, images 532–34, file 158, Yad Vashem Testimonies (M.1.E) (translated from Yiddish).

DOCUMENT 5-18:[101] Extracts from the file of Chaim Chajet, Warsaw, on accusations of wartime collaboration, September–December 1946, USHMMA Acc. 1996.A.0223, RG 15.189M, Central Committee of Jews in Poland, People's Courts collection, SYG 313, file 14 (translated from Polish).

DOCUMENT 5-19:[102] "Spoils, Restitution, Reintegration," *Bulletin du Centre Israélite d'Information* (Paris), December 1, 1946, USHMMA RG 68.066M, reel 50 (Selected Records from the AJJDC Archives, Jerusalem) (translated from French).

DOCUMENT 5-20:[103] Selection from the memorial book for Jewish victims in Tunisia edited by Gaston Guez, *Nos martyrs sous la botte Allemande. Ou' les ex-travailleurs juifs de Tunisie racontent leurs souffrances* (Tunis: G. Guez, 1946) (translated from French and Judeo-Arabic).

DOCUMENT 5-21:[104] Lyrics by Samson Först, *Der Grager. Gesriben in Lager* (Bucharest, 1947), for the Purim holiday, USHMMA Acc. 2010.343 (translated from Yiddish).

---

98. *Jewish Responses to Persecution*, 5:*1944–1946*, Document 3–6.
99. *Jewish Responses to Persecution*, 5:*1944–1946*, Document 11–10.
100. *Jewish Responses to Persecution*, 5:*1944–1946*, Document 12–1.
101. *Jewish Responses to Persecution*, 5:*1944–1946*, Document 8–9.
102. *Jewish Responses to Persecution*, 5:*1944–1946*, Document 9–7.
103. *Jewish Responses to Persecution*, 5:*1944–1946*, Document 10–4.
104. *Jewish Responses to Persecution*, 5:*1944–1946*, Document 10–7.

DOCUMENT 5-22:[105] Letter by Rachel Nordheim, near Leiden, the Netherlands, to her children in the Kfar Hassidim settlement, Palestine, December 19, 1946, USHMMA Acc. 2007.510.1, Moshe and Chaya Nordheim collection (translated from Dutch).

DOCUMENT 5-23:[106] Jacob Pat, *Ashes and Fire* (New York: International Universities Press, 1947), 248–54, on the Jewish past and future in Poland.

---

105. *Jewish Responses to Persecution*, 5:*1944–1946*, Document 4–5.
106. *Jewish Responses to Persecution*, 5:*1944–1946*, Document 6–9.

CHRONOLOGY

This chronology, collated from the five volumes of the *Jewish Responses to Persecution* series, furnishes additional context for the documents presented in this volume. Most of the casualty figures mentioned here are estimates.

1933

January 30, 1933: Reich president Paul von Hindenburg appoints Adolf Hitler as Reich chancellor in a coalition government. Hitler's cabinet initially includes only two Nazi Party officials, Wilhelm Frick as Reich interior minister and Hermann Göring as Reich minister without portfolio; the latter also serves as Prussian interior minister (until May 1933; after April 1933, as Prussian prime minister) and chief of the Prussian police, including the Gestapo (until November 1934).

February 1, 1933: Hindenburg dissolves the German national parliament (Reichstag); election is set for March 5.

February 4, 1933: Hindenburg issues the Regulation for the Protection of the German People (*Verordnung zum Schutze des deutschen Volkes*), allowing restrictions of personal rights and freedoms.

February 28, 1933: Following an arson attack on the Reichstag building on February 27, Hindenburg issues the Regulation for the Protection of the People and the State (*Verordnung zum Schutze von Volk und Staat*), which allows further restrictions of personal rights and freedoms, including indiscriminate arrests labeled "protective custody" (*Schutzhaft*), first in Prussia, then after March 5 in the other German states as well.

March 5, 1933: Reichstag elections are held; Hitler's National Socialist German Workers' Party (NSDAP) gets 43.9 percent of the popular vote, partly due to a massive propaganda campaign and intimidation by the Sturmabteilung (SA) and other Nazi Party organizations.

March 6–7, 1933: Local Nazi Party activists start a wave of anti-Jewish attacks, especially boycotts of Jewish businesses and assaults on Jewish lawyers, in Berlin and the Rhine-Ruhr area, then later also in Chemnitz (March 9), Breslau (March 12), Gleiwitz (March 27), Görlitz (March 28), and other German cities. These attacks continue with varying intensity at the local and regional levels until early July 1933.

March 8, 1933: Reich interior minister Frick announces the creation of concentration camps for political prisoners and persons taken into "protective custody" (*Schutzhaft*). That same month, transfer begins of the first prisoners to camps at Dachau (near Munich), Oranienburg (near Berlin), and a range of other places, mostly on the basis of initiatives by local and regional party functionaries. While most of the early prisoners come from the left of the political spectrum, guards often single out Jews for especially brutal treatment.

March 13, 1933: Joseph Goebbels is appointed Reich minister for popular enlightenment and propaganda (*Reichsminister für Volksaufklärung und Propaganda*).

March 17, 1933: Hjalmar Schacht is appointed president of the German National Bank (Reichsbank).

March 21, 1933: The newly elected Reichstag opens.

March 23, 1933: Representatives of all Reichstag parties—except Social Democratic Party delegates, who oppose the measure—provide the required two-thirds majority to pass the Enabling Act (*Ermächtigungsgesetz*, or *Gesetz zur Behebung der Not von Volk und Reich*), which, despite a term limit of four years and assurances from the government to observe constitutional guarantees, effectively provides the basis for Hitler's dictatorship.

March 25, 1933: German Jewish leaders, including the president of the Centralverein deutscher Staatsbürger jüdischen Glaubens (CV), Julius Brodnitz, meet with Göring to discuss the public protests against Nazi measures in the United States and other countries. In late March, many German Jewish organizations, including the CV and the Zionistische Vereinigung für Deutschland (ZVfD), publish appeals to Jews abroad to refrain from "anti-German demonstrations"; at the same time, these organizations intervene with German government agencies against anti-Jewish agitation and discriminatory actions in Germany.

March 28, 1933: The Nazi newspaper *Völkischer Beobachter* publishes an anti-Jewish boycott call. Hitler establishes a specially appointed boycott committee, headed by *Der Stürmer* editor Julius Streicher, to organize regional and local actions.

March 29, 1933: German Jewish community leaders headed by Leo Baeck send a letter to Hitler protesting the anti-Jewish boycott call.

April 1, 1933: Under the official leadership of Streicher's committee, the SA and other Nazi organizations conduct boycott actions against Jewish businesses, doctors, and lawyers throughout Germany.

April 4, 1933: The German Jewish veterans organization Reichsbund jüdischer Frontsoldaten (RjF) appeals in a letter to Hitler against hardships facing Jewish veterans and their families as a result of anti-Jewish agitation.

April 7, 1933: The Law for the Restoration of the Professional Civil Service (*Gesetz zur Wiederherstellung des Berufsbeamtentums*), or Civil Service Law, calls, among other things, for the forced retirement of officials "not of Aryan extraction" with the exception of World War I veterans and their relatives. The Law for Admission as a Professional Lawyer (*Gesetz über die Zulassung zur Rechtsanwaltschaft*) facilitates the withdrawal of permissions to work as lawyers from persons of "non-Aryan extraction."

April 11, 1933: The first supplementary decree (*Durchführungsverordnung*) to the Civil Service Law defines as "non-Aryan" any person "who descends from non-Aryan, especially Jewish, parents or grandparents." Subsequently, private businesses, sports clubs, and other organizations throughout the German economy and society increasingly adopt this "Aryan clause" to exclude persons labeled as Jews.

April 13, 1933: German Jewish organizations found the Zentralausschuss der deutschen Juden für Hilfe und Aufbau (ZAHA) to coordinate relief work.

April 21, 1933: The Germany-wide Law on the Slaughter of Animals (*Gesetz über das Schlachten von Tieren*) outlaws the butchering of animals according to Jewish religious laws (*Schächten, shechitah*), which individual German states had previously disallowed.

April 22, 1933: A new law (*Gesetz über die Bildung von Studentenschaften*) excludes Jews from membership in university student fraternities.

A new regulation (*Verordnung über die Zulassung von Ärzten zur Tätigkeit in den Krankenkassen*) terminates the admission of "non-Aryan" doctors (except war veterans) to the health-insurance-covered treatment of "Aryan" patients.

April 25, 1933: The Law against Overcrowding German Schools and Universities (*Gesetz gegen die Überfüllung deutscher Schulen und Hochschulen*) introduces a *numerus clausus* of maximum 5 percent for Jewish students. Exemptions for the families of war veterans protect roughly 75 percent of Jewish students.

May 10, 1933: Nazi activists organize public book burnings in many German cities and the screening of libraries for books written by leftist, pacifist, and Jewish authors.

May 17, 1933: A Jewish committee (Comité des Délégations Juives) submits the so-called Bernheim Petition to the League of Nations in Geneva regarding Jewish minority rights in Upper Silesia, a region in eastern Germany protected by international agreements until May 1937.

May 29, 1933: The association of German Jewish communal bodies (Reichsvertretung der jüdischen Landesverbände) issues a public statement, protesting as a representative body the denouncing of Jews in Germany and the danger of their loss of rights. On June 6, 1933, the protest is sent to Hitler but fails to prompt a response.

June 16, 1933: The founding of the Kulturbund deutscher Juden creates an umbrella organization for Jewish cultural activities that caters to exclusively Jewish audiences, first in Berlin and later in many other German cities.

June 21, 1933: A proclamation by the ZVfD regarding the status of Jews "in the new German state" stresses its hope for a viable relationship between the Jewish and the German peoples.

June 30, 1933: According to official U.S. immigration statistics and based on the immigration laws of 1921 and 1924, which established maximum annual levels of immigration from each European country (quotas) as well as various qualifications for immigrants, the United States admitted a total of 2,372 Jewish immigrants, 3.04 percent of them German Jews, in 1932 and 1933.

July 6, 1933: In a speech to his representatives in the German states (*Reichsstatthalter*), Hitler declares the Nazi "revolution" over and announces a shift toward further "evolution" of its principles.

July 14, 1933: The Law for the Prevention of Hereditarily Sick Offspring (*Gesetz zur Verhütung erbkranken Nachwuchses*) allows compulsory sterilization of persons deemed hereditarily ill. Up to the end of the war, roughly four hundred thousand persons, including

Jews, Sinti, and Roma, are sterilized under that law in Germany and the annexed territories.

The Law for Revoking Naturalizations and Withdrawing German Citizenship (*Gesetz über den Widerruf von Einbürgerungen und die Aberkennung der deutschen Staatsangehörigkeit*) allows the denaturalization of persons who became German citizens during the years of the Weimar Republic. The law and a decree, enacted July 26, 1933, subsequently target Jews from eastern Europe (*Ostjuden*).

August 25, 1933: Representatives of Jewish organizations in Palestine and of the German government sign the Ha'avara Agreement, which facilitates the immigration of Jews to Palestine in combination with the transfer of funds from Germany to Palestine.

September 8, 1933: In a letter to the German Industrial and Trade Association (Deutscher Industrie- und Handelstag), Reich economics minister Kurt P. Schmitt claims his ministry does not differentiate between "Aryan" and "non-Aryan" businesses and stresses the damaging effect of anti-Jewish boycott actions on the German economy.

September 17, 1933: German Jewish leaders found the Reichsvertretung der deutschen Juden as the central organization of most major Jewish communal bodies and organizations. Leo Baeck becomes the organization's president and Otto Hirsch its director.

September 22, 1933: The Reich Culture Chamber Law (*Reichskulturkammergesetz*) excludes Jews from membership in professional arts associations.

October 14, 1933: The German government leaves both the League of Nations and the international disarmament conference.

November 12, 1933: In the Reichstag elections, after the disallowance of all other political parties, Hitler's NSDAP receives 92.2 percent of the vote (turnout 95.2 percent). A simultaneously held referendum confirms Germany's withdrawal from the League of Nations and the international disarmament conference, with 95.1 percent voting yes and 4.9 percent voting no (turnout 96.3 percent).

November 24, 1933: The Reich Labor Ministry passes a regulation against laying off Jewish employees in private companies. The regulation also confirms the nonexistence of "exclusionary laws" (*Ausnahmegesetze*) aimed against Jews; the Reich Interior Ministry issues a similar decree on January 17, 1934. In reality, however, Jewish businesses and employees experience discrimination to varying degrees all across Germany on a daily basis.

December 16, 1933: A circular by the Reich Economics Ministry demands noninterference with Jewish businesses during the Christmas shopping season.

1934

January 24, 1934: A new national labor law (*Gesetz zur Ordnung der nationalen Arbeit*) excludes Jewish employees from holding leading positions in German firms and from membership in the German Labor Front (Deutsche Arbeitsfront).

February 26, 1934: The German army (Reichswehr) implements the "Aryan clause" of the Civil Service Law, which leads to the dismissal of roughly seventy servicemen, despite protests from the Reichsbund jüdischer Frontsoldaten to Reich president Hindenburg.

April 20, 1934: Göring appoints Schutzstaffel (SS) chief Heinrich Himmler as Gestapo head in Prussia.

May 1, 1934: *Der Stürmer* publishes a special issue on "ritual murder." The Reichsvertretung had already protested publication of this issue to the Reich Interior Ministry on April 26.

May 15, 1934: The Reichsvertretung (Baeck, Hirsch) writes a letter to Goebbels protesting his May 11 speech blaming Jews for anti-German boycotts abroad.

May 18, 1934: An amendment to the existing law regarding the "Reich flight tax" (*Reichsfluchtsteuer*) reduces the amount exempt from taxation that émigrés may take out of the country from RM 200,000 to RM 50,000. On June 23, 1934, the amount of foreign currency persons emigrating may exchange is reduced from RM 10,000 to RM 2,000.

June 26, 1934: A circular by the chief of the Prussian secret state police office (Gestapa), Reinhard Heydrich, disallows "Jewish gatherings" without prior permission and reinforces the need for Gestapo surveillance of organized Jewish events.

June 30, 1934: According to official U.S. immigration statistics, in 1933 and 1934, the United States admitted a total of 4,134 Jewish immigrants, 43.20 percent of whom were German Jews.

June 30–July 2, 1934: Hitler orders the murder of the SA leadership and other conservative regime critics and dresses the event up as the squashing of an attempted coup (*Röhmrevolte*, "Night of the Long Knifes"). In some instances, these crimes coincide with local actions against Jews.

July 18, 1934: New guidelines by the Reich sports leader (*Reichssportführer*) restrict membership of Jews to the Jewish sports clubs Makkabi and Schild (affiliated with the ZVfD and RjF, respectively).

July 30, 1934: Reichsbank president Schacht is appointed Reich economics minister.

August 2, 1934: The death of Hindenburg allows Hitler to combine the offices of Reich president and Reich chancellor in his capacity as "Führer und Reichskanzler" and leads to the German army's swearing an oath of loyalty to Hitler. During a referendum held on August 19, an overwhelming majority of voters approve the unification of the two offices (yes, 89.9 percent; no, 10.1 percent; turnout, 95.7 percent; invalid votes, 2 percent).

August 16, 1934: A decree by Deputy Führer Rudolf Hess prohibits contacts between party members and Jews.

November 15, 1934: In interministerial discussions, leading state and party functionaries acknowledge the negative diplomatic implications of Germany's racial policy but reach a consensus that even intense outside pressure should not lead to a revision of Nazi principles. To alleviate some problems, they suggest replacing the concept of "non-Aryan" with "Jewish" in future laws and regulations.

December 12, 1934: In a letter to the Reich interior minister, referring to Frick's decree of January 17, 1934, Reich economics minister Schacht protests the new wave of anti-Jewish boycotts and other violent actions. As a result, two weeks later Frick calls on Göring to end such actions.

1935

January 13, 1935: In a plebiscite held in the Saar on the question of whether the region should return to German rule, 90.8 percent vote yes. Subsequently, roughly five thousand regime opponents leave the Saar to avoid targeting by anti-Jewish regulations and other discriminatory measures already valid in the Reich.

February–August 1935: A wave of grassroots antisemitic outbursts—boycotts, agitation against "race defilement" (*Rassenschande*), acts of physical violence—and state-sponsored measures sweep through the Reich, with regional variations in terms of intensity, as a result of heightened anti-Jewish propaganda and local pressures for action.

March 16, 1935: Germany reintroduces compulsory military service.

April 1, 1935: ZAHA and other German Jewish relief organizations voluntarily integrate into the Reichsvertretung for the purpose of increasing efficiency.

April 11, 1935: The Deputy Führer (Hess) prohibits "individual actions" (*Einzelaktionen*) against Jews and reiterates the prohibition against having contact with Jews for all party members.

May 15, 1935: In an article on the introduction of compulsory military service, the SS journal *Das Schwarze Korps* predicts the exclusion of Jews in the coming Defense Law (*Wehrgesetz*).

May 18–25, 1935: During riots and anti-Jewish, anti-Catholic actions in Munich, the police arrest SA and SS men. Criticism from high-ranking Nazi officials (i.e., Frick, Reich justice minister Franz Gürtner) leads regional party officials to temporarily turn down the violence.

May 21, 1935: The new Reich Defense Law requires "Aryan" descent for military service. A decree issued on July 25, 1935, excludes "non-Aryans" from active military service under the new law.

June 14, 1935: Hess orders the maintenance of "party discipline" in fighting "ideological opponents."

June 18, 1935: Germany and Britain sign a naval agreement.

June 21, 1935: A decree by the Reich Interior Ministry orders the removal of anti-Jewish slogans from road and other official signs in preparation for the 1936 Olympic Games in Germany.

June 30, 1935: According to official U.S. immigration statistics, in 1934 and 1935, the United States admitted a total of 4,837 Jewish immigrants, 34.80 percent of whom were German Jews.

July 16, 1935: Frick advises local registrar officials (*Standesbeamte*) throughout the Reich not to perform "racially mixed marriages." The passage of the Nuremberg Laws on September 15, 1935, formally disallows these unions.

July 22–28, 1935: Nazi activists stage anti-Jewish riots on Berlin's Kurfürstendamm.

July 30, 1935: The Berlin city administration agrees with party and police offices to disallow new Jewish businesses and to mark "Aryan" shops.

August 6, 1935: The Reichsvertretung issues a "word of consolation" (*Trostwort*) to Jewish communities for the first Sabbath after 9th Av, with reference to the recent "wave of abuse" (*Flut von Beschimpfungen*) and an appeal not to succumb to depression and embitterment among German Jews.

September 6, 1935: A new Gestapo decree calls for the creation by the secret state police of a "Jewish file card catalogue" (*Judenkartei*) containing names of members of Jewish organizations.

September 15, 1935: During the Nazi Party congress, the Reichstag passes the so-called Nuremberg Laws comprising:

> Reich Citizenship Law (*Reichsbürgergesetz*): Article 1: "A 'subject of the state' [*Staatsangehöriger*] is anyone who enjoys the protection of the German Reich and who,

in return, has particular obligations to the Reich"; Article 2: "A 'citizen of the Reich' [*Reichsbürger*] is only that subject who is of German or related blood and who, by his conduct, demonstrates that he is both willing and suited to serve faithfully the German people and Reich." This law forms the basis for a plethora of anti-Jewish measures based on thirteen supplementary decrees enacted over the period up to July 1943.

Law for the Protection of German Blood and German Honor (*Gesetz zum Schutze des deutschen Blutes und der deutschen Ehre; Blutschutzgesetz*): Article 1: "Marriages between Jews and nationals of German or related blood are prohibited"; Article 2: "Extramarital relations between Jews and nationals of German or related blood are prohibited"; Article 3: "Jews are not permitted to employ in their households female nationals who are of German or related blood and who are under the age of 45"; Article 4: "Jews are forbidden to display the Reich and national flag or the colors of the Reich" but are "allowed to display the Jewish colors."

September 17, 1935: The CV changes its name to Centralverein der Juden in Deutschland. On September 22, 1935, the Reichsvertretung changes its name to Reichsvertretung der Juden in Deutschland; other Jewish organizations adopt similar name changes in the wake of the Nuremberg Laws. The Reichsvertretung also issues a declaration expressing its will to help create, as announced by Hitler in his Nuremberg address, a basis on which a "tolerable relationship between the German and the Jewish people is possible" and calls for its acceptance as an "autonomous Jewish leadership" by the government.

September 25, 1935: Reichsvertretung president Leo Baeck circulates to German communities his speech for Kol Nidre (the night prior to Yom Kippur), criticizing "the lie turned against us; the slander used against our religion and its testimonies." As a result, the speech is prohibited; the Gestapo arrests Baeck and Hirsch and releases them after a short incarceration in early October 1935.

September 30, 1935: The forced retirement of all German Jewish public servants until then exempt under the clauses of the Civil Service Law enacted on April 4, 1933, takes effect.

October 15, 1935: The national German winter relief system excludes the Jewish Winter Relief (Jüdische Winterhilfe).

October 18, 1935: The Law for the Protection of the Hereditary Health of the German People (*Gesetz zum Schutze der Erbgesundheit des deutschen Volkes*) mandates a prenuptial "marriage fitness certificate" (*Ehetauglichkeitszeugnis*) that includes racial criteria.

November 14, 1935: The first supplementary decree to the Reich Citizenship Law enacted on September 15, 1935, defines Jews and "mixed breeds" ("*Mischlinge*"):

Paragraph 2: "A Jewish *Mischling* is anyone who is descended from one or two grandparents who are racially full Jews. [. . .] A grandparent is considered a full-blooded Jew if he or she belonged to the Jewish religious community."

Paragraph 4: "A Jew cannot be a citizen of the Reich. He has no right to vote on political matters and he cannot hold public office. Jewish civil servants will retire by December 31, 1935."

Paragraph 5: "A Jew is anyone who is descended from at least three grandparents who are racially full Jews. [. . .] Also deemed to be a Jew is a Jewish *Mischling* who is descended from two fully Jewish grandparents, who belonged to the Jewish religious community at the time this law is issued, or joined the community at a later date, who was married to a Jew when the law was issued or marries one subsequently, who is the offspring of a marriage with a Jew as defined in section 1 of this paragraph and which was entered into after the Law for the Protection of German Blood and German Honor became effective, who is the offspring of an extramarital relationship with a Jew as defined in section 1 of this paragraph and was born out of wedlock after July 31, 1936."

Paragraph 7: "The Führer and Reich Chancellor can grant exemptions from the regulations laid down in this supplementary decree."

The first supplementary decree to the Law for the Protection of German Blood and German Honor enacted on September 15, 1935, paragraph 2, prohibits marriage "between Jews and subjects of the state who are *Mischlinge* with one fully Jewish grandparent." Paragraph 3 prohibits marriages between "subjects of state who are *Mischlinge* with two fully Jewish grandparents," and a person "of German or related blood or a subject of the state who is a *Mischling* with one fully Jewish grandparent" must receive permission from the Reich interior minister (Frick) and the Deputy of the Führer (Hess) or his designated representative. Paragraph 4 prohibits marriages "between state subjects when each are *Mischlinge* with one fully Jewish grandparent." Paragraph 6 states, "No marriage shall be concluded if it is feared that its offspring will endanger the purity of German blood." Paragraph 11 extends prohibitions to "sexual relations." Paragraph 12 restricts the employment of "female subjects of the state who are of German and related blood" in "Jewish households" with a Jewish male as head or member to women at least thirty-five years old on December 31, 1935. Paragraph 16 allows the Führer and Reich chancellor to make exemptions and calls for permission by the Reich ministers of justice and the interior prior to the criminal prosecution of a foreign citizen under the law.

November 26, 1935: A decree by the Reich Interior Ministry replaces "non-Aryan" (*Nichtarier*) with "Jew" (*Jude*) and "Aryan descent" (*arische Abstammung*) with "German and related blood" (*deutsches und artverwandtes Blut*) in legal and administrative texts.

1936

February 4, 1936: Jewish student David Frankfurter assassinates Wilhelm Gustloff, Nazi leader in Switzerland as an act of protest.

February 5, 1936: The Reich Justice Ministry prohibits "individual actions" against Jews after the murder of Gustloff prior to the Olympic Winter Games, held from February 6 to 16, 1936, in Garmisch-Partenkirchen, Germany.

March 7, 1936: The German army (newly renamed the Wehrmacht) moves into the Rhineland area demilitarized following the Versailles Treaty.

A new national electoral law (*Gesetz über das Reichstagswahlrecht*) excludes Jews from voting. Reichstag elections and a referendum held on March 29, 1936, yield a 99 percent yes vote for Hitler's foreign policy.

June 17, 1936: Hitler appoints SS chief Himmler as head of the German police. Himmler appoints Heydrich as chief of the Security Police (Sicherheitspolizei), comprising the Gestapo and the Criminal Police, and Kurt Daluege as chief of the Order Police (Ordnungspolizei).

June 30, 1936: According to official U.S. immigration statistics, in 1935 and 1936, the United States admitted a total of 6,252 Jewish immigrants, 52.53 percent of whom were German Jews.

July 13, 1936: A circular decree by the Reich Education Ministry allows the establishment of retraining schools for Jews in preparation for their emigration.

August 1936: Hitler establishes the Office of the Four-Year Plan, headed by Göring, to coordinate the regime's preparations for war.

August 1, 1936: Hitler opens the Eleventh Summer Olympic Games in Berlin.

August 12, 1936: A decree by the Reich Interior Ministry announces the marking of hospitals and medical institutes owned or run by Jews.

September 8–14, 1936: A Nazi Party congress is held in Nuremberg, and the Four-Year Plan is announced.

October 25, 1936: The German-Italian alliance ("axis Berlin-Rome") is signed.

November 25, 1936: Japan signs the Anti-Comintern Pact with Germany.

December 1, 1936: A new regulation excludes Jewish welfare agencies from tax exemption.

December 30, 1936: The Gestapo dissolves the CV-affiliated Jewish youth organization Der Ring Bund Deutsch-Jüdischer Jugend.

1937

January 30, 1937: In a pro forma vote, the Reichstag extends the Enabling Act passed March 23, 1933, for another four years.

March 18, 1937: The Gestapo Berlin decides on more strict supervision of "assimilationist" German Jewish organizations, especially the CV and the RjF.

April 15, 1937: A decree by the Reich education minister prohibits Jews from obtaining doctoral degrees at German universities.

June 12, 1937: A secret decree by the head of the Security Police (Heydrich) instructs local police to take Jews who have been convicted of "race defilement" (*Rassenschande*) and released from prison into "protective custody" (*Schutzhaft*) and to incarcerate them in concentration camps.

June 30, 1937: According to official U.S. immigration statistics, in 1936 and 1937, the United States admitted a total of 11,352 Jewish immigrants, 59.46 percent of whom were German Jews.

September 5, 1937: Schacht takes a leave of absence from the post of Reich economics minister (resigning formally in November). Göring acts pro tem until the appointment of Walther Funk in February 1938.

September 13, 1937: A decree by Himmler (chief of the German police) allows the release of Jews from "protective custody" (*Schutzhaft*) in concentration camps if they can provide evidence of their imminent emigration.

November 4, 1937: The Reich Justice Ministry forbids Jews to utilize the "German salute" (*Deutscher Gruss*) at court and in similar legal settings.

November 8, 1937: Reich propaganda minister Goebbels opens the antisemitic exhibition "The Eternal Jew" (*Der Ewige Jude*) in Munich.

December 13, 1937: The Reichsvertretung forms a Central Office for Jewish Emigration (Zentralstelle für jüdische Auswanderung) to better plan and coordinate the work of already existing Jewish organizations that promote and facilitate the emigration of Jews from Germany.

December 16, 1937: A Reich Interior Ministry regulation restricts issuance of passports to

Jews to exceptional cases (e.g., emigration, travel in the economic interest of Germany, serious illness or death of next of kin, own illness, or visits to children in schools abroad).

1938

January 5, 1938: Himmler orders the expulsion of Soviet citizens, except accredited diplomats, from the Reich within ten days.

The Law on the Modification of Family and First Names (*Gesetz über die Änderung von Familien- und Vornamen*) prohibits the change of family names for Jews and "*Mischlinge*" in order to prevent them from hiding their ancestry.

February 4, 1938: As part of the planning for war, Hitler takes over the supreme command of the German armed forces.

March 12, 1938: German troops invade and annex Austria ("Anschluss"), which triggers a massive wave of anti-Jewish actions, including arrests, assaults, and expropriations.

March 28, 1938: The Law on the Legal Relationships of the Jewish Cultural Associations (*Gesetz über die Rechtsverhältnisse der jüdischen Kultusvereinigungen*) reduces the status of Jewish communities from public law entities (*Körperschaften öffentlichen Rechts*) to registered associations (*Vereine*) by April 1, 1938. The new law has a massive effect on Jewish communal organizations in Germany and prompts the Reichsvertretung to restructure (see February 17, 1939).

April 12, 1938: A new family law (*Gesetz über die Änderung und Ergänzung familienrechtlicher Vorschriften und über die Rechtsstellung der Staatenlosen*) allows state prosecutors to open court proceedings to establish a person's (Jewish or non-Jewish) ancestry.

April 22, 1938: A new regulation imposes penalties for "covering up" the Jewish ownership of a business.

April 26, 1938: The Regulation Regarding the Registration of Jewish Assets (*Verordnung über die Anmeldung jüdischen Vermögens*) requires all Jews to register assets exceeding RM 5,000 in value. Hitler empowers Göring's Office of the Four-Year Plan to expropriate these assets "in the interest of the German economy."

May 20, 1938: The Reich officially introduces the Nuremberg Laws in annexed Austria.

May 31, 1938: Hitler orders the Wehrmacht to prepare for the invasion of Czechoslovakia.

June 1, 1938: A decree by the Reich Economics Ministry excludes Jewish schools from tax exemption.

June 13–18, 1938: Across the Reich, the police arrest roughly ten thousand "work-shy" (*Arbeitsscheue*) and "asocials," including more than twenty-two hundred Jews, incarcerating them in concentration camps.

June 14, 1938: The Reich Economics Ministry revokes its earlier regulations on the nonapplication of the "Aryan clause" to the private economy.

The third supplementary decree to the Reich Citizenship Law introduces the concept of Jewish enterprises (*jüdische Gewerbebetriebe*) and stipulates their registration and marking.

June 20, 1938: A decree by the Reich Economics Ministry excludes Jews from attending the German stock exchange.

June 30, 1938: According to official U.S. immigration statistics, in 1937 and 1938, the United States admitted a total of 19,736 Jewish immigrants, 60.38 percent of whom were from Germany and Austria.

July 6–15, 1938: US president Franklin D. Roosevelt convenes an international conference on the refugee crisis, held at Évian-les-Bains, France, with representatives from thirty-two countries and two dozen organizations. While doing little to remedy the plight of Jews trying to escape the Reich, the conference leads to the creation of an Intergovernmental Committee for Refugees headed by US diplomat George Rublee.

July 23, 1938: A regulation by the Reich Interior Ministry orders German Jews to report to police by December 31, 1938, to receive special ID cards (*Kennkarten*). After this date, they must present the IDs in all dealings with government officials.

July 25, 1938: The fourth supplementary regulation to the Reich Citizenship Law prohibits Jewish doctors from practicing and relegates a small number to serve as "caretakers of the sick" (*Krankenbehandler*) for Jews only.

July 27, 1938: A decree by the Reich Interior Ministry orders the renaming of streets named after Jews and first-degree "*Mischlinge.*"

August 17, 1938: New family law regulations (*Gesetz über die Änderung von Familien- und Vornamen*) require Jews to use the compulsory middle names "Sara" for women and "Israel" for men as of January 1, 1939.

August 20, 1938: Adolf Eichmann at the Viennese Security Service (Sicherheitsdienst, or SD) establishes a Central Office for Jewish Emigration to speed up the forced emigration of Jews from former Austrian territory.

August 22, 1938: A new police regulation (*Ausländerpolizeiverordnung*) allows the withdrawal of permission to stay in Germany for non-German and denaturalized Jews.

September 1938: An international crisis over German claims regarding the Sudetenland in Czechoslovakia triggers a new wave of antisemitic violence in the Reich that culminates in "*Kristallnacht*" (see November 9–10, 1938).

September 29–30, 1938: The Munich Agreement forces Czechoslovakia to cede the Sudetenland to the Reich.

October 1–10, 1938: German troops occupy the Sudetenland; Jewish inhabitants flee across the border into Czechoslovakia.

October 5, 1938: A decree by the Reich Interior Ministry voids German passports issued to Jews and orders restricted reissuance of passports stamped with the letter *J*.

October 6, 1938: The Italian Grand Council of Fascism approves racial laws along German lines announced by Benito Mussolini in July 1938.

October 28, 1938: German police arrest fifteen to seventeen thousand Polish Jewish citizens in various German cities and deports them over the border to Poland. Thousands of deportees get stranded in the border area, some entering Poland, others returning to Germany.

November 1938–February 1939: Negotiations similar to the Ha'avara Agreement (see entry for August 25, 1933) take place between George Rublee, head of the Intergovernmental Committee for Refugees established at the Évian conference, and German government officials (especially Schacht) to facilitate large-scale Jewish emigration from Germany to destinations yet to be determined.

November 7, 1938: In protest of the expulsion of Polish Jews from the Reich, Jewish student Herschel Grynszpan shoots German embassy official Ernst vom Rath in Paris.

November 9–10, 1938: "*Kristallnacht.*" The Nazi Party–instigated pogrom in Germany results in the murder of more than a hundred Jews, the mass arrest of at least twenty-six thousand Jewish men and their incarceration in prisons or concentration camps, the closing of Jewish organizations, and the massive destruction of synagogues and other buildings and other property owned by Jews. An estimated one thousand Jews arrested die as a result of their imprisonment.

November 12, 1938: A series of regulations calls for payment by German Jews of RM 1 billion as "compensation for damages" during "*Kristallnacht*," excludes Jews from the German economy by closing all Jewish businesses and workshops, and bans Jews from public theaters, cinemas, and exhibitions.

November 15, 1938: Jewish children are banned from German schools.

November 19, 1938: A new regulation (*Verordnung über die öffentliche Fürsorge der Juden*) reduces public welfare for Jews to exceptional cases.

November 23, 1938: After the abolishment of Jewish periodicals in Germany, the first issue of the *Jüdisches Nachrichtenblatt* published by the Reichsvertretung informs readers about government regulations.

November 29, 1938: The Reichsvertretung officially resumes its work after the shutdown or abolishment of Jewish organizations in the wake of "*Kristallnacht*."

December 2, 1938: The first *Kindertransport* from Berlin arrives in Harwich, England, with two hundred children from a Jewish orphanage destroyed during "*Kristallnacht*." The British cabinet eventually allows approximately eleven thousand unaccompanied Jewish children into Britain from Germany, Austria, and Czechoslovakia.

December 3, 1938: The Regulation on the Use of Jewish Assets (*Verordnung über den Einsatz jüdischen Vermögens*) systematizes the forced sale of Jewish businesses, real estate, and other assets.

December 12, 1938: A new foreign currency law (*Gesetz über Devisenbewirtschaftung*) restricts the possessions emigrants may take out of Germany (including money and jewelry) to items of personal use.

December 20, 1938: Moving beyond forced-labor regulations initiated locally earlier on, the Reich Labor Ministry decrees labor duties for unemployed Jews.

December 22, 1938: The Hungarian government submits a bill to Parliament designed to further restrict economic and other activities by Jews in the country.

December 27, 1938: The Nuremberg Laws formally take effect in the Sudetenland, ceded to Germany by Czechoslovakia following the Munich Agreement of September 29–30, 1938.

1939

January 1, 1939: Name changes for German Jews take effect based on the law enacted on August 17, 1938.

January 2, 1939: The Romanian government decides to foster the emigration of Jews from Romania and to contribute to a "solution of the Jewish question on an international basis."

January 16, 1939: In a conversation with the Hungarian foreign minister and against the background of the negotiations between Rublee and Schacht, Hitler suggests an international financial agreement to remove "every last Jew" from the Reich.

January 24, 1939: Göring authorizes Heydrich to coordinate Jewish emigration from the Reich by all possible means, according to procedures already established by Eichmann in Vienna and making use of a newly created Reich Central Office for Jewish Emigration

(Reichszentrale für jüdische Auswanderung). That same day, a confidential German-Polish agreement takes effect by which Poland accepts five to six thousand of the women and children expelled by Germany in October 1938; the two governments can reach no agreement regarding the seven to eight thousand Jews holding Polish passports but still living in Germany.

January 30, 1939: On the sixth anniversary of his appointment as chancellor, Hitler states in a speech to the Reichstag, "Today I will once more be a prophet: if the international Jewish financiers in and outside Europe should succeed in plunging the nations once more into a world war, then the result will not be the Bolshevizing of the earth, and thus the victory of Jewry, but the annihilation of the Jewish race in Europe (*Vernichtung der jüdischen Rasse in Europa*)!"

February 1939: Senator Robert F. Wagner (D-NY) and Representative Edith Nourse Rogers (R-MA) jointly propose a bill in the US Congress that, in a major liberalization of the 1924 Immigration Act, would effectively permit twenty thousand German Jewish children into the United States over a two-year period. Although the hearings attract widespread public attention, the bill fails in June due to insufficient congressional support and public opinion polls indicating a negative attitude toward increased immigration.

February 7, 1939: In a speech to diplomats and members of the diplomatic corps in Germany, leading Nazi Party official Alfred Rosenberg declares that the "Jewish question" will only be solved for Germany "once the last Jew has left the territory of the Third Reich" and that "the question of a decisive emigration" has become "a world-political problem of the most acute order."

February 9, 1939: Italian Royal Law Decree No. 126 establishes a corporation for taking over, managing, and selling "that part of the property exceeding the limits permitted to Italian nationals belonging to the Jewish race." Italy subsequently places further limitations on Jewish ownership of property and industrial and commercial activity. On the same day, Bulgaria enacts anti-Jewish regulations that include the forced removal of six thousand Jews with foreign citizenship.

February 17, 1939: The Jewish public in Germany learns of the replacement of its former central organization (Reichsvertretung) with the Reich Association of Jews in Germany (Reichsvereinigung der Juden in Deutschland), which the regime controls closely; on July 4, 1939, the authorities officially recognize the Reichsvereinigung as the sole body responsible for "the promotion of Jewish emigration" and supervising the Jewish school and welfare system in Germany. All persons defined as Jewish under the Nuremberg Laws (except foreign nationals and Jewish female spouses in "mixed marriages" with children) must join the Reichsvereinigung, which until its dissolution in 1943 remains under the control of Heydrich's Security Police and SD apparatus.

February 20, 1939: The Italian Fascist Party excludes persons of "Jewish race" from membership.

March 14–15, 1939: Following the Slovak government's declaration of independence from Czechoslovakia, German troops occupy the Czech lands (including the capital, Prague, with more than thirty-one thousand Jewish residents and a further twenty-five thousand refugees) and establish the Protectorate of Bohemia and Moravia. Both Hungary and Poland benefit from the German landgrab by acquiring their own parts of Czech territory. Hitler proclaims, "Czechoslovakia has ceased to exist."

March 22, 1939: German troops occupy the region of Klaipėda (German: Memel) in Lithuania, lost by Germany after World War I.

April 1, 1939: The Spanish Civil War officially ends following the victory of General Francisco Franco's Nationalist forces, heavily aided by military support from Nazi Germany and Fascist Italy, over the last Republican forces. The civil war claims an estimated 250,000 dead and forces tens of thousands of Spaniards into exile, many of whom end up in French internment camps.

April 18, 1939: The Slovak state enacts its first anti-Jewish law, defining who is a "Jew" and introducing restrictions on access to professions. More than eighty-five thousand Jews live in Slovakia.

April 27–28, 1939: Germany cancels its nonaggression pact with Poland (concluded in January 1934) and its naval agreement with Britain (concluded in June 1935).

April 30, 1939: A new German law restricts the rights of Jewish tenants (*Gesetz über die Mietverhältnisse der Juden*), providing the legal basis for the concentration of German Jews into so-called Jew houses (*Judenhäuser*) in German cities.

May 4, 1939: Hungary adopts a Second Jewish Law, more radical than the first passed in May 1938; it spells out further restrictions on employment, civil rights, and educational opportunities for Jews in Hungary.

May 13, 1939: The German ship SS *St. Louis* sails from Hamburg bound for Havana, Cuba, with 938 refugees on board (most of them German Jews). After Cuba and the United States deny it admission, the ship returns to Europe on June 17, with the refugees finding haven in Belgium, the Netherlands, Britain, and France.

May 17, 1939: Great Britain issues a white paper limiting Jewish migration to Palestine to fifteen thousand per year for the next five years. Simultaneously, the British government offers to accept ten thousand Jewish children from the Reich and Czechoslovakia, while a government commission suggests the settlement of up to five thousand Jewish immigrants in British Guyana.

June 30, 1939: According to official U.S. immigration statistics, in 1938 and 1939, the United States admitted a total of 43,450 Jewish immigrants, 69.27 percent of whom were from Germany and Austria.

July 4, 1939: The Reichsvereinigung der Juden in Deutschland is officially recognized (see entry for February 17, 1939).

July 26, 1939: In line with the Viennese and Berlin models, Eichmann's office establishes a Central Office for Jewish Emigration in Prague for Jews living in the Protectorate of Bohemia and Moravia.

August 19, 1939: The Italian government bars entry to Italy for Jews from Germany, Poland, Hungary, and Romania (and later Slovakia). At the same time, the government begins preparations for interning all foreign Jews found in Italy or confining them to small towns, with arrests beginning in June 1940.

August 23, 1939: The governments of Germany and the Soviet Union sign a nonaggression pact, also called the Molotov-Ribbentrop Pact, which includes a secret protocol regarding the division of eastern Europe into German and Soviet "spheres of interest."

August 26, 1939: Due to heightened international tensions, the Twenty-First Zionist Congress closes in Geneva, Switzerland, earlier than planned.

September 1, 1939: German troops invade Poland and defeat the Polish army within weeks. The Luftwaffe's shelling and bombing of Polish cities causes heavy casualties among the civilian population. Warsaw surrenders to the Germans on September 28, 1939. Subsequently, Poland disappears from the political map, with some parts of German-controlled Poland annexed to the Reich (e.g., as Reichsgau Wartheland, or Warthegau), while others are incorporated into the Generalgouvernement established in October under Hans Frank (see entry for October 10, 1939). Of the roughly four hundred thousand Polish POWs, the Germans take an estimated sixty thousand Jews captive, twenty to twenty-five thousand of whom perish. During the military campaign, units of the German army and the SS, particularly the *Einsatzgruppen* of the Security Police and the SD, commit atrocities against civilians. Of the sixteen thousand Poles executed by German units in September 1939, at least five thousand are Jewish.

September 8, 1939: Following an order by Heydrich targeting all male Jews with Polish citizenship living in Germany, police arrest roughly two thousand Jewish men for transfer to concentration camps.

September 17, 1939: The Soviet Union invades eastern Poland, with the Bug River becoming the new demarcation line for the partition of German- and Soviet-occupied Poland. After Germany and the Soviet Union agree to the final boundaries of their "spheres of interest" on September 28, 1939, approximately two million Polish Jews are trapped in German-occupied Poland, with the remaining 1.3 to 1.5 million under Soviet rule.

September 21, 1939: Heydrich instructs the *Einsatzgruppen* chiefs on how to deal with the Jewish population, including the establishment of Jewish Councils (*Judenräte*; sing. *Judenrat*) in Polish towns and cities.

September 23, 1939: Radios owned by Jews in Germany are confiscated.

September 27, 1939: Formation of the Reichssicherheitshauptamt (RSHA) in Berlin integrates the Security Police and Security Service under Heydrich into one bureaucratic apparatus within which Eichmann and his office coordinate anti-Jewish policies.

October 4, 1939: The German military administration of Warsaw (replaced in late October by civil administrators of the Generalgouvernement) establishes a *Judenrat* in the city. Adam Czerniaków becomes head of the twenty-four-member Jewish Council responsible for implementing German orders for the city's roughly 360,000 Jews.

October 7, 1939: Hitler appoints Himmler as Reich commissioner for the strengthening of Germandom (*Reichskommissar für die Festigung deutschen Volkstums*) in charge of the Germanization of the newly occupied areas, including the expulsion of unwanted elements among their populations and the resettlement of ethnic Germans (*Volksdeutsche*) into the Reich.

October 8, 1939: The German mayor of Piotrków Trybunalski (German: Petrikau), a town located in the Radom district of what will become the Generalgouvernement, issues orders to establish a Jewish ghetto, the first in German-controlled Poland, and mandates that the roughly fifteen thousand Jews (of the fifty thousand total inhabitants) must move into a dilapidated part of town by October 31.

October 10, 1939: The Generalgouvernement under Hans Frank, with Kraków (German: Krakau) as capital, officially replaces the German military administration.

October 13–14, 1939: The German administration of the city of Łódź appoints Mordechai Chaim Rumkowski Eldest of the Jews (*Älteste der Juden*). The city has some 233,000 Jewish residents on the eve of the war, tens of thousands of whom flee or are deported to the Generalgouvernement in late 1939.

October 18–27, 1939: As part of plans for a "Jewish reservation" developed by Eichmann's office, deportation transports with almost five thousand Jews from Vienna, Ostrava (in the Protectorate), and Katowice (in German-annexed East Upper Silesia) leave for Nisko in the Lublin district of the Generalgouvernement.

October 25, 1939: The German city administration in Włocławek (German: Leslau) in the Warthegau orders Jews to wear a yellow cloth triangle on the back of their outergarments. In the following months, German local and regional administrations issue similar regulations regarding the marking of Jews.

October 26, 1939: Frank introduces forced labor for all Jews between the ages of fourteen and sixty in the Generalgouvernement, forming the basis for subsequent regulations and running parallel with the ongoing expropriation and theft of Jewish property.

November 9, 1939: The city of Łódź (renamed Litzmannstadt), incorporated into the Reich as part of the Warthegau, subsequently gets drawn into Himmler's large-scale, though mostly unsuccessful plans to force resettlement of six hundred thousand Jews and four hundred thousand Poles. In the middle of November, German authorities destroy the main synagogues in Łódź.

November 12, 1939: Based on guidelines issued by Himmler and in anticipation of the resettlement of ethnic Germans from Soviet-controlled areas, German authorities begin the deportation of Jews from the incorporated Polish territories, forcing almost ninety thousand Jews out of the Warthegau into the Generalgouvernement during the first half of December 1939.

November 23, 1939: A decree issued by Frank orders that, by December 1, 1939, all Jews over the age of ten residing in the Generalgouvernement must wear white armbands bearing a Star of David on their right sleeve.

November 28, 1939: Frank decrees the establishment of Jewish Councils in towns and cities of the Generalgouvernement, with details left to the local and regional German authorities.

December 7, 1939: At the Dziekanka asylum in the formerly Polish province of Posen, an SS unit murders 1,172 inmates. The massacre forms part of the wider killing of the mentally ill in German-dominated Poland, conducted independently of the clandestine murder of hospital inmates in the Reich since the beginning of the war ("Aktion T4"), which by the summer of 1941 will have claimed the lives of an estimated seventy thousand men, women, and children.

1940

February 8, 1940: German authorities in Łódź decree the forced resettlement of the remaining 160,000 Jews into a ghetto in a small section of the city without proper sanitation or running water.

February 12, 1940: In a meeting presided over by Göring, leading members of the German regime discuss "eastern questions" (*Ostfragen*). Göring favors an "orderly emigration of Jews" over an unsystematic Jewish expulsion into the Generalgouvernement without the consent of Frank or his administrators.

February 15, 1940: Against the backdrop of Himmler's deportation plans targeting unwanted minorities but largely resulting from local Nazi officials' initiatives, the Reich deports more than eleven hundred Jews from the east German city of Stettin into the Lublin region of the Generalgouvernement. Due to the inhumane conditions in the Lublin district, approximately 30 percent of those transported die within six months of their arrival. This is the first deportation of Jews from Germany proper (*Altreich*), followed by the forced removal of roughly 160 Jews from the city of Schneidemühl in the German province of Pomerania on March 12, 1940.

March 8, 1940: German administrators in Warsaw shelve the idea of creating a ghetto in the city, officially to avoid negative economic repercussions. While Jewish leaders around Czerniaków have successfully petitioned the Germans to revoke their decision in this instance, the ghetto is established later that year (October 12, 1940).

March 13–14, 1940: The King-Havenner Bill, designed to facilitate refugee settlement in Alaska and supported by Secretary of the Interior Harold L. Ickes, is introduced in the US Congress. Facing strong opposition from nativist groups, the State Department, and Alaskans themselves, the bill ultimately dies in subcommittee.

March 23, 1940: Göring prohibits further deportations into the Generalgouvernement without his or Frank's prior approval, effectively ending the deportations to the Lublin district that had begun in October 1939.

March 26, 1940: The American Jewish Joint Distribution Committee (AJJDC or the Joint) office in Warsaw announces that German authorities have granted it permission to import matzos to Warsaw for the upcoming Passover holiday. An estimated 250,000 Jews in Warsaw receive some form of Passover relief from the Joint in 1940.

March 27, 1940: The Warsaw Jewish Council receives German orders to begin construction of a wall around a "plague-infected area" in the Jewish residential section of Warsaw. By the beginning of June, a large part of the wall has gone up.

April 8, 1940: The Wehrmacht High Command orders the exclusion from the German army of "*Mischlinge* of the first degree" as well as the husbands of Jewish or "first-degree *Mischling*" women.

April 8–11, 1940: Soviet units execute over twenty thousand Polish army officers and other prisoners, burying them in mass graves in the Katyn Forest near Smolensk in the Soviet Union.

April 9, 1940: German troops invade Denmark and Norway. At that time, roughly six thousand Danish Jews and fifteen hundred Jewish refugees reside in Denmark, and about eighteen hundred Jews live in Norway, including three hundred refugees.

April 24, 1940: The Protectorate of Bohemia and Moravia officially issues racial laws defining who is and is not a Jew or person of "mixed blood," affecting more than ninety thousand people.

April 27, 1940: Heydrich orders the deportation of twenty-five hundred German Sinti ("gypsies") into the Generalgouvernement. That same day, Himmler orders the creation of a concentration camp in Auschwitz in German-annexed East Upper Silesia; on April 30, SS Captain Rudolf Höss is appointed camp commander. The first 728 Polish prisoners arrive on June 14, 1940.

May 7, 1940: Łódź Jewish Council head Rumkowski receives the final ordinance from German authorities sealing off the city's ghetto. This completes a process commenced in February 1940, confining over 160,000 people into a severely overcrowded area of Łódź.

May 10, 1940: German troops invade the Netherlands, Belgium, Luxembourg, and France. British prime minister Neville Chamberlain resigns, and Winston Churchill succeeds him. The Wehrmacht overruns Luxembourg in one day; the Netherlands capitulate on May 15, and Belgium fights for eighteen days before surrendering. In Belgium, roughly 90,000 Jews, only 10 percent of them Belgian citizens, fall into German hands; 140,000 Jews live in the Netherlands, including 14,000 refugees from the Reich, while many of the 3,500 Jews in Luxembourg have fled to Belgium and France prior to the German advance.

May 26, 1940: The Allies begin evacuating over three hundred thousand British and French forces at Dunkirk in the face of the German invasion of France, ending the process by June 6. With the subsequent German advance on Paris, Chief Rabbi of France Isaïe Schwartz, the main leaders of the Israelite Central Consistory (Consistoire Central), and the heads of Jewish immigrant organizations follow the departure of the French government from the capital. Nearly one hundred thousand French Jews and German Jewish refugees stream to the south of the country, many seeking to cross the frontier into Spain. By June 22, Germany occupies the country except for southern France. Of the approximately three hundred thousand Jews in France, almost 50 percent were born outside that country.

June 6, 1940: A memorandum created in the German Foreign Office proposes several options for solving the "Jewish question," including mass deportations to Madagascar, a French colony off the coast of East Africa.

June 10, 1940: Italy declares war on Great Britain and France. One month later the Italian air force launches bombing raids on targets in Tel Aviv and Haifa, killing and wounding hundreds.

June 14, 1940: German forces enter Paris.

June 15–17, 1940: In accordance with the Molotov-Ribbentrop Pact and its demarcation of German-Soviet "spheres of interest," Soviet troops occupy the Baltic states of Estonia, Latvia, and Lithuania before their formal incorporation into the Soviet Union.

June 22, 1940: France signs an armistice with Germany, which provides for the German military occupation of the northern half of the country and permits the establishment of a collaborationist regime in the unoccupied south (see entry for July 10, 1940).

June 24, 1940: In a letter to Reich foreign minister Joachim von Ribbentrop, Heydrich requests involvement in German Foreign Office plans regarding the "solution of the Jewish question" and states that the scope of the "overall problem," with 3.25 million Jews under German rule, calls for replacing emigration with an unspecified "territorial final solution" (*territoriale Endlösung*).

June 27, 1940: Under German pressure, Romania cedes the regions of Bessarabia and northern Bukovina to the Soviet Union. The forced Romanian withdrawal triggers numerous acts of anti-Jewish violence by Romanian forces and leads thousands of Jews to flee across the border into the Soviet Union.

July 3, 1940: Eichmann summons representatives of the Reichsvereinigung and the Vienna and Prague Jewish communities to inform them about an "overall solution to the European Jewish question" (*Gesamtlösung der europäischen Judenfrage*) planned for after the war and affecting 4 million Jews. Eichmann demands a memo within forty-eight hours regarding how to achieve the "removal" of all Jews from the Reich. That same day, the German Foreign Office drafts a more concrete plan for the resettlement of all European Jews to the French island of Madagascar after the war.

July 4, 1940: The Berlin police president reduces the time during which Jews in the city can purchase food to between 4:00 p.m. and 5:00 p.m.

July 10, 1940: Marshal Henri-Philippe Pétain, a World War I hero, becomes head of a new French government. Establishing its seat in the spa town of Vichy in the southern, unoccupied part of the country, the regime adopts a reactionary program of "national renovation," which effectively supplants the ideals of liberty, equality, and fraternity.

July 12, 1940: Hans Frank reports to Generalgouvernement officials about plans to "transport" all Jews from the Reich, the Protectorate, and the Generalgouvernement to Madagascar immediately after the war.

July 16, 1940: Following Germany's annexation of Alsace-Lorraine, the Reich forces Jews in the city of Colmar across the border into France.

July 22, 1940: The Vichy regime passes a law that allows the denaturalization of all persons who acquired French citizenship after 1927.

July 28, 1940: Hitler urges the Slovak leadership to adopt a more radical anti-Jewish policy. In August, the Reich appoints an "advisor on Jewish affairs" to put additional pressure on the Slovak government, which, starting in September, enacts a range of measures targeting Jews in the country.

August 1940: The German air force begins its massive attacks on Britain in preparation for a ground invasion. Despite falling short of its goal of achieving air supremacy, the Blitz continues. The German bombing of British cities up to May 1941 kills more than forty thousand civilians.

August 9, 1940: The Romanian regime passes a "Jewish statute" that revokes the citizenship of Jews, prohibits "mixed marriages," and massively restricts Jews' economic and social status; among the exceptions are World War I veterans and their wives and children.

August 16, 1940: The deadline for the sixty to eighty thousand Jews living in Kraków to "voluntarily" leave the capital of Frank's Generalgouvernement passes; after this date all Jews, except for roughly fifteen thousand people holding jobs, are gradually expelled.

August 30, 1940: As part of the Second Vienna Award enforced by Germany, Romania cedes Northern Transylvania to Hungary, putting 150,000 more Jews under Hungarian control. Taking into account the prior loss of northern Bukovina and Bessarabia to the Soviet Union, Romania's Jewish population drops from 728,000 to 302,000.

September 6, 1940: Following the resignation of King Carol II of Romania, the extreme right-wing Iron Guard Legionnaires join Ion Antonescu's military government. Anti-Jewish measures continue even after Antonescu has forced the Iron Guard into illegality in January 1941.

September 9, 1940: In Luxembourg, where roughly two thousand Jews remain, German administrators introduce anti-Jewish regulations similar to those in the Reich.

September 27, 1940: The German military administration in the occupied part of France orders the registration of Jews. That same day, Germany, Italy, and Japan sign the Tripartite Pact ("Axis Berlin-Rome-Tokyo"), joined in November by Slovakia, Romania, and Hungary.

October 2, 1940: German city officials in Warsaw decide to concentrate the city's Jews in a ghetto and order all Jews in the city to move into the ghetto by the end of the month.

October 3, 1940: Coinciding with Rosh Hashanah, the Jewish New Year, the Vichy regime, on its own initiative, enacts the Statut des Juifs (Jewish Statute), which excludes Jews from public functions and duties and defines a "Jew" as a person with three grandparents "of the Jewish race" or with two Jewish grandparents and a Jewish spouse. The law provides the basis for the subsequent marginalization of Jews in French society and the economy. French-controlled Algeria, Morocco, and Tunisia thereafter introduce similar measures.

October 4, 1940: The Vichy regime authorizes internment of foreign Jews in "special camps" or assigns them to reside in remote locations under police surveillance.

October 6, 1940: The German administration of the Netherlands restricts the employment and membership of Jews in public institutions.

October 7, 1940: The Bulgarian government decides to introduce a law for the "protection of the nation," which includes anti-Jewish regulations to take effect in January 1941.

October 22, 1940: Registration of Jewish businesses in the Netherlands begins, accompanied by a more detailed definition of who is "Jewish."

October 22–23, 1940: Following orders by regional Nazi Party leaders (*Gauleiter*), more than 6,500 Jews from southwest Germany (Baden, Saar-Palatinate) are deported to unoccupied southern France over the protests of Vichy authorities, who intern the deportees in the Gurs camp. From October 22 until the end of January 1941, roughly 650 Luxembourg Jews are forced over the border into Vichy-controlled territory.

October 27, 1940: In the Warthegau, 290 Jewish inmates of the Kalisz asylum are murdered using carbon monoxide (see entry for December 7, 1939).

October 28, 1940: The German military administration for Belgium and northern France orders the registration of all Jews and Jewish businesses, as well as the exclusion of Jews from public office. Forty-two thousand Jews are affected; an estimated ten thousand avoid registration.

October 29, 1940: Following the Italian attack on Greece, British forces land in the country. The Axis defeats Greece only in the spring of 1941, after Germany joins its ally Italy in the military campaign.

November 15, 1940: According to a report by Heydrich, almost three hundred thousand Poles have been forced out of the annexed Polish territories into the Generalgouvernement up to November 1940; in addition, Frank's fiefdom becomes the destination of six thousand Jews "resettled" from Prague, Vienna, Ostrava, and Stettin, as well as 2,800 "gypsies." In the west, more than fifty thousand Frenchmen and Jews are forced out of Germany into France.

November 15–16, 1940: German authorities seal off the Warsaw ghetto, with its roughly 380,000 residents, thereby confining approximately 30 percent of the city's population to about 2.4 percent of Warsaw's total area. Tens of thousands of additional refugees are later sent from elsewhere in German-controlled Poland to the Warsaw ghetto.

December 18, 1940: Hitler signs the order for Operation Barbarossa, the German attack on the Soviet Union planned to begin on May 15, 1941. Due to the German military campaign in the Balkans (see entry for March 27, 1941), the attack on the Soviet Union is delayed until June 22, 1941.

1941

January 1941: Cut off from adequate supplies by the Germans, Jews in the Łódź ghetto in Warthegau experience a severe food shortage that heightens mass starvation, disease, and demonstrations against Rumkowski's *Judenrat*.

January 8, 1941: During a meeting at the RSHA, Heydrich pushes for speedy evictions of Poles and Jews (including sixty thousand from Vienna) into the Generalgouvernement to make room for ethnic Germans from the east in the German-annexed Polish territories. Altogether, this intermediate part of the "Germanization" plan for Poland envisages the forced "resettlement" of more than one million people, mostly Poles, despite objections voiced by Hans Frank and his officials. In reality, between January and March

1941, fewer than thirty thousand people, including five thousand Jews from Vienna, are deported to the Generalgouvernement.

January 10, 1941: The German civil administration in the Netherlands orders the registration of all Jews residing in that country.

January 21–23, 1941: During the revolt of the Iron Guard in Romania, over a hundred Jews are murdered in the capital of Bucharest. With German support, Ion Antonescu quashes the Iron Guard uprising and establishes himself as dictator.

January 30, 1941: In his speech in Berlin commemorating the anniversary of his appointment as German chancellor in 1933, Hitler harks back to his "prophecy" made on January 30, 1939, according to which a world war would result in the "annihilation of the Jewish race in Europe," and he expresses his hope for a "front against international Jewish exploitation and the spoliation of peoples" (*Front gegen die internationale jüdische Ausbeutung und Völkerverderbung*).

Early February 1941: Following Italian military setbacks in Libya against British divisions, the Wehrmacht begins dispatching German troops to North Africa ("Afrika-Korps").

Mid-February 1941: Following a confrontation between Dutch Nazis and anti-fascists in Amsterdam, the Germans close the Jewish quarter in the city, appoint a Jewish Council, and arrest hundreds of Jewish men.

March 1, 1941: Bulgaria joins the Axis.

March 13, 1941: Hitler empowers Himmler's SS and police to execute "special tasks" after the beginning of the attack on the Soviet Union to ensure German control over the newly occupied territory.

March 27, 1941: Following a coup in Yugoslavia against the pro-Axis regime and in light of Italian setbacks, Hitler opts for a military campaign against Yugoslavia in conjunction with an attack on Greece. As a result, the beginning of Operation Barbarossa is postponed.

April 6, 1941: German troops begin their attack on Yugoslavia and Greece. Within days, they occupy the Greek city of Salonika, which has fifty thousand Jewish residents. Yugoslavia surrenders on April 17; Greece, on April 23. The dismemberment of Yugoslavia leads to the creation of the Independent State of Croatia under fascist (Ustaša) leader Ante Pavelic (April 10) and the occupation of other parts of the country by Germany, Italy, and Hungary.

April 12, 1941: German troops order the registration of Jews in Belgrade. Following a wave of arrests beginning in July and executions in German "reprisal" actions, almost all six thousand male Jews in Serbia perish by the end of 1941.

April 24, 1941: Bulgaria occupies northern Greece (Thrace).

May–June 1941: The new Croatian regime introduces a range of measures targeting ethnic minorities in the country, especially Serbs, Jews, and Roma, and joins the Axis (on June 15).

May 2, 1941: In a planning meeting on food supply, high-ranking German government officials discuss the extraction of raw materials from to-be-occupied parts of the Soviet Union to ensure provisions for German troops and the German population, expecting "umpteen millions" (*zig Millionen*) to starve to death in the affected regions. These projections form the basis for guidelines issued by German planners later in May for the economic exploitation of the occupied regions of the Soviet Union.

May 8, 1941: Alfred Rosenberg, the designated Reich minister for the eastern occupied territories (to be conquered by the Wehrmacht as part of Operation Barbarossa), issues preemptive instructions to his chief administrators (*Reichskommissar Ostland* and *Reichskommissar Ukraine*) regarding the exploitation, "Germanization," and pacification of the Soviet Union as part of an "ideological struggle in which the last Jewish-Marxist enemy has to be defeated."

May 13, 1941: The Wehrmacht High Command limits the application of punitive measures for atrocities committed against civilians during Operation Barbarossa to acts committed by individual Wehrmacht soldiers that undermine troop discipline. It encourages collective punishment, reprisals, and preemptive measures to ensure the "pacification" of the occupied territory.

June 1941: The Vichy regime expands the range of regulations against Jews in the country and introduces discriminatory measures in French North Africa.

June 6, 1941: The Wehrmacht High Command issues regulations for Operation Barbarossa on the treatment of Red Army "political commissars": if caught in battle, they are to be shot; if captured in the rear army areas, they are to be handed over to Himmler's *Einsatzgruppen* attached to each army group. Before the beginning of the attack, the guidelines are passed on to Wehrmacht divisions deployed at the eastern front.

June 22, 1941: Operation Barbarossa begins with more than 3.2 million German soldiers and another 700,000 Axis (mostly Romanian) troops pushing eastward across the German-Soviet border on a front line stretching from the Baltic Sea in the north to Ukraine in the south. In a proclamation, Hitler presents the attack as a preemptive strike against Stalin's "Jewish-Bolshevist" regime.

June 24–early July 1941: German police units start executing Jews and other alleged Communists and partisans in the German-Lithuanian border area. German troops occupy Vilna, Lithuania, with its fifty thousand Jews, and appoint a Jewish Council (July 4), followed by mass executions of five thousand mostly male Jews at the Ponary killing site near Vilna.

Immediately following the occupation of Białystok (June 27), German policemen murder two thousand Jews, including women. Up to mid-July some four thousand more Jews in Białystok are killed.

In conjunction with the German advance, the local population commits pogroms behind the front line, particularly in Lithuania and Western Ukraine, that claim the lives of an estimated forty thousand Jews.

Mass executions by *Einsatzgruppen*, police, and army units increase in frequency, on occasion including women and children; German reports legitimize these murders as "reprisals" and anti-Communist measures.

June 28–29, 1941: Romanian troops stage a pogrom in the Moldovan city of Iași and force more than four thousand survivors into two trains without water or food, causing the deaths of at least half of them. Overall, more than four thousand Jews from Iași are murdered.

July 1941: In the Warsaw ghetto, with its over four hundred thousand Jews, the number of recorded deaths for July reaches 5,550, mostly from starvation and disease, having steadily increased from 900 in January 1941.

July–August 1941: Following the occupation of Bukovina and Bessarabia (Moldova), Romanian and German units murder at least 150,000 Jews. Up to the summer of 1942, Antonescu's regime kills more than 250,000 Jews and tens of thousands of Roma.

July 2–6, 1941: Following pogroms in Lwów, Ukraine, that claim the lives of four thousand Jews, *Einsatzgruppen* units kill an additional three thousand Jews outside the city.

July 9, 1941: During the encirclement battle of Białystok/Minsk, Wehrmacht Army Group Center captures 323,000 Red Army prisoners.

Mid-July 1941: Hungary starts deporting eighteen thousand Jews, primarily those deemed "foreigners," over the border toward German-occupied Ukraine.

July 16, 1941: German and Romanian troops occupy Kishinev and start killing several thousand of the six thousand Jews in the Bessarabian capital.

July 17, 1941: Hitler appoints Rosenberg as Reichsminister for the occupied eastern territories (*Reichsminister für die besetzten Ostgebiete*) in charge of the civil administration of Reichskommissariat Ostland (comprising the Baltic states and parts of Belorussia; created July 25, 1941) and Reichskommissariat Ukraine (created August 20, 1941), while Himmler retains his authority to implement "special tasks" and "ethnic cleansing" in the regions under civil administration.

In agreement with the Wehrmacht, Heydrich orders his Security Police and SD to screen camps for Soviet POWs and to kill all those who could pose a danger to the Reich, including all devout Communists and all Jews.

Frank instructs officials in the Generalgouvernement not to allow the creation of more ghettos because Hitler had decided in June to remove all Jews from the region.

July 31, 1941: Based on his decree from January 24, 1939, Göring issues Heydrich with a letter charging the Security Police and SD chief with preparing an "overall solution of the Jewish Question" (*Gesamtlösung der Judenfrage*) for German-controlled Europe.

Late July 1941: As "reprisals" for resistance acts in Serbia, the Wehrmacht arrests and executes several hundred Serbian "Communists and Jews."

Based on the encouragement or consent of their superiors, units of the *Einsatzgruppen* in German-occupied Belorussia, Lithuania, and Eastern Galicia start shooting an increasing number of Jewish women and children, thus extending the scope of mass murder beyond male Jews of military age all along the front line and passing another threshold toward genocide.

August 1, 1941: The Białystok-Grodno district comes under the administration of East Prussia, and the Galicia district is added to the Generalgouvernement.

As part of an operation to "cleanse" the area of the Pripet Marshes of potential partisans and "bandits," Himmler orders his Waffen-SS cavalry units to shoot all Jews and "drive all Jewish women into the swamps" (*Sämtliche Juden müssen erschossen werden. Judenweiber in die Sümpfe treiben*). Up to mid-August, an estimated twenty thousand civilians, predominantly Jews, are murdered in the Pripet region, including in the city of Pinsk.

August 5–8, 1941: At the end of the battles encircling Smolensk/Roslavl and Uman, the Wehrmacht captures more than 450,000 Red Army soldiers.

August 9–12, 1941: During the Atlantic Conference, President Roosevelt and Prime Minister Churchill discuss U.S. contributions to the British war effort.

August 15, 1941: During a meeting at the Reich Ministry for Propaganda, Eichmann states that Hitler has ruled out the "evacuation" of all Jews from the Reich but that Heydrich is working on a plan for deportations from large cities and that Hitler is considering a proposal for the marking of Jews in the Reich. That same day, Himmler observes a mass execution of Jews and alleged partisans near Minsk.

August 20, 1941: Goebbels notes Hitler's approval for the marking of Jews, increasing the number of working Jews in Berlin from twenty-three thousand (out of seventy-eight thousand) and deporting all Jews from Berlin immediately after the end of the campaign in the East to make the city "Jew-free." The decree for the marking of Jews, issued on September 1, taking effect on September 15.

August 23, 1941: Expressions of public discontent lead to official termination of the "Aktion T4" program after the murders of seventy thousand people (see entry for December 7, 1939). The SS later uses some of its staff for the creation and operation of death camps in the Generalgouvernement, while "euthanasia"-related murders in the Reich continue until after the war's end.

August 26–29, 1941: Following discussions with the Wehrmacht, SS General and Higher SS- and Police Leader (HSSPF) Friedrich Jeckeln orders and supervises the mass execution of 26,500 Jewish men, women, and children in Kamyanets-Podilsky, among them, four- teen thousand Jews forced over the border into German-occupied Ukraine by Hungary.

September 1, 1941: In the Reich, a new police regulation orders Jews older than six years of age (except those living in "privileged mixed marriages") to wear a yellow star marked with the word *Jude* beginning on September 15.

September 2, 1941: In conjunction with the ghettoization of the Jews in Vilna, German police and local auxiliaries murder more than 3,700 Jews at Ponary, including 2,019 women and 817 children.

September 10, 1941: According to a report by the *Einsatzgruppen* unit operating in Lithuania, 76,355 people, predominantly Jews, have been executed.

September 15, 1941: Antonescu orders the deportation of the remaining 150,000 Jews from Romanian-occupied Bukovina and Bessarabia to Transnistria. A large percentage of the deportees are murdered along the way or die at their destination. In German-occupied Berditchew, police units execute more than eighteen thousand Jews outside the city, leaving four hundred "work Jews" and their families.

Marking of Jews with a yellow star takes effect in the Reich.

Mid-September 1941: During the encirclement battle near Demjansk, the Wehrmacht cap- tures thirty-five thousand prisoners.

September 18, 1941: Himmler writes to the chief administrator in the Warthegau, Reichsstat- thalter Arthur Greiser, that based on Hitler's desire to "free" Germany and the Protec- torate from Jews, he plans to deport sixty thousand Jews to the Łódź ghetto before they are transported "further to the east" during the coming spring. Between October and early November 1941, twenty transports with one thousand Jews each, as well as five transports of Sinti and Roma from Austria, arrive in Łódź. Logistical problems and interagency rivalries lead to the rerouting of transports to other destinations in the east.

September 19, 1941: German troops occupy the Ukrainian capital, Kiev. Most of the city's Jews have escaped to the east, but sixty thousand remain. A week later, at the end of the encirclement battle near Kiev, Wehrmacht Army Group South captures 665,000 Red Army soldiers.

September 27, 1941: Heydrich is appointed acting *Reichsprotektor* for Bohemia and Moravia. In a speech to Protectorate officials one week later, Heydrich stresses the close connec- tion between military and political plans and his determination to implement "Germanization."

September 29–30, 1941: As a "reprisal" for resistance activities and a means to alleviate the housing problem in Kiev, HSSPF Jeckeln orders the city's Jews to gather near the ravine of Babi Yar. According to German reports, German police murder 33,711 Jews.

October 1941: In the Warthegau, an SS unit previously used for the murder of hospital patients starts setting up a killing facility in Chełmno near Łódź.

October 1–December 22, 1941: German police and local auxiliaries murder more than thirty-three thousand Jews from the Vilna ghetto.

October 2, 1941: Start of Operation Typhoon, the code name for the attack on Moscow by Army Group Center. During the battle of Wjasma und Brjansk, the Wehrmacht captures more than 670,000 Red Army soldiers.

October 2–3, 1941: The murder of more than twenty-two hundred Jews in Mogilev marks the beginning of the liquidation of all major ghettos in the rear area of Army Group Center. Roughly one week later, more than sixteen thousand Jews from the Vitebsk ghetto are executed.

October 4, 1941: Romanian agencies start deporting Jews from the Kishinev ghetto to Transnistria, and many of the deportees are murdered along the way. In Kovno, German Security Police and SD murder more than eighteen hundred Jews, mostly women and children.

October 10, 1941: Heydrich meets with Eichmann and others in Prague to discuss measures pertaining to Hitler's wish to have all Jews removed from the Reich. They plan the deportation of fifty thousand Jews to Minsk (Belorussia) and Riga (Latvia), then both in Reichskommissariat Ostland, as further alternatives to Łódź. They earmark Theresienstadt as the deportation destination for the Protectorate; Sinti and Roma will go to the Reichskommissariat Ostland. Following the meeting Heydrich announces in a press statement the "final goal" of "resettling" the Jews of Europe outside the continent and, as its first stage, the deportation of Jews from the Protectorate, beginning with five thousand in the following week.

At the end of the encirclement battle near Melitopol and Berdjansk, Army Group South captures one hundred thousand Red Army soldiers.

The commander of the Wehrmacht's Sixth Army, Field Marshal Walther von Reichenau, issues an order stressing the necessity for "harsh but just punishment of the Jewish sub-humans" (*harten, aber gerechten Sühne am jüdischen Untermenschentum*). Hitler applauds this as an exemplary stance. Other Wehrmacht commanders subsequently issue similar orders.

October 12, 1941: Romanian agencies begin the mass deportation of fifty-seven thousand Jews from Bukovina to northern Bessarabia and Transnistria.

October 13, 1941: *Einsatzgruppen* units murder more than ten thousand Jews in Dnjepropetrowsk (Ukraine).

October 14, 1941: At the end of the battle of Vjas'ma/Brjansk, 193 kilometers (120 miles) west of Moscow, Army Group Center captures more than 660,000 Red Army soldiers. The death rate of Soviet POWs taken by Army Group Center since mid-October increases drastically, rising to 15 to 20 percent per month. One year after the start of Operation Barbarossa, 2 million of the 3.5 million Red Army soldiers in German custody have perished, mostly due to starvation and disease.

October 15, 1941: Einsatzgruppe A reports that its units have executed 135,567 people, predominantly Jews, by this date. It committed most of these murders—more than eighty thousand—in Lithuania.

Mid-October 1941: The first deportation wave from the Greater Reich, the Protectorate, and Luxembourg to the Łódź ghetto starts. Up to November 9, twenty-five transports deport twenty thousand Jews and five thousand "gypsies" to Łódź. German units murder more than half of the deported Jews and all of the Sinti and Roma by the spring of 1942 in Chełmno.

October 23, 1941: Himmler orders a halt to Jewish emigration, except in individual cases determined by the RSHA. According to RSHA statistics, 537,000 Jews have emigrated from Greater Germany (360,000 from Germany proper, 147,000 from Austria) and the Protectorate (30,000) between January 1933 and the end of October 1941. At the beginning of 1942, more than 130,000 Jews still live in Germany proper. The Gestapo closes the Reichsvereinigung's emigration office, effective January 1, 1942.

October 23–25, 1941: Following bomb explosions in the newly occupied city of Odessa, Romanian units murder twenty-five thousand Jews.

October 28, 1941: German police and local auxiliaries select ninety-two hundred of the twenty-five thousand Jews in the Kovno ghetto (including more than forty-two hundred children) and execute them the next day.

November 1, 1941: German troops occupy Simferopol on the Crimean Peninsula. In the following days, the remaining thirteen thousand Jews are ordered to report for forced labor and to wear a yellow badge. Einsatzgruppe D murders most of the Crimean Jews in the first weeks of the German occupation.

November 3, 1941: Einsatzgruppe C, deployed in Ukraine, reports that it has executed seventy-five thousand Jews by this date.

November 7 and 20, 1941: In preparation for the arrival of Jews from the Reich, German SS and police kill nineteen thousand Jews in the Minsk ghetto.

November 7–8, 1941: Germans shoot more than fifteen thousand Jews in a forest near the Ukrainian city of Rovno; five thousand remain in the ghetto.

November 8, 1941: In conjunction with the creation of a ghetto in Lwów, five thousand of the city's Jews are executed.

The second deportation wave to "the east" begins and continues through the end of the month. Thirty-three transports, carrying a total of thirty-three thousand Jews, are sent to Minsk (Belorussia), Riga (Latvia), and Kovno (Lithuania).

November 14, 1941: Einsatzgruppe B, deployed in Belorussia, reports having executed forty-five thousand Jews.

Late November 1941: Due to Wehrmacht claims of transport problems caused by the planned deportation of twenty-five thousand Jews to Minsk, only seven transports with seven thousand Jews from the Reich are sent to Minsk. The first five transports scheduled for Riga are rerouted to Kovno, where all Jewish men, women, and children are murdered upon arrival.

November 25, 1941: The eleventh supplementary decree to the Reich Citizenship Law stipulates that Jews living outside the Reich lose their citizenship and their assets. The decree provides a basis for the state-sanctioned theft of the remaining property of deported Jews, some of which the RSHA uses to finance the deportation transports.

November 29, 1941: The Vichy regime replaces the existing Jewish organizations in France with a new central association, the Union Générale des Israélites de France (UGIF), controlled by the government.

Late November–early December 1941: Jeckeln oversees the mass murder of Jews in Riga in the Rumbula forest. The thirty-eight thousand Jewish victims include ten thousand recently arrived deportees from the Reich.

December 1941: The severe cold and problems with digging mass graves halt execution actions in many places behind the front line until the spring.

The first Jewish deportees from the Protectorate arrive in Theresienstadt.

After the execution of six thousand men by the Wehrmacht in Serbia, 8,500 Jewish women and children are transported to the Sajmište camp. They are murdered in the spring of 1942 in gas vans brought in from Berlin.

December 5, 1941: The start of the Red Army's counteroffensive ends the Wehrmacht's advance on Moscow and leads to a partial German withdrawal.

December 7–8, 1941: Following the Japanese attack on Pearl Harbor, the United States declares war on Japan. A massive Japanese offensive gets underway in the Pacific region.

Hitler's "night-and-fog" directive calls for the capital punishment and deportation of "enemies of the Reich."

December 8, 1941: Mass murder in Chełmno begins, targeting first the Jews in the area, followed by Jews and "gypsies" from the Łódź ghetto. Up to the spring of 1944, a small German unit murders more than 150,000 persons, mostly Jews, primarily in gas vans.

December 11, 1941: Germany and Italy declare war on the United States.

December 12, 1941: Einsatzgruppe D reports it has killed fifty-five thousand persons, mostly Jews, since the start of Operation Barbarossa.

December 14, 1941: The German military commander in France orders the arrest of one thousand Jews in Paris and the execution of ninety-five men as a reprisal for attacks on German troops. On March 27, 1942, the detainees are deported to the Auschwitz concentration camp.

December 21–31, 1941: Romanian and German units murder thirty thousand Jews, mostly deportees from Odessa, in the camp of Bogdanovka in Romanian-administered Transnistria. Up to March 1942 additional murders in other camps bring the number of executed Jews in the region up to seventy thousand.

1942

Early 1942–March 1944: Hungarian Jewish men are forced to fulfill their military service by serving in the unarmed Labor Service. Between twenty-five and forty thousand Hungarian labor servicemen perish on occupied Soviet territory or in Soviet captivity.

January 5, 1942: The Reich orders Jews in Germany to hand over their winter clothing and sports equipment for use by German troops in the east.

January 9, 1942: A third wave of deportations to Riga begins, affecting (up to February 6) ten thousand Jews from the Reich and the Protectorate.

January 10, 1942: The German Foreign Office informs the RSHA that the governments of Romania, Slovakia, and Croatia have agreed to the deportation of their Jewish citizens living in Germany.

January 13, 1942: At a conference in London, representatives of nine governments of countries under German occupation (Poland, Czechoslovakia, France, the Netherlands, Belgium, Luxembourg, Norway, Yugoslavia, and Greece) protest war crimes committed by Nazi Germany and call for postwar punishment without referring specifically to the mass murder of Jews.

January 14, 1942: German authorities in the Netherlands begin concentrating Jews outside urban areas in Amsterdam.

January 16, 1942: Deportations from the Łódź ghetto to the Chełmno death camp start. Up to the end of May, fifty-five thousand Jews from the ghetto, among them twenty thousand deportees from the Reich, perish in the camp's three gas vans.

January 20, 1942: Wannsee Conference. Originally planned by Heydrich for December 1941, fifteen state secretaries and other high-ranking German officials gather at a villa in the Wannsee suburb of Berlin to discuss and coordinate the implementation of the "Final Solution." Because German anti-Jewish polices in occupied eastern Europe had already shifted to mass murder in the second half of 1941, the conference did not mark the beginning of the Holocaust. Heydrich convened it to secure support from government ministries and other interested agencies for his lead role in solving the "Jewish question" across and beyond German-controlled Europe.

January 31, 1942: The RSHA issues a decree to all Gestapo offices regarding the "Final Solution of the Jewish question" through deportations of Jews from the Greater Reich and the Protectorate "to the east." Exceptions are made for Jews living in "mixed marriages," Jews older than age sixty-five, sick or disabled Jews between fifty-five and sixty-five, Jews of foreign nationality, and Jews working in industries critical for the war.

February 16, 1942: The Protectorate issues a decree regarding Theresienstadt. Up to the end of the war, more than 140,000 Jews, half of them from the Protectorate, are deported to Theresienstadt; thirty-three thousand die on-site, and eighty-eight thousand are transported to death camps.

March 1942: Deportations begin (and last until October 1942) of fifty-seven thousand Jews from Slovakia to Auschwitz and to the Lublin area, and eventually from there to death camps.

March 1, 1942: Construction work starts on the Sobibór death camp in the Lublin district. Mass transports with Jews start to arrive in early May 1942. Up to the end of July 1942, as many as one hundred thousand Jews, mostly from the Generalgouvernement, the Netherlands, and Slovakia, are murdered there using carbon monoxide.

March 2, 1942: German police murder more than five thousand Jews from the Minsk ghetto.

March 17, 1942: Gassings in the Bełżec death camp near Lublin begin. Up to December 1942, 435,000 Jews are murdered there, mostly from the Lublin and Galicia districts of the Generalgouvernement.

March 20, 1942: The first gassing of Jewish deportees from East Upper Silesia takes place in Auschwitz II–Birkenau, in a modified former farmhouse.

March 27, 1942: The first transport of Jewish deportees from France arrives in Auschwitz, originally scheduled by Wehrmacht officials for December 1941 as a "reprisal" for attacks on German soldiers in France. Other RSHA transports from France follow in rapid succession.

April 27, 1942: According to comments by the Reich Ministry for the Eastern Occupied Territories on "Germanization" plans developed by Himmler's SS, at least 30 million people in Poland and the Soviet Union are to be "evacuated to the east" to make room for racially suitable settlers from Germany, the Netherlands, and Scandinavia.

April 29, 1942: German authorities in the Netherlands order the marking of Jews, starting on May 3.

May 18, 1942: A Communist resistance group led by the German Jew Herbert Baum commits an arson attack on the Nazi propaganda exhibit "The Soviet Paradise" in Berlin. The Gestapo quickly arrest or kill many of the group's members, including Baum. As a "reprisal" and with Hitler's approval, 500 Berlin Jews are arrested; 250 are immediately shot and the rest transferred to the Sachsenhausen concentration camp.

May 22, 1942: The London-based Polish government-in-exile receives a report from the Polish Jewish Socialist "Bund" in Warsaw estimating the number of Jews murdered in German-controlled Poland between June 1941 and April 1942 at seven hundred thousand and demanding action from the Allies. In the next days, British and U.S. newspapers carry the story; on June 2, 1942, the BBC reports on a press conference with Polish politicians in exile on German atrocities in Poland, with estimated numbers for Jews murdered of up to 1 million.

May 27, 1942: In Prague, Czech partisans shoot RSHA chief and acting *Reichsprotektor* Heydrich; he dies on June 4.

May 28, 1942: German police deport six thousand Jews from the Kraków ghetto to Bełżec, where they are murdered.

June 1942: The RSHA assigns a special SS commando code-named "1005" the task of removing evidence of prior mass killings by opening up mass graves in German-controlled Poland and later in the occupied Soviet Union. Jewish forced laborers dig up the corpses, burn them, and crush the bones that remain; at the end of their assignment, the SS kills them and replaces them with new laborers.

June 7, 1942: According to decrees by the German military administration in France and Belgium, Jews over the age of six must wear the yellow star in public.

June 10, 1942: As a "reprisal" for the assassination of Heydrich, German forces raze the Czech village of Lidice, killing more than 260 men and women, and deport 1,000 Prague Jews to the Majdanek concentration camp.

June 22, 1942: Eichmann notifies the German Foreign Office of the RSHA plan to begin deporting forty thousand Jews from France, forty thousand from the Netherlands, and ten thousand from Belgium to Auschwitz in mid-July/early August "for labor deployment."

June 28, 1942: The advance of German and Italian troops in North Africa reaches El Alamein in western Egypt, threatening Jews in the Yishuv. German occupation officials in Libya institute forced labor for all male adult Jews in the country.

July 1942: Based on initiatives by Szmul Zygielbojm and Ignacy Schwarzbart, the two Jewish members of the Polish National Council in London, the British press and the BBC report on the extermination of the Jews in eastern Europe.

July–September 1942: Germany and its Axis partners launch a new offensive in the Soviet Union. German troops fight their way into Stalingrad on the Volga River by mid-September and penetrate deep into the Caucasus Mountains after securing the Crimean Peninsula.

July–October 1942: After the deportation of fifty-four thousand Jews from Slovakia to Auschwitz between March and July 1942, the Germans deport another four thousand to Auschwitz, where most are killed by gassing. The deportations are then halted until the fall of 1944.

July 2, 1942: The *New York Times* (on page 6) reports on news sent to the Polish government-in-exile that seven hundred thousand Jews have been slaughtered in German-occupied territories (see entry for May 22, 1942).

July 4, 1942: During the first "selection" of new arrivals in Auschwitz, less than a third of Jewish deportees from Slovakia are admitted to the camp; the majority die by gassing.

July 6, 1942: The Soviet Jewish Anti-Fascist Committee publishes the first issue of its Yiddish-language journal *Eynikayt* (Unity).

July 11, 1942: The Germans order all Jewish men aged eighteen to forty-five in Salonika to report to Liberty Square. Of the nine thousand Jews who report, only two thousand are assigned work. The Jewish communities in Salonika and Athens must pay a large ransom for release of the remaining Jews.

July 13, 1942: Five thousand Jews from the Rovno ghetto, Ukraine, are shot in a forest near the city.

July 16–17, 1942: Raids in Paris result in the arrest of thirteen thousand Jews, who are held in the Drancy camp and the Vélodrome d'Hiver sports arena before being transported to Auschwitz or other French camps.

July 17, 1942: Following German roundups in Amsterdam, the first two transports with two thousand Jews from the Dutch camps Westerbork and Amersfort arrive in Auschwitz; 449 men and women are immediately gassed.

July 17–18, 1942: On a visit to Auschwitz, Himmler views a "selection" of arriving deportees and their murder in the camp's gas chamber.

July 19, 1942: Himmler orders the "resettlement" of all remaining Jews in the Generalgouvernement before the end of the year, except indispensable workers concentrated in "collecting camps" in Warsaw, Lublin, Radom, Kraków, and Czestochowa. This murder wave, referred to in German documents as "Aktion Reinhard," extends until October 1943 and claims the lives of more than 2 million Jews.

July 21, 1942: Twenty thousand people attend a rally organized by the American Jewish Congress, B'nai B'rith, and the Jewish Labor Committee at Madison Square Garden in New York to protest Nazi atrocities. Churchill and Roosevelt send messages of support to the organizers. The U.S. president writes, "The Nazis will not succeed in exterminating their victims any more than they will succeed in enslaving mankind."

July 22, 1942: Mass deportations begin from the Warsaw ghetto to Treblinka. The overwhelming majority of the roughly 265,000 Jews deported from the ghetto over the next two months are murdered immediately upon arrival; some 10,000 Jews are killed in the ghetto itself. It is estimated that over eight hundred thousand Jews from the Generalgouvernement, as well as from Slovakia and Bulgarian-occupied Yugoslav Macedonia and Greece, perished in Treblinka before its dissolution in the fall of 1943.

July 23, 1942: The head of the Warsaw Jewish Council, Adam Czerniaków, commits suicide.

July 28, 1942: Zionist youth groups create the Jewish Combat Organization (Żydowska Organizacja Bojowa, ŻOB) to wage armed resistance in the Warsaw ghetto.

July 28–31, 1942: German SS and police officials and their auxiliaries murder between eighteen and thirty thousand Jews from the Minsk ghetto in mass shootings.

August 8, 1942: Gerhart Riegner, the World Jewish Congress representative in Switzerland, sends a cable, through British and American diplomatic channels, detailing the "Final Solution" to Rabbi Stephen S. Wise, president of the World Jewish Congress, and British member of Parliament Sidney Silverman. Wise publicizes the contents of the telegram in a press conference on November 24, 1942.

August 10–31, 1942: For three weeks, SS and police units, aided by Ukrainian volunteers, round up more than forty thousand Jews from the Lwów ghetto. They are deported to Bełżec or sent to the SS-run Janowska Street forced labor camp. Many are killed in the city itself.

August 12, 1942: From the ghettos in Bedzin and Sosnowiec in East Upper Silesia, Germans deport eleven thousand Jews (mostly women with children, the sick, and the elderly) to Auschwitz over several days; they send nine thousand Jews fit for work to forced labor camps.

August 13, 1942: Switzerland no longer allows Jewish refugees to enter across its border with France.

August 26, 1942: The Bulgarian government issues a decree that establishes the Commissariat for Jewish Questions and introduces a number of other anti-Jewish measures.

August 26–28, 1942: Seven thousand Jews are arrested in Vichy France.

September 5, 1942: Over one week, the Germans deport more than fifteen thousand children, elderly, and infirm Jews from the Łódź ghetto to their deaths at Chełmno.

September 24, 1942: The Jews of Korzec (Ukrainian: Korets) set their homes on fire to defy Nazi deportation plans.

October 5, 1942: Himmler issues an order that all Jews from concentration camps in Germany be sent to the Auschwitz and Majdanek concentration camps.

The first of five deportation trains departs from the Theresienstadt ghetto in the German Protectorate of Bohemia and Moravia for Treblinka.

October 7, 1942: A proposal for a United Nations Commission for the Investigation of War Crimes is announced in the House of Commons in London. The commission begins its work in 1943.

October 16, 1942: The Generalgouvernement administration reduces the Jewish Social Self-Help to an "Aid Center for Jews" and withdraws the organization's permission to organize relief work in the ghettos.

October 28, 1942: Jewish leaders in the Warsaw ghetto meet with Jan Karski, a courier for the Polish Underground, to implore him to report to the Polish government-in-exile and the West that the Germans are systematically murdering the Jews.

October 28–December 16, 1942: The Płońsk ghetto is liquidated and some twelve thousand Jews deported to Auschwitz.

October 29, 1942: The British Board of Deputies sponsors a rally at the Royal Albert Hall in London on behalf of European Jewry.

November 4, 1942: German forces of the "Afrika-Korps" withdraw from El Alamein, Egypt, a major turning point in this theater of war and a decisive reduction of the risk to the Yishuv.

November 6, 1942: The Vichy government establishes a history chair at the Sorbonne to study the "Jewish question."

November 8, 1942: Operation Torch, the British-American invasion of French North Africa, begins. The United States breaks off diplomatic relations with Vichy France when the Germans occupy the "free zone" in southern France.

November 26, 1942: More than five hundred Jews from Oslo are deported in cargo ships from Norway to Germany and sent on to Auschwitz.

December 1942: Killings at Bełżec cease after the murders of up to five hundred thousand Jews and an undetermined number of Poles and Roma. As part of operation "1005" (see June 1942), bodies were later exhumed and burned in the late spring of 1943 by Jewish forced laborers who were subsequently murdered.

December 2, 1942: Jews in thirty countries observe a day of prayer and fasting for European Jews, called by American Jewish organizations in New York.

Hungarian prime minister Miklós Kállay's government rejects German demands to mark and deport the Jews from Hungary.

December 16, 1942: Himmler orders all German "gypsies" (Sinti and Roma) sent to Auschwitz.

December 17, 1942: The Allied governments announce in a BBC broadcast that Jews in Europe face extermination at the hands of Nazi Germany and that those responsible for these crimes will not escape retribution at the end of the war.

British foreign secretary Anthony Eden tells the House of Commons about the "bestial policy" of mass executions of Jews by the Nazis.

1943

January 14–24, 1943: The Allied powers hold a conference in Casablanca, Morocco, to develop and coordinate strategies for the next phase of the war. Roosevelt and Churchill demand the unconditional surrender of Germany and its allies.

January 18, 1943: The Germans begin their second wave of deportations of Jews from the Warsaw ghetto. The ŻOB clashes with the Germans. This is the first occurrence of armed resistance in the ghetto.

January 23, 1943: The British Eighth Army under Commander Bernard Montgomery enters Tripoli. Axis powers lose control over Libya.

January 27, 1943: Senior officials of the Reichsvereinigung, including Rabbi Leo Baeck, are deported to Theresienstadt.

January 31–February 2, 1943: The German Sixth Army surrenders at Stalingrad, marking a decisive turning point in the war on the eastern front.

February 1943: Japan orders the creation of the Shanghai ghetto to house up to twenty thousand Jews, mostly refugees from Germany, Austria, Czechoslovakia, and Poland.

February 5, 1943: In a large roundup in the Białystok ghetto, the Germans deport, over a week, up to ten thousand Jews to Treblinka; they murder about two thousand Jews in the ghetto.

February 18, 1943: "White Rose" resisters Hans and Sophie Scholl and Christoph Probst are arrested in Munich. They are executed on February 22, 1943.

February 24, 1943: The Germans force the largest Greek Jewish community of Salonika into a newly established ghetto.

February 27, 1943: As part of a push to remove the remaining Jews from the Reich, during the "Fabrik-Aktion," the Gestapo seize and deport some eleven thousand Jews across the Reich, including more than eight thousand from Berlin.

March 1, 1943: Jewish, Christian, and labor organizations hold a mass rally in New York's Madison Square Garden, calling on the United Nations to end Nazi atrocities and rescue the Jews of Europe. The event draws as many as seventy-five thousand participants.

March 4, 1943: Bulgarian authorities start rounding up some four thousand Jews in Bulgarian-occupied Thrace and later deport them to Treblinka.

March 11, 1943: Bulgarian authorities start gathering more than seven thousand Jews in Bulgarian-occupied Yugoslav Macedonia and deport them to Treblinka in late March.

March 13–14, 1943: The Germans liquidate the Kraków ghetto and transport some eight thousand Jews to the Płaszów labor camp; those who remain they kill or send to Auschwitz.

April 16–17, 1943: Hungarian regent Miklós Horthy meets with Hitler at Klessheim near Salzburg. They discuss Axis prospects to win the war and Hungary's anti-Jewish policies.

April 19, 1943: The Warsaw Ghetto Uprising begins. Jewish resistance fighters attack police and SS auxiliary forces who enter the ghetto to carry out a final liquidation. The Germans suffer casualties and retreat but return with a much larger and more effective force. The Jewish fighters continue their resistance for several weeks but are ultimately defeated. The Jewish Fighting Organization's surviving leaders, including their commander, Mordechai Anielewicz, commit suicide when the Germans discover their hiding place. Subsequently, the Germans destroy the ghetto systematically.

Belgian Jewish partisans ambush a train carrying some sixteen hundred Jews to Auschwitz between Boortmeerbeek and Haacht. More than two hundred deportees ultimately escape the train.

British and U.S. officials open the Bermuda Conference, where they discuss the plight of Jewish refugees.

May 7, 1943: British forces enter Tunis; several days later, the Axis troops there surrender, and the Allies take final control of North Africa.

May 12, 1943: Szmul Zygielbojm, Bundist member of the Polish government-in-exile, commits suicide in London to protest Allied inaction in the face of the murder of Polish Jewry.

May 26, 1943: Nazi and Dutch police raid Amsterdam's old Jewish quarter, deporting some three thousand Jews to the Westerbork transit camp; most are then sent to Sobibór.

June 1943: In early June, the Germans start the liquidation of the Lwów ghetto. After an attempt to resist deportation, some three thousand Jews are murdered in the ghetto, and around seven thousand are taken to the Janowska camp.

June 11, 1943: Himmler orders the liquidation of all Jewish ghettos in Poland. On June 21, 1943, he expands this order to include all ghettos in the Soviet Union; it is implemented in stages.

June 26, 1943: The Germans start to liquidate the Częstochowa ghetto. ŻOB fighters under the command of Mordechai Zylberberg resist the Germans. Some fifteen hundred Jews die in the fighting and mass executions that ensue. Zylberberg commits suicide in one of the bunkers. Some Jews manage to escape the ghetto and join the partisans.

July 2, 1943: A German-Hungarian agreement is signed that allows transfer of Jewish labor companies to work in the copper mines of Bor in German-occupied Serbia.

July 4, 1943: The Germans launch Operation Citadel against the Red Army. The Soviet counterattack prevails, defeating the last major German offensive on the eastern front.

July 10, 1943: U.S. and British troops land on Sicily. The Allies control Sicily by mid-August.

July 16, 1943: Yitzhak Wittenberg, Jewish resistance leader of the partisan organization in the Vilna ghetto, dies in the city's Gestapo prison.

July 25, 1943: The Italian Grand Council of Fascism, after a vote of no confidence, deposes Mussolini. He is then arrested, enabling Marshal Pietro Badoglio to form a new government.

July 28, 1943: Jan Karski, courier in the Polish Underground, delivers a detailed report to President Roosevelt about the "Final Solution."

August 2, 1943: Prisoners revolt in Treblinka. Hundreds try to escape by running toward the main gate. SS and police guards shoot many, but more than three hundred get away. The SS and police track down and murder most of the escapees.

August 11–17, 1943: The Germans evacuate Sicily.

August 16, 1943: Several hundred Jews mount a revolt against the Germans in the Białystok ghetto. Many Jews die in the uprising, but a few ghetto insurgents break free and join partisan units in the forest. Deportation transports subsequently take more than twenty-five thousand Białystok Jews to Auschwitz and Treblinka.

August 18, 1943: As part of operation "1005," over six weeks Jewish and non-Jewish prisoners exhume and burn corpses at the mass killing site of Babi Yar, outside Kiev.

August 19, 1943: SS guards force surviving prisoners in Bełżec to remove all remaining traces of the camp's existence. The SS then shoot the remaining prisoners. Treblinka II, where between 870,000 and 925,000 people perished, is dismantled in the fall of 1943.

September 6, 1943: A large transport of some five thousand Jewish prisoners leaves Theresienstadt for the newly established "family camp" at Auschwitz II–Birkenau.

September 8, 1943: Armistice between Italy and the Allies is announced. The Germans soon seize control of Rome and northern Italy, establishing a puppet Fascist regime under Mussolini, whom German commandos free from imprisonment on September 12.

September 9, 1943: Some 250 inmates of the Italian Jewish internment camp on the Adriatic island of Rab proclaim the formation of a Jewish battalion. They immediately join Yugoslav partisans, who then evacuate some twenty-five hundred Jews from the former camp and protect them for the rest of the war.

Allied troops land on the beaches of Salerno near Naples.

September 10, 1943: German forces occupy Rome.

September 14, 1943: The Gestapo executes the chairman of the Vilna *Judenrat*, Jacob Gens.

September 22, 1943: Soviet partisans assassinate Wilhelm Kube, head of the German civil administration (*Generalkommissar*) for Belorussia in Minsk.

September 23, 1943: Mussolini establishes the Italian Social Republic, a Nazi puppet state in the northern Italian town of Salò.

September 23–24, 1943: The Vilna ghetto is liquidated. Abba Kovner, leader of the United Partisan Organization (FPO), and about a hundred FPO fighters escape from the ghetto.

September 25, 1943: Soviet troops recapture Smolensk.

September 29, 1943: The Gestapo announces the abolition of the Jewish Council (*Joodse Raad*) in Amsterdam, after all remaining members, including its leader, Abraham Asscher, have been sent to Westerbork.

October 1, 1943: After Hitler orders the arrest and deportation of all Danish Jews, Sweden announces that it will grant them asylum. The rescue operation of the Danish Underground leads to the successful evacuation of some seventy-two hundred Danish Jews to Sweden.

October 13, 1943: Italy declares war on its former Axis partner, Nazi Germany.

October 14, 1943: Some six hundred prisoners attempt to escape from Sobibór. About half initially succeed, but of these, only fifty manage to evade German capture. Following the revolt, the Germans close and bulldoze the camp.

October 16, 1943: The Germans round up the Jews of Rome, assembled at a nearby military school, and subsequently deport about one thousand to Auschwitz.

October 20, 1943: A United Nations War Crimes Commission is established at the Foreign Office in London during a meeting of Allied government representatives (excluding the Soviet Union).

October 21, 1943: The Minsk ghetto is liquidated. Approximately two thousand Jews are shot to death at Maly Trostinets, on the outskirts of Minsk.

October 30, 1943: Roosevelt, Churchill, and Joseph Stalin jointly issue the Moscow Declaration. It pledges continuation of the war until the unconditional surrender of Germany, the eradication of fascism in Italy, the annulment of Austria's annexation by Germany, and the prosecution of crimes committed by Germany.

November 2, 1943: The Germans start the liquidation of the Riga ghetto. More than two thousand remaining Jews are shot.

November 3–4, 1943: The Germans shoot more than forty-three thousand Jewish forced laborers during "Aktion Erntefest" (Operation Harvest Festival) in the Lublin district of the Generalgouvernement.

November 6, 1943: Soviet troops liberate Kiev.

November 19, 1943: *Sonderkommando* prisoners stage an uprising at the Janowska camp in the suburbs of Lwów. Most of the inmates are murdered, but a few escape to the surrounding forests.

November 28–December 1, 1943: Stalin, Roosevelt, and Churchill meet for the Tehran Conference, held at the Soviet embassy in Tehran. The western Allies commit to opening a second front against Germany in Europe.

November 29, 1943: The Anti-Fascist Council of National Liberation in Yugoslavia establishes a provisional government under Josip Broz Tito.

December 15–18, 1943: Three German Gestapo officers and a Russian collaborator stand trial in Kharkov, in Soviet Ukraine, for crimes against Soviet citizens. They are sentenced to death and hanged publicly on December 19. This is the first prosecution for German crimes committed in World War II.

December 18, 1943: The former Jewish Eldest in Theresienstadt, Jakob Edelstein, is deported to Auschwitz. He and his family are shot on June 20, 1944.

1944

January 4, 1944: In its westward advance, the Red Army crosses the former eastern Polish border.

January 22, 1944: Allied troops land at Anzio, close to Rome, but their advance is arrested for months.

President Franklin D. Roosevelt establishes the War Refugee Board, the U.S. government agency tasked with aiding the victims of Nazi persecution.

January 27, 1944: The Red Army breaks the 872-day German siege of Leningrad. Hundreds of thousands of Soviet soldiers and civilians have died.

March 19, 1944: The German army invades Hungary. Adolf Eichmann and his deportation experts (*Sondereinsatzkommando*) arrive in Budapest.

March 21, 1944: German authorities order creation of the Central Council of Hungarian Jews led by Samu Stern, president of the Pest Israelite Congregation.

March 22, 1944: Former Hungarian ambassador in Berlin Döme Sztójay forms the new collaborationist cabinet. The government soon forces Jews to wear the yellow star and decides to physically segregate them.

March 24, 1944: The Gestapo lures about eight hundred Athenian Jews to a synagogue with promises of food but instead interns and deports them to Auschwitz.

March 27, 1944: The Germans seize about two thousand Jewish children and a few remaining elderly Jews in the Kovno concentration camp (previously the Kovno ghetto), where most are killed or deported to Auschwitz.

April 4, 1944: The Hungarian Ministry of the Interior orders the Jews of Hungary to undergo obligatory registration, and Hungarian authorities begin to confiscate 1,500 Jewish apartments in Budapest to house non-Jewish Hungarians who have lost their homes in Allied bombings.

April 7, 1944: Hungarian officials issue a confidential decree for the concentration of Jews. Until April 13, 1944, German and Hungarian leaders reach agreement about the scale of deportations (one hundred thousand Jewish men capable of working).

April 10, 1944: The Red Army liberates Odessa.

April 16, 1944: Ghettoization of Jews in Hungary begins in what later becomes Deportation Zone I (Carpatho-Ruthenia). The government issues a decree on the registration and confiscation of Jewish assets.

April 22, 1944: In the Szentkút agreement, German and Hungarian officials arrive at a final decision on the deportation of all Hungarian Jews to Auschwitz.

April 25, 1944: Eichmann summons Joel Brand, a member of the Hungarian Aid and Rescue Committee, to discuss a deal between the SS and the Allies, in which the Nazis would release one million Jews in exchange for ten thousand trucks and other supplies.

May 9, 1944: The Red Army liberates Sevastopol, Crimea's largest city.

May 15, 1944: Mass deportations to Auschwitz by the Hungarian authorities begin.

June 4, 1944: Allied troops liberate Rome.

June 6, 1944: Operation Overlord, the Allied landing in Normandy, begins. By September, more than three million Allied troops are in France.

June 22, 1944: The Red Army launches a massive offensive in Belarus, reaching westward to the Vistula across from Warsaw by August 1.

June 25, 1944: Hungarian authorities force the Jews of Budapest into 1,948 designated buildings ("yellow-star houses") by this date.

June 30, 1944: King Gustav V of Sweden sends a cable to Horthy, calling on him to save Hungarian Jewry.

July 2–3, 1944: The remaining three thousand Jews from working camps near Vilna are taken to Ponary and executed.

July 3, 1944: The Red Army liberates Minsk.

July 4, 1944: Rabbi Michael Dov Weissmandl secretly transmits to Switzerland the so-called Vrba-Wetzler report, a twenty-six-page document compiled by Jewish escapees detailing the killing methods at Auschwitz II–Birkenau. George Mantello (George Mandel), a Hungarian Jew who became the first secretary of the consulate in El Salvador, translates it into English.

July 6, 1944: Horthy orders the deportations from Hungary to halt, effective July 9. Until this date, more than 437,000 Jews have been deported from Hungary.

July 8, 1944: The Kovno concentration camp is liquidated.

July 13, 1944: The Red Army liberates Vilna.

July 19, 1944: Despite Horthy's order of July 6, Eichmann's unit deports 1,220 Hungarian Jews from the Kistarcsa internment camp to Auschwitz.

July 20, 1944: Inside Hitler's headquarters near Rastenburg, East Prussia, an assassination attempt on the Nazi Führer fails.

July 22, 1944: In Lublin, the Communist-led Polish Committee of National Liberation proclaims itself the only legitimate Polish government and assumes administration of liberated Polish territory.

July 23, 1944: The International Red Cross visits Theresienstadt, which the Germans disguise as a benign camp with tolerable conditions for the duration of the visit.

The Polish Home Army (Armia Krajowa) begins an uprising in Lwów, liberating the city from the Germans after several days. The Soviets soon take Lwów over.

July 24, 1944: The Red Army liberates Majdanek.

About fifteen hundred Hungarian Jews from the Sárvár internment camp are deported to Auschwitz.

July 25, 1944: Anglo-American forces break out of the Normandy beachhead and push toward Paris.

July 27, 1944: The Red Army liberates Białystok and Lwów.

August 1, 1944: The Warsaw Uprising, a major operation of the Polish Underground, begins. The non-Communist Polish Home Army rises up against the Germans in an effort to liberate Warsaw before the arrival of Soviet troops. The Soviet advance halts on the east bank of the Vistula. On October 5, the Germans accept the surrender of the remnants of the Polish Home Army forces fighting in Warsaw. Approximately one thousand Jews, most of them ŻOB fighters in hiding, take part in the combat. Up to two hundred thousand civilians perish, and hundreds of thousands flee the city.

The Red Army liberates Kovno.

August 2, 1944: The Germans liquidate the "gypsy family camp" at Auschwitz II–Birkenau, murdering nearly three thousand Roma and transferring approximately fifteen hundred to Buchenwald.

August 6, 1944: With the start of the liquidation of the Łódź ghetto, over seventy-four thousand Jews are deported to Auschwitz.

August 17, 1944: Allied troops liberate Drancy, a major deportation center for Jews in France. More than sixty-five thousand French and other European Jews were ultimately deported from Drancy to their deaths.

August 19, 1944: An uprising against the German occupation begins in Paris as the Allied troops reach the city. Six days later, the troops of the Free French forces, supported by Allied troops, enter the French capital.

August 21, 1944: The Dumbarton Oaks Conference begins in Washington, DC. Over one and a half months, the Allied leaders and China negotiate the basic structure and functions of the United Nations.

August 23, 1944: The Red Army reaches the Prut River, and the Romanian opposition overthrows the Antonescu regime. Romania switches sides in the war.

August 24, 1944: Horthy refuses to hand over Budapest's Jews to the Germans. Eichmann's special unit is called back to resume deportations.

August 25, 1944: French Free forces, led by General Charles de Gaulle, liberate Paris.

August 29, 1944: Horthy dismisses Prime Minister Döme Sztójay, and a new government forms under Horthy loyalist General Géza Lakatos.

With the beginning of the German occupation, a Slovak uprising, supported by many of the remaining Slovak Jews, erupts, causing heavy civilian casualties. It is quashed by October 28, 1944. Between September 1944 and the end of the year, German units, including a special *Einsatzkommando*, deport approximately 12,600 Slovak Jews, most of them to Auschwitz, Theresienstadt, and other camps in Germany.

September 12, 1944: Romania signs an armistice with the Soviet Union.

September 13, 1944: The U.S. Air Force bombs Auschwitz III–Monowitz (Buna).

October 2–3, 1944: After a sixty-three-day siege, the Polish Home Army surrenders to the Germans in Warsaw. The Warsaw Uprising is crushed.

October 7, 1944: At Auschwitz II–Birkenau, Greek Jews of the *Sonderkommando* and others revolt, kill three SS guards, and blow up Crematorium IV.

October 14, 1944; British forces liberate Athens.

October 15–16, 1944: Horthy attempts to negotiate an armistice with the Allies; the fascist Arrow Cross movement under Ferenc Szálasi deposes him in a coup.

October 18–20, 1944: Eichmann's *Sondereinsatzkommando* returns to Budapest.

October 20, 1944: Yugoslav Communist leader Josip Tito's partisans liberate Belgrade.

November 6, 1944: Forced marches of Budapest Jews to Hungary's western border begin.

November 17, 1944: Szálasi creates two ghettos in Budapest.

November 25, 1944: Himmler orders the destruction of the Auschwitz II–Birkenau gas chambers and crematoria.

December 10, 1944: Eichmann orders the Budapest ghetto sealed.

December 16, 1944: The Germans launch a final offensive in the west, known as the Battle of the Bulge, in an attempt to reconquer Belgium and split the Allied forces along the German border. By January 1, 1945, the Germans are in retreat.

December 24, 1944–February 13, 1945: The Red Army besieges Budapest. Arrow Cross militiamen terrorize and massacre Jews in the city.

December 31, 1944: Following the Soviet takeover of the country, Hungary's Provisional National Government declares war on Germany. On January 20, 1945, the Hungarian government signs an armistice agreement with the Allies in Moscow.

1945

January 16, 1945: The Red Army liberates Łódź.

January 17, 1945: The Red Army liberates Warsaw.

    The SS evacuates Auschwitz and send approximately sixty-six thousand prisoners on death marches.

    The last forty-eight Jewish prisoners at Chełmno, part of operation "1005," revolt against the SS. Only three survive.

January 19, 1945: Soviet troops liberate Kraków, the capital of the Generalgouvernement.

January 27, 1945: Soviet troops liberate Auschwitz, freeing seven thousand prisoners. Jews make up a very small percentage of the survivors.

February 4–11, 1945: At the Yalta Conference, Stalin, Churchill, and Roosevelt discuss the division of Germany into Allied occupation zones, the setting of postwar borders in Europe, and the repatriation of an estimated 11 million displaced persons (DPs), that is, civilians uprooted by Nazi Germany, among them slave laborers and concentration camp prisoners.

February 13–15, 1945: The Allies bomb Dresden, destroying most of the city and killing approximately twenty-five thousand people, among them Allied POWs and forced laborers.

March 1945: The National Committee for Attending Deportees (Deportáltakat Gondozó Országos Bizottság, or DEGOB) testimony project is founded in Budapest.

March 16, 1945: The Protectorate sends its last deportation transport of Jews to Theresienstadt.

April 1945: Partisan units, led by Tito, capture Zagreb and topple the Ustaše regime. The top Ustaše leaders flee to Italy and Austria.

April 3–4, 1945: The SS forces approximately thirty thousand Buchenwald inmates on a death march, during which thousands perish.

April 4, 1945: American troops discover mass graves when they liberate Ohrdruf, a subcamp of Buchenwald. On April 5, 1945, Generals Dwight D. Eisenhower, Omar N. Bradley, and George S. Patton view the camp.

April 11, 1945: In anticipation of liberation, prisoners at Buchenwald seize control of the camp and storm the watchtowers. Later that afternoon, U.S. Third Army troops liberate Buchenwald, freeing twenty-one thousand prisoners. Of Buchenwald's more than 230,000 inmates, approximately 50,000 perished.

April 12, 1945: U.S. President Roosevelt dies, and Harry S. Truman takes over the presidency.

April 15, 1945: The British 11th Armored Division liberates Bergen-Belsen.

April 16, 1945: The Soviets launch their offensive on Berlin, encircling the city.

April 20, 1945: The U.S. Seventh Army captures Nuremberg.

April 22, 1945: One thousand prisoners of the Jasenovac concentration camp (in the former Independent State of Croatia) stage an uprising. A small number succeed in escaping, but most are killed by Ustaše guards.

April 23, 1945: American army units liberate Flossenbürg concentration camp and the approximately fifteen hundred remaining inmates.

April 26, 1945: The SS takes approximately seven thousand Jewish prisoners from Dachau on a death march; most are shot or die from various ailments along the way.

April 27, 1945: The Landsberg displaced persons camp is formed and becomes the second largest in the American zone of occupation. By October, it will function as an exclusively Jewish camp.

Representatives of the major Austrian parties declare the country's independence from Germany, revoking the 1938 "Anschluss."

April 30, 1945: Hitler commits suicide.

May 1, 1945: The U.S. Army opens the Feldafing displaced persons camp, which will become the first all-Jewish DP camp in the American zone.

May 4, 1945: The first Jewish DP newspaper, *Tkhies hameysim* (Resurrection of the dead), appears in handwritten Yiddish, three weeks after the liberation of Buchenwald.

May 5, 1945: American forces liberate Mauthausen.

May 7, 1945: Effective May 8, Germany surrenders to the western Allies at Reims, in north-western France. The German unconditional surrender is confirmed on May 8 at the Berlin headquarters of the Soviet Fifth Army.

May 8, 1945: The Red Army liberates Theresienstadt, freeing approximately seventeen thousand prisoners.

American troops capture Göring in Berchtesgaden.

May 23, 1945: Himmler commits suicide.

June 1945: The Föhrenwald displaced persons camp is established and becomes one of the largest Jewish DP camps. It was also the last Jewish DP camp to close, in 1957.

June 9, 1945: The Soviet Military Administration in Germany is created for the zone occupied by the Red Army.

June 15, 1945: Jewish DPs in Germany found the Central Committee of Liberated Jews.

July 17–August 2, 1945: At the Potsdam Conference convened by the United States, Great Britain, and the Soviet Union, Truman, Churchill (proceeded by Clement Atlee during the conference), and Stalin meet to discuss how to establish a basis for a postwar order, including the punishment of Nazi crimes.

August 1945: Jewish ethnographer M. I. Beregovskii conducts interviews with survivors of the concentration camps in Transnistria.

August 3, 1945: Earl G. Harrison, American envoy to the Intergovernmental Committee on Refugees, submits a report to President Truman that sharply criticizes DP camp conditions in Germany and Austria, especially those facing Jewish DPs. As a result, the United Nations Relief and Rehabilitation Administration (UNRRA) takes over DP camp administration, leading to improved conditions.

August 6, 1945: The United States drops an atomic bomb on Hiroshima.

August 8, 1945: The Soviet Union declares war on Japan and invades Manchuria.

August 9, 1945: The United States drops an atomic bomb on Nagasaki.

August 30, 1945: The Allied Control Council is created to set occupation policy in Germany.

September 2, 1945: Having agreed in principle to unconditional surrender on August 14, 1945, Japan surrenders formally, ending World War II.

September 29, 1945: The Office of Military Government, United States is created under U.S. Army general Lucius D. Clay as the governing body in the U.S. occupation zone in Germany.

October 1, 1945: UNRRA assumes responsibility for the administration of displaced persons in Europe.

November 28, 1945: The Central Historical Commission is founded in Munich as a subdivision of the Central Committee of Liberated Jews in Bavaria.

December 20, 1945: Following the Allies' Moscow Declaration of October 30, 1943, and the London Agreement of August 8, 1945, Control Council Law (CCL) No. 10 is enacted to create the legal basis for trials dealing with crimes against peace, war crimes, crimes against humanity, and membership in criminal organizations. CCL No. 10 is applied in the occupation zones of the three western Allies until 1951 and in the Soviet Zone until 1955.

1946

March 29, 1946: A riot breaks out in the Stuttgart displaced persons camp between local German police and the Jewish DPs residing there. One survivor dies due to the incident.

July 4, 1946: A Polish civilian mob carries out a pogrom against Jewish survivors in Kielce. Following a ritual murder accusation, the mob kills forty Jews and wounds dozens of others. After the attack, Jews from Poland and eastern Europe migrate en masse to DP camps in Germany, Austria, and Italy.

July 29, 1946: Psychologist David Boder starts his audio-recorded oral history interviews with Jewish survivors at the Organisation Reconstruction Travail (ORT) training school in Paris. It is the first such oral history interview project.

August 1946: The first edition of *Fun letstn khurbn* (From the last extermination), a periodical devoted to the history of the Jewish people during the Nazi regime, is published in Munich.

October 1, 1946: The International Military Tribunal passes judgment on major Nazi war criminals on trial in Nuremberg, Germany, convicting eighteen and acquitting three. Eleven of the defendants receive death sentences.

October 16, 1946: In accordance with sentences handed down after the convictions, ten of the Nuremberg defendants are executed by hanging; earlier, Göring had committed suicide in his cell.

Index

Page numbers followed by "n" indicate footnotes. Page numbers in *italic* indicate illustrations and photographs. Cities and countries are listed according to current borders.

About the Editors

Jürgen Matthäus is director of the Applied Research Division at the Jack, Joseph and Morton Mandel Center for Advanced Holocaust Studies of the United States Holocaust Memorial Museum.

Emil Kerenji is an applied research scholar at the Jack, Joseph and Morton Mandel Center for Advanced Holocaust Studies of the United States Holocaust Memorial Museum.